A Dilemma
of English Modernism

A Dilemma of English Modernism

Visual and Verbal Politics in the Life and Work of C. R. W. Nevinson (1889–1946)

Edited by
Michael J. K. Walsh

DELAWARE

Newark: University of Delaware Press

Associated University Presses
2010 Eastpark Boulevard
Cranbury, NJ 08512

The paper used in this publication meets the requirements of the American National Standard for Permanence of Paper for Printed Library Materials Z39.48-1984.

Library of Congress Cataloging-in-Publication Data

A dilemma of English modernism : visual and verbal politics in the life and work of C. R. W. Nevinson (1889–1946) / edited by Michael J. K. Walsh.
p. cm.
Includes bibliographical references and index.
ISBN-13: 978-0-87413-942-6 (alk. paper)
ISBN-10: 0-87413-942-2 (alk. paper)
1. Nevinson, C. R. W. (Christopher Richard Wynne), 1889–1946—Criticism and interpretation. I. Walsh, Michael J. K., 1968–
ND497.N4D55 2007
759.2—dc22 2006022576

PRINTED IN THE UNITED STATES OF AMERICA

For Erin Zoë and Aleea Victoria

Contents

Illustrations

Acknowledgments

FIRST AND FOREMOST I WOULD LIKE TO THANK THE contributors who have worked tirelessly with the editor for several years to produce this volume of essays. Its origin lies in the conference "C.R.W. Nevinson: Life, Art and Legacy" which was held at the University of Greenwich in 2002, and which was generously supported by an Educational Programme Grant from the Paul Mellon Centre for Studies in British Art (Yale University). My thanks go to Angela V. John for co-organizing, and co-hosting, the event. Thanks too to David Peters Corbett who chaired the day and who suggested the idea of collecting the essays, and others, into a publishable volume. A Research Support Grant from the Paul Mellon Centre for Studies in British Art (Yale University) made the continuation of the project throughout 2003–4 possible and the finishing touches were added during my period as Visiting Research Collaborator at Princeton University and simultaneously as Visiting Assistant Professor of Art History at Central Connecticut State University in 2005–6. At the former I would like to thank Patricia Fortini-Brown for my invitation and at the latter I would particularly like to thank Cassandra Broadus-Garcia and everyone at the Department of Art, and at the International Office, for offering such a warm welcome.

Other individuals and institutions which have been helpful along the way include the Harry Ransom Humanities Research Center at the University of Texas at Austin, where L. Christine Amos, in particular, has been a pleasure to work with; the staff at the Hyman Kreitman Research Centre at the Tate, London; the Imperial War Museum, London; and the Bodleian Library, Oxford University. My thanks also to Jonathan Black for inviting my contribution to *Blasting the Future: Vorticism in Britain 1910 -1920* (Philip Wilson, 2004) and for sharing his findings, and offering his opinions on mine, over the last seven years. The Vice-Rector for Research at Eastern Mediterranean University, Professor Ayhan Bilsel, also deserves thanks for his continued support of publishing, conference and research activities, and for procuring both leave and funds with which to make them happen. Thanks go to Lisa Goldreich (Art Historian and Digital Image Archivist) in Connecticut for enormous patience and professionalism in managing the image preparation for this volume. I would like to thank Johann Pillai for his useful comments on the early versions of the introduction and also Dan Frodsham, Anber Onar and Tamas Kiss, for more general, and always useful, conversations. My thanks go, as always, to John and Ann Walsh and also to Lee and Cathy Wortman. Gül İnanç has been a constant support and the source of many suggestions (though rarely ridicule), as has Erdal Barkay, particularly in assisting with the bibliography.

Last but not least, and on the occasion of his retirement, I extend my thanks to John Rimmer for introducing me to the world of British art as an undergraduate more years ago than either of us would care to admit.

Michael Walsh
Famagusta and Princeton
2005.

A Dilemma of English Modernism

Introduction

Michael J. K. Walsh

A GLANCE AT THE OBITUARY COLUMNS THE DAY after Christopher Richard Wynne Nevinson's death on October 7, 1946, provides some sense of both the diversity, and intensity, of contemporary opinion aroused by this controversial and high-profile English artist who, having come to prominence at the age of twenty-two, had played such an important role in the development of British visual and written culture in the first half of the twentieth century. Over his three-and-a-half-decade career he had been a member of one of the most dynamic classes ever to attend the Slade School of Art; participated in the dying days of prewar Edwardian bohemianism in Paris and London; been toasted and vilified as "England's only Futurist" and served on the western front where he had made his reputation as *the* modern artist of modern war. After the Armistice he had taken his brand of modernism to New York at the outset of the Jazz Age; been hailed as a celebrity at the heart of London in the Roaring Twenties; railed as a provocateur against the Royal Academy and simultaneously against fascism during the Great Depression; and then faced the inevitable next war with the cynicism of a man who had seen it all before. He died in his studio the year after the war ended and was cremated with no service or ceremony.

As a painter, social commentator, novelist, journalist, and society host par excellence, Nevinson had always been widely known (at one time, perhaps, more so than any other artist in England), though he had not always been held in great affection. But the obituaries let no personal prejudices or ill feelings eclipse his importance, and so the *Evening Standard* could sum up, "Nevinson was a rebel. He was at perpetual loggerheads with the respectable and conventional in art";[1] the *News Chronicle* ran the headline "Nevinson, the fighting artist, dies";[2] while the *Liverpool Daily* honored him by suggesting he was "one of the most provocative artists of the century."[3] The *Daily Mail* remembered him as the "fearless artist and commentator on life"[4] while the *Scotsman* concluded its eulogy with a happy ending, in which he was portrayed as "A rebel in art who lived to be acclaimed as a classic."[5] Socially and artistically Nevinson had come, albeit circuitously, "home," and this was acknowledged in an article dedicated to him seven months after his death, entitled "Prodigal's Return: A Romantic Painter Who Strayed but Came Back to the English Tradition."[6] In short, he had not slipped away unnoticed, nor had his achievements gone unrecognized.

What *is* surprising then is that Nevinson's name drifted into obscurity in the years after his death, and it is hard to say how this happened. This was, after all, the friend (or foe) of such notables as: Roger Fry, Clive Bell, Dora Carrington, Mark Gertler, Virginia Woolf, F. T. Marinetti, Amadeo Modigliani, Edward Elgar, H. G. Wells, Charlie Chaplin, T. S. Eliot, Paul and John Nash, Jacob Epstein, Wyndham Lewis, the Sitwells, Rupert Brooke, Ezra Pound, George Bernard Shaw, Emmeline Pankhurst, Augustus John and Aleister Crowley. In the latter years of his life the ex-rebel had also become a full member of the New English Art Club, an Associate of the Royal Academy, a member of the Royal Institute of Oil Painters and *Chevalier de la Legion d' Honneur* in France. But there had always been inconsistencies in all of this, not least to the artist himself, and so his lifelong sense of exclusion, combined with an acute persecution complex, might have led him to believe that his being sidelined from the history of art after his death was an inevitability. In his own estimation he had been the most celebrated and simultaneously the hardest done-by artist of his generation; the hater of the "mob" (who had won acclaim from them) and also of the "high-brow"; the rebel and "lone wolf" who had ended up comfortable in the leather chairs of the Savage Club. He had seen himself as an intellectual, though he had lived in the shadow of his father; and he had been viewed by others as both violent and wildly outspoken, while privately he had been cursed with timidity and an ultrasensitive (easy-to-wound) personality. Art had brought with it a lifetime of misery and this could be felt in a letter to Dame Laura Knight shortly before his death "I love painting for its own sake too much, and I detest all the lying Curators, and Officials, Courtiers and general 'art' chi-chi so much that it makes me loathe the profession of painting."[7] Accordingly he instructed his wife, in his Last Will and Testament, to destroy any works of art that were not worthy of his name and reputation after his death—but on no account to ask an artist should she be in any doubt. With his living presence no longer at the helm to create self-promoting publicity, controversy, and high-profile pronouncements, the retreat into the shadows that he had so expressly forbidden in his own lifetime was finally permissible.

In anticipation of this he had gone some way to creating his own legend and left, he hoped, his interpretation of his worth for posterity, principally through his autobiography *Paint and Prejudice*, and fourteen volumes of edited press cuttings, later bequeathed to the Tate Gallery. Yet this very conscious image-making within the autobiography, coupled with his perpetual self-positioning as "outsider" within his own lifetime, may well have eclipsed many of his legitimate achievements and led to the heavily buttressed image collapsing upon his death. Or perhaps he had simply been, for the generation that followed him, the last of a bygone generation who had had their day in a world that had begun before the Boer War and ended at the outset of the Cold War—a relic of a forgotten, if not despised, era. In fact his artistic lifespan (ca. 1909–46) could hardly have been more relevant to the modernization of the society that surrounded him, and the aforementioned volumes of press cuttings in the Tate Archive, and a formidable catalog of painted works (and prints), suggest that this "forgotten artist" had been pivotal within it and had had plenty to say about it.

Subsequent trends in art history have not helped the survival of his name and reputation either, with a prevalent orientation toward continental modernist innovation and its subsequent path to abstraction. Overlaid with this framework Nevinson's early work can be mainstreamed and authenticated with a rubber stamp of approval, leaving the postwar work doomed, by the same criteria, to cultural irrelevance and the artistic periphery. Such art histories, I would suggest, have created little space for the value of individualism and personal conviction on the part of a committed "modern" (an attribute so vital to modernism itself), in preference for doctrinal adherence to formal qualities of the finished canvas. Such readings regard a return to realism as an irrefutable sign of defeat and retreat, while the artistic eclecticism that characterized Nevinson's later work is read as a sure sign of a lack of conviction and/or focus. However, should an alternative perspective be adopted in which postwar painting can be more clearly read in a context that downplays Clive Bell's "otherworldliness" in preference for the tangible "residues of the day," the artist's experience, articulated in whatever way, might yet be valued within a critique that adhers to Nevinson's own ethos of "art rules the artist." But this has not been the case and Lisa Messinger's question ("Why then is there such a great disparity in the amount of public and critical recognition Nevinson received during the two distinct parts of his career?"[8]) remains fairly easy to answer. Nevinson himself had acknowledged this and written in despair in 1936 that the interwar era was "the fallow ground from which the weeds of sensationalism, exploitation, and disillusionment sprang: the weeds which now choke us."[9]

A Dilemma of English Modernism: Visual and Verbal Politics in the Life and Work of C. R. W. Nevinson (1889–1946), takes an important step in reevaluating the artist's place in, and contribution to, the history of English twentieth-century art, and in rethinking his contribution to the shifting tides of a seemingly beleaguered modernism in a convalescent, yet ever modernizing society. Despite the fact that Nevinson's name has appeared in literally hundreds of books, very few of these raise any original points or question any of the assumptions arrived at in the 1970s and 1980s in the writings of Richard Cork, William Wees, and Charles Harrison. Richard Cork especially wrote extensively and influentially on the art of the period, and Nevinson featured in many of these discussions, most notably in the two-volume *Vorticism and Abstract Art in the First Machine Age* (University of California Press, 1976). For Cork, Nevinson was to be respected, principally for his Futurist polemics, though treated eventually as a traitor to the modernist cause and the pariah who abandoned his prewar experimentation to attain popular success in the latter stages of the conflict and thereafter. In *A Bitter Truth: Avant-Garde Art and the Great War* (Yale University Press, 1994) Cork assured Nevinson his place at the very center of British art history, where he has remained to this day, but as a Futurist and war artist, whose career ended around 1917. William Wees, in *Vorticism and the English Avant-Garde* (University of Toronto, 1972), also created space for the importance of Futurism in England and Nevinson's contribution to it; but again, and quite traditionally, his emphasis lay on the success of Vorticism, not Futurism, and those associated with it. Wees, too, suggested that the Great War represented the zenith of Nevinson's career, eclipsing the relative wilderness he experienced after the Armistice. Charles Harrison, in *English Art and Modernism 1900–1939* (University of Indiana Press, 1981) presented a more catholic history when he depicted the prewar avant-garde advancing over a wide "front," and not in the narrow linear trajectory as proposed by Cork. This provided some lateral space for accommodating an artist like Nevinson as a key figure before and during the conflict, although again, Harrison found no place at all for him in any cultural evaluation of postwar London. Besides, for Harrison, there was a natural bias toward what was happening in Paris—a far from perfect mode of evaluating Nevinson's output in London, leading David Peters Corbett and Lara Perry to ask in their introduction to *English Art 1860–1914: Modern Artists and Identity*, why English modernism should be bound by, or judged on, the priorities of other nations. David Peters Corbett, in *The Modernity of English Art 1914–1930* (Manchester University Press, 1997), had previously examined Nevinson, or at least allowed him a place in the discussion, after the war and throughout the twenties, even if his role had been seen as symptomatic of the general decline the arts experienced in this convalescent era. Sue Malvern's book *Great Britain, Modern Art and the Great War* (Yale University Press, 2004) has, once again, thrust Nevinson into the limelight and, rather temptingly, even started to analyze the artist's work up to and including the 1930s.

Other subcurrents of scholarly activity have existed at the hands of a few notable curators, a small group of essayists, and several PhD students;[10] and through these Nevinson's important role in English culture, though seriously downplayed, has not been entirely sidelined. If the 1988 exhibition "C. R. W. Nevinson: A Retrospective Exhibition of Paintings, Drawings and Prints" at Kettle's Yard Gallery, Cambridge, UK, took the first step in returning him to his rightful place closer to the heart of the English modernist experiment, the truly giant leap was made in 1999 and 2000 with the traveling exhibition (Imperial War Museum and Yale Center for British Art) of the most comprehensive collection of the artist's painting yet assembled, entitled "C. R. W. Nevinson: The Twentieth Century." Extensive reviews both in Great Britain and in the United States of America rekindled discussions on the artist and his art in the press on a scale perhaps only witnessed before in his own lifetime, and with these controversy reemerged, resulting in comments both complimentary and biting. John Russell Taylor, for example, claimed "If this show of 140 pieces does not return him to the pantheon of 20th century art, nothing will,"[11] while another reviewer talked of the "long-overdue reassessment of the artist's significant contribution to twentieth century art."[12] Brian Sewell, on the other hand, in his comments on "the forgotten man of early 20th century British painting," mocked Nevinson as "a fat hypochondriac living in a caravan, ranting like a jingoist," before concluding that "few painters' ends, [however], were as sterile as his own."[13] It seemed that Nevinson, over half a century after his own death, still divided opinion in no uncertain way, and yet was ever present—impossible to dismiss entirely.

In 2002, the conference "C. R. W. Nevinson: Life, Art and Legacy," organized by Professor Angela V. John and myself, brought the handful of scholars working on Nevinson together for the first time, and it was at this event that David Peters Corbett suggested the collection of essays that now forms this volume. On the same day, and at the same event, the Yale University Press launched my study of Nevinson's work in his Futurist and Great War periods, between 1912 and 1919, entitled *C. R. W. Nevinson: This Cult of Violence*. The critical reception that followed was very positive, but as complimentary as the accolades were, for me they simply highlighted the self-satisfied fact that the rest of Nevinson's career should remain unstudied, unpublished, and still outside any significant discourse within the history of art of the period. It seemed that my own work was reinforcing the myth that by 1919 the artist was a spent force, and that no further time need be applied to the study of the last twenty-seven years of his life and work. It is this limiting *terminus ad quem* that this collection of essays aims to shift, for however justified the criticisms in the context of keeping up with continental modernism and the formal or aesthetic developments and achievements of Paris and New York, Nevinson still represented something more than timorous and socially disengaged image-making in the interwar period. On the contrary, his subjects were England, modernity, and art—and his results, though not pursuing the historically desirable path to abstraction, far from valueless.

A Dilemma of English Modernism then sets out to conduct two major investigations: first, to rethink existing notions concerning early English modernist image-making and rhetoric, specifically in the prewar and war years; and second, to write a first history of an important subcurrent of English modernism in the interwar period, seen through the eyes of one of its key (or "-ex") protagonists. No prosopographical reconstruction of the era, I would argue, can claim to be authoritative without some reinvigorated attempt to understand this important artist's life and work in relation to the pressures acting upon him and influencing cultural production and consumption in the interwar period. The "dilemma" referred to in the title then suggests an inability to be content with the explanation that Nevinson was simply a spent force after the war, or indeed an artist who epitomized only a general retreat from, and denial of, prewar and war modernisms. Likewise, the essays consider his own "dilemma" in both adapting and abandoning the formal qualities of modernism, in order to present and interpret the modern experience. In the light of these findings, can a wider aperture not be applied to observe a more general rejection of extreme and radical vocabulary, attributable not only to this individual, but to the history of English modernism in general, and in so doing question Nevinson's return to the conservative "right" as a homecoming to the Englishness of English art, to a native tradition that had merely flirted with foreign ideologies and goals, before returning to a more stable and logical destination? Whatever the medium used, Nevinson was a modern painter of a modern society, and though his brief *dalliance* with a historically or artistically conventional modernist dialect was over early in his career, his critical evaluation and investigation of the society in which he lived was not. The ambitions of a modern painter had changed, but the social and cultural relevance of his work had not, even if he had renounced all previous associations in pursuit of "legitimate art." Reshifting the emphasis, then, from an exclusive examination of formal qualities of paint on canvas, the essays in this collection explore the identity, positioning, output, and reception of an important modern artist in a country debating its relationship with both modernism and modernity over four vital decades in its history.

If the omission of C. R. W. Nevinson's name from its rightful place of prominence in cultural histories of the time and place is a mystery, then so too is the case of both his parents. Three out of four members of the Nevinson family left behind autobiographies, amounting to six volumes in all, and in addition to this, Henry Woodd Nevinson, known as "the king of war correspondents," was the author of more than thirty books. His wife Margaret, as well as writing several of her own, was a prominent suffragette and one of Britain's first female magistrates, while his second wife, Evelyn Sharp, was also a noted writer and feminist. The Nevinsons' Hampstead home, therefore, was a hub of debate concerning the suffragette movement, the Ulstermen of Carson, the decline of the Liberal Party, the continuing domestic threat caused by Britain's trade unions, as well as far flung issues relating to Russia, Greece, India, Ireland, Albania, Georgia, and even Angola. The young C. R. W. Nevinson, therefore, grew up in the realization that a new ideological climate existed in Britain, perhaps even predating Virginia Woolf's famous claim that it had all begun in (or around) December 1910.[14] Sir Charles Petrie had also observed that "The year 1910 . . . does seem to associate itself with an unwelcome change in the country's state of mind,"[15] while George Dangerfield had observed "the old order, the old bland order, was dying fast."[16] Nevinson's parents were not only observers of and commentators on this turbulent era; they were activists instrumental within it and in many cases close personal friends of the protagonists, such as Emmeline Pankhurst, Ramsay MacDonald, Herbert Asquith, W. B. Yeats, H. G. Wells, and a host of others. The link to protest and polemic seems obvious when the familial context is appreciated, and it is no surprise that father and son should have gone to the western front in each other's company. On a domestic level, however, such socially committed parents could often neglect their children to the point that their daughter Philippa is scarcely mentioned in all the volumes of memoirs combined, and C. R. W. Nevinson's reminiscences of them are often far from complimentary. Angela V. John ("A Family at War: The Nevinson Family") explores this relationship between Nevinson and his social milieu, evaluating how "journalism claimed him," and bringing to light the link to the arts, through his father, which was more than coincidental or peripheral in importance. Through this important chapter it becomes clear why contemporary observers could comment "He is the son of H. W. Nevinson, the war correspondent, who also has a rebellious temperament. The father, however, confines his violent revolutionism to politics and journalism, while the son finds more colour for his views in the paint-box."[17] Professor John's own biographical study of Henry Nevinson, entitled *War, Journalism and the Shaping of the 20th Century. The Life and Times of Henry W. Nevinson*, was published in 2006.

For three years Nevinson was schooled at the Slade School of Art (hereafter: the Slade) with the "who's who" of early twentieth-century art in England, where he was the friend and "admirer" of Dora Carrington and best friend of Mark Gertler—himself a flamboyant and charismatic character. In fact Gilbert Cannan based his novel *Mendel* around these three young artists in the wider context of the school during its prewar triumphal flow, or in Henry Tonks's words, the Slade's "second crisis of brilliance." C. R. W. Nevinson was very much a part, if not at the head, of a peer group that included David Bomberg, John Currie, Paul Nash, Edward Wadsworth, and Stanley Spencer, as they received an education both within, and outside of, the walls of the institution. David Boyd Haycock ("A Crisis of Brilliance: C. R. W. Nevinson, Henry Tonks and the Slade School of Art, 1909–12"), examines the role of the Slade, and in particular the teachings of Henry Tonks, in formulating Nevinson's development as an artist (despite their reciprocal loathing), and evaluates the internal and external influences acting on him and his fellow students in the years before the Great War. In particular, Haycock assesses the importance of Roger Fry's first Postimpressionist exhibition in 1910, and identifies, perhaps surprisingly, the stronger influence that came from Renaissance sources and led to the rise and fall of the Neo-Primitives, before graduation in the year 1912. The Slade was vital to the creation of the avant-garde in prewar London, and in turn to the war art of the nation several years later, and so deserves this timely preliminary analysis before Haycock's full study is presented in the forthcoming book *A Crisis of Brilliance: Five Young British Artists, 1908–1919*.

Few would argue that Futurism was the peacetime zenith for Nevinson and his work, and the manifesto *Vital English Art* (written in collaboration with F. T. Marinetti) the crowning achievement. By late 1913 or early 1914 there could be little doubt that in the art world, as much as in other walks of life, a substantial and irreversible change was becoming inevitable; and Futurism was there, at the heart of these changes, to confront the past and catalyze the arrival of the future. Nevinson would not have been far from the mind of Sir Osbert Sitwell when the latter wrote: "A ferment such as I have never since felt in this country prevailed over the world of art. It seemed as if at last we were on the verge of a great movement."[18] Likewise, Ezra Pound observed that these "new masses of unexplored arts and facts are pouring into the vortex of London."[19] And so, having lived the student life of the Slade, and the bohemian life of the café and the theater in Paris, Nevinson returned to London and there found precisely the movement he had been looking for, albeit from Milan. Italian Futurism promised all the bombast, publicity, and polemic that he could have desired and a timely alternative to the London Group, the Camden Town Group, the NEAC, and the Bloomsbury Group. Nevinson now became, through direct association with F. T. Marinetti and Gino Severini, perhaps the only English artist who "unmistakably deserved the label 'Futurist'"[20] and on that trajectory got to work violently rejecting the past, universities, snobs, the inhabitants of Chelsea, the professors at the "stinking" Royal Academy, and above all else, *passéism*. Now his desire was to replace all of this with a new love of violence, danger, industry, skyscrapers, traffic, and noise, in a celebration of the era of Morse, Edison, Bell, Ford, aviation, and mass production. Art, he felt, had a duty to acknowledge, if not embrace, this very simple fact if it was to remain relevant to the society in which it existed.

In releasing a Futurist Manifesto for England, however, Nevinson went a step too far and split the English avant-garde, catalyzing the formation of the Vorticist Group under Wyndham Lewis, who chose to reject the Italian ethos as it stood and to create, instead, a British version of it. The results artistically, both Futurist and Vorticist, were an outrage to London society, though today they hang in the Tate Gallery as vital icons of the adventurous and pioneering spirit that characterized British culture in the prewar era. But barring superficial glimpses, the manifesto itself, so crucial in the development of the prewar avant-garde, has gone unstudied until now. A close reading of the document has been undertaken by Johann Pillai and Anber Onar ("Tracing the Performative: F. T. Marinetti, C. R. W. Nevinson, and the English Futurist Manifesto") for the first time, from the perspective of its literary value and performative potentialities, as well as in terms of the artistic implications inherent within the text, and the impact of "foreign" modernist ideologies on a homegrown avant-garde. Onar and Pillai have placed their study within a literary, artistic, and historical framework on both national and international levels, with parallel readings of French and Italian translations, to clarify many of the existing misconceptions surrounding the relationship between Lewis and Nevinson/Futurism and Vorticism. In so doing, and also in assessing the impact of the "manifesto-as-performed," they offer an intriguing and thorough rereading of this episode in the history of English art, on the eve of a war that augured doom for both Futurism and extreme modernist rhetoric of this nature. It was, to use the vocabulary of the manifesto itself, a final "hurrah" at the zenith of the modernist experiment in London, before the "deluge" that the following months and years were to bring.

Recontextualizing the Futurist Vorticist schism, and that of the two chief protagonists, provides an engaging starting point for Paul Edwards's discussion in the following chapter ("Artists as Activists: C. R. W. Nevinson and Wyndham Lewis"), using as a starting point their own autobiographies: Nevinson's aptly named *Paint and Prejudice*, and Lewis's *Blasting and Bombardiering*. Though Lewis's book has been studied and analyzed in the interim years, Nevinson's account of himself has been allowed to form the virtually unquestioned basis of our understanding for over half a century. But this is symptomatic of the critical attention the former has received in comparison to the latter, and typical of the total eclipse of one by the other in scholarship in subsequent years—a balance that Paul Edwards in this chapter goes some way to redress. Through an analysis of the autobiographies in relation to one another, the historical inaccuracy or intentional deceit that both utilized in order to reinforce their self-images during a lull in their careers, and using other published accounts (some disguised in the form of novels), Edwards has attempted to validate and question the claims made by both Nevinson and Lewis concerning the fates of both modern art and artists in interwar England. This new understanding is vitally important in appreciating the work of these prewar rivals and for rethinking the pressures on modernist coteries in prewar and interwar London, especially for rebels-at-arms, who became, in difficult times, the best of enemies.

Following the polemics of his Futurist days, and after the destruction of the Great War, Nevinson decided to go in search of a positive modernity, which he believed could be found in New York City, and this is the focus of my essay ("'A Veiled and Virgin Shore': C. R. W. Nevinson and the (end of an) American Dream"). Not wishing to be caught up in the general European-wide *rappel a l'ordre* he sailed for the United States in 1919, and returned a second time in 1920, to confront what was both triumph and tragedy on a grand scale. He was in awe of New York City, and viewed it as a refreshing break from the war scenes with which his name had become inextricably linked. The nightclubs, the fashions, the dances, and the skyline would make a welcome change from the western front, and accordingly he enthused, "Where the Venetians drove stakes into his sandbanks to overcome nature, the American has pegged his city to the sky. No sight can be more exhilarating and beautiful than this triumph of man."[21] Additionally, he was given a celebrity's welcome, though he spoiled things somewhat when inexplicably, and rather undiplomatically, he told his assembled American hosts that there was no such thing as American art and declared that their idea of an artist was a plumber; their idea of art, a well-appointed bathroom. It was not long before he was in the headlines in the new world, every bit as much as he had been in the old, and at the center of some very similar storms. An indication of this can be sensed in C. Lewis Hind's introduction to the catalog for Nevinson's second one-man show in New York City in 1920, which read, "It is something, at the age of thirty one, to be among the most discussed, most successful, most promising, most admired, and most hated of British artists." Nothing has previously been published on Nevinson and his brief relationship with American modernism, and so this essay charts the artist's last great chance to convert his work into a peaceful, yet relevant and innovative language that might yet interpret, criticize, celebrate, or challenge the modernity of his era. Moreover, it explains how that chance was lost.

Nevinson's work in the years following his return from the USA (1920–46) has been totally eclipsed by his earlier output in all published art histories of the era. In most cases it has been ignored entirely. Neglected particularly are his studies of London and Paris where, in the time-honored role of *flaneur,* he was well known and widely respected as the type of genius who could emerge from the horrors of the last four years to tackle the urban utopia of the Roaring Twenties, the Flapper, the Charleston, and so on. [Such was the respect he commanded, he was chosen to represent the fine arts of Great Britain, together with H. G. Wells for literature and Edward Elgar for music, in the peace delegation to Prague in 1921]. The social commentator, the art critic, the cynic, the Café Royal-ist, the giver of legendary society parties (which were reported as far away as Delhi, Melbourne, and Buenos Aires, and which Stanley Spencer reminisced were "like a wonderful love affair"[22]), was now running the very real risk of becoming an artistic "has-been," but very much "in" as a *boulevardier* and *bon viveur.* A veritable icon of his age, Nevinson was reengaging in the cultural and social developments of the 1920s to which he was so eminently suited, wielding a pen in some cases more effectively than the brush. Indeed, both as a writer and literary character, Nevinson was not insignificant or peripheral in interwar London. The bohemian of three cities (two after the New York fiasco) was, however, privately consumed by a depression following the death of his infant son, and by his gradually being sidelined by the art establishment of London. From here began his very public, sometimes personal, written attacks on the Royal Academy, the New English Art Club, and even on icons of the age, and family friends, such as George "Barnum" Shaw, Henry "Henrietta" Tonks, Muirhead "Bonehead" Bone, the "Gloomsburies," and Sir Kenneth "Napoleon" Clark. In fact Nevinson now began to refocus on writing entirely, as Lewis was doing, and this was to be the start of a long and prodigious output which is today housed in fourteen volumes of press cuttings at the Tate Archive, and in many other archives throughout the world. On a much more substantial scale, in addition to cowriting the novel *Exodus Ad: A Warning to Civilians* with Princess Troubetzkoy, and his autobiography *Paint and Prejudice,* he was also written about, appearing in numerous novels and literary works of the era such as *Back to Montparnasse* and *Mr. Paname* by Sisley Huddleston; *Mendel* by Gilbert Cannan; *The Power of the Dead* and *Phoenix Generation* by Henry Williamson; and *Impressions* by Ethel Mannin. More importantly he featured in an early draft of *The Waste Land* by T. S. Eliot (later modified by Ezra Pound), that read:

> He the young man carbuncular will stare,
> Boldly about in London's one café,
> And he will tell her with a casual air,
> Grandly, I have been with Nevinson today.

In other essays, such as *The Seven Pillars of Fire,* Nevinson preached of a terrifying future for civilization, to parallel the slipping control of the League of Nations and the inevitable and imminent outcome that was to manifest itself in the Second World War. It would not be long before Nevinson could watch at first hand that terrible premonition realized, firstly in the Blitz of London, Coventry, and Liverpool, and then reciprocally in the RAF firestorms at Dresden and Hamburg. Nevinson, now manically depressed and despairing for civilization, even said that he was glad his son had died in infancy as, at the age of seventeen, he would merely have been bred for slaughter. As a living artist he was hardly more optimistic when he said he would "rather be a Jew in Germany than an artist in England." Christopher Martin ("Nevinson and Fiction: A Survey") has produced the first study of Nevinson and his relationship to literature and the written word. From the pronouncements of a playboy, to the "warnings of Cassandra," there is, in this chapter, a valuable resource concerning Britain, literature, and society in the interwar years, culminating in a close study of *Exodus AD*—a valuable parallel to Nevinson's apocalyptic images from the 1930s, discussed further in chapter 9.

Neither has there been any attempt to study Nevinson's considerable career as a printmaker, even though it spanned his most productive periods on the western front, in Manhattan, Paris, and London, and, of course, in the English/Welsh countryside. In fact, it is quite commonly believed that his achievements in this field were often more notable than his works on canvas and so the absence of even a *catalogue raisonné* remains a glaring omission in the history of British visual culture. Jonathan Black ("Beauty, Rhythm, Strength: C. R. W. Nevinson as a Printmaker ca. 1916–32") has produced an essay that will stand as a valuable and long overdue "first" in this genre, analyzing Nevinson's total output of approximately 155 images, all completed before 1932, and concluding, "Nevinson ought to be considered one of the major British artistic talents of the twentieth century." His chapter demonstrates this beyond any reasonable doubt.

Scrutinizing not only what Nevinson saw, but how he saw it, Ben Jones ("Denying the 'Foe-to-graphic': C. R. W. Nevinson and Photography") has produced a solid piece of analytical observation, based on rigorous archival research, the results of which are not mildly surprising. Far from the artist armed only with sketchbook (on one occasion preparing to jump from a balloon basket high over the western front), and always staring the subject eyeball to eyeball, Jones finds some far from coincidental similarities between Nevinson's most celebrated works, and photographs published or exhibited at the same time. His essay therefore looks at Nevinson's dual use of the photographic image; initially, in the production of his more complex works of art, but also in the theatrical creation of his own public image. The results are groundbreaking, not only in terms of the mode of production, but as a sociologically sensitive account of how Nevinson built his rebel, then prodigal, image throughout his life. The camera, it turns out, despite his protestations to the contrary, was a recurrent creative crutch in creating both modern art and the modern artist.

London, and in particular Nevinson's Hampstead, was regrouping too, to become home to Ben Nicholson, Barbara Hepworth, Henry Moore, Walter Gropius, Wells Coates, Nuam Gabo, Piet Mondrian, and a host of others, some of whom were coming from a progressively intolerant European mainland. And yet, despite having plenty to say about both art and politics, Nevinson, now an "old hand," remained outside group identities that might have lured him toward Constructivism, Surrealism, Mass Observation, or Social Realism. Quite the contrary, it was in the 1930s that Nevinson started a decadelong association with the Royal Academy that would see fifty-five of his works exhibited before his death, despite his open detestation of the institution. That said, in the 1930s Nevinson remained as belligerent as ever, to the point that the *Star* newspaper called him "eternally the bad boy . . . among the artists." This is the starting point for Sue Malvern ("Nevinson's 'bad boy' Modernisms and Fascism in the 1930s") and her analysis of Nevinson's exhibited series of allegories, sometimes called his "problem pictures," that became increasingly political as the threat of fascism became more overt. In this chapter Malvern unpicks the contradictions in Nevinson's politics and practice in the 1930s, to argue that the artist's work played off the propaganda of dictatorships, particularly Mussolini's Italy, to perform a preposterous masculinity that functioned as a critique of fascism. Malvern observes "Nevinson's absence from artists' antiwar and antifascist activism in the 1930s raises the question of the perplexity and elusiveness of his political position, especially in an age when it was not possible to be neutral about the pressures that faced intellectuals and artists." Her chapter, the first published on Nevinson's work in the 1930s, as international relations began their descent into the second global catastrophe of the twentieth century, is a welcome critical appraisal (which works closely with Christopher Martin's study), and will undoubtedly foster further debate.

Nevinson lived to see both the beginning and the end of the Second World War, helping as a stretcher-bearer when the Blitz came, painting the conflict as it returned to the skies over London, and died one year after VE and VJ Days. In his *New York Times* obituary he was immediately remembered as a "genius, playboy and war hero," and though this was undoubtedly tongue-in-cheek, I think he deserved much of that accolade. There could have been no more dedicated and conscientious artist than he, and it is here in this collection of essays that many of his achievements, neglected, forgotten, or never studied, are reevaluated or indeed approached for the first time. It is beyond doubt that Nevinson retreated stylistically from the aggressiveness of the avant-garde after the Great War and paid scant regard to Anglo-French formalism throughout the rest of his career. That is not to say, however, that he detached himself entirely from social and cultural engagement. If we are determined to adhere to the belief that his role after the Great War *is* a disappointment or an evasion from all that had gone before, then as a barometer of cultural welfare he acts as a very important constant, even in retreat. On the other hand we can view Nevinson's interwar period in the same way that Sir Osbert Sitwell did (appendix, "C. R. W. Nevinson," 1925) when he described him as a "born explorer," and an "an almost legendary figure of violence." Critic T. W. Earp went so far as to call him a "traveller amongst tourists,"[23] and accordingly, this volume of essays views art in England through the eyes of both the "explorer" and "traveller," observing the individual and collective "dilemma of English modernism" at this time.

In September 1942, Winston Churchill wrote to Nevinson thanking the artist for a painting he had given to him, saying: "I am sure the young men who are fighting regard you as part of the England they defend."[24] I should like to present this collection of essays with every bit the same gravitas and centrality suggested by Churchill in his positioning of Nevinson at the heart of Englishness and English culture in the first half of the twentieth century.

Notes

1. *Evening Standard*, October 7, 1946.
2. *News Chronicle*, October 8, 1946
3. *Liverpool Daily*, October 8, 1946.
4. *Daily Mail*, October 8, 1946
5. *Scotsman*, October 8, 1946.
6. *Cavalcade*, May 31, 1947.
7. Janet Dunbar, *Laura Knight* (London: Collins, 1975), 159–60.
8. Lisa M. Messinger "Nevinson in New York" (lecture, Yale Center for British Art, New Haven, CT, March 1, 2000).
9. C. R. W. Nevinson, "The Arts Within This Bellicose Civilisation," in *The Seven Pillars of Fire* (London: Herbert Jenkins, 1936), 181–220.
10. Some useful sources relating to Nevinson scholarship might include Sue Malvern's doctoral dissertation on the official war artist scheme in Britain in the Great War (S. Malvern, "Art, Patronage and Propaganda: British Modern Art Discourses and Official War Art During the First World War" [PhD diss., Reading University, UK, 1981]. Charles Doherty's doctoral dissertation provides a *catalogue raisonné* for part of the period in question and with it a useful introductory essay (C. Doherty, "Nash, Nevinson and Roberts at War: A Catalogue Raisonné of first World War Paintings, Drawings and Prints by Paul Nash, C. R. W. Nevinson and William Roberts" [PhD diss., University of Wisconsin, Madison, 1989]. Melissa Hall also dealt with Nevinson within a wider study of the political implications of a state-sponsored war art in Britain where she examined aesthetic discourses and critical debates relating to modernism (specifically to masculinity and militarism) during the war years. Nevinson appeared in her discussion, but again, like Malvern and Doherty, her research was neither based exclusively around Nevinson nor was it concerned with the person, rather the critical opinion, which his work inspired, and again, it was focused on the war years. (M. Hall, "Modernism, Militarism and Masculinity: British Modern Art Discourses and Official War Art During the First World War" [PhD diss., State University of New York at Binghampton, 1994]. Jonathan Black's essays, his curatorial achievements, and his doctoral dissertation have all added valuable pieces to the puzzle. See: " 'Neither Beasts, nor Gods, But Men': Constructions of Masculinity and the Image of the British Soldier (or "Tommy") in the First World War Art of: C. R. W. Nevinson (1889–1946); Eric H. Kennington (1888–1960) and Charles Sargeant Jagger (1885–1934)" [PhD diss., University College, London, 2003].
11. J. Russell Taylor, "The Big Show: C. R. W. Nevinson," *Times*, October 30, 1999.
12. "C. R. W. Nevinson," *Antiques and The Arts Weekly*, February 11, 2000.
13. B. Sewell, "Pictures that pack a punch," *Evening Standard*, November 19, 1999, 34.
14. V. Woolf, *Mr. Bennett and Mr. Brown*. Cited in H. Read, *Contemporary British Art* (Harmondsworth, UK: Penguin Books, 1951).
15. Sir C. Petrie, *The Edwardians* (London: W. W. Norton, 1965), 231.
16. Ibid., p. 67.
17. *T.P.'s Weekly*, August 7, 1915.
18. Sir O. Sitwell, *Great Morning*, 235. Cited in W. C. Wees, *Vorticism and the English Avant-Garde* (Manchester, UK: Manchester University Press, 1972), p. 61.
19. E. Pound, "Affirmations VI," *New Age* 16, no. 15 (1915): 411.
20. W. C. Wees, *Vorticism and the English Avant-Garde* (Toronto: Toronto University Press, 1972), 106.
21. C. R. W. Nevinson, "The Most Beautiful City: Which is it? London? Paris? New York?" *Daily Chronicle*, October 24, 1929.
22. Stanley Spencer, "My Romances," January 1942. Tate Archive Cat: 733.2.105.
23. T. W. Earp, *New Statesman*, October 13, 1928.
24. Winston Churchill to C. R. W. Nevinson, October 7, 1942, Private Communication, Churchill Archives Centre, Churchill College, Cambridge (Char 2/458).

A Family at War: The Nevinson Family

Angela V. John

In January 1909 the war correspondent, essayist, and campaigner for social justice, Henry Woodd Nevinson, wrote to the classical scholar Gilbert Murray about his son C. R.W. Nevinson. He explained to Murray that he would not be following in his own footsteps: "No, my son absolutely refuses to go to Oxford. He cares for nothing in the world but 'art.' It is a dreary prospect."[1]

Given his subsequent fame as an artist and the renewal of interest in his work today, Henry Nevinson's gloomy prognosis was clearly incorrect even though Richard (as his family called him) was not always appreciated by the art world. His father's disparaging tone is worth noting, as is his use of inverted commas. Yet Henry Nevinson was highly cultured and friendly with a number of artists and art critics. His somewhat disingenuous comments were partly tailored to the views of the letter's recipient, an Oxford don. As a father, Henry Nevinson also harbored misgivings about the prospects in such a precarious profession. The previous year he had gone to his son's studio and found him doing "that queer kind of work that seems so unlike work."[2] He did, however, recognize his talent, conceding that he had executed a fine, very Russian, charcoal portrait of a workman with a flag.[3]

This essay explores the familial dimension of Richard Nevinson's life, showing how and why many of his claims about his background were distorted. It concentrates especially on the complicated relationship between father and son, examining how their life stories, interests, and perspectives converged and diverged, and assesses their interdependence. The artist claimed that he was born in 1889 "into the most exquisite and intellectual ambience."[4] Both of his parents, Henry Nevinson (fig. 1) and Margaret Wynne Nevinson (née Jones) (fig. 2) were educated, successful, and independent thinkers living in London's Hampstead. They had one daughter, Philippa, who had been born in Germany and was five years older than her brother. Richard Nevinson's commitment to art and infamous posturing can in part be perceived as a reaction against his parents, especially his well-known, radical father. The relationship between father and son was a complex, symbiotic one that, time and again, revealed them to be more similar than either acknowledged.

And despite Henry Nevinson's remarks to Gilbert Murray, this was a family for whom art mattered. Some of Richard Nevinson's relatives had been amateur artists, for example, his grandfather George Nevinson, a Leicester solicitor. He also collected English landscapes and one of his sketchbooks survives.[5] Richard's great-uncle, Charles Woodd, drew skillfully and his uncle, Edward Bonney Nevinson, became an architect. Moreover, some of Henry Nevinson's publications involved close collaboration with artists. He provided a number of sketches for his own books and articles[6] and wrote the text and introduction for *Pictures of Classical Greek Landscape and Architecture* (1897), which he jointly authored with the artist and architect John Fulleylove RI.[7] A lover of Greece, he was personally familiar with all but one of the locations depicted in its thirty-eight black-and-white plates. Fulleylove was a neighbor and gave the young Nevinson (a friend of his son's) some private tuition in drawing.

In 1904 Henry Nevinson wrote nearly a hundred pages of text to accompany the French section of *Sketches On The Old Road Through France to Florence*, a lavish work by the publisher and amateur artist John Murray.[8] Henry Nevinson followed the course of the watercolors reproduced in this volume (using the latest development in the photographic three-color process) before writing the text and introduction. After World War I, both father and son recognized the potential of the American market. In 1920, during the first of several lecturing and journalistic assignments in the United States,[9] Henry Nevinson worked on arrangements for his son's forthcoming exhibition at New York's Bourgeois Galleries.[10] Ten years later he published an analysis of English society primarily for American readers. Entitled *The Natives of England* (and *Rough Islanders* in Britain) it included sixteen plates depicting Richard's work.[11]

Henry, Margaret, and Richard—three of the four Nevinsons—published autobiographies. The parents wrote their accounts in the 1920s and their son's appeared a decade later, producing a total of six volumes in all. It has long been recognized that the artist's autobiography, *Paint and Prejudice*, published in 1937 after his mother's death and when his father was in his early eighties, is far from being the most reliable of sources. It evinces both pride and prejudice,

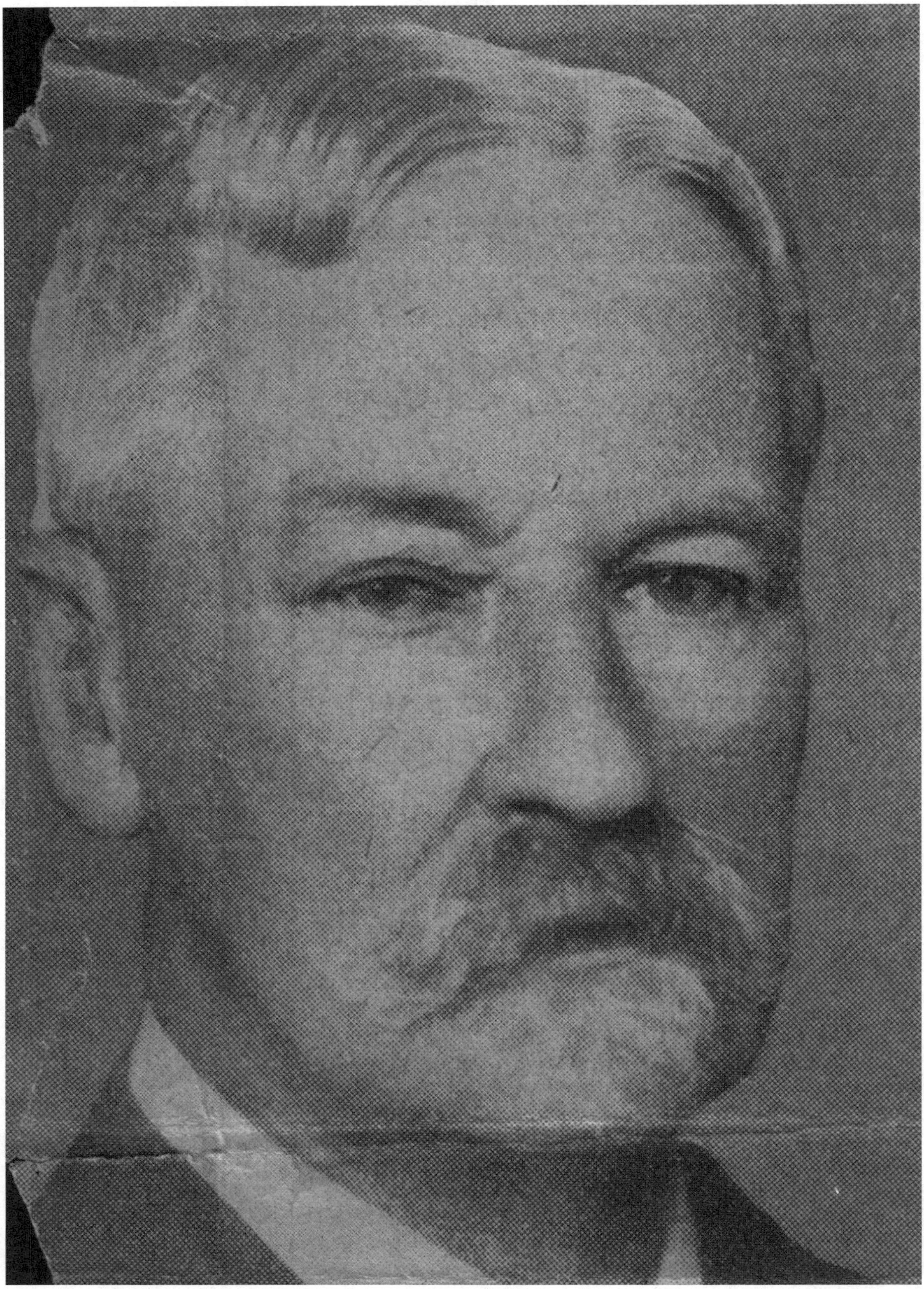

1. The artist's father, Henry W. Nevinson, *Daily Herald*, August 27, 1932 (Private Collection).

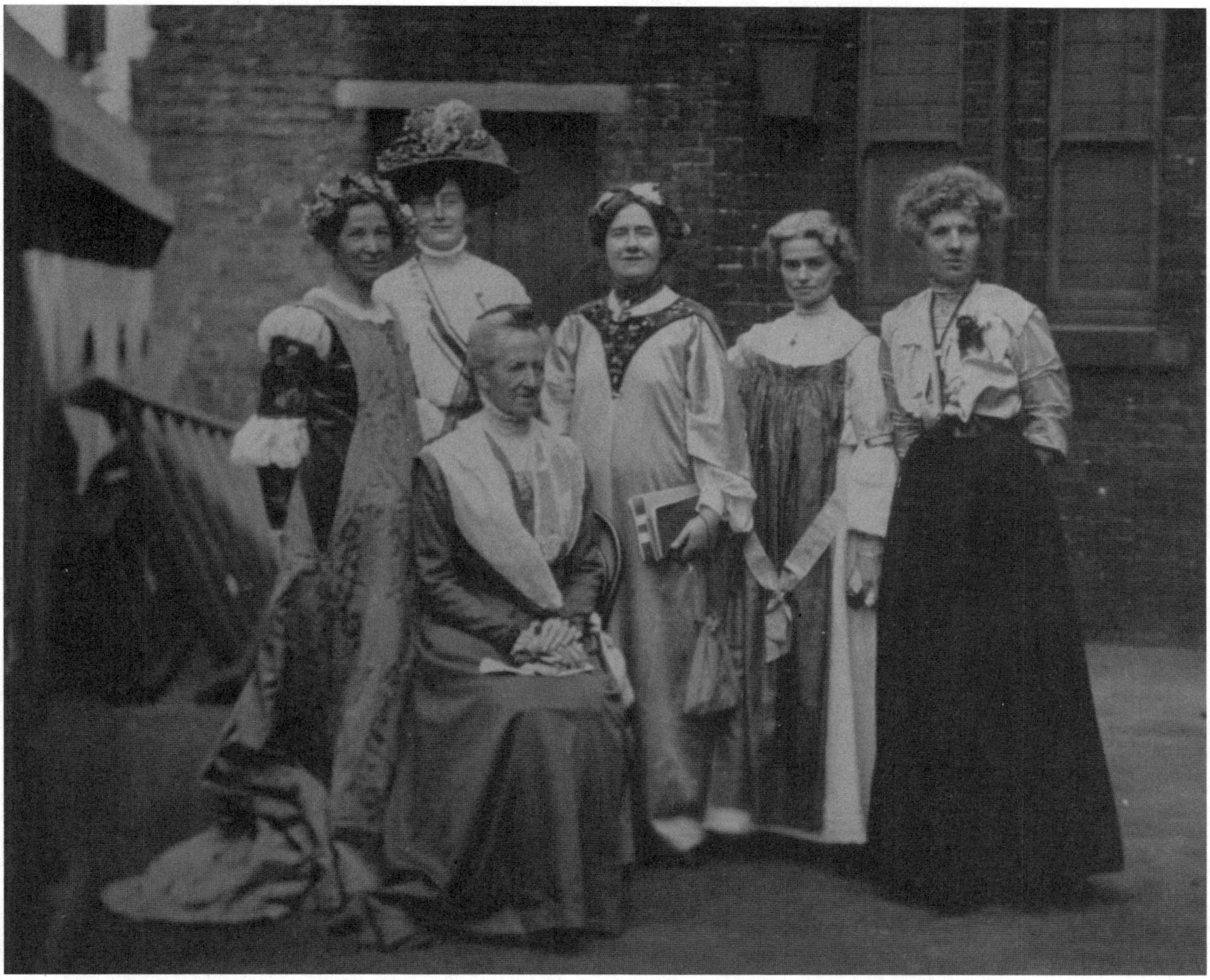

2. The artist's mother, Margaret Wynne Nevinson, dressed for a Women's Freedom League suffrage pageant ca. 1910. Margaret is standing with books in her hand. (Private Collection: Myrna Goode)

is frequently inaccurate and fascinatingly, deliberately misleading. The picture it composes of family life cries out for alternative perspectives. But his parents' memoirs also require critical reading. The silences in both Henry Nevinson's triple-decker contribution[12] and in his wife Margaret's autobiography[13] are especially revealing and these books unwittingly say much about a family whose members led outwardly successful lives but which was actually, by any standard, dysfunctional. War may have been the key subject for the work of both father and son but here was also a family that was far from harmonious and whose members were rarely at peace with each other.

Margaret Nevinson published short stories and pamphlets. Her husband wrote over thirty books and thousands of articles. But for insight into this troubled family, a far richer source is Henry Nevinson's voluminous diary, now in the Bodleian Library, Oxford. It was meticulously sustained from the early 1890s until just before his death in 1941. Although highly subjective, it is a valuable corrective to his own and his son's published utterances. The lack of a comparable source for his wife does, however, raise questions about how to discern her perspectives.

Today Henry Nevinson is less well known than is his son. Yet for much of C. R. W. Nevinson's life, his father was the famous one.[14] He was friendly with writers, diplomats, soldiers, and political dissidents across the world. Acknowledged as the "King of war correspondents," he had been in Ladysmith at the time of the siege. He witnessed upheavals in the Russian Empire and the Balkans and made an intrepid journey into the heart of Portuguese Angola. His excoriating prose exposing the persistence of the Angolan slave trade provoked unease in British diplomatic circles, worried cocoa manufacturers, and stirred radical opinion. This was part of his trademark. In India he followed in Keir Hardie's footsteps but was considered by the British authorities to be more subversive than the founder of the Independent Labour Party. He was committed to the rights of small nations and especially concerned about the fate of Ireland and Georgia. Despite his age, he was still reporting during the First World War and, when nearly sixty, was wounded at Gallipoli. He was present at Mons when the Armistice was announced in 1918 and lived until his mid-eighties, assiduously fashioning and refashioning images of himself over time. At home he was a passionate defender of women's suffrage, chaired the most militant of the men's support groups, was thrown out of suffrage meetings, arrested, and resigned his post on the *Daily News* because of the paper's problematic stance on the forcible feeding of suffragettes in prison. He was known as the champion of lost causes though he argued that this was not true since the causes he espoused tended to be won—eventually.

Nevinson Senior was admired and envied because, unlike many associated with military matters, he was also a man of literature. He edited the Literary Page of the *Daily Chronicle* when this Liberal paper was at its height, published exquisite essays, and wrote short fiction and biographical studies of Herder, Schiller, Goethe, and Hardy. He was a hard act for a son to follow. And much of the latter's behavior can be seen as a reaction against the world his father inhabited. Predictably, he sought to emulate as well as ridicule. Richard Nevinson's fashioning of his own identity—from his name to his notoriety—told a tale about his need to be appreciated in his own right.[15]

In 1912, he told fellow art student Dora Carrington that "I, who was born for Oxford & the army in a hotbed of intellectualism, religion & the classics, found refreshment in ugliness & the uncouth."[16] Choosing, like his father, to be seen as a rebel, Richard Nevinson was positing his conception of the modern against parents steeped in classical education. When asked by the BBC to describe the age he would most like to have lived in, Henry Nevinson opted for Periclean Athens.[17]

Margaret Nevinson had an external degree from St. Andrews University, Scotland, and had taught classics at South Hampstead High School.[18] She was also a writer and feminist, a leading figure in the suffrage Women's Freedom League, a school manager for twenty-five years, and long-standing and committed Poor Law Guardian. In 1920 she became one of Britain's first women magistrates and was the first woman in London to adjudicate at Criminal Petty Sessions. Her son liked to give the impression that she was immersed in public rather than domestic life: "if my mother does happen to be in for a meal she is so engrossed in other things that she hardly hears and certainly never takes in a word I say."[19]

Richard Nevinson's autobiographical depiction of his family as part of the Hampstead intelligentsia provided a fitting background for the budding artist. But it is complicated by tensions within the family. His parents came from religious families based in Leicester though the Nevinsons saw themselves as socially superior to the Joneses. They were also committed Evangelicals whereas the Reverend Jones (Margaret's father) and his family were High Church Anglicans. Henry Nevinson reacted against this. He came to reject many of the trappings of organized religion and certainly did not share his wife's fervent Anglo-Catholicism. And although the couple shared a love of the classical world (which was reflected in their publications),[20] greatly admired Thomas Carlyle and German culture, and actively supported women's rights, their politics and perspectives were frequently at variance with one another.

Both seem to have regretted marrying. Margaret Nevinson's writings resonate with bitterness. Her 1922 volume *Fragments of Life* (her husband's abridged version of his memoirs was carefully entitled *Fire of Life*) mixes fact and fiction. Dedicated to her son, it includes a story called "An Everyday Tragedy." Here a woman explains how she endured her husband's affairs since "I had my son, you see I could not leave him."[21] The story "Port After Stormy Seas" stresses how the wives of literary men "must get used to being forgotten."[22]

Margaret and Henry Nevinson's autobiographies are best read contrapuntally. They both refer only sparingly and formally to their respective spouses. The writer and suffragette Evelyn Sharp who had figured in Henry Nevinson's life since the start of the century, features more prominently than does his wife.[23] He married her seven months after Margaret died. Even on the day of his wife's death in 1932, Henry Nevinson's diary referred to their "dismal marriage" in 1884 and how she was "little suited to me."[24] He had been involved in several serious relationships lasting for many years, the first when his son was a few years old. At the start of the new century the family moved to a third home in the Hampstead area and although Margaret and Henry Nevinson never formally separated, this large Downside Crescent house enabled the couple to inhabit separate space within their home. They led semidetached (but never suburban) lives in their semidetached house. Henry Nevinson was frequently absent during his son's youth: working nights as a literary editor, reviewing plays, abroad as a newspaper correspondent, reporting or giving talks on a range of causes. He represented, in an extreme form, the "flight from domesticity" which the historian John Tosh sees as prevalent among late Victorian middle-class Englishmen.[25] In 1919 Henry described Christmas Day with Margaret, Philippa, and Richard as "terrible." His son was "obsessive," taking "all the wrong aggressive approaches."[26] Henry Nevinson chose to spend subsequent Christmas celebrations in England with friends instead of family.

The young Richard Nevinson inhabited a predominantly female household composed of his mother, various maids, and sister Philippa. The family home in Hampstead was in John Street (now Keats Grove), in a house chosen for location rather than luxury: damp and lacking the basic facilities of their previous artisans' dwellings in Whitechapel. After her son's birth Margaret contracted puerperal fever and almost died. Unlike many women of her time and class, she was prepared to admit that she did not adapt easily to the constant demands of small children and in her memoirs stated that "it is a terrible thing to be a mother."[27]

Richard Nevinson's looks were "pure Jones, not Nevinsonian."[28] Philippa Nevinson also resembled her mother though inherited her father's ruddy complexion. She is largely conspicuous by her absence in the Nevinson memoirs. Henry Nevinson's diaries sometimes refer to skating, playing cricket, and walking with his son, and occasional holidays such as a ski trip to Switzerland and France together in 1909, but there are only scanty references to his daughter. She was a talented pianist and singer and studied at the Royal College of Music and at the Milan Conservatoire, yet mention of her was generally accompanied by criticism. Brother and sister never seem to have been close. The attention given to Richard may have soured sibling relations in the longer term. Their stepmother Evelyn Sharp was well aware of their feuds. After their father's death and the bomb-damaged house in Downside Crescent needed to be sold (the money from the sale was to be divided between Evelyn and the children) Philippa initially rejected an offer for the house. Evelyn Sharp suspected that this was due to "her horrible desire to hurt Richard whenever she can." In her opinion, the origin of "all her difficult behaviour" lay "buried in her childhood."[29] But Philippa's later years were also marred by other problems. She and her architect husband, Sidney Caulfield, faced some financial difficulties, exacerbated by the fragile mental state of her son Toby who spent most of his life in asylums, dying when he was twenty-five.

To many outsiders the Nevinson family appeared not only cultured and progressive but also united. Arnold Bennett's journal records dining at the home of H. G. Wells in December 1909. Mrs. Nevinson was one of the guests and "agreeably disagreeable of demeanour at first. I soon broke down her barriers by talking about H.W.N.'s *Neighbours of Ours*."[30] Yet there were serious differences of opinion between the Nevinsons as to the true author of this collection of "slum stories" dating from the 1880s when they lived in London's East End. The literary style was indisputably Henry's but Margaret had worked as a rent collector in two large blocks of artisans' dwellings in Whitechapel and probably supplied much background material. She maintained that she should have received credit for her contribution.[31]

Richard Nevinson's education reflected his parents' lack of agreement. Henry Nevinson had gone to a public school himself. He remembered his own misery when first entering Shrewsbury School, though he had soon flourished. His diary suggests that he, along with many other men of his time, believed that such an experience would "make a man" out of his son.[32] And there is evidence of some irritation with Richard's "slack" and "loafing" ways.[33] The choice of Uppingham School, Rutland, a public school with a reputation for sport, was not, however, the most appropriate for a boy like Richard Nevinson who was uninterested in games. Moreover, he had recently begun to enjoy art at the Junior Department of University College School. *Paint and Prejudice* stresses an ability to paint imaginary and historical subjects at this time.[34] However, the recent discovery of his Nature Studies Exercise Book (fig. 3) from University College School does not suggest anything outstanding about his drawing.[35] As a day-boy Richard had, however, flourished generally and become a monitor. Uppingham was another story. He spent three miserable years there, exacerbated by ill health culminating in an emergency appendectomy.

The Uppingham episode is revealing in the way it was later used by the Nevinsons. Richard Nevinson retold it as a story of extreme abuse and neglect. Like other public schools it was spartan and undoubtedly a shock for a sensitive boy. The experience is recounted as unremitting: "I withered. I learned nothing; I did nothing."[36] His graphic account is bounded by short sentences, which serve to emphasize the horrors: The darkness starts with "Then came the *débâcle*. I was sent to Uppingham" and finally there is light when "From Uppingham I went straight to heaven: to St John's Wood School of Art, where I was to train for the Royal

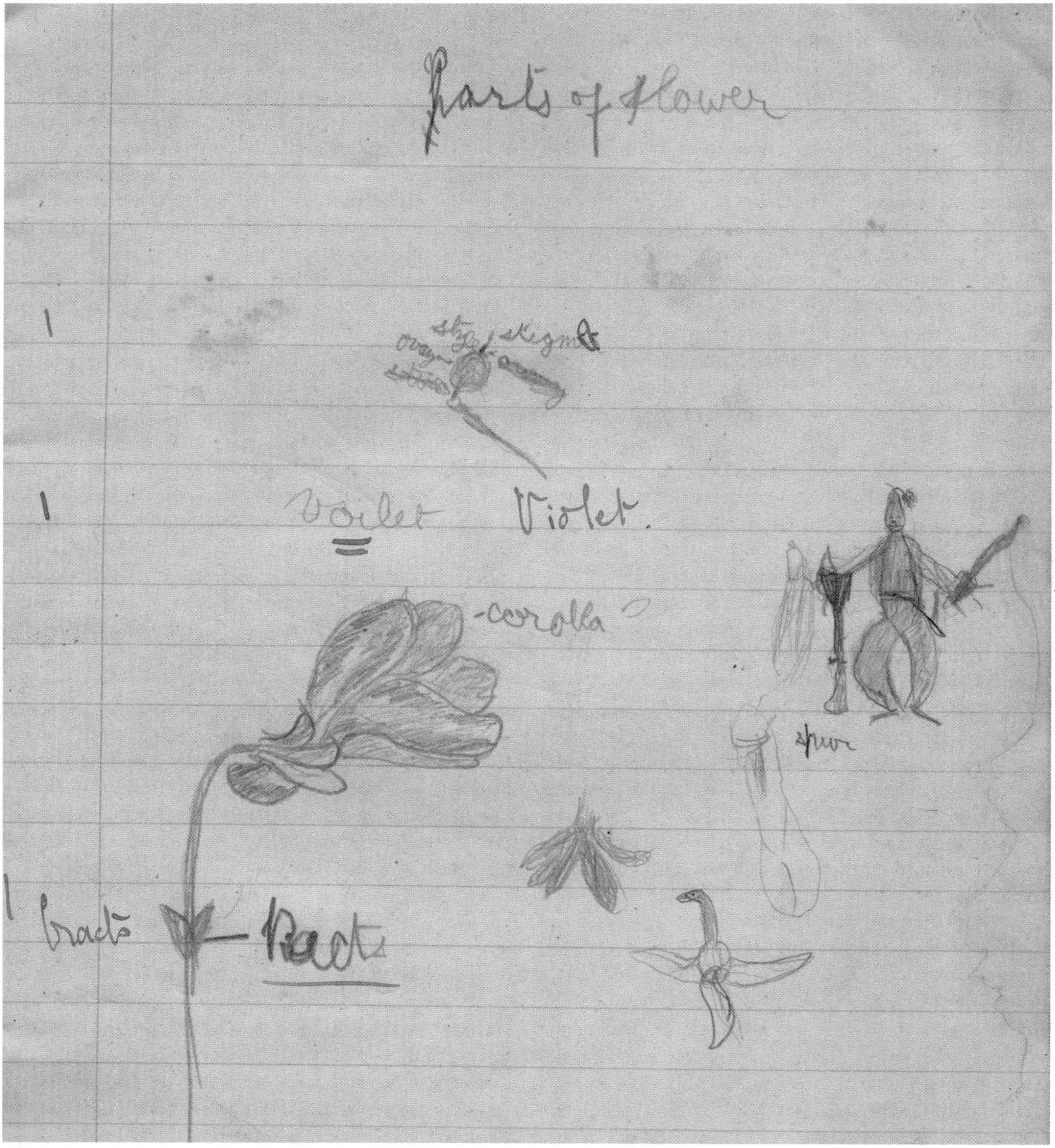

3. Pages from the Nature Studies Exercise Book of C. R. W. Nevinson while a pupil at the Junior Department of University College School, London. (Private Collection: Harish Chandra Banazi)

Academy Schools."[37] He also claimed that the decision to send him to Uppingham was taken by his mother in his father's absence and implies that his parents were too concerned with their own lives to pay much attention to him.

Henry Nevinson's diaries challenge this claim effectively. He describes leaving his son at Uppingham on the first day of his first term in September 1903: "A day of choking sadness to me & us all."[38] A fortnight later he was haunted by his son's descriptions of "bullying, filth, thieving, underfeeding & every torment."[39] He was undoubtedly troubled by his homesick son's unhappiness and continued to express consternation, though his claim that "I can hardly live for sorrow"[40] needs to be read as typical of this journalist's tendency to dramatize his own feelings in his private writings. Nevertheless, Henry Nevinson spent time visiting his son and Selwyn, the headmaster. He was infuriated when the latter made light of Richard's drawing and asked if Nevinson Junior "had not 'blood' enough to go out into the world like me."[41] Yet he did not withdraw Richard from the school.

In his autobiography, Henry Nevinson claimed that "most unhappily, I was induced to send him to a Public School for three years, and I might just as well have sent him for three years to hell."[42] The implication is that his wife was to blame. Yet Richard Nevinson's name had, according to Margaret Nevinson's memoirs, been down for Uppingham since birth! Moreover, he claims that his son declined the offer to leave and go to Shrewsbury instead. Margaret Nevinson confirms this, stating that he "elected to stay and endure."[43] She sets her retrospective account of her son's unhappiness at public school within a chapter on the problem of education. She suggests that she felt she was doing wrong in sending him to Uppingham and that she had made "a cowardly concession to convention and persuasion."[44] The parents blamed each other and their son developed the story.

In 1937, a review of Richard Nevinson's autobiography revived the guilt and blame of this episode for Henry Nevinson. Criticized in the *New Statesman* for his choice of schooling, he indignantly retorted that while arrangements were being made, he was in Africa and Russia. Yet Richard went to Uppingham in the autumn of 1903 and it was over a year before Henry left for Angola. His travels in the Russian Empire were in late 1905–6. He stressed his son's refusal to leave, arguing that the "abominations" he suffered there "partially wrecked his healthy nature." He now claimed that "unless a boy shows aptitude for sport" it was "a crime to send him to a Public School."[45]

In Gilbert Cannan's novel *Mendel: A Story of Youth* (1916), the Nevinsons are parodied as Mr. and Mrs. Mitchell, the ultimate "do-gooders" who had "a platform manner of speaking and "seemed to have their fingers in innumerable reforms."[46] Yet their views did not converge so neatly. Not only did Margaret Nevinson hold and articulate opinions distinct from those of her husband but they also disagreed about politics and policies. Although interested in Fabianism in the 1890s and disillusioned with Prime Minister Asquith's stance on women's suffrage in the following decade, Margaret Nevinson nevertheless became a committed Liberal. In the 1880s Henry Nevinson flirted with the socialist Social Democratic Party. He had intimate friends in anarchist circles, became nominally a member of the Liberal Party for a time, then publicly renounced their policies, especially over Russia and women's suffrage. After the First World War he joined the Labour Party. But he was never really a party political figure, preferring to plow his own furrow.

Richard Nevinson's autobiography is concerned to stress the international and intellectual atmosphere in which he grew up, rather than emphasizing his parents' differences. He does, though, briefly acknowledge their divergent views on the South African War of 1899–1902, though erroneously suggests that when this war began, his father attended pro-Boer meetings in Hampstead. In fact Henry Nevinson sailed to South Africa before war broke out and was there when it started.[47] He endured the siege of Ladysmith and wrote about it, and also familiarized himself with the sufferings of Boer and black Africans in concentration camps. To his intense annoyance, when Emily Hobhouse's report on these camps was published it was "received with jeers & laughter by my family—encouraged by their mother."[48] Margaret had become markedly anti-Boer. When she heard Canon Scott Holland preach a pro-Boer sermon at St. Paul's Cathedral she was so angry and disappointed that "I had an impulse to throw my shoe at him."[49] At this juncture relations between the couple were at their nadir. So dismissive was he of his wife that he could not even name her: "usual abuse & contempt at home from the woman who lives here & spends all her time speaking evil of me to her friends & children."[50]

Both of the Nevinson parents were committed to women's suffrage. Yet here too they differed in their adherence. Margaret Nevinson began as a constitutionalist and sat on the Hampstead branch committee of the National Union of Women's Suffrage Societies. She was briefly active in the militant Women's Social and Political Union but in 1907 joined the new breakaway organization, the Women's Freedom League (WFL). She would write and speak for them well into the 1920s, was national treasurer of the Women Writers' Suffrage League as well as an active member of both the Church League for Women's Suffrage and the London-Welsh Cymric Suffrage Union. In contrast Henry Nevinson was, for a number of years, much more sympathetic to the Pankhursts than was his wife. He chaired the militant Men's Political Union for Women's Enfranchisement and declared the WFL to be dull.

Whereas Margaret's suffrage activities show her drawing upon her Welshness as a crucial constituent of her identity (her father was a Welsh speaker from Lampeter in west Wales and her mother half Welsh), Henry focused on Irish nationalism. To his wife's disapproval, he campaigned tirelessly and ultimately unsuccessfully, for the reprieve from execution for treason of the Irish nationalist and erstwhile hero in the Congo, Sir Roger Casement.

Richard Nevinson's upbringing was one in which his parents lived public and separate lives. Despite finding motherhood difficult at first, Margaret Nevinson seems to have adored her only son. He, rather than her husband, was her companion on holidays to Europe in his youth. Even when he was an adult she referred to him as "my boy." His cousin John L. Nevinson, from a much more traditional home, described the Nevinson offspring as spoiled, dismissing Richard as "simply intolerable."[51] Henry Nevinson was predictably disparaging about his wife's efforts to promote their son's career. She was the secret purchaser of *The Railway Bridge, Charenton*. It was Richard Nevinson's first sale and his father feared that his son's apparent ease in obtaining a purchaser would place him in a fool's paradise, giving him false hope.[52] When Margaret died in 1932, Henry Nevinson claimed that "For Rich she laboured incessantly & cared for no one else."[53] Yet he had long been dismissive of most of his wife's actions and was hardly a dispassionate critic.

But even he was saddened by his son's treatment of her in the postwar years. The elderly Henry Nevinson dreaded his son's weekly visits to Downside Crescent. A manic depressive, his "profound depression & persecution mania" added "terror to every Sunday."[54] Margaret still doted on him yet he made her "very wretched" by venting his rage on her: "It is all vanity & want of self-confidence at bottom." Henry believed that his volatile and aggressive son had lost the artistic inspiration provided by war. War itself and "others' jealousy" had also "diminished his charm & attraction" and, as he put it, "taken the sunshine out of him." In the mid-1920s Richard was threatening suicide. The presence of Philippa (who suffered from thyroid problems) only exacerbated the tension in her father's opinion and they were lucky if they got through Sunday lunch "without disturbances." Adapting a biblical reference, in May 1928 Henry Nevinson made the poignant comment that "Children are a quiverful of arrows that pierce the parents' hearts."[55]

Margaret Nevinson had a weak heart and was in poor health for some years. In the 1920s she continued to take holidays separately from her husband and spent a considerable time with her widowed sister-in-law in Northampton (her brother Lloyd had been Canon of Peterborough). By the early 1930s she was in severe mental as well as physical distress, even attempting to drown herself in the bath. She suffered from delusions and believed there was a plot to poison her and Richard. The latter now believed that she should be institutionalized but his father resisted this. As he told his old friend, the writer and former actress, Elizabeth Robins, "To send her to a mental home among strangers seems to me cruel, but all are urging it in hopes of reducing the great expense."[56] He had his way and she died at home in June 1932. Henry Nevinson lived to see the outbreak of the Second World War, surviving until late 1941 when he was eighty-five. He spent his last few years in Chipping Campden, having been bombed out of his Hampstead home. His son seldom visited yet his father, hating the enforced exile, wanted badly to spend time with him. His diary admits, "Most I regret the entire absence of Richard."

Richard Nevinson and his father had long enjoyed a wary relationship with each other. The latter expended considerable energy and ingenuity in seeking to assist his son. Being part of the media and with numerous friends in the arts, he was in a good position to do this. Some of the key critics who promoted the young Nevinson's artistic career were old friends such as Charles Lewis Hind, Frank Rutter, and William Rothenstein (who made several drawings of Nevinson Senior). Connections with important political and military figures such as Charles Masterman and Sir Ian Hamilton also impacted his son's opportunities.

From the seminal Leicester Galleries exhibition of 1916 through to a show of "British Artists Since Whistler" at the National Gallery in 1940 when Henry Nevinson was in his eighties, he networked to get his son's pictures seen, reviewed, and bought. It was he who enabled his son to meet figures such as Gino Severini, Roger Fry, Clive Bell, and Walter Sickert. By the time of the 1940 exhibition, organized by Sir Kenneth Clark, the artist had alienated so many in the art world, including the exhibition's curator, that it was necessary to adopt increasingly camouflaged interventions. Henry therefore wrote to Sir Michael Sadler, asking him if he would lend one of his Nevinson's: "It is a matter of reputation for my son to be seen among his contemporaries" and Sir Kenneth "appears to have forgotten him."[57] And he persuaded Edward Marsh to lend a tiny Nevinson to the show.

Richard Nevinson was ambivalent about such interventions. He desperately wanted to be revered (though never to defer) but long felt in the shadow of his famous father. One way of handling this was to dismiss his values and to spurn, even as he sought, his father's world of journalism. Thus, apparently casually, he remarked that "Journalism seemed a great lark to me." In his autobiography he stressed that scientists appealed to him rather than writers: "Unlike literary people, scientists know what people are really like."[58] Sometimes he protested just that bit too much to be convincing. And, after the war, journalism claimed him. Richard Nevinson contributed numerous "lifestyle" articles to magazines and newspapers.

His parents' lives had an impact on his work in all sorts of ways. In 1912 during the First Balkan War, Henry Nevinson stayed in a remote Bulgarian town with a group of war correspondents. Here too was the flamboyant Italian Futurist artist, Filippo Marinetti, with whose name his son was to be closely associated. Over the following year or so Henry wrote several articles about his "performance art." The creed of Futurism with its problematic relationship to History as Henry Nevinson knew it, actually ran counter to many of his beliefs. But its rebellious edge, the way in which Marinetti could get to the heart of what war was about and the fact that his son, his personal future, was identifying himself with Marinetti's approach, meant that Henry Nevinson was prepared, for the time being, to endorse it. His mother had reviewed Marinetti's speech to London's Lyceum Club in 1910. She had been offended by his denunciation of women though it seemed to stop short of the Suffragettes in his audience.[59] It was another three years before her son met him. The two Nevinson men are famously linked through their various interpretations of war.[60] Henry Nevinson had drilled working-class cadets in London's East End in the late nineteenth century and even advocated a form of conscription. He became disenchanted with such views just as the public (as a result of the South African War) caught up with them. His direct experience of conflict across the globe, his espousal of rebels which encompassed conscientious objectors, his relationship with the pacifist Evelyn Sharp, and his anti-statist stance, led him to reject militarism and hatred between races.

Father and son were together in November 1914 when Richard Nevinson gained his first direct experience of war. This was with the Quaker Ambulance Unit of the Red Cross tending the wounded at Dunkirk in old railway sheds known as The Shambles. Indeed, it was due to Henry Nevinson contacting Dr. Hector Munro that they were both there together.[61] Richard would use this harrowing experience to great effect in his paintings. He became an ambulance driver and then a nursing orderly at Malo-Les-Bains though early in 1915, according to his autobiography, "crocked up," and returned home.[62]

His father could empathize with his son's rheumatic fever, having himself intermittently suffered ill health ever since being struck by malarial fever in South Africa. The younger Nevinson's medical problems seem to have afforded him an opportunity to circumvent military action. His mother told a friend just after his return home that he actually "looks very well."[63] He then refused to return to the Quaker Unit though he did work as an orderly for the Royal Army Medical Corps at the Third London General Hospital at Wandsworth.

Henry Nevinson, in contrast, saw illness as an irritant since it inhibited the dangerous war reporting he so enjoyed. Both men used the fact that they became wartime casualties, albeit in differing ways. When the aging war correspondent was struck on the head by a shell at Gallipoli he was proud of this vicarious sacrifice and made much of it in prose and poetry. Indeed, his Australian colleague Charles Bean noting that "A good deal has been made out of Nevinson's wound," even briefly toyed with the idea of using his own leg wound to help promote his literary work.[64]

However, Henry Nevinson was primarily a commentator on war rather than a participant. A well-known radical campaigner, he objected to restrictions of freedom including conscription. These concerns came close to home when there were changes in the laws concerning military service. His diary in 1917 shows him fearful that his son might not be exempted from returning to active service. Yet, thanks largely to the pressure he exerted both directly and indirectly, Richard became an official war artist.

But all this does not mean that father and adult son had a cozy relationship. Far from it. Henry Nevinson badly wanted his offspring to succeed but found it increasingly difficult to handle when his son's name began to be better known than his own. In 1918 toward the end of the First World War when Philip Gibbs was on sick leave, Henry Nevinson took his place as a war correspondent on the western front. He wrote in his diary, "Rich now the well known one." Reading one week earlier the introduction to *The Great War Fourth Year* had probably prompted his comment. Written by J. E. Crawford Flitch, it claimed that the Nevinson war paintings told the truth from the trenches. This was seen as a corrective to the work of journalists that, by implication, was seen as fanciful. Moreover, the artist was quoted as saying he could paint because he had "an unjournalistic mind."[65] Henry was stung by such criticism, seeing it as "needlessly harsh" on journalists and war correspondents."[66]

In the same year Major Beecher Wilson told him, that Richard had "eclipsed his father."[67] At an exhibition of his son's work in 1920 four women asked him if he was "the Nevinson." When he explained, one told him that "she was glad I was not as she much preferred ordinary people."[68] His contemporaries, though, sought to put the record straight. Just over a decade later the journalist W. R. Titterton suggested to his editor that he interview Nevinson: "What, the artist? said the editor. 'No,' said I, fuming slightly, 'H. W. Nevinson, the greatest war correspondent of modern times.' The editor frowned thoughtfully. 'Oh, yes,' he said at length. 'The father of the artist, isn't he?' I told him he was misinformed; the artist was H. W. Nevinson's son."[69] Richard Nevinson found his father useful—his connections helped open doors—but the two men seem always to have been conscious of the other's public standing and concerned how they might be judged by each other. Nevinson Junior knew that he could never really pass muster when it came to serious intellectual discussions with his father and his friends who included international statesmen, political scientists, lawyers, and literary figures. So it was easier to disparage his world than appear to take it seriously. And it suited him to cast his retrospective life story in a way which suggested that his father was absorbed in his own interests rather than promoting his son's. Thus in *Paint and Prejudice* when he mentions his marriage to Kathleen Knowlman, he says, "My own father, *of course*, was in Gallipoli" [my emphasis].[70] He adds a few pages later that they then went to live in Downside Crescent: "My father was then in Egypt, and I don't think had even heard of my marriage."[71] In fact he was in Turin on the day of the wedding and just two days earlier had dined at home "to say goodbye to Rich before his sudden marriage next week."[72] From a ship off the coast of southern Italy he wrote to his son "for his wedding."[73]

Yet we also need to treat with caution the consternation frequently expressed in Henry Nevinson's diary about his son's health and fluctuating fortunes. Henry Nevinson would dramatize in this diary almost anything personal. He was a mercurial, romantic individual who liked to see himself as free from familial ties (though he became very fond of his one granddaughter, Margaret Caulfield). When Richard and Kathleen Nevinson's baby was born in May 1919, Richard was in America. He never saw his son who died before he reached home: Margaret met him at Southampton with the news. Henry Nevinson mentioned the baby boy's birth but then made no further reference to him until early June. Such absence does not necessarily denote callousness and may even have signified fear but when Anthony Christopher Wynne Nevinson lay dying, just a few weeks old, his grandfather used a curious adverb: "I was strangely unhappy at the thought."[74]

Henry Nevinson earned, over the years, a reputation as a fiery rebel. His son shared his dislike of authority and also courted rebelliousness but lacked his father's social conscience and commitment to radicalism. Richard Nevinson's flamboyant behavior and the criticism it engendered increasingly distressed his father. The hedonistic pursuit of publicity and self-destruction gathered pace as his creative ability became less appreciated. Incidents such as striking an old friend in the Gargoyle Club (for calling him a failure) must have reminded his father of his own brother Basil. This older brother had been a very talented cellist who used to play with Edward Elgar. The composer named one of his Enigma Variations—B.G.N.—in honor of him. Yet "Bas," who liked to mix with socially significant people and frequented the Savage Club, became an alcoholic and died young. His Tory politics had helped alienate the brothers, but it was his dedication to self-destruction that really drove a wedge between them. In 1925 Henry Nevinson confided in his diary that he feared his son was becoming middle-aged and losing his imagination, partly from not reading or associating with "great minds."[75]

Richard Nevinson's politics also concerned his father. He was opposed to the General Strike of 1926. During this time Henry Nevinson posed the question "Why have I two reactionary children?"[76] His son even defended the British Union of Fascists when they hounded a speaker on Hampstead Heath.[77] But Henry was delighted when, in 1939, Richard was finally elected a Fellow of the Royal Academy, calling it "a splendid triumph" even though his application had been rejected on four previous occasions. On the eve of war Richard Nevinson was once more plunged into depression, unable to work and suicidal. By December 1939 his father was writing, "No one has brought me such unhappiness as he."[78]

Despite recurrent bouts of fever Henry Nevinson had a strong constitution. Indeed, without this he would not have survived some of the appalling conditions in which he lived when reporting on wars, revolutions, and famine in different parts of the world. Richard Nevinson, like his maternal grandfather and his mother, had heart problems. He suffered from rheumatic fever and a bad hip as well as being a depressive and always fearing the worst. In 1932, he thought he had tuberculosis then cancer. He was proved wrong on both counts but he was seriously ill and in this same year he lost his mother.

A year later he paid his father a rare tribute. A luncheon had been arranged at the Criterion Restaurant in London to honor the war correspondent's achievements. About four hundred and fifty people gathered there, including Albanian, Bulgarian, and Greek ministers. John Masefield, Sir Ian Hamilton, Dr. Louisa Garrett Anderson, and Sir T. B. Sapru were among those who spoke in praise of his varied achievements in different parts of the world. Richard Nevinson was too ill to attend but sent a statement. It characteristically dwelt on self-image yet it did, for once, acknowledge his debt. And when Henry Nevinson read his son's memoirs he paid him a compliment, noting that it was "all brilliantly done." He did, though, admit that the book revealed how little "I really knew of him."[79]

But both Henry Nevinson and his son died in the 1940s within five years of each other. One was in his mid-eighties, the other still in his fifties but debilitated in his last years from successive strokes. In many ways the two men were more alike than they usually cared to admit. Both had periods when they felt unappreciated though this could not be divined from *Paint and Prejudice* which, in the interwar years, rewrote the Nevinson family history. In reality the older Nevinson had not stepped easily or quickly into being well known. He was not, as his son's autobiography claims, a professor at the University of Jena in the mid-1880s, merely a postgraduate student, spending a year in Germany studying philosophy. And it was many years before he got his first real break, covering the Greco-Turkish war of 1897. In the meantime he took jobs where he could, teaching (which he hated) and working as secretary to the London Playing Fields Association. He was middle-aged before he was able to eke out a living from writing and he was never wealthy.

Where the son was sardonic, the father was deeply ironic. Ethel Mannin wrote that Richard Nevinson had "a perfect genius for being misunderstood,"[80] and his father was not dissimilar. Mannin also saw the artist as utterly insincere in his disregard for criticism.[81] Henry Nevinson too was much more sensitive than many realized. Both were mercurial and quick to anger. Henry Nevinson's diaries show him fulminating and upset when, for example, he received the occasional bad review. Yet he was spared public embarrassment, both because, unlike his son, he worked to maintain friends and he raged privately about his own affairs, saving his public indignation for matters of injustice to others. His son, however, found it harder to accept criticism, engaging in public spats with literary heavyweights from George Bernard Shaw to the Bloomsbury Group. He harbored grudges and retorted quickly at the slightest provocation. When he was attacked in print, as for example, in the *Times Literary Supplement* at the end of 1937, he threatened libel action.[82]

Both were sensual men though Henry Nevinson was acknowledged time and again to be, unlike his son, a dashing, handsome figure. They could be irrationally jealous of each other since both courted fame, albeit less flamboyantly in Henry Nevinson's case. Despite the latter's concern for others, he too displayed traits of the self-centeredness that was so evident in his son, though any individual who leaves a diary is likely to perceived in such a way. Both were prone to exaggerate, though much of the time Nevinson Senior knowingly combined this with self-deprecation, ironic wit and critical social comment. Thus in the first volume of his autobiography, he reflected back on his earlier arguments for a national army. Now, in the 1920s, he disparaged his own earlier beliefs so, writing about his early article on the subject, and commented that "For about a week, as the most detested person in England, I was almost famous."[83] Yet he and his son were easily depressed. Henry Nevinson felt that he was too cerebral for some of the military figures he admired yet too obviously associated with the world of action for serious literary appreciation. Carefully cultivating the role of the inveterate rebel, he was involved in numerous causes and campaigns on behalf of others. He also operated on a very wide international canvas. His son, in contrast, focused more on self and dedicated himself primarily to his art though, as Christopher Martin shows,[84] he too had some literary ambitions, wrote a novel and, like his father, was parodied in print.

Both men came to hate war yet in a sense were made and sustained by it. War also managed, in differing ways, to dislocate both men's lives but to supply them with superb copy which work in peacetime could never quite match. In 1913, fresh from Bulgaria and the First Balkan War, Henry Nevinson published one of his many unsigned "Middles" in the *Nation.*[85] It was on the subject of "The Lie in War." Here he exposed the problem of historical accounts of war asking "What can we really know of Carthaginian & Barbarian wars with Rome or of Kossovo and the repeated battles with the Turk?" But he also scotched the notion that eyewitnesses and modern developments in the media dealt with the truth. Censorship and competition among correspondents compounded the problem. The demand for instant news encouraged some to cut corners. Henry had discovered that a fellow correspondent in Bulgaria had faked his presence at the front. And, Henry added, the best liars were painters and that "no battle-picture we have seen has ever borne the smallest resemblance to the reality of war."

But within a few years his son was challenging the common representation of war in a way that was very different from his father but also questioned and disturbed. An article on C. R. W. Nevinson's war pictures in the *Westminster Gazette* in 1916 linked together father and son, suggesting something of what they both brought to their respective work: "Had there been Nevinsons in the world at the time of the Napoleonic Wars we should possess fewer pictures of a romantic Emperor on a white charger, or of Grenadiers sleeping picturesquely on the snow; but we should have known a good deal more of what war is like."[86] Depicting and questioning through their work the destructive nature of war even while they sought to create romantic images of themselves (Henry Nevinson had been known to ride around north London on a "white charger") characterized this father and son. They had much in common besides a passion for their work and their undoubted talent in their own artistic fields. Yet neither would acknowledge this, perhaps because they never really liked the aspect of themselves that they saw reflected in the other.

Richard Nevinson cultivated that seemingly modern construction, the celebrity. His apparent determination to behave badly and alienation of significant art critics came to camouflage his real achievements as an artist. Understanding the tale of his imagined upbringing and how it can be squared with other representations of life in the Nevinson household and, in particular, his relationship with his father, helps illuminate Richard Nevinson's creation of himself as a public figure. Yet the resurgence in appreciation of his work, especially that produced in wartime, fortunately demonstrates that the legacy of the artist C. R. W. Nevinson is far more substantial than the legend.

Notes

1. The Bodleian Library, University of Oxford, Gilbert Murray Papers, MSS 15, fol. 87, Nevinson to Murray, January 18, 1909. This chapter is an expanded version of the paper I gave to the "C. R. W. Nevinson. Life, Art and Legacy" conference held at the University of Greenwich, July 2002. See *Nevi(n)son News* 7 (2002): 4–6.

2. The Bodleian Library, University of Oxford, Henry Woodd Nevinson Papers, Diaries, MSS Eng. Misc. e615/1, October 8, 1908.

3. Henry Nevinson had been in Russia in 1905–6 during the "Days of Liberty" and the subsequent repression.

4. C. R. W. Nevinson, *Paint and Prejudice* (London: Methuen, 1937, New York: Harcourt Brace, 1938), 5.

5. In the Society of Antiquaries, Burlington House, London. Nevinson Papers.

6. For example, see his pencil sketch of the fort at Loanda with which he opened his series of articles on "The New Slave-Trade" of Portuguese Africa in *Harper's Monthly Magazine* 111, no. 663 (1905): 43 and his sketch of Newby Hall that is the frontispiece to H. W. Nevinson, *Changes and Chances* (London: Nisbel, 1923).

7. J. Fulleylove RI and H. W. Nevinson, *Pictures of Classic Greek Landscape and Architecture* (London: Dent, 1897).

8. A. H. H. Murray accompanied by H. W. Nevinson and M. Carmichael, *Sketches On The Old Road Through France to Florence* (London: John Murray, 1904).

9. The first was for a lecture tour. He also covered (for the *Manchester Guardian*) the 1920 Republican Convention in Chicago and the Washington Disarmament Conference of 1921–22. In 1929, he accompanied Prime Minister Ramsay Macdonald on his historic trip to the United States for talks with President Hoover, the first visit from a British prime minister to an American president. For discussion of this and other aspects of Henry Nevinson's life, see my biography: *War, Journalism and the Shaping of the 20th Century. The Life and Times of Henry W. Nevinson* (London: I.B. Taurus, 2006).

10. *Christian Science Monitor*, June 16, 1920.

11. H. W. Nevinson, *The Natives of England* (New York: Alfred A. Knopf, 1930); *Rough Islanders* (London: Routledge, 1930).

12. Nevinson, *Changes and Chances*; *More Changes, More Chances* (London: Nisbet, 1925); *Last Changes, Last Chances* (London: Nisbet, 1928). *Fire of Life* (London: Nisbet with Victor Gollancz, 1935) was an abridged one-volume edition of the autobiography.

13. M. Wynne Nevinson, *Life's Fitful Fever* (London: A. C. Black, 1926).

14. Angela V. John, "Imag(in)ing H. W. Nevinson: war correspondent, literary journalist and rebel," in *Representing Victorian Lives*, ed. M. Hewitt (Leeds: Leeds Centre working papers in victorian studies, 1999), 140–51; and *War, Journalism and the Shaping of the 20th Century*.

15. Christopher Martin has pointed out that, at the Slade, Richard Nevinson was known as C. R. Nevinson, *Nevi(n)son News* 6 (2001).

16. Harry Ransom Humanities Research Center, Austin, Texas, Nevinson to Carrington, January 14, 1913. I am grateful to Dr. Paula Bartley for this reference.

17. *Listener*, August 8, 1940, 193–94.

18. Angela V. John, "Margaret Wynne Nevinson: Gender and National Identity in the Early Twentieth Century," in *From Medieval to Modern Wales: Historical Essays in Honour of Kenneth O. Morgan and Ralph A. Griffiths* G. H. Jenkins and R. R. Davies ed., (Cardiff: University of Wales Press, 2004).

19. Harry Ransom Humanities Research Center, Nevinson to Carrington, January 14, 1913.

20. For example, H. W. Nevinson, *The Plea of Pan* (London: John Murray, 1901); Mrs. H. W. Nevinson, "Juvenal on Latter-Day Problems: an Unscholarly Gossip," *Fortnightly Review* 87 (1907): 913.

21. M. Wynne Nevinson, *Fragments of Life* (London: George Allen & Unwin, 1922), 70.

22. M. Nevinson, *Fragments of Life*, 119.

23. See W. Harris, "H. W. Nevinson, Margaret Wynne Nevinson, Evelyn Sharp: Little-Known Writers and Crusaders," *English Literature in Transition* 45, no. 3 (2002): 291.

24. Nevinson Diaries, e625/4, June 8, 1932.

25. J. Tosh, *A Man's Place. Masculinity and the Middle-Class Home in Victorian England* (New Haven, CT: Yale University Press, 1999).

26. Nevinson Diaries, e620/4, December 25, 1919.

27. Margaret Wynne Nevinson, *Life's Fitful Fever*, 113.

28. Society of Antiquaries, Nevinson Papers, John Lea Nevinson Diaries, 111, September 15, 1924.

29. Bod.L, Evelyn Sharp Nevinson Papers, Diary 1, d668, September 21, 1942. I am currently writing a book about Evelyn Sharp.

30. A. Bennett, *The Journals*, ed. F. Swinnerton (Harmondsworth, UK: Penguin, 1971), 274. The book was published in 1885. In the United States it was called *Slum Stories of London*.

31. Nevinson Diaries, e611/1, January 23, 1901.

32. See, for example, Nevinson Diaries, e612/1, October 10, 1903 and e612/3, May 5, 1904.

33. Nevinson Diaries, e612/1, May 20, 1903.

34. Nevinson, *Paint and Prejudice*, 6.

35. I am grateful to Harish Chandra Banazi for letting me see the Exercise Book and School Magazine.

36. For his account see Nevinson, *Paint and Prejudice*, 6–20. See too M. J. K. Walsh, *C. R. W. Nevinson. This Cult of Violence* (New Haven, CT: Yale University Press, 2002), 6–9.

37. Nevinson, *Paint and Prejudice*, 21.

38. Nevinson Diaries, e612/2, September 18, 1903.

39. Nevinson Diaries, e612/2, October 4, 1903.

40. Nevinson Diaries, e612/2, October 7, 1903.

41. Nevinson Diaries, e613/3, October 5, 1906.

42. Nevinson, *Changes and Chances*, 310–11.

43. Margaret Wynne Nevinson, *Life's Fitful Fever*, 155.

44. Ibid.

45. *New Statesman*, December 11, 18, 1937.

46. G. Çannan, *Mendel. A Story of Youth* (London: T. Fisher Unwin, 1916), 186–87.

47. Nevinson, *Paint and Prejudice*, 7.

48. Nevinson Diaries, e611/2, June 23, 1902.

49. British Library MSS RP2679(ii), Wynne Nevinson to John Lea (the brother of Henry Nevinson's sister-in-law), April 10, 1900.

50. Ibid., August 1, 1902.

51. John Lea Nevinson Diaries, V11, December 23, 1926. In fact this young man hardly knew him and many of his opinions reflected rather the views of his parents. His father was Henry's younger brother.

52. Nevinson Diaries, e617/1, February 24, 25, 1912.

53. Ibid., e625/4, June 6, 1932.

54. For his concern about his behavior, his wife's health, and the difficult domestic situation see Ibid., e 21/1, December 25, 1919; e621/2, April 1, 1920; e622/1 February 1, July 31, 1921; e622/3, May 14, 19, 1922.

55. Ibid., e624/4, May 14, 1928.

56. The Fales Library, Elmer Holmes Bobst Library, New York University, Elizabeth Robins Papers, Nevinson to Robins, June 4, 1932, Series 2B, Box 6, folder 136.

57. Bod.L MS Eng. Misc. c549, Nevinson to Sadler, March 14, 1940.

58. Nevinson, *Paint and Prejudice*, 226.

59. *Vote*, December 31, 1910. See, too, J. Lyon, "Militant Discourse, Strange Bedfellows: Suffragettes and Vorticists before the War," *Differences: A Journal of Feminist Cultural Studies* 4, no. 2 (1992): 100–133.

60. See Walsh, *C. R. W. Nevinson*, chapters 6 to 9, and John, *War, Journalism and the Shaping of the 20th Century*, chapters 7 to 8.

61. This was Henry Nevinson's second visit there.

62. Nevinson, *Paint and Prejudice*, 104.

63. The Women's Library, London, Margaret Wynne Nevinson to Edith How Martyn, February 11, 1915. Walsh points out that he was officially discharged for "Business Reasons" after returning home on leave. Walsh, *C. R. W. Nevinson*, 95.

64. K. Fewster (ed.), *Gallipoli Correspondent. The Front-line Diary of C. E. W. Bean* (Sydney: George Alen & Unwin, 1983), 165.

65. J. E. Crawford Flitch, *The Great War: Fourth Year, by C. R. W. Nevinson* (London: Grant Richards, 1918), 10.

66. Nevinson Diaries, e620/4, August 16, 1918.

67. Ibid., e623/6, December 25, 1918.

68. Ibid., e621/2, January 21, 1920.

69. W. R. Titterton, *A Candle To The Stars* (London: Grayson & Grayson, 1932), 178.

70. Nevinson, *Paint and Prejudice*, 109.

71. Ibid., 113.

72. Nevinson Diaries, e619/2, October 30, 1915.

73. Ibid., e619/2, November 1, 1915.

74. Ibid., e621/1, June 3, 1919. See too the somewhat callous comments of his son, Nevinson, *Paint and Prejudice*, 186.

75. Ibid., e623/5, March 1, 1925.

76. Ibid., e624/1, May 16, 1926.

77. Ibid., e627/3, February 28, 1939.

78. Ibid., e627/4, December 6, 1939.

79. Ibid., e627/2, November 22, 1937.

80. E. Mannin, *Confessions and Impressions* (London: Jarrolds, 1930), 196.

81. Ibid., 200.

82. Nevinson Diaries, e627/2, December 31, 1937, January 11, 1938.

83. Nevinson, *Changes and Chances*, 74.

84. See chapter 6 below.

85. *Nation*, January 4, 1913, 598–99.

86. *Westminster Gazette*, October 2, 1916, 7.

"A Crisis of Brilliance": C. R. W. Nevinson, Henry Tonks, and the Slade School of Art, 1909–12

David Boyd Haycock

It was largely to professor Henry Tonks and his star pupil, Augustus John, that the Slade School of Drawing, Painting, and Sculpture in London owed its prominence in the years before the Great War. By 1912 their combined reputations had attracted a range of sharp young talents to Gower Street, and Richard Nevinson's fellow students would include Mark Gertler, Stanley Spencer, Edward Wadsworth, Paul Nash, David Bomberg, Dora Carrington, Ben Nicholson, and William Roberts. Other highly promising contemporaries included John Currie and Maxwell Gordon Lightfoot, who both committed suicide before achieving full recognition, and Adrian Allinson, who never quite lived up to his early promise. It was this group of students that Tonks would later describe as the Slade's second "crisis of brilliance"—the first had been the years of Gwen and Augustus John, Selwyn Image, William Orpen, and Wyndham Lewis in the 1890s. It was also of this second group that a former student, Randolph Schwabe, would write in 1943: "Suicide, madness, disease and war exacted a heavy toll on them. Much talent and some genius were born into their generation, and their loss, even for those who were not bound to them by ties of friendship, is deplorable in its tale of waste and unfulfilment."[1] It is this circle of famous but often ill-fated students, and their influential drawing master, that I shall examine in this chapter, casting some light on the cultural and artistic influences that were operating around them at the time of Nevinson's attendance at the school (fig. 4).

After his loathed public school education at Uppingham, Nevinson successfully evaded possible futures as an engineer or at Oxford, and enrolled as a student at the St John's Wood School of Art. It was here, in 1908, that his attention was first drawn to the Slade. The previous year John Fothergill had published an illustrated magazine, *The Slade: A Collection of Drawings and Some Pictures done by Past and Present Students*. It was in this little pamphlet that Nevinson saw Augustus John's remarkable work for the first time. "These drawings completely upset my apple-cart," he would later recall in his (unreliable) memoir, *Paint and Prejudice*. He took them to show one of his teachers at St John's Wood "who, something to my horror, dismissed them as no good. John was simply a posing charlatan who wore gold earrings, 'long hair like Christ' and a Salvation Army jersey."[2]

With this critical analysis, one of Nevinson's many periods of self-doubt descended. For over a year he had been training with a single objective in mind: the Royal Academy. But what was the academy if not another Uppingham, a bulwark of tradition and conventionality, a bastion of Englishness upholding all the standards he and his radical parents were supposedly so set on undermining? He was already reading the novels of Tolstoy, Dostoevsky, Zola, "and a host of others whose work shouted for a better appreciation of art."[3] These were not, it would have appeared, the tastes or sentiments of a future Royal Academician. So when John Singer Sargent, "the god of St John's Wood," declared that Augustus John "was the greatest draughtsman since the Renaissance," Nevinson's mind was made up. It became "obvious" that John's former school was the only place to study, and he "abandoned any attempt to get into the Royal Academy Schools, a grave step which I took lightly."[4] It was no doubt the right move. As he recorded in his autobiography, at St John's Wood, "I was running before I could walk . . . I was an appallingly bad student."[5] Indeed, his teachers reported to Henry Nevinson that his son had "no true style," was trying to do things "every way," and lacked "concentration."[6] If anyone was going to whip Nevinson into shape as a draughtsman and focus his attention as an artist, it was surely the remarkable Henry Tonks.

"A picture is an accident in our lives," the writer George Moore observed, "but in Tonks's it is an event."[7] His friend lived for art: "never was a man more anxious to learn and to teach than Tonks," Moore reflected in 1924: "He read everything that was written about drawing; he listened to all that his friends had to say; he thought about drawing, and he practiced drawing, praying that the secret might be vouchsafed to him, for art has become Tonks's religion."[8]

Henry Tonks was born in Birmingham in 1862, and was, like Nevinson, the unwilling victim of an English public school: after nine years' "education" he left having learned little. Though already in love with the idea

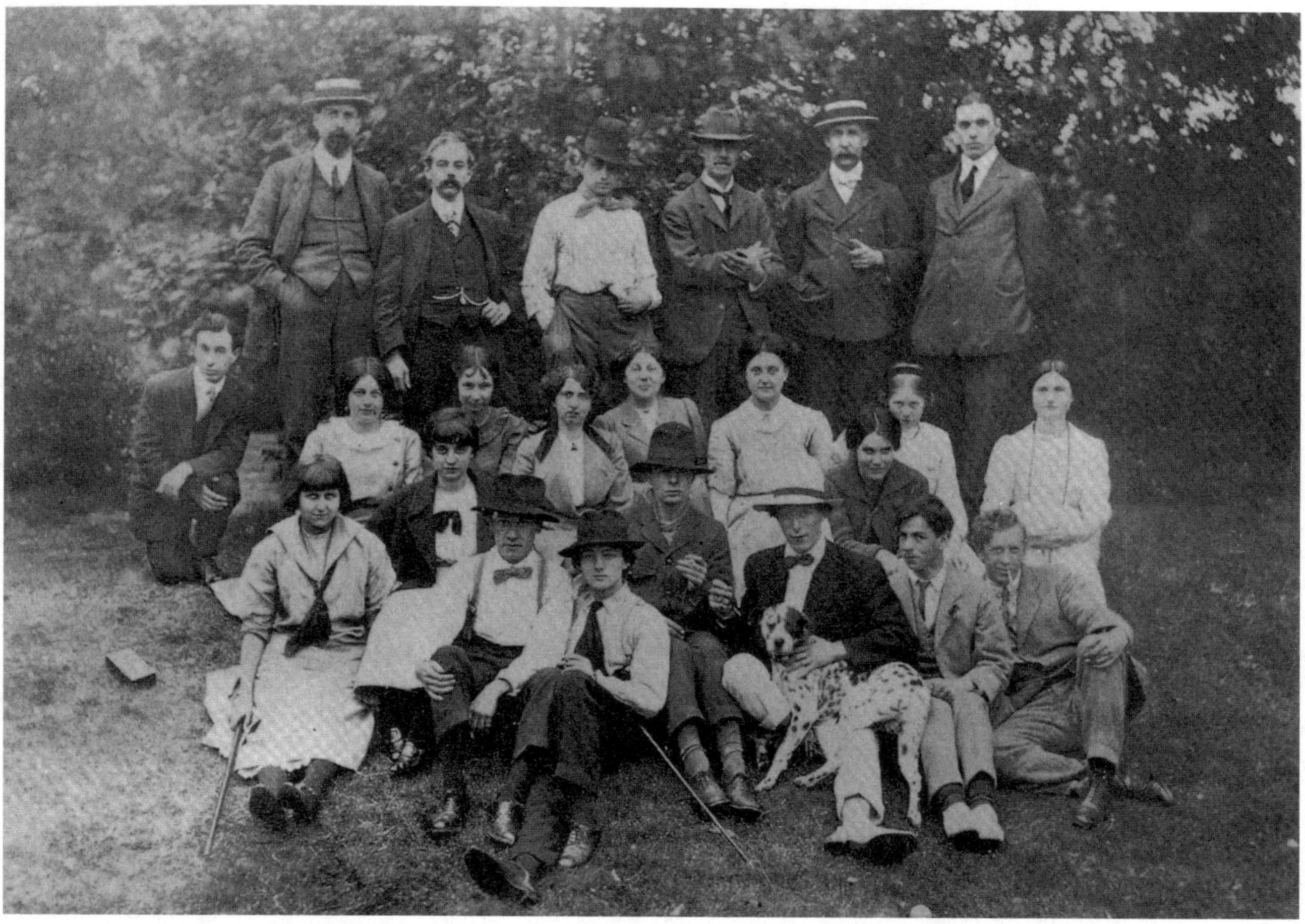

4. The Slade Summer Picnic, 1912. Reproduced by kind permission of the Tate Archive, London. Nevinson is seated at front left, wearing a bow tie.

of being an artist, he began a career as a doctor. But at a teaching hospital in Brighton he met a fellow student who shared and encouraged his passion for art. When Tonks moved to a hospital in London he used his developing talent in anatomy classes, and drawing became his "absorbing passion." On the ward rounds "each patient had a double interest, that of the disease which brought him there, and his possibilities as a model and how I would express them."[9] Like Mark Gertler, Tonks was inspired to finally become an artist by reading the life of a Victorian artist, in his case Randolph Caldecott, who quit a job as a bank clerk in Manchester to become a successful artist and illustrator in London. Thus in 1888, the same year he was appointed Senior Medical Officer at London's Royal Free Hospital, Tonks began studying part-time with Fred Brown at the Westminster Art School. Brown was so impressed by Tonks's draughtsmanship and dedication that when he was offered the Slade professorship he invited Tonks to join him as drawing master.[10] In the opinion of John Rothenstein, Tonks's "impact upon the Slade was that of a bracing wind"—though he also noted that Tonks's "ability to distinguish great talent from promise was far from unerring." It was only with "reluctance," for example, that he had recognized the abilities of Augustus John.[11] But such was Tonks's influence on his students that in the opinion of Paul Nash "Tonks was the Slade and the Slade was Tonks."[12]

Like many strict teachers, Tonks loved his work and loved his students. A "towering, dominating figure," well over six feet tall, a student later recalled that there "was about him an aura of incorruptible nobility of purpose and he was . . . respected by all the students and feared by many."[13] Tonks later modestly wondered why it was that he had been called upon to help so many in their first steps to becoming artists, and thought the key was that he had "enough honesty to urge my students to strengthen themselves where I am weak."[14] Or perhaps it was actually Tonks's great skill as an anatomist, which allowed him almost to see inside the human body: "in fact I have often wondered since what the figure looks like to anyone who has not this knowledge."[15]

Deeply influenced by the art of the Italian Renaissance, Tonks encouraged a style that drew on the great European tradition of meticulous observation and flawless line work. Titian, Rubens, Velasquez, and Ingres were his paragons. According to Helen Lassore, a student at the Slade in the 1920s, one of Tonks's chief beliefs, "from which sprang all his teaching and the way he ran the school," was in "the great European traditions as seen in the Italian Renaissance and a period following it. He believed in the methods of drawing as practiced in Italy—more particularly in Florence and Umbria—from the Quattrocento onwards, and of painting as it developed in North Italy towards the end of the Renaissance, mainly in Venice, and continued through Rubens and Velasquez." According to Lassore, "The atmosphere that prevailed in the school was one of high-minded devotion to Art, untainted by the breath of Commerce."[16]

New students at the Slade had first to draw from antique casts before progressing to the life classes. Some, like Nevinson, who had served this apprenticeship at St John's Wood, were allowed to skip this requirement. Tonks's teaching routine was to come round the classes on Monday, Tuesday, and Wednesday, distributing words of advice and occasionally making his own sketches in the corner of the student's work to illustrate his ideas. His hands clutching the lapels of his suit jacket, he moved from student to student, quietly disseminating his doxology of drawing with a few well-chosen words. Gilbert Spencer, who followed his brother Stanley to the Slade in 1912, wrote how Tonks "talked of dedication, the privilege of being an artist, that to do a bad drawing was like living with a lie, and he proceeded to implant these ideals by ruthless and withering criticism. I remember once coming home and feeling like flinging myself under a train, and Stan telling me not to mind as he did it to everyone."[17] Paul Nash would have concurred. Shortly after his arrival at the Slade in the autumn of 1910 he told his friend Gordon Bottomley, "one learns a great deal from [Tonks] but until one gets used to it, his manner & sarcastic comments rather damp hope. He never praises and can find more faults in five minutes than another man could think of in a fortnight."[18] Yet in spite of his criticisms, the professor's strong ideals meant that many students learned a great deal from him. "I think Tonks is a good man for young men to know," Stanley Spencer reflected in 1912. "I think he brings them to their senses without putting anything unnecessary into them."[19]

After lunch Tonks would be available for an hour or so for individual students to visit him with their drawings for "thorough criticism." They would sit outside his room "with batches of work and called in one after another, as at a doctor's surgery."[20] Tonks told Lassore "that women made the best students because they were clever and did what you told them, whereas the men might argue and want to try things out in different ways, but it was they who did better after leaving."[21] Like many great teachers, Tonks (who never married) showed favoritism, particularly to female students (of whom there were many: the ratio of female to male students at the Slade ranged between three and four to one). Tonks's Victorian attitude to female beauty is apparent in his oil paintings of young ladies portrayed in drawing rooms and country gardens, twee and slightly syrupy in their English Impressionism. They reveal a different, more sentimental side to the stern face he presented to his students. His interest in women was often reciprocated in a strange hero worship, with William Rothenstein observing that while young ladies "of the best families were known to weep at Tonks's acid comments on their works," they still "flocked to the Slade to throw themselves before Tonks's Jaganath progress through the life rooms. There was a time when poor Tonks had to walk the streets not daring to go home, lest ladies be found at his door awaiting his arrival with drawings in their hands, whose easels had been passed by, and in whose hearts was despair."[22] Some students might have idolized Tonks, but others, like Nevinson, came to loathe him.[23]

The precise methodology of Tonks's theory of drawing was laid out in John Fothergill's essay that accompanied his Slade magazine, and it appears Nevinson had already imbibed the lessons of Fothergill's essay by the time he arrived at the Slade. When Tonks first came up to Nevinson in the Life Room he "was not unpleasant. He asked me to define drawing, a thing I was fortunately able to do to his satisfaction, as I neither mentioned tone nor colour in my stammering definition but kept on using the word outline. But he nevertheless managed to shatter my self-confidence, and I was wringing wet by the time he left me to go on to Stanley Spencer."[24]

According to William Coldstream, who was at the Slade in the 1920s, Tonks encouraged his students to visit the Print Room at the British Museum and the library at the Victoria and Albert Museum, and to make copies of the paintings at the National Gallery. The letters of Carrington, Gertler, Nash, Nevinson, and Spencer confirm that things were much the same in the first years of the century. Though the names of many

Slade students would soon become synonymous with the English avant-garde, they were happy to learn from the Old Masters. To Gertler and Bomberg, Michelangelo was the pinnacle of artistic achievement, and Richard Cork has written that at the Slade Bomberg benefited from the emphasis that Tonks and Brown "laid on the firm underlying structure of draughtsmanship." In Cork's opinion their influence "pervades Bomberg's few surviving drawings of this period, with their sculptural severity and clear sighted concentration on the essentials of form alone."[25]

Tonks was supportive of students with clear talent and the determination to improve their draughtsmanship: both Spencer and Gertler received praise and encouragement, and he arranged for them to spend time during the summer vacations drawing in the countryside. A less naturally gifted draughtsman, Nevinson was less favored. "Oh I would love to prove I could draw," he told Carrington. "I think I would shoot myself to prevent any deterioration." His life while at the Slade was "hell," he confessed to her, "with exquisite moments of heaven."[26] Nevinson's father recorded in his diary in July 1909 that he had bumped into Richard as he was going out to draw, and "felt very sad about it, perhaps without reason." Though he considered Tonks to be a "remarkable man with wide sympathies & knowledge," Henry Nevinson must have thought that his son had made the wrong decision in attempting to become an artist, as he was receiving little or no encouragement from Tonks.[27]

But Nevinson was not alone in his struggle to reach the high standards Tonks demanded. Paul Nash and Ben Nicholson both left the school within a year, Nash going on to find true inspiration in nature, with trees becoming symbolic substitutes for the female nude. Out of doors, he discovered that he could draw a springtime oak as he "felt" it, the "red swollen buds" on the branches, the round trunk in the sunlight "as white as paper. I did not find it difficult to draw this tree, as I had found the models at the Slade difficult to draw. An instinctive knowledge seemed to serve me as I drew, enabling my hand to convey my understanding. I could make these branches grow as I could never make the legs and arms of the models move and live."[28] Ben Nicholson also rejected Tonks's regime. A reluctant young student, instead of attending lessons he lunched with Nash before passing his afternoons playing billiards. The abstract formality of the green baize and the constantly changing relationships of the balls were, he later claimed, of more appeal to his aesthetic sense than "the fustiness of the classrooms at the Slade."[29] But despite Tonks's criticisms—and, indeed, his advice toward the end of his third year at the school that he should abandon his attempt to become an artist (advice that briefly led him to consider a career as a journalist)—Nevinson proved his strength of character by remaining the full four years.[30]

It has been noted that many of the well-known artists Tonks taught "have reputations quite independent of the international trends of Modern Art," and William Coldstream agreed that Tonks was "against commercialism," meaning that "the Slade did give artists a certain independence of fashion."[31] But this independence could also be taken as a commitment to Slade values. Isaac Rosenberg, who was at the school with Nevinson complained in 1914 that "the paradox of the Slade" was the push "to attain to a completeness of vision" which resulted in "a total sinking of all conscious personality, a complete absorption and forgetfulness in nature."[32] He quit the Slade and devoted his creative attention to poetry and drama instead. Even Gertler would complain to Carrington of "that awful ghost Tonks,"[33] while Nevinson, after his early adulation, would come to criticize Augustus John for his failure to overcome the school's influence. In 1912 he told Carrington that John's latest work struck him "as being by a symbolic Slade man who is a marvellous exponent of Slade teaching, conventions and eccentricities, but somehow not quite art."[34]

Stanley Spencer appears to have been one of the few prominent students from this era to have retained a positive view of Tonks's guidance—though even he had considered leaving the school in his third year.[35] In 1917, while on active service, he told Lady Ottoline Morrell that he was thinking of spending another term at the Slade after the war in order to rehone his drawing technique, "that is if Tonks is still master." Nevertheless, he too felt that there was something to be overcome from his education there, somewhat enigmatically telling Ottoline in the same letter that in his recent portrait drawings he had "got over a lot of my Slade-ish ways, though not all."[36] In due course, Spencer did return to the Slade for a term in the early 1920s.

To get on the wrong side of Tonks was potentially disastrous, as his influence over students extended beyond the life classes to the hanging committee of the New English Art Club. Many Slade students and alumni exhibited there, and it was to the NEAC that Gertler and Nevinson aspired to first show their work. Their correspondence with Carrington contains regular references to their attempts—and frequent failures—to get exhibited at the "New English." Nevinson generally, and perhaps unfairly, blamed Tonks: in 1919 he would complain that he expected nothing of "New English" artists "but spite, jealousy, & intrigue," accusing Tonks of having "for the past 8 years always shown me the greatest personal opposition."[37] John Rothenstein, for one, was sympathetic, and would write that Tonks's hostility "intensified" Nevinson's "crushing sense of the world's ill-will, a sense which from that time onwards was ever on the alert."[38] Gertler did not have much sympathy for Tonks, either. When the NEAC rejected his painting, *The Creation of Eve* in 1915 he told Carrington "it did not upset me much. What can you expect from a committee that has a mean little rascal like Albert R[othenstein] on it? or Tonks!"[39] In fairness to Tonks, however, much of his dislike of Nevinson stemmed from the young student's hedonistic private life. (In order to keep up with the sexual antics of Nevinson and Wadsworth, Adrian Allinson felt compelled to spend some of the money he won with his Slade scholarship on visiting a prostitute.) In 1911 Nevinson proposed to a Slade model who had become pregnant, and he was one of three possible men who fathered a child with another Slade model in 1915.[40] In August 1911 he told Carrington that "Tonks has been saying about me that he has never in all his life heard of any man behaving worse than I have done."[41]

With the foundation of the London Group in late 1913, however, the NEAC was eclipsed as the principal place of exhibition for many of the most ambitious young Slade graduates. An amalgam of the Camden Town and Fitzroy Street groups, and with Nevinson and Wadsworth both among its founder members, the appearance of the London Group reflects the emergence in England of an alternative aesthetic which cut across the traditional principles Tonks attempted to imbue in his students: Postimpressionism. This "new" movement came directly from modern continental art, and it was advocated by one of the Slade's own teaching staff, Roger Fry. Fry had arrived at the school at the beginning of the autumn term of 1910 as lecturer in art history. His principal influence on the Slade students came not from his lectures, however, but from his revolutionary exhibition that opened at the Grafton Galleries that November. As a student at Cambridge and as a young man Fry had, like Tonks, been deeply moved—and influenced as a painter—by the canon of Italian Renaissance artists. But by 1910 Fry's interests were ranging beyond the Renaissance and Old Masters, and like a number of key European avant-garde artists and critics he was taking an interest in the pictorial and sculptural works of what were considered more primitive civilizations. In the spring of 1910 he reviewed a book on drawings by African Bushmen for the *Burlington Magazine*, admiring their sharpness of perception and intelligence of design.[42] These drawings, he felt, could in no way be considered inferior works, though they clearly differed from the traditions of Western painting. Fry was starting to open up his awareness to a wider sphere of artistic expression, though it was not one that would win him friends among more traditionally minded peers. As Tonks told the critic Robert Ross, "I say, don't you think Fry might find something more interesting to write about than Bushmen, Bushmen!!"[43]

Though Fry was, like Tonks, a member of the NEAC hanging committee, he had recently helped establish the Contemporary Art Society, and he participated in Vanessa Bell's Friday Club. Bell had briefly been at the Slade, and her club offered an alternative exhibiting venue to the NEAC. Fry also felt an obligation to assist what he called *les jeunes*, "the younger and more vigorous" British artists, telling William Rothenstein in 1911 that with his position as adviser to the Grafton Gallery, "I can give them a chance they never had before of being well seen."[44] This was true, and Fry would act upon it, particularly with the establishment of the Omega Workshops, which provided a much needed regular income for often impoverished and struggling young artists. Through these establishments, as well as Ottoline Morrell's Bedford Square Thursday salons, the emergent Bloomsbury Group, the Camden Town Group, was offered an alternative to the conventions of English Impressionism and Renaissance standards of draughtsmanship expounded by Tonks and the Slade. But Fry, with Clive Bell and Duncan Grant, advocated their own particular aesthetic of "significant form." Fry's support and influence were not always welcomed, however. Nash considered him "Dangerous to work with or for but frightfully shrewd and brilliant brain,"[45] while Wyndham Lewis accused him of being "a shark in aesthetic waters."[46] Nevertheless, in the opinion of Paul Nash's friend, Robert Trevelyan, "Fry was without doubt the high priest of art of the day, and could and did make artistic reputations overnight."[47]

Fry's soon-to-be-infamous exhibition of modern continental art opened to the public on November 8, 1910, under the title "Manet and the Post-Impressionists," a collective phrase he coined especially for the show. It was dominated by Manet, Cézanne, Gauguin, Van Gogh, and Matisse, and included such works as Matisse's *Femme aux Yeux Verts*, Manet's *Un Bar aux Folies-Bergeres*, Van Gogh's *Crows in a Wheatfield*, and Picasso's *Portrait of Clovis Sagot*. These paintings rejected the narrative and literary inspirations of the traditional Western art canon since the High Renaissance, and although some pictures were already twenty or even thirty years old—and four of the five major artists represented were dead—they were new to most Londoners. The show was going to be quite an eye-opener for an insular audience brought up on the traditional verisimilitude of the classical tradition, exemplified by such painters then working in Britain as John Singer Sargent, William Rothenstein, William Nicholson, and Augustus John. Only Walter Sickert, and before him Rex Whistler, seemed to be offering anything akin to the "new" art across the Channel. Fry knew there would be trouble: "I am preparing for a huge campaign of outraged British Philistinism," he told a friend in October.[48]

As anticipated, the exhibition met with widespread derision. The critic for the high-class *Pall Mall Gazette* described the paintings as "the output of a lunatic asylum,"[49] while Robert Ross, writing in the *Morning Post*, pointed out that Van Gogh had been "a lunatic," and that the "emotions of these painters . . . are of no interest except to the student of pathology and the specialist in abnormality." The exhibition, Ross declared, revealed "a widespread plot to destroy the whole fabric of European painting."[50] Paul Nash recalled that one critic, Sir Claude Phillips of the *Telegraph*, "the most honest and uncompromising of them all," on leaving the show "threw down his catalogue upon the threshold of the Grafton Galleries and stamped on it."[51] The reviewer from the *Times* observed that such work "throws away all that the long-developed skills of past artists had acquired and bequeathed. It begins all over again . . . and stops where a child would stop."[52] The venerable painter Sir William Blake Richmond, meanwhile, wrote of his "fierce feeling of terror lest the youth of England, young promising fellows, might be contaminated" by "this unmanly show,"[53] while the aging poet and travel writer Wilfred Scawen Blunt rejected claims that the show paralleled the response to the Pre-Raphaelites' first appearance at the Royal Academy in the late 1850s: "these are not works of art at all," he wrote in his diary, "unless throwing a handful of mud against a wall may be called one. They are works of idleness and impotent stupidity, a pornographic show."[54]

These hostile responses have to be set not only against the ongoing revolution in all the arts, but against the wider social contexts of contemporary Britain: contexts important for understanding the world in which the young Slade artists were growing up and working. For both socially and politically these were years of crisis and anxiety. The decade before the Great War is often seen, nostalgically, as a period of peaceful innocence and tranquillity. In one sense this was true—for no one could have predicted the contrasting horrors that would be wrought in the trenches of Passchaendale and the Somme, and the millions of hopeless deaths which that pointless war would bring only a few years later. Yet in 1910, Edwardian England was not wholly at ease with itself. The previous year had seen the fraught divisions caused by the Liberal government's "People's Budget." While this was a major first step towards the creation of a modern welfare state, it had enraged the landed classes whom Prime Minister Asquith and his chancellor, Lloyd George, expected to fund it. The House of Lords had unsuccessfully opposed the budget—indeed, the government had questioned the Lords' continued existence, and in 1910 an Act of Parliament seriously curtailed their powers. The old Tory order, it seemed, was on the brink of collapse.

But it was not only the Liberal government that seemed to be threatening the status quo. In Wales and northwest England the labour unions, with links to socialist, Marxist, and anarchist movements, were in full and militant action, demanding radical social as well as political change. On November 8, the same day Fry's exhibition opened to the public, there was a serious riot in Tonypandy, with shops looted and a miner killed. The home secretary, Winston Churchill, was forced to send policemen and soldiers from London in an effort to restore order. The disquiet continued to simmer and occasionally boil over through the rest of the year and on into the long hot summer of 1911. In Ireland, meanwhile, calls for Home Rule and independence were getting ever louder, the threat of civil war between Protestants and Catholics looking ever likelier.

And in London the suffragette movement was becoming more vocal and forceful in its demands—and meeting even stronger government opposition. On November 18, only a few days after Wilfred Blunt visited the Gratfton Galleries and described the exhibition there as "pornographic," truncheon-wielding policemen in Parliament Square broke up a vocal crowd of protesters demanding votes for women. On what became known as "Bloody Friday," some two hundred and eighty protesters were arrested, and many were injured. Both of Nevinson's parents were closely involved in the suffragette movement, and Paul Nash's future wife was a suffragette. Noel Carrington believed Nevinson and his family's influence was important on his sister's development. Though he was uncertain if Carrington actually joined the movement, he thought the new friendship "marked the beginning of her later dislike for feminine weakness and for the restrictions which custom then imposed upon women . . . It was almost certainly at the Nevinsons' house in Hampstead that she began to acquire the feeling that a woman's role in life must not be one of subservience."[55]

Did Postimpressionism not actually reflect many of these social upheavals? Fry was surprised that the "accusation of anarchism was constantly made" against the "new" artistic movement. He believed that from an aesthetic point of view "this was, of course, the exact opposite of the truth, and I was for long puzzled to find the explanation of so paradoxical an opinion and so violent an enemy." Fry thought the opposition arose from class and snobbery. To become an authority on Chinese porcelain or Renaissance painting demanded education, erudition, and time devoted to study, "but to admire a Matisse required only a certain sensibility. One could feel fairly sure that one's maid could not rival one in the former case, but might by a mere haphazard gift of Providence surpass one in the second."[56] This, perhaps, was true—but Fry seems to have missed the bigger social picture.

Heavily morally and culturally loaded as it was, the first Postimpressionism show was quite an exhibition. Back at the Slade, Tonks was having none of it. As Nash observed, his fellow students were "by no means a docile crowd and the virus of the new art was working in them uncomfortably. Suppose they all began to draw like Matisse?"[57] Tonks gathered them together and called on their "sporting instincts," explaining that while he couldn't prevent them visiting the Grafton Galleries, he could tell them "how very much better pleased he would be if we did not risk contamination but stayed away."[58] In private Tonks was equally hostile. When George Moore suggested he allow more openness to the new style at the Slade, Tonks retorted bluntly: "I cannot teach what I don't believe in. I shall resign if this talk about Cubism doesn't cease; it is killing me."[59] According to Moore, in Tonks's opinion Postimpressionism was "an evil thing that had seduced the most gifted of the Slade students, those very ones that Tonks had relied upon to continue the tradition of Turner and Gainsborough and Constable."[60]

Like most of the Slade's younger student's, Paul Nash ignored Tonks's request to stay away from the exhibition, though he left it "untouched," writing long afterward "I remained at the point I had reached and continued to make my monochrome drawings of "visions."[61] The responses of his colleagues were at this stage equally cool. One Slade student declared in the University College magazine his opinion that "The principles advanced in the catalogue of the Exhibition at the Grafton Galleries were certainly interesting, but surely more as a revival than as an innovation. They express nothing more than has been the aim of artists from time immemorial."[62] Nevinson, who had already spent some time traveling in France, knew of the Postimpressionist artists long before 1910. On November 26 he and Gertler went to what was being called this "ultra-modernist" exhibition with Nevinson's father, Henry. They ran into Henry's friend Charles Lewis-Hind, a critic for the *Art Journal* and *Daily Chronicle*, and Henry Nevinson recorded in his diary afterward that "The ribald scorn of the fatted rich who knew nothing of art even stirred Hind's rage."[63] But as Michael Walsh has shown, the exhibition made only a limited impact on Nevinson, with his artistic ambitions remaining, even in 1912, "conservative and really quite modest."[64] Like Nash, he would not yet be joining the ranks of the European avant-garde, or even, apparently, wanting to.

In fact, William Rothenstein told Fry he considered the first Postimpressionist exhibition to have been "a brilliant and gallant charge of the light brigade . . . a glorious episode, but leaving things very much where they were before."[65] This seems to have been true, at least at first, for the youngest generation of artists. But while their immediate elders, including Vanessa Bell, Duncan Grant, and the Fitzroy Street painters such as Spencer Gore, were all soon displaying the influence of Postimpressionism in one form or another, Nevinson, Gertler, Spencer, and some of their other Slade colleagues were still finding greater influence in the National Gallery's collection of Renaissance paintings than in the Postimpressionists at Dover Street. In 1910 Augustus John had made his first visit to northern Italy, where he had seen the works of such Italian "primitives" as Signorelli at Orvieto and Giotto at Padua. Their influence had quickly appeared in his paintings, which were exhibited on his return to England. The critic Laurence Binyon, writing in the *Saturday Review*, actually considered them better than the Gauguins on show at the Postimpressionist exhibition,[66] and the young Slade artists appear to have followed John's lead, not Fry's.

Indeed, according to Nevinson by 1911 a group of Slade students, including himself, Gertler, Currie, and Stanley Spencer were no longer going by their earlier mantle of the "Slade Coster Gang," but were using the much more artistic sounding title of "the Neo-Primitives." Certainly, they all were drawing artistic influence directly from the early to mid-Italian Renaissance, including Duccio, Cimabue, Giotto, Masaccio, Fra Angelico, Piero della Francesca, and Sandro Botticelli—artistic sources of which Tonks would undoubtedly have approved and encouraged, and may well have been the instigator.[67] The works of this period thus stand in distinction to Gertler and Nevinson's pre- and early Slade work: Nevinson's oil paintings from ca. 1908–11, such as *The Railway Bridge, Charenton* (Manchester City Gallery), and *The Towing Path, Camden Town* (Ashmolean Museum, Oxford) used an English Impressionist style to tackle gritty urban subjects, while

Gertler's portraits represented his Jewish neighbors in Whitechapel in a not dissimilar style. But as Gertler explained in an interview with the *Jewish Chronicle* in February 1912, Piero della Francesca's *Nativity* in the National Gallery was "assuredly one of the finest pictures in the world," filled with "music and rhythm" of color. He added that Botticelli had also "helped me a great deal to see clearly in that direction." He doubted whether these Old Masters would ever be equaled in this respect: "There is too much visualism, and not enough brain, in modern art," he complained. "People do not think enough before they put brush to canvas, and then we are not such keen craftsmen as they were in the old days."[68] When the reporter asked him what he thought of modern art, Gertler explained "I say this, that until we begin to paint in the same sincere spirit that they did, we have no chance of approaching them as painters." Augustus John was the *only* modern artist he spoke of *by name* as being "really great."[69] In August 1913 Gertler would tell another Slade student, Dorothy Brett, "*do* study Giotto! & at once—He is tremendous!!! Study also Dürer—*the* draughtsman. These men are a constant cause of inspiration to me. It will never do, unless we too, express ourselves with such knowledge & emotion."[70] Nevinson's thinking clearly lay in the same direction. His beautifully finished self-portrait of 1911 shows the clear influence of Botticelli's *Portrait of a Young Man* in the National Gallery. He also rated Piero della Francesca highly, though he held that it was Whistler who was "undoubtedly our last Artist," and that "John is useless compared to him emotionally."[71] Interestingly, however, the exact dating of Nevinson's "Neo-Primitive" and Neo-Impressionist periods is hard to ascertain, and they may even have overlapped. This characteristic of painting in different styles at the same time according to taste or subject matter would continue, controversially, throughout his career.

The apotheosis of the Slade students' "primitive" spirit was John Currie's tempera group portrait, painted in 1912. It pictured him standing alongside Gertler, Nevinson, Wadsworth, Allinson, and the proprietress of the Petit Savoyard café in Soho, one of their favored haunts. With a deftly Renaissance style and an Italianate backdrop (a critic would speak of the "Florentine lucidity" of Currie's figures),[72] he titled this scene *Some Later Primitives and Madame Tisceron.* It was a remarkable work, well received when exhibited at the NEAC later that year. But it could not be called modern in terms of what was happening across the Channel—or indeed in terms of what was happening across Oxford Street in Bloomsbury and Camden Town. Thus in December 1912 when the Chenil Gallery in Chelsea exhibited Nevinson, Gertler and Currie alongside Augustus John, the critic for the *Observer* perceived that "when their modernity is closely investigated it seems to belong more to the fifteenth century than to the twentieth century. Indeed the most "advanced" of the exhibits take us back to the days of Giotto."[73] But by then the "Neo-Primitives" were breaking up. Nevinson had already warned Carrington in July of his fear that Currie and Gertler were becoming too "early Italian & costumy," telling her "we must guard against raking up the past." He felt that such "academic art" was "second hand & therefore lifeless." Though he looked to the past, he wanted "to paint this present age."[74] Gertler and Currie soon followed suit, though the break up of the "Neo-Primitives" no doubt also owed much to Gertler and Nevinson's falling out over their romantic feelings for Carrington. The split left Nevinson bitter, feeling that Gertler had simply used him "as a stepping stone" to help him move in "decent society."[75]

It must be noted that Fry perceived a link between at least some Postimpressionists and the "Primitives." In a lecture given at the Grafton Galleries at the close of the Postimpressionist exhibition, he suggested that in his "feeling for plastic form and strict correlation of planes," Cézanne's work "becomes in this respect singularly near to that of certain primitive Italian artists, such as Piero della Francesca, who also relied almost entirely upon linear design for producing this effect."[76] Though not a Postimpressionist, Puvis de Chavannes used a sparseness of palette that seems to reflect Piero della Francesca's, and he may perhaps be considered a greater influence on Spencer's *John Donne Arriving in Heaven* than any of Fry's Postimpressionists. Despite Spencer's claims not to be influenced by contemporary movements in art, when in May 1911 he took this remarkable little painting to the Slade, Tonks opined that it was "influenced by a certain party at the Grafton Gallery a little while ago." Spencer was annoyed by this reference to Fry's exhibition, and called Tonks a "damn liar!"[77] Yet Spencer's painting was the only work by his generation of Slade students to be hung in Fry's second Postimpressionist exhibition in 1912. (Gilbert Spencer believed that Tonks's anger at Fry's inclusion of Stanley's painting in the exhibition contributed to Fry's departure from the Slade.) In fact, despite this apparent early success as a recognized "modern," among the Slade "Neo-Primitives," it was Spencer who remained the most influenced by the early Renaissance Italians, and he later earned Gertler's wrath by responding to the question of what he thought of Picasso by replying, "I haven't got past Piero della Francesca yet."[78] Gertler and Nevinson soon moved beyond their interest in the so-called Primitives; Spencer with his love for Giotto, famously, did not.

In spite of his claims in his autobiography, Nevinson's conversion to the new Modernist movement would not come until *after* he had left the Slade—as is to be seen in the fractured cubism of *The Departure of the Train de Luxe* of 1913 and *The Arrival* (Tate Gallery) of 1913–14. Here the influence of the Futurists, and not Fry, was foremost. Fry's 1910 exhibition of Postimpressionism cannot, therefore, be taken as the single catalyst that redirected the young Slade students away from the traditions of Western art history advocated by Tonks. In fact, over the subsequent four years, a number of exhibitions of avant-garde art gradually influenced and redirected the young Slade students. The arrival of the Futurists in London in 1910, with their manifestos, lectures, and wild antics, lent a sense of both chaos and excitement to the promotion of contemporary art. Nevinson was quickly participating in their activities, and learned much from them—both as an artist and a self-promoter. Other Slade artists were either influenced by, or increasingly involved in, the emergence of this exciting new art scene that snowballed in the years after 1910. In November 1911 the short-lived Stafford Gallery in London held an exhibition of works by Cézanne and Gauguin, and there was, of course, Fry's Second Post-Impressionist Exhibition. Then in October 1913 Frank Rutter organized an exhibition of Postimpressionist and Futurist art at the Doré Galleries. It included works by Cézanne, Van Gogh, Gauguin, Camille Pissarro, Signac, Bonnard, Vuillard, Matisse, as well as German art from the collection of Michael Sadler pieces by six artists from the Camden Town Group, and works by Nevinson and Wadsworth.[79] This was followed in turn by the "Camden Town Group and Others" exhibition at Brighton Public Art Galleries in December 1913. Nevinson, Wadsworth, Bomberg, Nash, and Wyndham Lewis were all among the former Slade students who exhibited there. Then there was the "Twentieth Century Art" show at the Whitechapel Art Gallery, from May to June 1914—which was effectively a review of all the recent modern movements. There was the Omega Workshops, the Rebel Art Centre, and Vorticism—the first edition of *Blast* appeared in June 1914, and the London artists were fighting with each other and with themselves. As Nevinson later wrote in 1919, "I think it can be said that modern artists have been at war since 1912. Everything in art was in turmoil . . . the whole talk among artists was of war."[80]

It is difficult, from this mass of cultural episode and incident, to judge exactly the extent to which the Slade students were the masters or slaves of circumstance. The presence at the school of such a rich crop of students was both unprecedented and unrepeated. This must, in part, have been chance; but as I suggested in my opening paragraph, it must also have owed something to the combined reputations of Tonks and John. Despite the resentment held by some of his students, Tonks encouraged—or enforced—strong technique. With his promotion of primitivism and Postimpressionism, Roger Fry was also, clearly, an important aid and influence, as was the arrival of Marinetti and his Futurist cohort. The art scene in London was ripe for change, and the Slade students took full advantage of the exciting opportunities and influences available. But equally important was their influence upon each other. According to Edward Wadsworth's daughter, it was the "freedom of expression and exchange of ideas" with his fellow students, rather than the Slade's teaching staff, that was "all-important" to Wadsworth's early development as an artist. Indeed, she writes that her father found the staff "on the whole dull, with Tonks actually worse than this, in Edward's estimation; he was rude and arrogant."[81]

The clear evidence of influence can be detected in the works of many of the Slade artists through this period, and even up until the end of the war. They watched each other work, sometimes exchanged or bought drawings, and advice was sought—or more often simply given. Spencer and Gertler, for example, fell out badly in 1913. Gertler complained to the prominent collector Edward Marsh (who bought important early works by Gertler, Currie, Bomberg, and the Spencer and Nash brothers, though not, it appears, by Nevinson) that Spencer "seems to have already adopted the 'Great Man' attitude . . . He has had much praise lately and he is spoilt. I will have nothing more to do with him."[82] Almost all the Slade students had their own theories on how great art could or should be produced, with Spencer, Lightfoot, and Wadsworth being amongst the most fervent in advancing their ideas and advising their peers. Spencer didn't mind encouragement from the amiable and precociously talented, Lightfoot, but in 1914 he explained to Gwen Darwin that while at the Slade he "used to go, for ages every day, to lunch with Nevinson & Wadsworth, & Wadsworth used to get me to study the anatomy of his 'thoughts' upon art & how to paint & draw in a practical way, mind. This sort of thing went on for what seemed to me years until at last one day Wadsworth came in absolutely desperate." Wadsworth didn't think Spencer knew enough about "Art," and advised him to give it up altogether, explaining

"I have had experience; you have not. I have passed through all the stages an artist can go through; Rembrandt & all the rest." He went on like this & Nevinson looked very glum. It is extraordinary, but on this occasion I was silent. I thought perhaps he was ragging, until one day I asked Nevinson & he said Wadsworth was doing the same thing to him; delivering these lectures. I thought when I heard Wadsworth going on, "If you had not interfered you would never have got yourself into a muddle" for Wadsworth is a horrible man to me. You understand I only tell you this to show you that it was more or less through listening to these people's rubbish that made me so prejudiced against thought in every way . . . I agree with you that my work has suffered on account of this prejudice.[83]

The electric nature of these youthful exchanges is vividly portrayed in the novel written by Gertler's friend, the promising young author Gilbert Cannan. Based on long and intimate conversations, the roman a clef, *Mendel* was first published in 1916. There Nevinson was depicted by Cannan as Mitchell, "a fine young Englishman, pink and oozing robustious health, ease, refinement, and comfort," but living "under his father's shadow." According to Cannan, it was Gertler (as the eponymous Jewish hero Mendel) who set off Nevinson's "revolt against his Public School training," and Nevinson and his family who "shocked" Carrington "into thinking and gave her a sense of liberation." And it was "Mitchell" who introduced Mendel to John Currie, whose exciting conversation made the Slade seem like "a girls' school" in comparison. Cannan depicted Currie as a brilliant rabble-rouser filled with "furious energy," but slowly sliding into insanity. In Cannan's novel it is the Blake-like Currie who encourages Gertler to end his friendship with Nevinson. "He is a liar and a coward, and he will never be an artist, because he is too weak," are the words Cannan puts into Mendel's mouth. "He is not true. He is not good. . . . I wanted him to be my friend, but it is impossible."[84] Remarkably true to the life stories of Gertler and his colleagues, *Mendel* caused a stir in the literary world, with one reviewer being particularly impressed by Cannan's rendering of the life of a struggling painter: "We have always felt an artists' temperament must be an uncomfortable possession, but never has the belief been quite so irresistibly forced on us as after reading Gilbert Cannan's odd, brilliant study of a Jewish artist."

But life lived at the highly charged pace depicted in *Mendel* was too much, and, like Spencer, Gertler tired of these endless discussions and the strange, unhinged force of Currie's talent. He complained to Carrington in September 1912 of watching his fellow artists "talking art, Ancient art, Modern art, Impressionism, Post-Impressionism, Neo-Impressionism, Cubists, Spottists, Futurists, Cave-dwelling, Wyndham Lewis, Duncan Grant, [Frederick] Etchells, Roger Fry! I looked on and laughed to myself . . . and I walked home disgusted with them *all*."[85] As another, anonymous Slade student acknowledged in the *UCL Magazine* in 1911, with this mass of artistic ideas clambering for attention, these were tricky times, and wondered, "Are we indeed to be thankful for living in this century? . . . Not every student can bear with equanimity the burden of dozens of semi-digested principles, the bewilderment of theories innumerable, each claiming for itself superiority over all others."[86]

Ultimately, the Slade students had to find their own way. Yet it was the success of many of them in doing just this, of overcoming together the "crisis" of their collective brilliance and finally breaking away from Tonks's stern, invaluable guidance and judging their own course and their own futures among such a welter of chance and influence, that made their generation one of such remarkable excellence. That the many facets of the Slade at that time helped to model the great artist inside Nevinson is undoubtable: the painter who would have emerged had he stayed at St John's Wood and gone on to the Royal Academy would have been a very different being. But then, Nevinson could never have been that man; he could never have stood still long enough to keep such a conventional course. He was always, always, upsetting his apple cart.

Notes

1. Randolph Schwabe, "Reminiscences of Fellow Students," *Burlington Magazine* 82 (1943): 6, 9. Schwabe succeeded Tonks as Professor of Drawing and then as director of the Slade.

2. C. R. W. Nevinson, *Paint and Prejudice* (London: Methuen, 1937), 18.

3. Ibid., 19.

4. Ibid., 20–21.

5. Ibid., 15.

6. Michael J. K. Walsh, *C. R. W. Nevinson: This Cult of Violence* (New Haven, CT: Yale University Press, 2002), 11.

7. George Moore, *Conversations in Ebury Street* (London: Heinemann, 1924), 120.

8. Moore, *Conversations*, 118.

9. Henry Tonks, "Notes from 'Wander Years,'" *Artwork* 5, no. 20 (1929): 224–29.

10. Tonks, "Notes," 235.

11. John Rothenstein, *Modern English Painters: Sickert to Moore* (London: Eyre & Spottiswoode, 1957), 89.

12. Paul Nash, *Outline: An Autobiography and Other Writings*, with a preface by Herbert Read (London: Faber & Faber, 1949), 89.

13. Helen Lessore in *Henry Tonks and the "Art of Pure Drawing"* Lynda Morris, ed. (Norwich, UK: Norwich School of Art Gallery, 1985), 8.

14. Tonks, "Notes from 'Wonder Years,'" 235.

15. Ibid., 230.

16. Helen Lessore, in Morris, *Henry Tonks*, 8.

17. Gilbert Spencer, *Memoirs of a Painter* (London: Chatto & Windus, 1974), 31.

18. Paul Nash to Gordon Bottomley, November 15, 1910, in *Poet and Painter: Being the Correspondence Between Gordon Bottomley and Paul Nash, 1910–1946* Claude Colleer Abbott and Anthony Bertram, eds. (London: Oxford University Press, 1955), 13.

19. Stanley Spencer to Jacques and Gwen Raverat, December 13, 1912, Hyman Kreitman Research Centre, Tate Britain, London, TGA 8116.18.

20. Morris, *Henry Tonks*, 9.

21. Ibid., 10.

22. William Rothenstein, *Men and Memories: Recollections of William Rothenstein, 1900–1922* (London: Faber & Faber, 1932), 166.

23. Gertler to Carrington, September 24, 1912, in *Mark Gertler: Selected Letters*, Noel Carrington, ed. (London: Rupert Hart-Davis, 1965), 47.

24. Nevinson, *Paint and Prejudice* (1937), 24.

25. Richard Cork, *David Bomberg* (London: Tate Gallery, 1988), 12.

26. Nevinson to Carrington, n.d., Harry Ransom Humanities Research Center, University of Austin, Texas (hereafter HRHRC).

27. Walsh, *C. R. W. Nevinson*, 18.

28. Nash, *Outline*, 111.

29. James King, *Interior Landscapes: A Life of Paul Nash* (London: George Weidenfeld & Nicolson, 1987), 43.

30. Nevinson, *Paint and Prejudice* p. 30.

31. Morris, *Henry Tonks*, 13.

32. Ian Parsons, ed., *The Collected Works of Isaac Rosenberg: Poetry, Prose, Letters, Paintings and Drawings* (London: Chatto & Windus, 1979), 301.

33. Gertler to Carrington, September 24, 1912, HRHRC.

34. Nevinson to Carrington, probably August 1912, HRHRC.

35. Stanley Spencer to Jacques and Gwen Raverat, August 7, 1911, Hyman Kreitman Research Centre, Tate Britain, London, TGA 8116.6

36. Stanley Spencer to Lady Ottoline Morrell, June 9, 1917, HRHRC.

37. Richard Nevinson to Yockney, undated (December 1919?), Imperial War Museum, London, First World War Artists Archive, file 266 B/6, 150–52.

38. Rothenstein, *Modern English Painters*, 367.

39. Gertler to Carrington, November 13 (1915?), HRHRC.

40. Nevinson, *Paint and Prejudice*, 29, Diana Holman-Hunt, *Latin Among Lions: Alvaro Guevara* (London: Michael Joseph, 1974), 85.

41. Nevinson to Carrington, August 1912, HRHRC.

42. Helen Tongue, *Bushman Drawings*, in *Burlington Magazine* (May 1910): see Frances Spalding, *Roger Fry: Art and Life* (London: Granada Publishing, 1980), 129.

43. Margarey Ross, *Robert Ross: Friend of Friends* (London: Cape, 1952).

44. Fry to William Rothenstein, March 28, 1911, in Spalding, *Roger Fry*, 155.

45. Paul Nash to Gordon Bottomley, December 27, 1913, Abbott and Bertram, *Poet and Painter*, 68.

46. Nevinson, *Paint and Prejudice*, 56.

47. Nash, *Outline*, 162.

48. Roger Fry to G. L. Dickinson, October 15, 1910 in *Letters of Roger Fry* Denys Sutton, ed. (London: Chatto & Windus, 1972).

49. *Pall Mall Gazette*, November 10, 1910.

50. Robert Ross, *Morning Post*, November 7, 1910, in *Post-Impressionists in England* J. B. Bullen, ed. (London: Routledge, 1988), 100–4.

51. Nash, *Outline*, 93

52. *Times*, November 7, 1910.

53. W. B. Richmond, *Morning Post*, November 16, 1910, in Bullen (1988), 114–16.

54. W. S. Blunt, in Bullen, *Post-Impressionists*, 113–14.

55. Noel Carrington, *Carrington: Paintings, Drawings and Decorations* (London: Thames and Hudson, 1980), 22.

56. Fry, *Vision and Design*, 192–93.

57. Nash, *Outline*, 93.

58. Ibid.

59. Moore, *Conversations*, 137. By 1920 Tonks had decided he was "quite unable to appreciate modern art." The final straw was Dada, which he described as "the Art to end Art." Henry Tonks to Mary Hutchinson, April 1920, HRHRC.

60. Moore, *Conversations*, 131.

61. Nash, *Outline*, 93.

62. *University College Union Magazine* 2 (June 1911): 242.

63. Bodleian Library, Oxford, MS Eng. Misc. e. 616/2, November 26, 1910.

64. Walsh, *C. R. W. Nevinson*, 21–23. Also see Rothenstein (1957) 365 and 368–69, who also critiques some of Nevinson's myth making for this period of his career.

65. William Rothenstein to Fry, March 19, 1911, quoted in Spalding (1980), 155.

66. Laurence Binyon, *Saturday Review*, December 10, 1910, 747.

67. Nevinson, *Paint and Prejudice*, 33.

68. Quoted in John Woodeson, *Mark Gertler: Biography of a Painter, 1891–1939* (London: Sidgwick & Jackson, 1973), 335.

69. Quoted in Woodeson (1973), 336.

70. Mark Gertler to Dorothy Brett, August 1913, HRHRC.

71. Richard Nevinson to Dora Carrington, n.d., HRHRC.

72. *Times*, February 20, 1914.

73. Quoted in Woodeson (1973), 337. It may be noted that it was John who introduced Gertler to tempera.

74. Richard Nevinson to Dora Carrington, July 1912, HRHRC.

75. Richard Nevinson to Dora Carrington, August 14, 1912, HRHRC.

76. Bullen, *Post-Impressionists*, 177.

77. Stanley Spencer to Sydney Spencer, May 18, 1911, in Adrian Glew, *Stanley Spencer: Letters and Writings* (London: Tate Publishing, 2001), 34.

78. Spencer, *Memories*, 99.

79. Wendy Baron, *Perfect Moderns: A History of the Camden Town Group* (Aldershot, UK: Ashgate, 2000), 61.

80. Nevinson, *New York Times*, May 25, 1919, quoted in Rothenstein (1957), 379.

81. Barbara Wadsworth, *Edward Wadsworth: A Painter's Life* (Salisbury, UK: Michael Russell, 1989), 28.

82. Gertler to Marsh, October 1913, in Carrington (1965) 56.

83. Stanley Spencer to Jacques and Gwen Raverat, July 12, 15, 17, 1914, quoted in Glew, *Stanley Spencer*, 49.

84. Gilbert Cannan, *Mendel* (Lloyds: London, 1916), 57, 78, 102, 105, 108, 121–22.

85. Mark Gertler to Dora Carrington, September 24, 1912, HRHRC.

86. *University College Union Magazine* 5, no. 2 (June 1911): 242.

Tracing the Performative: F. T. Marinetti, C. R. W. Nevinson, and the English Futurist Manifesto

Johann Pillai and Anber Onar

> Meanwhile the excitement was intense. *Putsches* took place every month or so. . . . Marinetti brought off a Futurist *Putsch* about this time. / It started in Bond Street. I counterputsched. I assembled in Greek Street a determined band of miscellaneous anti-futurists. Mr. Epstein was there; Gaudier Brzeska, T. E. Hulme, Edward Wadsworth. . . . There were about ten of us. After a hearty meal we shuffled bellicosely round to the Doré Gallery. / Marinetti had entrenched himself upon a high lecture platform. . . . Gaudier . . . was sniping him without intermission, standing up in his place in the audience all the while. The remainder of our party maintained a confused uproar.
>
> The Italian intruder was worsted. There was another occasion (before he declared war on us, and especially on me) when Mr. C. R. W. Nevinson . . . assisted him. The founder of Fascism had been at Adrianople. . . . He wanted to imitate the noise of bombardment. It was a poetic declamation, which must be packed to the muzzle with what he called "la rage balkanique". So Mr. Nevinson concealed himself somewhere in the hall, and at a signal from Marinetti belaboured a gigantic drum.
>
> . . . And at last this man [Marinetti] attempted a *Putsch* against the "great London Vortex". He denounced me in letters to the Press, as the major obstacle to the advance of Futurism in England. And that was perfectly true. . . .
>
> Then Mr. C. R. W. Nevinson attempted a *Putsch*. He selected a sheet of "Rebel Art Centre" notepaper. The "Rebel Art Centre" in Great Ormond Street, founded by Miss Lechmere and myself, was the seat of the "Great London Vortex". Upon this notepaper Mr. C. R. W. Nevinson expressed Futurist opinions; he too, I think, went over into the Press, and I had to repudiate him as an interloper and a heretic.
>
> I have said enough to show that the months immediately preceding the declaration of war were full of sound and fury . . . Life was one big bloodless brawl, prior to the Great Bloodletting.
>
> —Wyndham Lewis, *Blasting and Bombardiering*

Some critical distance can be maintained from the sound and fury of London's art world in 1914 if it is understood as a dynamic series of shifting aesthetic allegiances arising from artists' dissatisfaction with the conservatism of the Royal Academy and art-historical tradition. In 1886 the New English Art Club (NEAC) was created to exhibit the work of artists under the influence of Impressionism. Its founding members, Whistler, Sickert, and Steer would soon be joined by Clausen, Stanhope Forbes, and Sargent; and by 1920 it would include Augustus John and Stanley Spencer. In 1911 the NEAC was challenged by the Postimpressionist-oriented Camden Town Group, which developed around Sickert and Lucien Pissarro, and included Wyndham Lewis. Two years later, members of the Bloomsbury Group of artists, writers, and intellectuals formed the Omega Workshops, a design collective organized as a company by the critic Roger Fry. The Omega group included Vanessa Bell, Duncan Grant, and initially, Lewis—who with Frederick Etchells, Cuthbert Hamilton, and Edward Wadsworth, then broke away to form a rival group, the Rebel Art Centre (RAC). In 1913 too, the Camden Town Group merged with other, smaller groups to form the London Group; the latter's first exhibition in 1914 included members of the RAC, which soon expanded to include Lawrence Atkinson, Henri Gaudier-Brzeska, Jessica Dismorr, Williams Roberts, Helen Saunders, Jacob

Epstein, David Bomberg, and C. R. W. Nevinson. The joint publication in 1914 by Nevinson and the Italian poet Marinetti of a Futurist manifesto would cause an even more dramatic shift in allegiances, giving impetus to a new movement emerging from the RAC under the guidance of Lewis, the poet Ezra Pound and the critic T. E. Hulme, and revolving around the periodical *Blast*: Vorticism.

The excitement Lewis describes in the artists' community of London in 1914 ironically anticipates the approaching political and physical chaos immortalized in William Butler Yeats's lines: "Things fall apart; the center cannot hold; / Mere anarchy is loosed upon the world."[1] The political *putsch* represents (at least theoretically) an attack on existing hierarchical order, an attempt at decentralization. Lewis's characterization of the artistic revolutions of the time as "putsches" is thus naturally couched in terms of political centralization: Marinetti is "the founder of Fascism," a centralized form of government; a "vortex" is a spiraling toward a center (in this case, London); and with unwitting irony, the organization Lewis cofounds is named the "Rebel Art *Centre*." Lewis himself acknowledges this in retrospect in his memoir: "Really all this organized disturbance was Art behaving as if it were Politics. But I swear I did not know it . . . I see that now. . . . I mistook the agitation in the audience for the sign of an awakening of the emotions of artistic sensibility. . . . And I concluded that as a matter of course some romantic figure must always emerge, to captain the 'group'. Like myself!"[2] Centrality presupposes hierarchy and a power differential between center and periphery; and as this differential is at its base ideologically determined, Lewis shifts from an aesthetic to a political register to characterize the activities of Marinetti and Nevinson in terms of nationalism ("the Italian intruder") and Christian dogma ("I had to repudiate him [i.e., Nevinson] as . . . a heretic"). Circumscribing these relations is a metaphorics of war, of a "bloodless brawl." It has physical moments—Lewis recalls that Gaudier "threatened at Ford's to sock Bomberg on the jaw"; that he himself "seized Hulme by the throat; but he transfixed me upon the railings of Soho Square"; and that "Mr. Epstein and David Bomberg kissed, to seal a truce" under a "piece of dynamic statuary"[3]—but for the most part it takes place in spoken and written language. Its indices are such expressions as "sniping," "confused uproar," "declared war," or "packed to the muzzle"; and its medium "a poetic declamation," denunciation in "letters to the Press," opinions on headed "notepaper," and other forms of "repudiation." It is in this linguistic context, following the logic of the pen rather than the sword, and informed by the play between centering and decentering, that F. T. Marinetti and C. R. W. Nevinson introduce the English Futurist manifesto, proclaiming the ideal of a "Vital English Art" (**VEA**).

The Context of Politics

The adjective "English" in the manifesto's title suggests a broader political framework of nationalism; and indeed, as Renato Poggioli noted in a classic treatise, traditionally there have been two senses of the "avant-garde": first, the "sociopolitical" (echoing the original military connotation of a *vanguard*) and second, the "cultural-artistic"—although in late nineteenth-century Europe "what had up to then been a secondary, figurative meaning became instead the primary, in fact the only, meaning."[4] This shift might today tempt one to treat Futurism merely as an aesthetic phenomenon; but, as Rosa Clough and others have argued, "Futurism was from the very beginning an aspect of Italian nationalism."[5] The Italian Futurists were active in election campaigns, and

> Futurist nationalism . . . became a recognized power in the political agitations that prepared the [1911] Tripolitan Campaign and the World War, and directed public opinion towards colonial enterprises, collaboration with England and France, and war against the Germanic nations. . . . Meetings, riots, speeches, poetic tournaments, everything was resorted to in an endeavor to convince the Italians of the necessity of the conquest of that African land which would satisfy the needs for colonial expansion and remove the cause of friction with France over the occupation of Tunis. . . . In March and April of . . . [1910] Marinetti spoke at the Lyceum Club in London. His subject was Futurism, but he did not lose the opportunity to emphasize his love for war and his hatred for Pan-Germanism in general and for Austria in particular.[6]

In June 1914, with war approaching, Italy was still involved with Germany and Austria-Hungary in the Triple Alliance, although its territorial rivalries with Austria-Hungary were increasing; it was only later that year that it declared neutrality, and not until 1915 that it aligned itself with the Allies. So Marinetti could declare: "Our hatred of Austria; our feverish anticipation of war; our desire to strangle Pan-Germanism. This is the corollary of our Futurist theorem!"[7] Meanwhile, the 1904 Entente Cordiale between Britain and France had expanded under the Anglo-Russian agreement of 1907 that created the Triple Entente. Neither Marinetti's Futurist statements and performances in England prior to the appearance of **VEA**, nor the manifesto itself, can therefore be separated from the politics of Italian and English national identity during this period.

The specific roots of such a politics may be traced in the local histories of nation-states; on a broader conceptual level, however, a "nation" must first be understood as an artificial ideological construct. In Benedict Anderson's terms,

> it is an *imagined political community*—and imagined as both inherently limited and sovereign. / It is *imagined* because the members of even the smallest nation will never know most of their fellow-members, meet them, or even hear of them, yet in the minds of each lives the image of their communion. . . . The nation is imagined as *limited* because even the largest of them . . . has finite, if elastic boundaries, beyond which lie other nations. No nation imagines itself coterminous with mankind. . . . It is imagined as *sovereign* because the concept was born in an age in which Enlightenment and Revolution were destroying the legitimacy of the divinely-ordained, hierarchical dynastic realm. . . . Finally, it is imagined as a *community*, because, regardless of the actual inequality and exploitation that may prevail in each, the nation is always conceived as a deep, horizontal comradeship.[8]

The primary force through which national imagined communities were invented, Anderson argues, was "the convergence of capitalism and print technology on the fatal diversity of human language." Widely disseminated books, pamphlets, and particularly newspapers, created new standardized and official versions of national vernaculars, enabling individuals to imagine they were part of a community unified by a common master tongue, past, and destiny. At the same time, the official propagation of national ideology in the form of "culture" led to the imagining of a common geography and of shared feelings of "deep, horizontal comradeship" within the general population.[9]

As against, then, the romantic figure of the individual, original, and visionary genius who captains the group—Lewis would later acknowledge, "it never occurred to me that left to itself a group might express itself *in chorus*"[10]—Anderson's argument suggests that it is the ethos of an imagined artistic-political community or group expressed through the individual that is at stake in Futurism. Creating such a communal ethos, however, is the function of the Futurist avant-garde; so it is essential that the movement's primary venues, "theaters of operations," be print media and performance. As Marinetti explained in 1913:

> Those people who today make use of the telegraph, the telephone . . . , the automobile . . . , the cinema, the great newspaper . . . do not realize that these various means of communication, transportation and information have a decisive influence on their psyches. . . . By reading a newspaper the inhabitant of a mountain village can tremble each day with anxiety, following insurrection in China, the London and New York suffragettes . . . The timid, sedentary inhabitant of any provincial town can indulge in the intoxication of danger by going to the movies and watching a great hunt in the Congo. . . . these facts are important modifiers of our sensibility because they have caused the following significant phenomena:
>
> 1. Acceleration of life to today's swift pace. . . .
> 2. Dread of the old and the known. Love of the new, the unexpected. . . .
> 9. A modification of patriotism, which now means a heroic idealization of the commercial, industrial, and artistic solidarity of a people.
> 10. A modification in the idea of war, which has become the necessary and bloody test of a people's force.[11]

In poetry and performance, the Futurist campaign focuses on subverting dominant *languages* of communication (this is the logic of *parole in libertà* or "words-in-freedom"); but for the actual *communication* of the campaign, it must needs employ those very languages that it would subvert. So Marinetti comments: "Philosophy, the exact sciences, politics, journalism, education, business, however much they may seek synthetic forms of expression, will still need to use syntax and punctuation. I am obliged, for that matter, to use them myself in order to make myself clear to you."[12] In newspaper or pamphlet form the Futurist text is circumscribed by additional factors, not least the spatial, sociocultural, political, and linguistic frames and boundaries within which it is printed and distributed. The subversion generated by the text operates primarily on a semantic level, through its content; the framing of this content, however—its genre, its form *as a manifesto*—creates another kind of disturbance, on formal and aesthetic levels as well as the political.

The Politics of Context

The Futurist manifesto "Vital English Art" (**VEA**) first appeared in English on June 7, 1914, in a London newspaper, the *Observer*. Nevinson writes in his memoir:

> This was published in the *Times*, the *Observer* and the *Daily Mail*, but we were not content with that and I used to go to the galleries of theatres and shower the manifestos on the heads of the unsuspecting people in the stalls and

> the dress circle. When I was located I was escorted from the building by the largest commissionaire. It would be untrue to say that this joint effort shook England to its foundations, but it certainly stirred the art world; and P. Wyndham Lewis, white hot, wrote to the *Times*, the *Observer*, and the *Daily Mail*, dissociating himself from Marinetti, to the great satisfaction of all and the derision of Fleet Street.[13]

We have thus far located seven roughly contemporaneous versions of **VEA**, which was published in various formats (although not, pace Nevinson, in the *Times* or the *Daily Mail*) and reprinted several times, with some significant textual variations:

1) The first version, printed in a single column on page 7 of the *Observer* (henceforth **VEA-OBS1-EN**).[14]
2) A reprint of this version with the *Observer*'s headlines in a book(let) of unknown source and date (**VEA-OBS2-EN**).[15]
3) An English pamphlet version of uncertain provenance, but possibly published in Italy in June (**VEA-PAM-EN**).[16]
4) A French pamphlet version, presumably printed in Italy, titled "Contre l'art anglais," and dated "LONDRES, 11 Juin 1914" (**VEA-PAM-FR**).[17]
5) An English version printed on the front and second page (209–10) of the Italian political-cultural journal *Lacerba*[18] on July 15, 1914 (**VEA-LAC-EN**).
6) An Italian translation of the above, titled "Manifesto Futurista," which appeared below it on pages 210–11 of the same issue of *Lacerba* (**VEA-LAC-IT**).[19]
7) An English version printed in 1938, in Nevinson's book *Paint and Prejudice* (**VEA-P&P-EN**).[20]

On June 12, 1914, Nevinson prefaced his reading/performance of the manifesto at the Doré Gallerie's with a lecture, "Vital English Art," which was printed in the *New Age* on June 18,[21] along with an ironic account of the performance in abbreviated transcript form by Charles Brookfarmer entitled "Futile-ism. Or, All Cackle and No Osses."[22] After this performance Marinetti traveled alone to Cambridge University,[23] where he read out a French text that presumably corresponds to **VEA-PAM-FR**.[24] At least one other performance is recorded in 1919 during Nevinson's visit to the United States: the New York *Sun* (May 17) and the *New York Times* (May 29) reported that he read out a version of **VEA** at the Kevorkian Gallery, 40 West Fifty-seventh Street, in the course of a lecture on "Art as a National Asset."[25]

The manifesto's existence in such a variety of forms and languages—as newspaper and journal article, as pamphlet, performance, transcript, reprint, and book chapter—calls for a study beyond the scope of this preliminary essay;[26] our primary focus here is on the manifesto's appearance as a column in a newspaper, where it is itself "news," and therefore circumscribed by the cultural and political attitudes and events of the day that "make the news."

The text of **VEA** first appeared rather unobtrusively on Sunday, June 7, 1914, on page 7 of the *Observer*, in the fourth column (of a seven-column page) under the general heading "ART & ARTISTS," along with notes on art exhibitions (John Lavery at the Grosvenor Gallery, Théophile Steinlen at the Leicester Galleries) and "Letters to the Editor," on a page bordered by advertisements for clothing, wedding presents, hair tonic, "Waterman's Ideal Fountain Pen," "Poulton and Noels English Ox Tongues," "Borwick's Baking Powder," and "Cockle's Antibilious Pills." Among the newsworthy items of the preceding and following days are Home Rule for Ireland, the activities of the Suffragettes and the arrest of Sylvia Pankhurst, political strikes in Italy, events related to the Triple Alliance, tensions between Turkey and Greece, the possibility of an European war, and—albeit on a lesser scale—discussions of Futurism.

As one moves down the fourth column, one encounters a series of centered headlines of progressively decreasing size, each separated by a line (//)—FUTURISM / AND / ENGLISH ART // SIGNOR MARINETTI'S / MANIFESTO // NEW IDEALS FOR OLD // "HURRAH FOR MOTORS!" // —followed by four lines of editorial introduction: "Signor Marinetti, who has acquired so much notoriety as the apostle of Futurism, has issued the following 'manifesto' to the English public:—" and then the headings "VITAL ENGLISH ART // FUTURIST MANIFESTO." The effect of this setup, whether deliberate or unconscious on the part of the editors, is subtly to condition the paper's readers to reject or ridicule the text that follows. First, the largest font is used for the words "English Art," immediately followed by the contrasting Italian title "Signor," which is calculated to suggest foreignness and tap into any latent feelings of nationalism or xenophobia in the readership. That such feelings exist is suggested by part of a conversation Wyndham Lewis recalls with Marinetti:

> You are a futurist, Lewis! he [Marinetti] shouted at me one day, as we were passing into a lavabo together, where

he wanted to wash after a lecture where he had drenched himself in sweat.

No, I said.

Why don't you announce that you are a futurist! he asked me squarely.

Because I am not one, I answered, just as pointblank and to the point.

Yes. But what's it matter! said he with great impatience.

It's most important, I replied rather coldly.

Not at all! said he. Futurism is good. It is all right.

Not too bad, said I. It has its points. But you Wops insist too much on the Machine. You're always on about these driving-belts, you are always exploding about internal combustion. We've had machines here in England for a donkey's years. They're no novelty to *us*.[27]

"Signor Marinetti's Manifesto" is further qualified by the next heading, "New Ideals for Old," an allusion to the familiar cry of the evil magician in the *Arabian Nights* who tricks Aladdin's princess into handing over the magic lamp by posing as a street vendor who will exchange "new lamps for old."[28] The final heading—"Hurrah for Motors"—although quoted from the manifesto, appears here out of context as a trivial slogan to invite ridicule; the editorial introduction then directly sets "the English public" against Marinetti's "notoriety."

Vital English Art I: The Nevinson Virus

The combined effect of the newspaper's headlines and introduction in the political context of the time is thus, at least on an unconscious level, to encourage its readership's opposition to **VEA**'s opening gambit and the attacks that will follow: "I am an Italian Futurist poet, and a passionate admirer of England. I wish, however, to cure English art of that most grave of all maladies—passéism. I have the right to speak plainly and without compromise, and together with my friend Nevinson, an English Futurist painter, to give the signal for battle." From its first line, the dominant voice in the text is Marinetti's, and given the editorial buildup, it is unlikely that any reader could take the evil magician of the tale to be a "passionate admirer of England"; further, that a notorious Italian should claim to have a cure for England (which has presumably been unaware, prior to this diagnosis, of its affliction with the "most grave of all maladies") suggests all the quackery of the traveling medicine show. It is in this context that "my friend Nevinson"—whose name appears as a coauthor's at the end of the manifesto, below Marinetti's—is introduced as an "English Futurist painter," as the supplement to the "Italian Futurist poet" Marinetti's "I." Marinetti's primary medium of aesthetic expression is verbal language—words and performance in Italian and French—while Nevinson's is visual representation: both are outsiders, albeit in slightly different ways, with respect to verbal political expression in the English language. Here, in a curious reversal of roles, Marinetti's "I" expresses itself in Nevinson's native language verbally, and in its supplementarity the "I" of Nevinson's language declares his identity as a Futurist—a declaration that Lewis refuses to make; through this play, the text establishes an imagined community of Futurists that transcends the national boundaries of both Italy and England.

Now by association the manifesto seems to move into a joint declaration; but it is Marinetti, in the persona of the "I," who has "the right to speak plainly and without compromise" (the French and Italian versions, perhaps closer to Marinetti's own voice, read: *parler haut et sans periphrases* [**VEA-PAM-FR**]; *parlare ad alta voce e senza perifrasi* [**VEA-LAC-IT**]—"speak loudly and without circumlocutions") while the joint action in which Nevinson participates is giving "the signal for battle."[29] Marinetti's signal must be understandable in the English cultural context, and so it is given jointly with the native English speaker; in this way the audience culture or readership can be drawn into what Lewis calls the "organized disturbance" of art functioning as politics. The stock modernist image of sickness used to characterize hidebound tradition or "passéism" thus gives way to a different kind of imagery: the proposed "cure" is couched in terms of a declaration of war on language and culture; in short, on the imagined community of the nation. For the general reader this is war not simply on English art but on the culture of "Englishness" and England, by what Lewis calls "the Italian intruder." And in this war Nevinson is placed—and, by his "signature" at the end of the manifesto, places himself—in the position of a translator (we recall the wordplay of the Italian maxim *traduttore-traditore*, "translator, traitor") or "collaborator" in both senses, with the "Wops."

Nevinson himself, at the Doré Galleries, describes the manifesto as a text "that Signor Marinetti and myself have drawn up together,"[30] and since the latter "spoke no English"[31] there is no doubt that the writing is Nevinson's; the narrative tone and style, however, suggest that it is largely a translation of Marinetti's words. It is interesting that Nevinson reverts to visual language in introducting the manifesto which his "I" supplements: it has jointly been "drawn up." One can only speculate on how differently the audience might have reacted had the dominant voice in the text been Nevinson's; as it is, the language of the manifesto—it is no coincidence that the French translation dated June 11, the day before this lecture, was titled *Contre l'art anglais*, or "*Against* English Art"—is calculated to strike, from outside, at the core of English traditions. The battle (significant variants in the French and Italian versions are shown in brackets below) will be

AGAINST:

1.—The worship of tradition and the conservatism of Academies, the commercial acquiescence of English artists, the effeminacy of their art and their complete absorption towards a purely decorative sense.

[**VEA-PAM-FR:** . . . *le culte de la tradition, le conservatorisme artistique des académies, la préoccupation commerciale des artistes anglais, la mièvrerie efféminée de leur art, et leurs recherches purement décoratives*]

[**VEA-LAC-IT:** . . . *il culto della tradizione, il conservatorismo delle accademie, la preoccupazione commerciale degli artisti inglesi, l'effeminatezza della loro arte e i loro sforzi in un senso puramente ed esclusivamente decorativo*]

2.—The pessimistic, sceptical and narrow views of the English public, who stupidly adore the pretty-pretty, the commonplace, the soft, sweet, and mediocre, the sickly revivals of mediaevalism, the Garden Cities with their curfews and artificial battlements, the Maypole Morris dances, Aestheticism, Oscar Wilde, the Pre-Raphaelites, Neo-primitives and Paris.

[**VEA-PAM-FR:** . . . *les goûts pessimistes, sceptiques et nostalgiques . . . le mièvre, le modéré, l'atténué, le médiocre, les ignobles Gardens* [sic] *Cities, Maypole, Morris dances et Fairy stories . . . et tout ce qui vient de Paris.* (the phrases "sickly revivals" and "with . . . battlements" are omitted)]

[**VEA-LAC-IT:** . . . *i gusti pessimisti, scettici e nostalgici . . . lezioso, moderato, attenuato, mediocre; le meschine ricostruzioni medioevali, le ignobili* Gardens cities, *Maypole*, Morris dances, Fairystories . . . *e Parigi.*]

3.—The perverted snob who ignores or despises all English daring, originality and invention, but welcomes all foreign originality and daring. After all, England can boast of Pioneers—in Poetry, such as Shakespeare and Swinburne; in Art, Turner and Constable (the original founders of the Impressionist and Barbizon School); in Science, Watts, Stephenson, Darwin, &c., &c.

[**VEA-PAM-FR:** . . . *le Snobisme mal canalisé qui ignore ou méprise toutes . . . Il ne faut pas oublier que l'Angleterre a eu des vaillants pionniers tel que . . . Turner, Constable, (qui fut le premier initiateur du mouvement impressioniste de l'école de Barbizon) Watts, Stephenson, Darwin, etc.* (the phrases "in Poetry," "in Art," "in Science" are omitted)]

[**VEA-LAC-IT:** . . . *lo snobismo mal canalizzato che ignora o disprezza tutte . . . Non si deve dimenticare che l'Inghilterra ebbe dei novatori quali Shakespeare e Swinburne nella poesia: Turner e Constable (che fu il primo iniziatore del movimento impressionista e della scuola di Barbizon) nella pittura; Watts, Stephenson, Darwin, ecc., nelle scienze.*]

4.—The sham revolutionaries of the New English Art Club, who, having destroyed the prestige of the Royal Academy, now show themselves grossly hostile to the later movements of the advance guard.

[**VEA-PAM-FR:** . . . *Club qui hérita le prestige de la Royal Academy* . . .]

[**VEA-LAC-IT:** . . . *Club, che annientò il prestigio della Royal Academy* . . .]

5.—The indifference of the King, the State and the politicians towards all arts.

6.—The English notion that Art is a useless pastime, only fit for women and schoolgirls, that artists are poor deluded fools to be pitied and protected, and Art a ridiculous complaint, a mere topic for table-talk.

[**VEA-PAM-FR:** . . . *l'art une maladie bizarre dont tout le monde peut parler;*]

[**VEA-LAC-IT:** . . . *l'arte una malattia bizzarra di cui tutti possono parlare;*]

7.—The universal right of the ignorant to discuss and decide upon all questions of Art.

8.—The old grotesque idea of genius—drunken, filthy, ragged, outcast; drunkenness the synonym of Art, Chelsea the Montmartre of London; the Post-Rossettis with long hair under the sombrero, and other passéist filth.

[**VEA-PAM-FR:** . . . *le vieil idéal brûlé du génie ivrogne, crasseux, débraillé et hors cadre* . . .]

[**VEA-LAC-IT:** . . . *il vecchio ideale grottesco del genio ubriacone, sordido, mal vestito, fuori classe* . . .]

9.—The sentimentality with which you load your pictures—to compensate, perhaps, for your praiseworthy utter lack of sentimentality in life.

[**VEA-PAM-FR:** . . . *le sentimentalisme dont vous bourrez vos tableaux pour compenser (et vous avez tort) votre absence d'affectuosité et de sentiment dans la vie;*]

[**VEA-LAC-IT:** . . . *il sentimentalismo di cui impregnate i vostri dipinti, per compensare (e avete torto) la vostra mancanza di affettuosità e di sentimento nella vita;*]

10.—Pioneers suffering from arrested development, from success or from despair, pioneers sitting snug on their tight little islands, or vegetating in their oases, refusing to resume the march, the pioneers who say: "We love Progress, but not yours"; the wearied pioneers who say: "Post-impressionism is all right, but it must not go further than deliberate naïveté" (Gauguin). These pioneers show that not only has their development stopped, but that they have never really understood the evolution of Art. If it has been necessary in painting and sculpture to have naïveté, deformation and archaism, it was only because it was essential to break away violently from the academic and the graceful before going further towards the plastic dynamism of painting.

[**VEA-PAM-FR:** . . . *les novateurs arrêtés de fatigue, de bien-être ou de désespoir . . . les novateurs exténués qui murmurent . . . (Gauguin etc.) . . . de la déformation et de l'ingénu à tout prix et de l'archaïsme . . . vers le dynamisme plastique de la peinture futuriste;*]

[**VEA-LAC-IT:** . . . *i novatori fermati dalla stanchezza, dal benessere dalla disperazione; . . . i novatori stanchi che dicono: «Ammiriamo e seguiamo i post-impressionisti; ma non vi va oltre l'ingenuità voluta (Gauguin, ecc.)» . . . dell'ingenuo ad ogni costo, della deformazione e dell'arcaismo . . . prima di andare più avanti verso il dinamismo plastico della pittura futurista;*]

Much of the tone here, and the general broadsides on tradition, commercialism, Academies (Item 1), and the idea of genius (Item 8), echo passages in earlier Futurist manifestos. Michael Walsh suggests that in the attacks on specifically English institutions Nevinson's voice appears, "acting perhaps for the first time in place of Marinetti's,"[32] but he then lists various contradictions: the manifesto's rejection of the Royal Academy (Item 4), which Nevinson had trained for and later joined; of the Neo-Primitives (Item 2), with whom he had been associated; of the influence of Paris (Item 2), where he had claimed artistic inspiration, met the Futurists, and set the *Train de Luxe*; of the New English Art Club (Item 4), which he had applied to, exhibited at, and would eventually join.[33] These contradictions seem to us to militate against the voice being Nevinson's except in the mode of translation; it seems more likely that his contribution here was simply to list institutions enshrined by the English art world, which were all then subjected to an equal barrage by Marinetti, in the style of other Futurist declarations.

The differences between the French and English versions, however—some are also found in the later, Italian version—suggest some negotiation between Marinetti and Nevinson on the exact phrasing and tone to be used in the English cultural context. The title of **VEA** in French, for example, translates as "Against English Art"—appropriate phrasing for a foreigner taking an antagonistic stance; while the more positively phrased English title, "Vital English Art," would be less likely to alienate an English audience. The French text, in keeping with its title, is occasionally blunter than the English: thus, instead of "the worship of tradition . . . commercial acquiescence . . . effeminacy," it reads (like the Italian): "the cult of tradition . . . commercial preoccupation . . . effeminate affectation" (Item 1). In some places the emphasis shifts: the "narrow views" ("nostalgic . . . tastes" in the French and Italian) of the English public in **VEA-OBS1-EN** reflect adoration of "the pretty-pretty, the commonplace, the soft, sweet, and mediocre," but in French and Italian these are "the affected, the toned-down, the attenuated, the mediocre" (Item 2). Similarly, the "old grotesque idea" of genius becomes, in French, "the old burned-out ideal" (Item 8); and the pioneers "suffering from arrested development" become "innovators halted by fatigue . . . exhausted innovators" (Item 10). A few phrases and sentences are absent in the French and Italian; others, absent in the English version, appear (e.g., "Fairy stories," in Item 2) or in their phrasing provide clarification of the original. Thus "Paris" in the English text is clarified in French as "all that comes from Paris" (Item 2); and the "ridiculous complaint" of Art in the original, unambiguously refers to sickness in the French and the Italian: "Art a bizarre malady" (Item 6). The French text mentions Turner (Item 3) but omits the English text's statement that he was the originator of Impressionism. The New English Art Club, which in **VEA-OBS1-EN** has "destroyed the prestige of the Royal Academy," appears in the French as having "inherited" its prestige. Another irony appears in Item 9, where the French and Italian read: "the sentimentality with which you load your pictures to compensate (and you are wrong) for your absence of affectedness and sentiment in life."

In addition to suggesting possible linguistic negotiations between Marinetti and Nevinson, these differences provide a sense of the shifting cultural codes that maintain the two signatories' relation of supplementarity. Our focus here, however, is on the English version of the manifesto, as it appeared for the first time in the *Observer*—addressing an English audience. The main characteristics of art to be rejected—and here it is not simply the philosophy of artists which is attacked, but the stupidity, the "pessimistic, skeptical and narrow views of the English public"—are "a purely decorative sense," "the pretty-pretty, the commonplace, the soft, sweet, and mediocre" (Items 1, 2) and "sentimentality" (Item 9). Luca Somigli sees this as "a clear reference to William Morris's Arts and Crafts movement and its successors, such as Roger Fry's Omega Workshop, in which art is supposedly returned to performing a social function by becoming mere ornament of everyday objects . . . [an] accusation [which], however, could have been levelled just as easily at the Rebel Art Centre whose members, for all the revolutionary rhetoric of the enterprise . . . ended up decorating 'handkerchieves, scarves, candles, and fans to be used as party favours.'"[34]

Also into these categories fall the traditional Maypole and Morris dances with their flowers and ribbons; as do the idealized suburbs or "garden cities" (Item 2) proposed by Sir Ebenezer Howard in 1898 and 1902—self-contained communities living in what were essentially council allotments surrounded by artificially created "natural environments."

In similar fashion, Chelsea—the site of the Earl's Court Exhibition Ground until 1914; the venue after 1913 of the "Royal Horticultural Society's Great Spring Show" (the Chelsea Flower Show); and famous for the Ranelagh Pleasure Gardens with their neoclassical Rotunda—is ridiculed as "the Montmartre of London" (Item 8). This comparison is not arbitrary: large areas of Montmartre, particularly the boulevards and the Opera, were reconstructed by Baron Haussmann (1809–91) under Napoleon III; and although the city is chiefly known today as a center for artists in the early twentieth century—Picasso, Degas, Toulouse-Lautrec, Modigliani, van Gogh, and others—it, like Venice, Rome, and Florence, had come under fire from Marinetti for living in the past. The attack on Venice, for example,

> began on July 8, 1910, when the Futurists hurled down from the Clock Tower of the Piazza San Marco 800,000 leaflets containing a scathing arraignment of Venetian life. Immediately afterwards Marinetti improvised a speech in which he demanded: trolley lines, automobiles, highways, broader and deeper canals, demolitions of palaces and utilization of their sites for wharves, factories and piers. Nor was his hatred of dead cities limited to those of Italy. Montmartre came in for a raking with the following compliments and suggestions: . . . "Il y a des morts qu'il faut qu'on tue. Il faut tuer Montmartre!" and "Le Moulin de la Galette disparaîtra fatalement dans une gare de Métro" [There are dead that have to be killed. Montmartre has to be killed . . . The Moulin de la Galette [dance hall] will disappear fatally into a station of the Métro].[35]

The attack on the "pretty-pretty" also alludes to the dandyism and decadence represented by "Aestheticism" and Oscar Wilde (Item 2), and would seem to confirm the charge of "effeminacy" (Item 1) in English art—and among Englishmen: Wilde's much-publicized trials for libel and homosexuality were held in April and May of 1895. However, Marinetti commented in his "Futurist Speech to the English" at the Lyceum in 1910:

> You are so custom-bound, in fact, as to believe firmly in this old wives' tale: that . . . chastity is a nation's most important virtue. But remember the dismal, ridiculous condemnation of Oscar Wilde. Intellectual Europe will never forgive you for it. Didn't all your newspapers cry out that it was time to throw open every window, because the plague was over?
>
> Naturally, in such an atmosphere of habitual and hypocritical formality, your young women are skilled in the use of their naïve elegance to carry on the most audaciously lascivious games. . . .
>
> As for your twenty-year-old young men, almost all of them are homosexual for a time. This highly respectable taste of theirs evolves through a kind of intensification of *camaraderie* and friendship, in athletic sports, before the age of thirty, the time for work and good order, when they show their heels to Sodom in order to marry a shamelessly licentious young lady, making haste to condemn the born invert severely, the counterfeit man, the half woman who fails to conform.[36]

The homophobia and sexism implicit in the term "effeminacy" are in context clearly there for ironic and tactical reasons, as is the "English notion," based on a hypocritical construct of masculinity, that "Art is a useless pastime, only fit for women and schoolgirls" (Item 6). Marinetti's own gender project, outlined in *Futurist Democracy* (1919), is remarkably reactionary given the historical period in which this was written: "We want to destroy not only the ownership of land, but also the ownership of woman. / Woman does not belong to a man, but rather to the future and the race's development. / We want a woman to love a man and give herself to him for as long as she likes; then, not chained by a contract or by moralistic tribunals, she should bear a child who society will educate physically and intellectually to a high conception of Italian freedom."[37] Similarly, while the use of what would in today's European cultural climate be considered sexist language is common in Futurist writing—for example: "When little boys and girls live together, the formation of the male character is always retarded. They are always attracted by the charm and willful seductiveness of the little woman, like little *cicisbei* or stupid little slaves"[38]—Marinetti's piece on the suffragettes, "Against *Amore* and Parliamentarianism," makes it clear that what he opposes are problems arising from "[w]oman, as she has been shaped by our contemporary society."[39] Thus "in her actual state of intellectual and erotic slavery, woman finds herself wholly inferior in respect to character and intelligence"; however, "As for the supposed inferiority of woman, we think that if her body and spirit had, for many generations past, been subjected to the same physical and spiritual education as man, it would perhaps be legitimate to speak of the equality of the sexes."[40]

The term "effeminacy" is therefore to be understood as an aesthetic stereotyping—of artificial subscription to "the pretty-pretty, the commonplace, the soft, sweet, and mediocre," as against its contrasting term which appears later in the call for "an English art that is strong, *virile* and anti-sentimental." It is similarly not a contradiction that the manifesto should extol Algernon Charles Swinburne (1837–1909)—along with Shakespeare (whom "our Futurist theater jeers at," Marinetti and his colleagues will say in 1915)[41]—as a "pioneer" of poetry (Item 3), despite Swinburne's reputation for being homosexual and his rumored engagement in practices ranging from masochistic flagellation to pederasty and bestiality. Again, the positive light on Swinburne here might seem ironic in view of the text's rejection of "sickly revivals of mediaevalism" (Item 2), since like his colleague Dante Gabriel Rossetti (1828–82) he was an accomplished medievalist who used medieval settings, subjects, and verse forms in his own writing. Yet Swinburne was best known in his time for metrical innovations in poetry, in particular his almost hypnotic techniques of rhythm; and in this regard he may indeed be considered a "pioneer." Similar ironies appear in the manifesto's rejection of the Pre-Raphaelites (Item 2), whose secret brotherhood was formed in 1848 in rebellion against the Royal Academy—as was, later, the New English Art Club (Item 4).

But this and other apparent ironies and contradictions are resolved if the text's praises are understood to refer to transient moments of revolutionary innovation, and its attacks directed primarily at the fossilization of modes of thinking and at the institutional immortalization of pioneers beyond the moment of their innovation. Thus the New English Art Club has lost momentum and is filled with "sham revolutionaries . . . who . . . now show themselves grossly hostile to the later movements of the advance guard" (Item 4); just as the late Victorian revivals of medievalism had by the late nineteenth century turned into the effete mannerisms caricatured by Gilbert and Sullivan's character Bunthorne in the comic opera *Patience* (1881):

> Am I alone, / And unobserved? I am! / Then let me own / I'm an aesthetic sham! / . . . Let me confess! / A languid love for lilies does *not* blight me! / Lank limbs and haggard cheeks do *not* delight me! / . . . I am *not* fond of uttering platitudes / In stained-glass attitudes. / In short, my mediaevalism's affectation, / Born of a morbid love of admiration! /
>
> . . . Be eloquent in praise of the very dull old days which have long since passed away, / And convince 'em, if you can, that the reign of good Queen Anne was Culture's palmist day. / Of course you will pooh-pooh whatever's fresh and new, and declare it's crude and mean, / For Art stopped short in the cultivated court of the Empress Josephine.
>
> . . . Though the Philistines may jostle, you will rank as an apostle in the high aesthetic band, / If you walk down Piccadilly with a poppy or a lily in your medieval hand.[42]

The problem with these revivals and revolutions is that they have ended up stagnant or static. In contrast, the "pioneers" of English science are named (Item 3) for their contributions to dynamism, evolutionary development, and motion: James Watt (1736–1819) who was, incidentally, Scottish, and for whom the unit of power, the "watt," was named, developed the high-pressure steam engine in 1769; George Stephenson (1781–1848) created the practical steam locomotive (1814) and the first passenger railway (1825); and his son Robert Stephenson (1803–59) constructed locomotives, railways, and bridges. The reference to Charles Darwin (1809–82) and his theory of evolution, a kind of perpetual motion by natural selection, further recalls the theories of Henri Bergson (1859–1941), elaborated in his *Creative Evolution* (1907) and frequently invoked by the Futurists: "Any division of matter into autonomous bodies with absolutely defined contours is an artificial division. . . . Any movement viewed as a transition from one state of rest to another, is absolutely indivisible."[43]

It is on this head that the manifesto rails against English institutions—on account of their *stasis*; for stasis characterizes *passéism*, "that most grave of all maladies." And so the third item focuses on "the perverted snob who ignores or despises all English daring, originality and invention but welcomes all foreign originality and daring." This plays on a double irony: first, it is a patronizing thrust at the English audience, who—in addition to being seduced by Paris (Item 2)—are welcoming "the Italian intruder" in that they are attending Marinetti's lectures and performances and reading the text he has written with Nevinson; and second, it inverts Marinetti's ostensible praise of English "pioneers," since all of the individuals listed, including (Item 3) the painters John Constable (1776–1837) and Joseph Turner (1775–1851), represent innovations that have already been institutionalized and immortalized. Impressionism, for example, took its cues from photography (and later, film), and produced instants of innovation in framing, in the representation of how light and color were perceived in moments of modern life, etc.; but today this is *passé* in that it is now commonplace: it must be re-presented in a new way if its pioneering moment is to be experienced again as such, in the present.

Marinetti's "wish . . . to cure English art" of its illness is thus indulged by a kind of shock therapy: treatment for the illness, which is partly due to an infection by a foreign element, will be a vaccination of more of the same through the manifesto—the introduction of *passéism* under the guise of novelty, to provoke the English aesthetic body, as it were, to reject it. As Marinetti remarks in his "Technical Manifesto . . ." (1912): "Microbes—don't forget—are essential to the health of the intestines and stomach. There is also a microbe essential to the vitality of *art, this extension of the forest of our veins*, that pours out, beyond the body, into the infinity of space and time."[44] Art, in other words, holds out both the disease and its potential to be cured. In this endeavor, the malady of Art must be taken seriously, so that it ceases to be treated as "a ridiculous complaint, a mere topic for table-talk" (Item 6). Here two things have to be eliminated: the art which by virtue of its immortalized stasis has become trivialized to the point where it is treated like an ache or pain discussed in small talk; and also the triteness of small talk, which at all levels of society reflects the philistinism of "the ignorant" (Item 7). One symptom of *passéism* is apathetic acceptance of tradition; and so the cure also requires national provocation, against "the *indifference* of the King, the State and the politicians towards all arts" (Item 5)—the apathy of the governmental representatives of the nation who have the power to establish or break with tradition. The inference is that the organs of the state should actively be involved in artistic revolutions—as they are (particularly in the Fascist context) in the organization of wars and propaganda. Marinetti raises his voice, the voice of the intruder, again in Item 9: "The sentimentality with which *you* load your pictures—to compensate, perhaps, for *your* praiseworthy utter lack of sentimentality in life." The apostrophe is addressed to his readers, but no less to the English nation: in destroying the artificialities, the sentimentality in English art, what will be made manifest through art is the people's *lack* of sentimentality, the reality of the modern English nation (and this is ironized again in the French and Italian versions of **VEA**).

The remedy for English art, then, what will restore its vitality, is to be administered by the foreign intruder; but it is "together with my friend Nevinson" that Marinetti will "give the signal for battle." English art is to be cured of its ailment by a battle *from within*, and the agent of the cure—the double agent, to be more precise—is "an English Futurist painter." Nevinson becomes the subversive Futurist cell within the body politic that through its self-destruction confirms the transience of the pioneering moment; for the battle/cure of English art will be directed against the stasis and permanence seen in such symptoms of "passéist filth" as the pretensions of "genius" (Item 8), and "immortality":

> 11.—The mania for immortality. A masterpiece must disappear with its author. Immortality in Art is a disgrace. The ancestors of our Italian Art, by their constructive power and their ideal of immortality, have built for us a prison of timidity, of imitation and of plagiarism. They sit there on grandfather chairs and for ever dominate our creative agonies with their marble frowns: "Take care, children, mind the motors, don't go too quick, wrap yourselves up well, mind the draughts, be careful of the lightning" . . .
>
> [**VEA-PAM-FR:** . . . *leur don d'immortalité* . . . *Ils sont toujours là sur leurs chaises de grands-pères vénérables et nous commandent. Leurs fronts de marbre pèsent toujours sur notre inspiration trépidante: «Prenez garde aux autos, mes enfants* . . . » . . .]
>
> [**VEA-LAC-IT:** . . . *loro immortalità* . . . *Sono sempre presenti sui loro seggioloni di nonni venerabili, e ci comandano. Le loro fronti di marmo pesano sempre sulle nostre giovani angoscie: «Schivate gli automobile, figliuoli! Copritevi! Evitate le correnti d'aria! Attenti al fulmine!»*

This last item in the list of "againsts" draws an analogy between the attack on tradition in English art and that needed on "our Italian Art." The voice here again is clearly Marinetti's; "immortality" represents the fossilization of tradition, and the power of "ancestors" to control and hold back the present. The oppressive force of past grand masters intimidates the new generation of Italian artists, forcing them to suppress their creative urges and do nothing more than imitate and plagiarize static, past models. Marinetti had already commented on derivative copying in the context of drama in "The Variety Theater" (1913)—"We are deeply disgusted with the contemporary theater . . . because it vacillates stupidly between historical reconstruction (pastiche or plagiarism) and photographic reproduction of our daily life; a . . . diluted theater worthy, all in all, of the age of the oil lamp"[45]—and had declared in *War, the World's Only Hygiene* (1911–15): "We *despise* in art, and especially in the theater, *every kind of historical reconstruction*."[46]

But the adjective "our" which modifies "our Italian Art" splits into another voice that extends beyond Italy to the traditions of European and British art: English artists, too, have been culturally colonized by the type of admiration for European traditions that is exemplified in the writings of John Ruskin. They see the Italian past as part of their own heritage, and continue to plunder and appropriate it as part of the colonial enterprise. As Marinetti commented in his "Futurist Speech to the English" (1910) at the Lyceum,

> . . . what you love in our dear peninsula is exactly the object of all our hatreds. Indeed, you crisscross Italy only to meticulously sniff out the traces of our oppressive past, and you are happy, insanely happy, if you have the good fortune to carry home some miserable stone on which our ancestors have trodden.

When, when will you disembarrass yourselves of the lymphatic ideology of that deplorable Ruskin . . . ?[47]

The longevity, immortality, and implacability of this dominating ancestral force in both Italian and English art are suggested in the classical image of monumental "marble frowns" that issue from the "grandfather chairs." The clichéd, overprotective grandparental warnings against technology, speed, fresh air, draughts, and storms represent the stasis of tradition, resistance to innovation, and a lack of understanding of the modern world. The reaction of Boccioni and others in the "Manifesto of the Futurist Painters" (1910) was: "1. Destroy the cult of the past, the obsession with the ancients, pedantry and academic formalism. 2. Totally invalidate all kinds of imitation. 3. Elevate all attempts at originality . . . Make room for youth, for violence, for daring!"[48]

Similarly, the response of the speakers of "Vital English Art" is a rebellion of the imagined community of youth against a generation that has forgotten its own youth and daring, a rebellion that rejects the injunctions of conservative tradition and rejoices in the confluence of natural forces (lightning, draughts of wind) and the man-made power of machines (the spark of the internal combustion engine, the wind that races past at the speed of the automobile)—the unifying ideology of its own technological modernity:

"Forward! HURRAH for motors! HURRAH for speed! HURRAH for draughts! HURRAH for lightning!"

[**VEA-PAM-FR:** *Allons donc! Vive les autos! Vive la vitesse! Vive les courants d'air! Vive la foudre!*]

[**VEA-LAC-IT:** *Via! via! . . . Viva gli automobili! Viva le correnti d'aria! Viva il fulmine!*]

Vital English Art II: The Futurist Vaccination

Giving the signal for this rebellion with Marinetti is Nevinson. The two sets of quotation marks surrounding the words of the rebellious youth and their ancestors represent a splitting of voices of ambiguous national origin within the tradition of art, and it is at this point that the roles of **VEA**'s cowriters come together; here that its text, written in the English of Nevinson, translator-traitor, becomes the joint declaration that will subvert the English tradition from within, using its own language. For in contrast to the anonymous "*AGAINST*" which introduced the list of attacks on tradition and seemed to reflect Marinetti's exercise of his "right to speak plainly and without compromise," the next section of the manifesto is introduced with the pronoun "we":

WE WANT:

1.—To have an English art that is strong, virile and anti-sentimental.

2.—That English artists strengthen their Art by a recuperative optimism, a fearless desire of adventure, a heroic instinct of discovery, a worship of strength and a physical and moral courage—all sturdy virtues of the English race.

[**VEA-PAM-FR:** . . . *que les artistes anglais cultivent l'optimisme régénérateur . . . l'héroïque instinct d'exploration, la passion du sport, l'adoration des muscles, le courage physique et moral* . . .]

VEA-LAC-IT: . . . *che gli artisti inglesi rinforzino la loro arte con un ottimismo rigeneratore . . . e con un eroico instinto d'esplorazione, col culto della forza e col coraggio fisico e morale* . . .]

3.—Sport to be considered an essential element in Art.

4.—To create a powerful advance guard, which alone can save English Art, now threatened by the traditional conservatism of Academies and the habitual indifference of the public. This will be an exciting stimulant, a violent incentive for creative genius, a constant inducement to keep alive the fires of invention and of art, so as to obviate the monotonous labour and expense of perpetual raking out and relighting of the furnace.

[**VEA-PAM-FR:** *réveillera . . . étouffé . . . un excitant alcool, un aiguillon acharné . . . une préoccupation constante . . . les chaufferies . . . des continuels déblais de scories et des continuels allumages*]

[**VEA-LAC-IT:** *salvare . . . minacciata di morte . . . un alcool eccitante, un pungolo accanito . . . una costante preoccupazione . . . i forni . . . dei continui sgomberi di scorie e delle continue riaccensioni*]

5.—A rich and powerful country like England ought without question to support, defend and glorify its advance guard of artists, no matter how advanced or how extreme, if it intends to deliver its Art from inevitable death.

[**VEA-PAM-FR:** *Nous voulons que l'Angleterre . . . soutienne, . . . ses artistes novateurs les plus révolutionnaires et les plus avancés, qui seuls pourront sauver son art d'une mort certaine.*]

[**VEA-LAC-IT:** *L'inghilterra . . . dovrà assolutamente sostenere . . . le sue avanguardie artistiche più rivoluzionarie e più avanzate, se vorrà salvare la sua arte da una morte sicura*]

[This paragraph (5) is not numbered in the French or Italian versions, and is added to Item 4 as the final paragraph of the manifesto]

6.—So we call upon the English public to support, defend, and glorify the genius of the great Futurist painters or pioneers and advance-forces of vital English Art—ATKINSON, BOMBERG, EPSTEIN, ETCHELLS, HAMILTON, NEVINSON, ROBERTS, WADSWORTH, WYNDHAM LEWIS. [This item is omitted in all versions except **VEA-OBS1-EN** and **VEA-OBS2-EN.**]

The "We want" that introduces this list of demands, constitutes the "signal for battle." Here both signatories are included—the Italian intruder and the English native; here Nevinson introduces himself both as part of the afflicted tradition and as its cure. His presence as an Englishman in the "we" means that it is from within the tradition of English art that the rejection of tradition is being proposed; and at this point the ambivalence of the personal pronoun marks a shift from the negativity of attacks "against" from without, to what appears to be a set of positive propositions; most of these still, however, are informed by the double irony of the attacks.

Against the artificial "effeminacy" of sentimentalism, there is a demand for virility in art (Item 1), which will presumably reflect, realistically, the "utter lack of sentimentality" in English life. Against the debilitating malady of *passéism* that afflicts the tradition, there should be a "recuperative optimism" (Item 2), a regaining of physical and moral vitality. Physically and politically, this represents a reinvigoration of national blood, a consolidation of the "sturdy virtues of the English race," in the same way that, as Marinetti and his colleagues will declare in "The Futurist Cinema" (1916): "Our great hygienic war, which should satisfy *all* our national aspirations, centuples the renewing power of the Italian race."[49] On an aesthetic level, it represents the reincarnation or recovery of a past moment of pre-plagiarism ancestral power. The wording of this demand seems to be contradictory—"heroic instinct" and "worship of strength" suggest classical ideas of the immortality (rejected in Item 11 of the "againsts") of the hero, and a blind, dogmatic faith in physicality, which might seem at odds with the "desire of adventure"—but what Marinetti and Nevinson are doing here, and throughout **VEA**, is rejecting existing systems and standards, and then repackaging them in new proposals, so that their original revolutionary and pioneering force may endlessly be reframed and experienced in a new form and context. The Futurist moment is thus one of continual death and rebirth—immortalized only in its constant self-destruction and self-renewal.

This is particularly apparent in the call for sport to be "an essential element in Art" (Item 3); reinforcing this, the French text (the Italian partially) significantly adds in Item 2 the demand that English artists "cultivate . . . the passion for sport, the adoration of muscles." The exaltation of sport dates back to classical times, to the ideal described by Juvenal in his *Satires* as *mens sana in corpore sano*,[50] a healthy mind in a healthy body; in Futurist terms, the body must become a perfectly coordinated and disciplined "virile" machine. Thus, the same year that **VEA** is published, Marinetti speaks of "a new beauty [that] is born today from the chaos of the new contradictory sensibilities that we Futurists will substitute for the former beauty, and that I call Geometric and Mechanical Splendour." Among the elements of this chaos are "hope, desire, controlled force, speed, light, willpower, order, discipline, method . . . ; the aggressive optimism that results from the cult of muscles and sport."[51]

In the English context, an imbalance between the mental and the physical has led to a lack of discipline and to dissipation. Marinetti has already referred ironically in his "Futurist Speech to the English" (1910) to homosexuality which, he claims, is common among young men in England and evolves "through a kind of intensification of *camaraderie* and friendship, in athletic sports." In the same speech he declares: "You invented the love of hygiene, the adoration of muscles, a harsh passion for effort, all of which triumph in your fine life of sport. But to your disgrace, you push your exaggerated cult of the body to the point of scorning ideas, and you care seriously only for the physical pleasures. Platonic love is virtually absent from among you, and that is good; but you too much love succulent meals . . . !"[52]

The need for sport in art is based not simply on maintaining health, but on aggression, on the competitive spirit that drives the individual beyond existing conditions. Thus in "Destruction of Syntax . . ." (1913) Marinetti argues that modern developments in mass consciousness such as newspapers and movies, which have increased awareness of others' achievements, are "important modifiers of our sensibility"; among the phenomena they have engendered are: "[13.] The passion, art, and idealism of Sport. Idea and love of the 'record.'"[53] And in "Electrical War" he explains: "Muscular work ceases to be servile, now having only three goals: hygiene, pleasure, and struggle—no longer needing to strive for his daily bread, man finally conceives the pure idea of the ascensional *record.* His will power and ambition grow immense."[54] The record, in short, represents an aesthetic limitation in that it is a standard, a "pure idea" to be broken for its own sake: through breaking records, human consciousness transcends its own boundaries. Human beings compete in sports in terms of brute power; but Marinetti sees the machine as surpassing both human and animal power—the power of machines, for example, is expressed in multiples of "horsepower." Organic growth and subjective aestheticization give way to technological or mechanical growth and measurable quantification; and the body becomes an aesthetic machine. "Vitality" is thus to be understood not in organic terms, but as the Marinettian aesthetic splendor of the mechanical.

English art is under threat from academic conservatism and "the habitual indifference of the public" (Item 4); it has become subjected to an ignorant complacency and table-talk stagnation based on the acceptance and institutionalization of existing aesthetic norms. To effect a cure for this stasis, current limitations must be transcended and records broken; there must be an "exciting stimulant, a violent incentive . . . , a constant inducement to keep alive the fires of invention and of art" (Item 4). The imagery in the French text (and to some extent the Italian) here is considerably more vivid: English art is to be revived from its "suffocation" by tradition; it needs an intense or "desperate spur," an "exciting alcohol."[55]

The "stoke-holds" of invention must be kept alight to obviate the need for a "continual cleaning out of slag and continual (re)lightings." What is required, in other words, is "a powerful advance guard" (Item 4) which will enable "a rich and powerful country like England" (Item 5) to break records within its own tradition, and compete with other nations as a matter of national pride. The nation will "deliver its Art from inevitable death" (Item 5) by reincarnating it in an art which constantly destroys tradition; what will be immortalized is not the "immortality" of ancestral tradition but the pioneering moments which gave rise to it, reconfigured as such in each moment of the present. Thus it will institutionalize—"support, defend and glorify" (Item 5, Item 6)—not its institutions, but, in its military, political, and aesthetic sense, the "advance guard of artists" (Item 5) who will bring about the destruction of its institutions.

It is "the genius of the great Futurist painters or pioneers and advance-forces of vital English Art" (Item 6), the agency of destruction itself, that is to be institutionalized—and here the terms that were rejected earlier in the manifesto are problematically reconfigured. "Genius" no longer represents the great name canonized by the art-historical tradition, but the spirit of the new individual who rejects all canonizations prior to his or her historical moment. And the new "pioneers" are not individuals "suffering from arrested development, from success [i.e., acceptance] or from despair," not artists like Gauguin who sets limits to art—e.g., "Post-impressionism . . . must not go further than deliberate naïveté"—but pioneers who understand that art has evolved through the breaking of limits: "If it has been necessary in painting and sculpture to have naïveté, deformation and archaism, it was only because it was essential to break away violently from the academic and the graceful before going further towards the plastic dynamism of painting" ("Against," Item 10). Here Postimpressionism receives the same treatment as Turner and Impressionism: its pioneering moment must be repackaged and reborn continually. The praise of the "advance-forces" shifts focus away from the individual genius and toward the group, the institution that denies institutionalization; and the avant-garde becomes the expression of national interest—it is to be supported and glorified by the imagined community of the English nation.

The final demand is thus, inevitably, a call for these pioneers to be exalted by "the English public"—the same public derided earlier for their "narrow views" and because they "stupidly adore . . . the commonplace, the . . . mediocre" ("Against," Item 2). Here the splitting of voices in the "we" that introduced the list of demands takes on a crucial role. The English public that "welcomes all foreign originality and daring" ("Against," Item 3) is to look to its own avant-garde for leadership, so at this point the names of "the great Futurist painters or pioneers" are listed: "ATKINSON, BOMBERG, EPSTEIN, ETCHELLS, HAMILTON, NEVINSON, ROBERTS, WADSWORTH, WYNDHAM LEWIS." The "we" that introduced the demands and included the public, is now separated from the public—"*we* call upon the English public . . ."—and Nevinson's own name is included, effectively in the third person, displacing the "we" into a generic and collective voice which includes the members of the Rebel Art Centre. The list is alphabetical, and the artists, thus given equal status, are all identified by surname with the exception of Lewis, whose middle name is added and who stands prominently at the end, adding authority to the manifesto along with the signatures of Marinetti and Nevinson which follow. It is this list of names, coupled with Nevinson's signature that will lead to the split between Nevinson and the Rebel Art Centre, and between Futurism and Vorticism in England.

Signatures and Authority

F. T. MARINETTI,
Italian Futurist Movement (Milan).

C. R. W. NEVINSON,
Art Rebel Centre (London).

—**VEA-OBS1-EN; VEA-OBS2-EN**

According to Lewis, **VEA** was written on "Rebel Art Centre" notepaper; however, since the text was published typeset and not in facsimile in the *Observer*, the association with the Centre is provided only by the list of names, and by the address under Nevinson's "signature"—which, in keeping with the manifesto's emphasis on pioneering individuals, is given not as "Rebel Art Centre" (which would suggest an art of rebellion) but as "Art Rebel Centre," suggesting a cohort of rebellious artists. The addresses continue an art-historical tradition in which artists—such as Leonardo "da Vinci"—included as part of their names the names of their places of origin. Here the names of the signatories take additional force from their respective affiliations, the "Italian Futurist Movement (Milan)" and the "Art Rebel Centre (London)": each group and city represents a center of artistic and political authority. It is not only this, but the logic of the signature, that will determine the future of the manifesto, which will be repudiated by the other members of the Rebel Art Centre.

The signature on a painting or other work of visual art has traditionally functioned somewhat differently from that on a political declaration such as a manifesto. Prior to the development of collage techniques in modernist art, the signature on a painting or other work of visual art typically served as a mark of authentication, indicating the work's provenance and its exchange value within the cultural economy of patrons and audiences in the "art world." However, in the basic Cubist collage, as Marjorie Perloff explains,

> pasted papers are literally placed in front of and on top of one another on an opaque picture surface, thus challenging the fundamental principle of Western painting from the early Renaissance to the late nineteenth century that a picture is a window on reality, an imaginary transparency through which an illusion is discerned. Collage also subverts all conventional figure-ground relationships, for here nothing is either figure or ground; rather, the collage juxtaposes "real" items—pages torn from newspapers, [etc.]—so as to create a curiously enigmatic pictorial surface. For each element in the collage has a dual function: it refers to an external reality even as its compositional thrust is to undercut the very referentiality it seems to assert.[56]

Later Cubist works would make use of painted representations of text, a development which problematically undermines the double logic of collage that Perloff describes, by returning to the representational framework of painting. However, in both cases, the incorporation of letters and words in painting brings these overlapping systems—the visual-aesthetic, the verbal, and the experiential "real"—together, with the result that the signature becomes a compositional element of the artwork, and its function as signature, as exterior and authenticating mark, becomes diminished. This play between systems is also apparent in the typographical and compositional experiments of many Futurist texts, which function both textually and visually so that style itself becomes representative of content. In **VEA**, the typeset "signatures" of Marinetti and Nevinson are very much part of the text in terms of style and form; but here they have a function beyond simple authentication or serving merely as compositional elements.

In Futurist collage,[57] any distinction between the aesthetic and the political is elided; the fragmentation of modern life through the interventions of technology and new modes of communication, and the subsumption of the individual into the masses, will find their expression in the conceit of "words-in-freedom" or *parole in libertà*; their correlative is the destruction of whatever represents unique individuality, any "I" or genius "captaining the group," and its displacement into the collective expression of experiential reality:

> Destroy the *I* in literature: that is, all psychology. The man sidetracked by the library and the museum, subjected to a logic and wisdom of fear, is of absolutely no interest. We must therefore drive him from literature and finally put matter in his place." (Marinetti, "Technical manifesto . . ." (1912).[58]
>
> To rid ourselves of this obsessive *I*, we must abandon the habit of humanizing nature . . . Instead we should express the infinite smallness that surrounds us, the imperceptible, the invisible, the agitation of atoms . . . (Marinetti, "Destruction of Syntax . . ." (1913)[59]
>
> We systematically destroy the literary *I* in order to scatter it into the universal vibration and reach the point of expressing the infinitely small and the vibration of molecules. (Marinetti, "Geometric and Mechanical Splendour . . ." (1914)[60]
>
> In the new Futurist lyricism . . . our literary *I* consumes and obliterates itself in the grand cosmic vibration, so that the declaimer himself must also somehow disappear in the dynamic and synoptic manifestation of words-in-freedom. (Marinetti, "Dynamic and Synoptic Declamation," 1916.[61]

Although the Marinetti-Nevinson manifesto does not display any of the formal games or typographical pyrotechnics of other Futurist texts, it is this very logic of displacement that is enacted in the listing of names at the end of "Vital English Art,"—through the subsuming of the individual "I" of Marinetti and that of Nevinson into a "we," followed by a group of artists' names, followed in turn by the association of the "Italian Futurist Movement (Milan)" with the "Art Rebel Centre (London)" in what can only be read as the signatures of these groups' representatives. "A masterpiece," the manifesto declares, "must disappear with its author"

("Against," Item 11); in the "Dynamic and Synoptic Declamation" we are told that "the declaimer himself must also somehow disappear in the . . . manifestation of words-in-freedom." It is through the repeated moment of mortality that Futurist "immortality" is maintained; and here the personae of the two signatories simultaneously destroy and reassert themselves in different ways.

Marinetti's name appears in **VEA** as the first signature, and so as the more authoritative of the two; it is thus, for the editors of the *Observer,* "Signor Marinetti's Manifesto." When therefore on June 14 the artists listed, who had not consented to the use of their names, wrote to the paper dissociating themselves from the ideas expressed in the manifesto, they did not mention Nevinson by name, relegating him to the status of a follower: "There are certain artists in England who do not belong to the Royal Academy nor to any of the passeist groups and who do not on that account agree with the Futurism of Signor Marinetti. An assumption of such agreement either by Signor Marinetti or by his followers is an impertinence."[62] At the same time, however, Marinetti is exteriorized in **VEA** by the geopolitical and national implications of the parenthetical "(Milan)" that appears under his name.

The deliberate omission by the artists of the Rebel Art Centre of the second signatory indicates that the real "joker in the pack" is Nevinson, whose name appears both "outside" the manifesto—first as "my friend Nevinson," in Marinetti's introductory comment; finally as a signature which completes the "signal for battle"—and inside it, as one of the listed pioneers of English art. This liminal position, by which Nevinson is situated both within and (by association with Marinetti) without English art, represents the self-alienated presence that the English tradition must reject in order to achieve its cure. As Nevinson himself points out in his letter to Lewis on June 13, "neither you nor the others have in the past objected to your names being used by Marinetti, but when my name appears also then you adopt your narrow minded and pompous tone. *There lies the cause of the trouble.*"[63]

Prior to the publication of "Vital English Art," the rebel art group had in fact admired Marinetti to the extent that they had held a dinner in his honor (on November 18, 1913) at which Nevinson and Wyndham Lewis had toasted him; Marinetti and Nevinson had performed together to Lewis's acclaim at the Doré Galleries on the last three evenings of April 1914; and Lewis had invited Marinetti to perform on May 6 and 8 at the Rebel Art Centre.[64] A week before the manifesto appeared, on May 14, Lewis himself had written an encomium in the *New Weekly* entitled "Marinetti. Man of the Week" in which he had called Marinetti "the intellectual Cromwell of our time"[65] and concluded:

> "Futurism" is largely Anglo-Saxon civilisation. It should not rest with others to be the Artists of this revolution and new possibilities in life . . .
>
> But England has needed these foreign auxiliaries to put her energies to rights and restore order. Marinetti's services, in this home of aestheticism, crass snobbery, and languors of distinguished phlegm, are great.[66]

For Michael Walsh, the title of Lewis's article here implies that Marinetti "would be gone and forgotten again soon; and the attribution of Futurism to "Anglo-Saxon civilisation," that "Marinetti, to some extent, was both a plagiarist and outdated in what he was saying."[67] However, the implication of Lewis's title and his admission of England's need for "foreign auxiliaries" as a temporary spur before English art restores itself to "order" confirms, consciously or unconsciously, Marinetti's own argument for the transitory nature of the avant-garde moment. Lewis's staking of a claim to Futurism in the name of Anglo-Saxon civilization also represents a defensive declaration against the "foreign auxiliaries" in the typical style of colonial nationalist discourse—claiming and appropriating the inferiorized other's past and history as a moment of one's own. It is the same condescending rhetorical ploy that occurs in Lewis's comment to Marinetti: "you Wops insist too much on the machine . . . We've had machines here in England for a donkey's years. They're no novelty to *us.*"

Yet this is precisely the kind of discourse that "Vital English Art" attempts to generate and stir up, with its appeals to nationalism and attack on the snob who "despises all English . . . , but welcomes all foreign originality and daring." Marinetti's position in the manifesto is thus vindicated, for toward the end of the text, as his "I" takes second place to the "we" of English artists associated with the "Art Rebel Centre"—the "Italian intruder" will not lead the English avant-garde—the attention shifts to Nevinson, whose "English daring, originality and invention" will be repudiated by Lewis and the other members of the Centre. Nevinson's self-inclusion in the manifesto is a crucial facet of the "signal for battle," and it confirms the argument of the text in several ways: it ensures that the English tradition will reject him; in the process English artists will both reassert their tradition and revive it in the form of a reconfigured futurism as "Vorticism"; and in this way the "foreign auxiliaries" will be replaced by an advance-guard of Vorticists, who will, in Lewis's phrase, "restore order." The Futurist moment of "Vital English Art" will thus serve as a catalyst for the vitalization of English art, and will demonstrate that Futurism as such could not be followed, could not become a passéist or superfluous model.

Nevinson's attempts to defend himself following the repudiation of **VEA** by the Rebel Art Centre—his letter to the *Observer* on June 21 claiming that his use of the center's address had been misunderstood, his plaintive note to Lewis[68]—suggest that he is unaware of the subtleties of the manifesto and unconscious of the interpretive limitations of his audience—and indeed, of the historic role that he is playing in the development of English art. For when he signs his name to the manifesto with Marinetti, he both christens himself and writes his own epitaph as a Futurist. The list of "Futurist painters or pioneers and advance-forces of vital English Art" is prophetic of the Vorticist movement, a species of English futurism from which he himself will be, for the most part, excluded; and so, although new lamps will in reality be exchanged for old through Nevinson's agency, the art-historical tradition, a public no less blind than he to his role and theirs in this moment, will perceive Nevinson's part in the success of this revitalization as merely the commission of an unfortunate faux pas that consigns him and English Futurism to near oblivion. Yet unlike the signature on a painting, Nevinson's signature on "Vital English Art" assumes an active responsibility that transcends his own historical moment. It functions, that is to say, not merely as a mark of authentication, but as a performative speech act.

Performance and Performativity

F. T. Marinetti,
ITALIAN FUTURIST MOVEMENT (MILAN).
C. R. W. Nevinson,
5, BELSIZE STUDIOS
HAMPSTEAD,
LONDON, N.W.

—**VEA-PAM-EN**

In speech act theory, as developed by J. L. Austin, John Searle, and others, a "performative utterance" is a statement or declaration which brings about a state of affairs by its being uttered, in the same way that the sentence "I now pronounce you man and wife" spoken in a particular context has actual consequences in the world. For a performative utterance to be felicitous—to succeed in its professed goal—various contextual conditions, including institutional conventions, have to be in operation; these include presuppositions that the intention of the utterance is sincere, that it is made with appropriate seriousness, that it is correctly understood by its audience, and so on.[69]

"Vital English Art" functions as performative language on several complex levels: as a Futurist manifesto, it presents itself as a statement which performs a political act by breaking with certain conventions of artistic tradition; it lays down new conventions; and it places the conditions for its own felicity in the hands of its readership—a success that can be measured by the extent to which the revolutionary movement of Futurism which it declares is perceived to fail. By defining its own prescriptions both against and in terms of traditional English and Italian artistic conventions, the manifesto becomes dependent on these conventions for its argument—so that the "futurist" break with the aura of tradition is essentially a repackaging and renewal of the revolutionary moments of that past, in its own moment. Crucial to this act is the performance of a statement, as suggested in Lewis's conversation with Marinetti: when asked "Why don't you announce that you are a futurist!" Lewis replies, "Because I am not one." Marinetti's impatient reply is: "Yes. But what's it matter!" From Marinetti's perspective, belief in Futurism is insignificant compared with the act of making a Futurist statement; his problem with Lewis is not that the latter does not believe in Futurism, but that he refuses to separate his belief from the process of declaration.

It is the act of declaration, regardless of the intention or sincerity of the declarer, that constitutes the Futurist performative; and there are also several different contexts in which "Vital English Art" is performed. There is the initial publication on June 7, 1914, in the *Observer*, which has been our primary focus, and then the reprintings in *Lacerba* and in *Paint and Prejudice*. There is Nevinson's prefatory lecture and reading of the manifesto at the Doré Galleries on June 12; and Marinetti's reading of the text in Cambridge shortly afterward. There is the reading of the manifesto at the Kevorkian Gallery in 1919. And then there are the various pamphlet versions of the text in French and in English, some of which may have participated in a performance "within a performance" if they were showered down on theater audiences' heads. These various modes of existence of **VEA** may all be considered performances, because it is in the nature of a manifesto to present itself as an ephemeral event of textual declaration, inserting itself momentarily into both written and spoken discourses, and generating opposition and reaction from its audience. In the case of **VEA**, relatively detailed information on the audience's reaction is readily available for only two of these performances: from Charles

Brookfarmer's account ("Futile-ism") in the *New Age* of the Doré Galleries lecture and performances by Nevinson and Marinetti; and from the various letters and responses to **VEA** that appeared in newspapers following its first publication.

The "Futile-ism" piece provides a sense both of the audience's profile and of its relative perceptions of Nevinson and Marinetti. Brookfarmer begins by setting the stage:

> (*Enter Student.* The hot room is full for the most part of elderly (passées?) ladies, including such half-forgotten crimes as Messrs. Cunninghame-Graham and Nevinson père. Barely twenty minutes late the lecturers arrive—ironical applause from frivolous audience. Sig. Marinetti rises and introduces "mon ami Nevinson," and refers to "les noise-tuners" whose performance is eagerly expected. . . .)

Nevinson gets up to speak, but from this point onward, it is not his speech (which is reported in fragments—the full text is reported on pages 160–62 of the same issue of the *New Age*), but, as the following excerpts suggest, Brookfarmer's parenthetical remarks and stage directions that recreate the performance—exclamation marks implying Nevinson's insecurity or incapacity as he *reads* his lecture; sniping by an artist (i.e., Gaudier-Brzeska, during what Lewis describes as his "counterputsch"); the disturbance caused by Nevinson's mispronunciation of "Vorticists"; the *sotto voce* comments of Brookfarmer himself, in the persona of a student, and his mental reaction as he recalls paintings by Kandinsky; the "special effects" as Nevinson extols lightning; the exclamation marks indicating Brookfarmer's raised eyebrows at Nevinson's presumption in including his own name among the "advance-forces" of art:

> *Mr. Nev.* (*reading his speech*—[!!!]: But he seems frequently to digress) [. . .] England to-day is no more a decadent country in art than in commerce.
> *Stud.* (*sotto voce*): Nor no less, neither.
> *Mr. Nev.*: . . . Compare him unfavourably with a second-rate Parisian painter, and say how much finer the latter is.
> *An Artist*: So he is!
> *Mr. Nev.*: You're a Russian! (*Commotion*) [. . .] The Futurists . . . their art, so vital, so intense and so complex . . . Vortickists. . . .
> *The Artist*: Vorticistes! (*Commotion.*)
> *Mr. Nev.*: [. . .] three paintings by Kandinsky at the Allied Artists' Association Salon, which to my mind are simply gorgeous! (Stud. shudders at the memory of formless yellow blobs.) [. . .] an engineer if he fails to make a woman understand the working of a simple piece of machinery (Audience: Oo-ooh!) [. . .] London, its chromatic crowds, red motor-'buses (etc.), through which some black limousine glides like a snake.
> *Stud.*: Where in futurity have I heard that before?
> *Mr. Nev.*: [. . .] barbarians of the West End (some giggles) [. . .] backwoods of Chelsea (more giggles) [. . .] (He reads the manifesto, in which occurs, "Immortality in art is a disgrace"!! As he cries, "Forward! hurrah for motors! hurrah for speed! hurrah for draughts! hurrah for lightning!" an assistant fires a small piece of magnesium wire. Tremendous Futurartistic effect. Then, "We call upon the English public [. . .] Atkinson, Bomberg, Epstein, Etchells, Hamilton, Nevinson [!!!] Roberts, Wadsworth, Wyndham Lewis." Mr. Nev. sits down amid laughter and shouting of names [. . .]).[70]

Brookfarmer's account suggests that the audience is at the performance to be entertained, rather than to participate in or object to a revolutionary aesthetic and political agenda; this impression is also a function of his stage directions and comments, which are aimed at entertaining the readers of the *New Age*. Yet the audience's perception of Nevinson's performance is in marked contrast to its perception of Marinetti's, although presumably Marinetti's name and the promise of the noise-tuners were the main attraction. The general response here to Marinetti's lecture (which is at a relative disadvantage, being delivered in French and lacking special effects such as Nevinson's magnesium flash) seems to be boredom; and Brookfarmer's condescension towards the sweaty and prosy foreigner, no doubt shared by others in the audience, shines through in his changing the latter's name to "Mr. Mario," making fun of his accent, and finally describing what he hears, through his "Student" persona, as "cackle":

> ([. . .] Marinetti rises and commences to wander on and on and on with much emphasis and gesture and mopping of sweaty brow.)
> *Mr. Mario* (*in French*): I am forced to repeat some of the arguments put forward by mon ami Nevinson . . . les passéistes . . . les passéistes [. . .] [they] call you a "cloon" [. . .] Mon ami Nevinson has already told you that modern sensibility must be introduced into modern art. (Tells it all again, with variations, explanations, enlargements, etc., etc., very, very prosily.) Mon ami Nevinson (proses) . . . [. . .] I have often said what I mean by detestable sentimentality in art. (Says it all again. Stud. dozes, in spite of Mr. Mario's waving of fists, etc.) . . . [. . .] The great speed of motors and limousines . . . (etc., etc., punctuated with innumerable "Voila la pointe importante"). (Stud. wishes he would cut the cackle and get to the noise-tuners.) [. . .] immortality is not merely a fault but a crime!

Stud.: So there's no futurity in Futurism!
Mr. Mario: Futurism (etc., etc.) . . . Futurism (etc., etc.) . . . Futurism is a sort of lava . . . Electricity which rules the world . . . ever to advance and never to look back. (Having thus wandered, prosily, volubly, and enormously quickly from one thing to another for about an hour, Mr. Mario sits down, his collar unstarched with sweat; the audience, too, is tired out with his prosiness and the heat. He pops up again.)
Mr. Mario: I am quite at the disposition of the audience. I'm not a bit tired. (The hideous rumour spread that, though the "noise-tuners" are present, they have not got their instruments and will not perform after all. The disappointed audience begins to disperse. Mr. Mario busily explains to Stud. and others some of the angular monstrosities that are shown as Futurist sculptures.) [. . .] (As Stud. departs, two small persons shake him enthusiastically by the hand. They are "les noise-tuners.")
Stud (*wearily*): All this cackle and no—Futurist—noises! (Exit Student.)[71]

What emerges from this portrayal of the two lectures and the reading of the manifesto at the Doré Galleries is a physical shift in the identities of the two signers of **VEA.** The signatures of Marinetti and Nevinson, as we have seen, pose a problem in determining the precise identity of the "I" that speaks in the manifesto; and here the physical, spoken performance of the text becomes determinative. In this act, what authenticates the text is not the signatures, but the presence of the speakers/performers themselves. When Marinetti reads out the manifesto in Cambridge to a British audience, he does so alone, in French, in his own voice, and as an outsider speaking "against English art"; Nevinson is present only as "mon ami," and in the text's list of artists, and signature; here at the Doré Galleries too, Marinetti is exteriorized, as the audience reaction illustrates. But when Nevinson performs the manifesto, he does so using Marinetti's "I" to exercise his "right to speak plainly"; and in this viral act of doubling which gives "the signal for battle"—and in which, as the audience's response suggests, Marinetti the outsider becomes secondary to Nevinson the insider and the agent of change—English art is turned, in theory, against itself.

This theoretical moment lasts, indeed, only a moment in speech or writing: for once the enunciation of the Futurist project is complete it has itself moved into the past, even if its effects persist in an "afterlife" granted by its audience. If its written text remains, it serves only as a trace of that ephemeral moment of declaration; as an obituary, an epitaph. And this, ultimately, is the status of the manifesto in print.

Imagined Artistic Communities

F. T. Marinetti
Italian Futurist Movement
(Corso Venezia, 61 — Milan)

C. R. W. Nevinson
(4, Downside Crescent — Hampstead — London)

—VEA-LAC-EN

A week after Marinetti and Nevinson's publication of "Vital English Art," the manifesto was repudiated in the now-famous letter of June 8 which was reported in the *Daily Mail* (June 11) and the *Times* (June 13), and printed in full, with some variations, in the *New Weekly* (June 13), the *Egoist* (June 15), and the *Observer* (June 14): "We, the undersigned, whose ideals were mentioned or implied, or who might by the opinions of others be implicated, beg to dissociate ourselves from the 'Futurist' manifesto which appeared in the pages of THE OBSERVER of Sunday, June 7."[72] The letter appeared under the heading "The Futurist Manifesto" and was signed by Richard Aldington, David Bomberg, Frederick Etchells, Ezra Pound, Edward Wadsworth, Lawrence Atkinson, Gaudier Brzeska, W. Roberts, and Wyndham Lewis; an editorial note explained that Bomberg was signing independently of the "Art Rebel Centre." A postscript above the address of the "Rebel Art Centre" added: "P.S.—The Direction of the Rebel Art Centre wishes to state that the use of their address by Signor Marinetti and Mr. Nevinson was unauthorised."

It is of some interest to note that three days earlier, the author of a short anonymous piece in the *Daily Express* of Thursday, June 11, entitled "Futurist Squabbles: English Artists' Counterblast to Signor Marinetti," had taken the time to wonder what all the fuss was about: "In reading through the manifesto it is difficult to see the reason which has caused some of the English advance guard to issue their counter-blast in the shape of a circular letter, in which they dissociate themselves from the Futurist manifesto. . . . Is it possible that the split in the fighting ranks has been caused by Signor Marinetti's condemnation of ostentatious Bohemianism and eccentric attire? . . . These rebel artists are Anarchists who resent any kind of leadership."[73]

In contrast to this relatively positive comment on the manifesto, an article entitled "Futurists and the Past" that appeared the same day in the *Times* echoes the very tone of Lewis's condescension toward Marinetti: "He gives the signal for battle—and against what? Among other things, against our aestheticism, our Pre-Raphaelites . . . Now all these things are not only passéist, but past. One would suppose that SIGNOR MARINETTI had been reading the *Punch* of LEECH and DU MAURIER or the Yellow Book; that he had visited London once in the eighties. . . . It is clear that SIGNOR MARINETTI has believed what he was told about England, but who can have told him what he believes?"[74]

Nevinson's own response to the Rebel Art Centre's letter, dated June 16 and printed in the *Observer* on June 21, is precise and pointed:

> Sir,—As a Futurist, the fight before me is too great to feel very interested in the petty and personal polemics or the meticulous technical differences that the directors of the Rebel Art Centre seem so much to enjoy.
>
> But, much as I should like utterly to ignore their letter, it is necessary for me to contradict a few mis-statements. I would point out:—
>
> (1) That there was no need for the artists mentioned in the manifesto to disassociate themselves from Futurism, as they were quite distinctly and invariably named as "Pioneers or advance-forces of vital English Art," which they undoubtedly are. Nor was there the slightest hint that they endorsed the ideals of either Signor Marinetti or myself.
> (2) We are at perfect liberty to praise (or criticise) an artist without his consent.
> (3) That Signor Marinetti never used the address of the R.A.C. as stated, but his address of the Futurist movement, Milan.
> (4) I willingly admit I made an error of judgment in using the address of the R.A.C., considering its autocratic constitution, but I used it simply as a member uses the address of his club, without the slightest evil intent, for I had no idea how very strongly the directors felt against Futurism. I even understood they professsed to teach it, and I know that in a prospectus they mention it as a vital form of Art.
>
> Yours, etc.
> C. R. W. Nevinson[75]

The reasons Lewis gives (as laid out in our epigraph) for repudiating Nevinson "as an interloper and a heretic" are all related to issues of group identity and expression—he writes on Rebel Art Centre notepaper, he goes to the press, he expresses Futurist ideas; the anonymous writer of "Futurist Squabbles" thus hits close to the mark when he identifies the problem as resentment of leadership. The **VEA** manifesto continued to exist, and was reproduced and reprinted in various versions, albeit with the final list of names removed ("We Want," Item 6). Marked by this correspondence and the ensuing debate in the public space of various newspapers, the split between Nevinson and Lewis's cohort is generally understood to have resulted in the "death" of Futurism in England and stimulated the development of the Vorticist movement that found its expression in Lewis's journal, *Blast.*

It is the publication of **VEA** that serves as a catalyst for this split. Unlike Lewis, who refuses to declare that he is a Futurist, Nevinson, by signing his name to the manifesto, performs this act of declaration; and by doing so with Marinetti, momentarily places himself in the Futurist "tradition." His name, in other words, becomes a supplementary text that will historically be associated with Futurism. This self-textualization of Nevinson as the "choral" expression of a group voice makes him the hidden force of the Vorticist revolution; at the same time, it produces his own epitaph. For unlike Marinetti, who continually resurrects himself in manifestos and performances repeated in new forms and contexts, Nevinson is unable to repackage himself after the publication and live performance of the manifesto. And although he claims he came up with the word *Blast* in 1913[76] and will later contribute to the second issue of the journal, Nevinson becomes the paradigmatic Futurist scapegoat, the unwitting revolutionary who embraces his own death, sacrificing himself for the cause of the revolution. It is the ultimate irony that he will be resurrected and immortalized as a Futurist at the end of the twentieth century by the art historical tradition.

But how exactly is the Vorticist philosophy different from the Futurist? Indeed, the graphic design of the journal owes much to the typographical art of *Lacerba*;[77] and the lists of "Blasts," "Curses," and "Blessings" reads like a parody of Marinetti and Nevinson's "Againsts" and "We Wants." The introductory "Great Preliminary Vortex" to the first issue of *Blast* tells us that its exponents "stand for the Reality of the Present—not for the sentimental Future, or the sacripant Past . . . We do not want to change the appearance of the world, because we are not Naturalists, Impressionists or Futurists (the latest form of Impressionism) and do not depend on the appearance of the world for our art." However its "Manifesto II" signed by, among others, Aldington, Gaudier-Brzeska, Hamilton, Pound, Roberts, Wadsworth, and Lewis, lists the following, which are essentially some of Marinetti and Nevinson's original arguments, and indeed, phrases, repackaged:

> [I. 3] Luxury, sport, the famous English "Humour," the thrilling ascendancy and idée fixe of Class, producing the most intense snobbery in the World; . . . these phenomena give England a peculiar distinction in the wrong sense, among the nations.

[I. 4] This is why England produces such good artists from time to time. . . .

[III. 2] But there is violent boredom with that feeble Europeanism, abasement of the miserable "intellectual" before anything coming from Paris, Cosmopolitan sentimentality, which prevails in so many quarters. . . .

[V.2] At the freest and most vigorous period of ENGLAND'S history, her literature, then chief Art, was in many ways identical with that of France. . . .

[VI.1] The Modern World is due almost entirely to Anglo-Saxon genius,—its appearance and its spirit.

[VI.2] Machinery, trains, steam-ships, all that distinguishes externally our time, came far more from here than anywhere else. . . .

[VII.1] Once this consciousness towards the new possibilities of expression in present life has come, however, it will be more the legitimate property of Englishmen than of any other people in Europe. . . .[78]

These statements suggest—and this is a common thread running through much of Lewis's writing—that Futurism, an Italian import, is to be rejected (or rather, appropriated) in the service of an imagined homegrown aesthetic. The Vorticist cohort thus becomes the mobilized army of the English avant-garde, and since armies not only advance boundaries but defend them, one that will defend art against the foreign army of the Italian Futurist avant-garde.

Yet despite these nationalistic rants, Lewis's main theoretical argument, as he articulates it in a piece titled "The Melodrama of Modernity," seems to be for art not to behave like politics: "Cannot Marinetti, sensible and energetic man that he is, be induced to throw over this sentimental rubbish about Automobiles and Aeroplanes, and follow his friend Balla into a purer region of art?"[79] The split between Futurism and Vorticism takes on an entirely new complexion in this light; for, as Walter Benjamin argued in his groundbreaking essay on "The Work of Art in the Age of Mechanical Reproduction," this kind of negative theological conceit of "art for art's sake," or a "pure art" removed from the field of social praxis, appeared as the initial reaction of the art world to the crisis of authenticity created by new technologies of reproduction such as photography, film, and the mass media.[80]

The alternative offered by Marinetti is the logic of Fascism, which Benjamin describes as "the introduction of aesthetics into political life . . . All efforts to render politics aesthetic culminate in one thing: war."[81] Lewis's reaction to Futurism should perhaps therefore be seen as a mode of escape—through a retreat into the "higher" aesthetic plane of a literary journal—from a confluence of social, cultural, and political factors giving shape to the crisis that he will later call "the Great Bloodletting." Benjamin also articulates a further thrust to this crisis of authenticity, one that unpicks another stitch in the rhetoric of *Blast*: the advent of technological reproduction "changes the reaction of the masses toward art. . . . The greater the decrease in the social significance of an art form, the sharper the distinction between criticism and enjoyment by the public. The conventional is uncritically enjoyed, and the truly new is criticized with aversion."[82]

Benjamin's overriding thesis is that as the "aura" or authenticity of a work, its unique spatial and temporal existence, is replaced by a multiplicity of reproduced images, the definition of art itself must change, and the reproduction be placed in the service of politics—to generate movement of the masses. This shaping of mass perception through the propagandization of art is already part of the modus operandi of the Futurist movement; and through the various modes of expression of **VEA** it manifests itself in the actions and reactions of imagined aesthetic communities within gallery audiences and newspaper readerships. As the former heckle the performers, so becoming part of the performance; and as the latter send letters to the editors of newspapers, so becoming writers: the distinctions between audience, artwork and artist become blurred, and it is no longer clear what would constitute the imagined community of Futurists—or, for that matter, Vorticists. But the Futurist manifesto, anticipating later twentieth-century conceptual art, exists, happens, as a performance in the public sphere; and a case can therefore be made for **VEA** to be considered an exemplar of Futurist art.

The Art of the Manifesto

F. T. Marinetti
DIRECTION DU MOUVEMENT FUTURISTE
Corso Venezia, 61 — MILAN

C. R. W. Nevinson
5, BELSIZE STUDIOS
Hampstead — LONDON, N. W.

—**VEA-PAM-FR**

The word "manifesto" derives from the Latin *manifestus*—clear, obvious, or "caught in the act"; this in turn is a compound of *manu festus*, meaning literally "struck by hand."[83] The etymology suggests that the public declaration of principles, policies, beliefs, or intentions which constitutes a manifesto is ultimately rooted in a deliberate act of violence or transgression; and since this act takes place through verbal communication, that the manifesto is a peculiar instance of a "performative utterance." Luca Somigli has argued that

> [b]orrowed from the practice of political propaganda, they [manifestos] do not belong clearly to either the realm of polemical writing, of aesthetic experimentation, or of theoretical reflection. In fact, their association with the political makes them an ideal means to reach out to a mass audience uninvolved with the relatively closed world of cultural production, and to attempt to bridge the perceived gap between art and life. . . . what made the manifesto such a supple and adaptable genre for the avant-garde was precisely its unstable generic nature, poised between politics and aesthetics, and between exposition and exhortation.[84]

In the case of **VEA**, as we have noted, the text does not display any of the typographical experimentation of other Futurist texts; however, its various modes of existence situate it on an unstable confluence of fault lines—between revolutionary pamphlet, article, advertisement, and letter to the editor; speech, lecture illustration, voice-over to special effects, and performance. Somigli lists nine characteristics of manifestos; and for the most part these seem to fit the logic of **VEA**: the manifesto is (1) an act of denial and (2) of affirmation, (3) "an unstable structure, the trace of a work in progress," (5) the ground where "the avant-garde producer and the audience confront," (6) a performative act "which establishes the avant-garde project in announcing its coming into existence," (7) constitutive of "the avant-garde as a projectual subject," (8) "the textual space in which the audience is produced," and (9) something that "by its rhetoric . . . undermines the distinction between artist and audience."

Somigli's fourth characteristic of manifestos, omitted above, seems to us to be somewhat limited: (4) "The avant-garde manifesto is neither a theoretical work nor an example of a new literary or artistic practice."[85] This is elaborated in glosses to the fifth and eighth characteristics, as follows:

> The manifesto plays upon its supplementary role by suggesting that the real work is being carried out elsewhere, and that its own purpose is that of bridging the gap between producer and consumer. As a supplement, it is ultimately unnecessary, to be replaced by the work which it announces and explains; however, it simultaneously leaves its mark by suggesting strategies of reading, by preparing a certain horizon of interpretation of the work. Thus, the manifesto capitalizes on its ambiguous status: on the one hand, it is other than the work, and therefore it is not bound by the necessity of "making it new" . . . On the other, it governs and directs the openness of the radically new, of the work itself, by offering strategies of reading which make it possible to approach the work from the point of view of its producer. . . .
>
> In its metaliterary, programmatic aspect, the manifesto serves the prosaic purpose of providing the tools through which the reader can suitably decode the new language of the properly artistic text.[86]

The problem here is that Somigli is distinguishing arbitrarily between the aesthetic qualities of the written text of a manifesto, and something arbitrarily designated as "the properly artistic text"—despite the fact that much of twentieth-century art and criticism has been concerned precisely with eliding boundaries of this sort, as could be illustrated by numerous examples from Dada to performance art. In making this distinction, and the related distinction between art and politics, Somigli is subscribing to a model not unlike Lewis's, where, as Marjorie Perloff puts it, "[i]t is assumed that the art object is not to be confused with the environment or its situation in the world and that its formal structure should be governed by such values as coherence and unity. The fact is, however, that, like it or not, most art and literature since the midsixties has moved away from the coherency model of High Modernism, and to dismiss such art wholesale as nonart or nonliterature is not particularly useful for criticism."[87]

This model, which is pervasive in the discipline of art history, establishes an arbitrary hierarchy between texts, considering some—such as newspapers, autobiographies, diaries, letters, and also artists' writings and manifestos—as existing irreducibly in "life," and as therefore serving as normative points of reference for the others—paintings, for example—that are assigned to the category of "art." The persistence of this model generally reflects a lack of understanding on the part of art historians of textual/literary genres considered as forms of aesthetic expression. Somigli's contention that the "metaliterary" nature of the manifesto deflects the reader's attention elsewhere misses the point that even a metaliterary text is a *text*, and therefore literary. As Perloff points out, "the real point is that the theory . . . *is* the practice in that the text foregrounds what Giovanni Lista calls 'the problematic of the precedence of project to work, of metalanguages to creation.' . . . To talk about art becomes equivalent to making it, and indeed most historians of Italian Futurism agree that the series of fifty-odd manifestos published between 1909 and Italy's entrance into the war in 1915 were the movement's literary form par excellence."[88]

As regards the "properly artistic text," one presumes that for Somigli this category would include, for instance, paintings. But in the case of Nevinson's "futurist" paintings, one would be hard pressed to find any techniques or thematic developments that are not simply imitative of the work of the Italian Futurists; indeed, Nevinson's works of visual art do not stand out at all as regards originality or technique in comparison to, say, the works of Boccioni or Balla. Nevinson and his paintings remain of interest today almost entirely as objects of ethnographic or anthropological study, or in the service of art-historical nationalism—by virtue of his association with other artists, his nationality and self-proclaimed status as an English Futurist, and the role he played with Marinetti, through the **VEA** manifesto, in the development of Vorticism.

But there is another reason why Nevinson's paintings, and the genre of painting in general, are of less consequence than the manifesto: as Walter Benjamin has argued, "Painting simply is in no position to present an object for simultaneous collective experience";[89] whereas, in the age of mechanical reproduction, it is textual dissemination through print and other media that provides the widest experiential access to the masses and establishes the role of art in the public sphere. In this context, politics behaves as if it were art, and the manifesto becomes foregrounded as the paradigmatic conceptual and popular art form of the age. In Perloff's terms, "To give one's text 'the form of Manifesto' . . . was to create what was essentially a new literary genre, a genre that might meet the needs of a mass audience even as, paradoxically, it insisted on the avant-garde, the esoteric, the antibourgeois. The Futurist manifesto marks the transformation of what had traditionally been a vehicle for political statement into a literary, one might say, a quasi-poetic construct."[90]

At the same time, art behaves as if it were politics. The manifesto should be written not in the mode of narrative—for that would make it merely an article; but rather, in that of declaration. Hence Marinetti's famous reply in 1913 to Severini, who had sent him a manuscript for a manifesto:

> I have read with great attention your manuscript, which contains extremely interesting things. But I must tell you that there is nothing of the *manifesto* in it. . . . The rest of the material is very good and very important, but to publish it as is would be to publish an article that is excellent but not yet a manifesto. I therefore advise you to take it back and reword it, removing all that I have already mentioned, and tightening it, recasting the whole new part in the form of *Manifesto* [*in forma di Manifesto*] and not in that of the review article about futurist painting.[91]

This act of declaration is the political performative of Futurism, a violent strike of the hand that transgresses the current norms of society and gives "the signal for battle." In **VEA**, this signal, ironically, is for the reactionary battle of England against its own past, and against its domination by the ancestral and current forces of Italian art, as represented by Marinetti; it therefore heralds a temporal reaction of the present against both the past and the future, and a spatial reaction of English art against foreign intrusion. As Renato Poggioli expresses it,

> for the moderns the present is valid only by virtue of the potentialities of the future . . . the "presentism" of the Zeitgeist stands to the futurism of contemporary art as romanticism does to avant-gardism. Furthermore, it was precisely by the term "presentism" that Wyndham Lewis defined the credo of the movement he founded and named "vorticism," by which he deceived himself into believing that he had surpassed Italian and French Futurism . . . In any event, the image used by Lewis *is* agonistic and nihilistic when, in his manifesto, he describes his movement as "the new vortex," which "plunges to the heart of the present."[92]

The declaration given by Marinetti and Nevinson is, in other words, the signal for the defensive rear-guard of an imagined Vorticist community to fight a national aesthetic struggle against the imagined encroachments of Italian Futurism; and the text-performance of the manifesto becomes simultaneously the rallying cry, swan-song, and epitaph of Nevinson and English Futurism.

The Future of Futurism

This triple thrust of the Marinetti-Nevinson declaration reflects the general logic of *activism* (motivated "for no other end than its own self") and *antagonism* (agitation "*against* something or someone," such as the academy or tradition); and the general dialectic of *nihilism* ("beating down barriers, razing obstacles, destroying whatever stands in its way) and *agonism* (ignoring, welcoming, or accepting "self-ruin as an obscure or unknown sacrifice to the success of future movements"), that Renato Poggioli famously identified as characterizing avant-garde movements.[93] The attitude of "agonism" ultimately constitutes a "futurism" that transcends "Futurism," since it is a general characteristic of imagined avant-garde communities united by a manifesto: "the futurist movement belongs to all the avant-gardes and not only to the one named for it . . . the so-named movement was only a significant symptom of a broader and deeper state of mind. Italian futurism had the great merit of fixing and expressing it, coining that most fortunate term as its own label."[94]

There is therefore an irony built into the very nature of the avant-garde movement, whereby it has the potential both to succeed and fail under its own momentum. As Poggioli comments,

> The case of [Italian F]uturism, because of the ambition of its programs and the extravagance of its claims, the vanity of its works and its incapacity to transform the letter into the spirit, its own attempt to survive itself, proves—as an extreme example—that each specific avant-garde is destined to last only a morning. When a specific avant-garde which has had its day insists on repeating the promises it cannot now keep, it transforms itself without further ado into its own opposite. Then, as happened with futurism, the movement becomes an academy.[95]

In the English context, as an epitaph, "Vital English Art" is carved in stone, so to speak, by virtue of being preserved in newspaper, journal, and book archives as a part of the art-historical tradition and past history; in contrast to the Italian movement, "English Futurism" *as such* never became institutionalized, although some of its arguments were reconfigured in the bromides of Vorticism. At the same time, however, the fact that **VEA** is a linguistic object means that the significance it had during its initial moment of performance is not final, and that its meaning, beyond its catalytic role in establishing the Vorticist reaction, remains open to reinterpretation as a function of future communities of readers. To assess its success in its own time and place would therefore be futile, as the logic of "futurism" is deeply related to "the sense or consciousness of belonging to an intermediate stage, to a present already distinct from the past and to a future in potentiality which will be valid only when the future is actuality";[96] any such assessment could only be made through the construction of a retrospective historical fiction.

In our present moment of reading, then, **VEA** serves, rather like the inscription on a tombstone, to signify the loss and hope its signs refer to; as the mark of an absence that is constantly supplemented with meaning added to it by subsequent generations. For "[i]f the real futurism is dead forever, ideal futurism is still living, precisely because it renews itself in the consciousness of each successive avant-garde."[97] As an epitaph, the manifesto "Vital English Art" circumscribes the gap between mortality and immortality, its literary *I*, in Marinetti's terms, "consuming and obliterating itself in the grand cosmic vibration." From the perspective of the present, the significance of **VEA** lies not in its enduring testament to a past moment of history, but in Marinetti and Nevinson's "immolation of the self to the art of the future[, which] must be understood not only as an anonymous and collective sacrifice, but also as the self-immolation of the isolated creative personality."[98] In this sense, supplemented by the *I* of Marinetti, the manifesto stands as the only genuinely Futurist work that can be attributed to Nevinson, whose own voice, caught in the self-consuming play between presence and absence, speaks its authority as signature, as a trace of the performative:

F. T. Marinetti
Direzione del Movimento Futurista
(Corso Venezia, 61 — Milano)

C. R. W. Nevinson
(4, Downside Crescent — Hampstead — London)

—**VEA-LAC-IT**

Notes

W. Lewis, *Blasting and Bombardiering* (London: Eyre & Spottiswoode, 1937), 33, 35.

1. Yeats, "The Second Coming," In *The Norton Anthology of English Literature*, 7th edition, vol. 2 (New York: W. W. Norton, 2000), 2106.

2. Lewis, *Blasting and Bombardiering*, 32.

3. Ibid., 35–36.

4. R. Poggioli, *The Theory of the Avant-Garde*, trans. Gerald Fitzgerald (Cambridge, MA: Harvard University Press, 1968), 10, 12.

5. R. T. Clough, *Futurism: The Story of a Modern Art Movement: A New Appraisal*, (Philosophical Library, 1961; repr. New York: Greenwood Press, 1969), 16.

6. Ibid., 20–21, 23.

7. Marinetti, "Electrical War" (A Futurist Vision-Hypothesis), from "War, the World's Only Hygiene" (1911–15), in *Marinetti: Selected Writings* trans. R. W. Flint and Arthur A. Coppotelli (New York: Farrar, Straus & Giroux, 1972), 104–8, 108.

8. B. Anderson, *Imagined Communities Reflections on the Origin and Spread of Nationalism* (London: Verso, 1983; revised repr. 1992), 6–7.

9. Ibid., 46, 44–45, 113–15.

10. Lewis, *Blasting and Bombardiering*, 32.

11. Marinetti, "Destruction of Syntax—Imagination without Strings—Words-in-Freedom 1913," in *Futurist Manifestos*, ed. U. Apollonio, trans. Robert Brain, R. W. Flint, J. C. Higgitt, Caroline Tisdall (New York: Vileing Press, 1973), 95–106, 96–97.

12. Marinetti, "Destruction of Syntax—Imagination without Strings—Words-in-Freedom 1913," in Apollonio, ed., *Futurist Manifestos*, 95–106, 95–96.

13. C. R. W. Nevinson, *Paint and Prejudice* (London: Methuen, 1937; and New York: Harcourt, Brace, 1938), 81.

14. Marinetti and Nevinson. "Futurism and English Art." [newspaper publication].

15. Marinetti and Nevinson. "Futurism and English Art." [digital image]. This can be viewed on the Yale University (Beinecke) Library's collection of Digital Images Online, under the "Marinetti Libroni" (Master CD Number: 0259-3231-0455; Carousel 8, Slots 20 and 69). The manifesto appears to be printed on two pages (19 and 20) of a booklet; the preceding page (18) contains the second half of Henry W. Nevinson's essay "Marinetti: The Apostle of Futurism" reprinted from the *Manchester Guardian.* (The first half of the essay is on page 16; page 17 contains two images of works by Boccioni [Carousel 8, Slots 65 and 21]).

16. Marinetti and Nevinson, "Vital English Art: Futurist Manifesto." [pamphlet].

17. Marinetti and Nevinson, "Contre l'art anglais, Manifeste futuriste" [pamphlet].This version is presumed to have been printed in Italy, as it bears a publisher's mark below the signatures, "STAB. TIP. TAVEGGIA—MILANO VIA OSPEDALE 3." Below the title is a subtitle: Manifeste futuriste / lu à la Doré Galerie (Exposition des / peintres futuristes Boccioni, Carrà, Rus- / solo, Balla, Severini, Soffici) et à l'Uni- / versité de Cambridge. — Juin 1914." The text is in the Yale University–Beinecke Library collection (Marinetti +M317 79).

18. Marinetti and Nevinson, "Vital English Art." [journal publication].

19. Marinetti and Nevinson, "Manifesto Futurista." [journal publication].

20. C. R. W. Nevinson, "A Futurist Manifesto: Vital English Art," in *Paint and Prejudice*, 79–81.

21. C. R. W. Nevinson, "Vital English Art, (A Lecture . . .)," 160–62.

22. Charles Brookfarmer, "Futile-ism Or, All Cackle and No Osses" (*New Age* 15, 7 [June 18, 1914]). The text is parenthetically subtitled: "Report of lectures on 'Vital English Art,' by Messrs. Marinetti and C. R. W. Nevinson, Doré Galleries, Friday evening, June 12." While some commentators regard this as a satire, a comparison of the fragments of Nevinson's words as reported against the text of the lecture reveals they are nearly exact quotations, with one or two minor exceptions; this suggests that not only Nevinson's but also the reported fragments from the speech of Marinetti, who spoke after Nevinson, are fairly accurately recorded. The latter also frequently reflect an English structure that bears the marks of French syntax, and which is consistent with Marinetti's French delivery.

23. M. J. K. Walsh, *C. R. W. Nevinson: This Cult of Violence* (New Haven, CT: Yale University Press, 2002), 87.

24. The subtitle of **VEA-PAM-FR**, when translated into English, reads: "Futurist manifesto / read at the Doré Gallery (Exhibition of / the Futurist painters Boccioni, Carrà, Rus- / solo, Balla, Severini, Soffici) and at the Uni- / versity of Cambridge.—June 1914."

25. Walsh, "The Eminent English Futurist: C. R. W. Nevinson and English Futurism in Peace and War." In *Blasting the Future: Vorticism in Britain 1910–1920*, ed. Jonathan Black et al. (London: Philip Wilson Publishers, 2004), 26.

26. Such a study would involve researching the the circulation and distribution histories of versions of **VEA** in different countries, establishing readership profiles in each medium, and analyzing the history of the text's popular and critical reception, from its first appearance to the present. It would also involve exploring issues of identities and boundaries raised in the cosigning of the manifesto by Marinetti and Nevinson: to what extent can the (often contradictory) intentions expressed in the text be attributed to either signer? what cross-cultural connections can be drawn between **VEA** and other futurist manifestos, or the relative movements of Futurism and of the conventions it purports to reject, in England and Italy? The publication in Italy of an English version of **VEA**, for instance, suggests the authors were considering not only the art world in England, but also the broader spectrum of English speakers in Europe, as their audience. And, to take another example, the manifesto published in a newspaper is contextualized by the other articles around it, whereas the pamphlet version is a self-contained work, handed out to people—or, if Nevinson can be believed—dropped on the heads of theatergoers; in this mode, the manifesto functions differently, as a fragment to which each reader can attach his or her own personal interpretation.

27. Lewis, *Blasting and Bombardiering*, 34.

28. The text of the *Arabian Nights* first appeared in English in 1704; the *Aladdin* tale was already well known in the eighteenth century; and Richard Burton's translation of *The Book of the Thousand Nights and a Night* was published in 1885–88.

29. One can get a sense of the sonorousness of this voice in its original tongue by reading aloud, loudly, in Marinettian fashion, the Italian version—*Io sono un poeta futurista italiano* . . . —and comparing it with the relatively flat sound of the English equivalent: *I am an Italian Futurist poet*. . . .

30. C. R. W. Nevinson, "Vital English Art, (A Lecture . . .)," 160.

31. Nevinson, *Paint and Prejudice*, 83, quoted in Walsh, *C. R. W. Nevinson*, 82. Marinetti himself confirms in another context: "In London where the English Futurist painters Nevinson Wyndham Lewis Wadsworth have distinguished themselves for their proposal to camouflage ships by using dynamic Futurist color patterns by that genius the Roman Futurist Giacomo Balla there took place before and after the concert other furious fistfights and encounters that didn't stop me at all but rather were inspiring as I dared explain even though I didn't know English and pronounced the few phrases I did know badly to the rich and well-educated London that mattered persuading them with gestures that they should respect Luigi Russolo's talent . . ." (Marinetti, "Aggressive Noisiness and Russolo's Noise Machines," 335–37 in Flint, ed., *Marinetti: Selected Writings*, 336).

32. Walsh, *C. R. W. Nevinson*, 78.

33. Ibid., 78.

34. L. Somigli, *Towards a Theory of the Avant-Garde Manifesto* (PhD diss., State University of New York at Stony Brook, 1996; DAI, 57, no. 11A [1996]: 4726), 207, quoting W. Wees, *Vorticism and the English Avant-Garde* (Toronto: University of Toronto Press, 1972), 69.

35. Clough, *Futurism*, 20.

36. Marinetti, "Futurist Speech to the English (1910)," 59–61 in *Marinetti: Selected Writings*, ed. Flint, 60.

37. Marinetti, "Futurist Democracy (1919)," 76–79 in *Marinetti: Selected Writings*, ed. Flint, 78.

38. Marinetti, "Marriage and the Family," from "Futurist Democracy (1919)," 76–79 in *Marinetti: Selected Writings*, ed. Flint, 78.

39. Marinetti, "Against *Amore* and Parliamentarianism," from "War, the World's Only Hygiene, 1911–1915," 72–75 in *Marinetti: Selected Writings*, ed. Flint, 74.

40. Marinetti, "Against *Amore* and Parliamentarianism," from "War, the World's Only Hygiene, 1911–1915," 72–75 in *Marinetti: Selected Writings*, ed. Flint, 73. For more on Futurism's complex attitudes toward gender, see the chapter on "Futurism and Women,"

in Tisdall, C., and Bozzolla, Angelo, *Futurism* (New York: Oxford University Press, 1978), 153–63.

41. Marinetti, "The Futurist Synthetic Theater (1915)," 123–29 in *Marinetti: Selected Writings*, ed. Flint, 127.

42. W. S. Gilbert, and A. S. Sullivan, *Patience*, in *The Complet Plays of Gilbert and Sullivan*. Illustrated by W. S. Gilbert (New York: Garden City, 1941; repr. New York: W. W. Norton, 1976), 168–69.

43. Quoted in Boccioni, Umberto. "The Plastic Foundations of Futurist Sculpture and Painting 1913," 88–90, in Apollonio, ed. *Futurist Manifestos*, 89.

44. Marinetti, "Technical Manifesto of Futurist Literature (1912)," 84–89 in *Marinetti: Selected Writings*, ed. Flint, 89.

45. Marinetti, "The Variety Theater (1913)," 116–22 in *Marinetti: Selected Writings*, ed. Flint, 116.

46. Marinetti, "The Pleasure of Being Booed (1911–1915)," 113–15 in *Marinetti: Selected Writings*, ed. Flint, 114.

47. Marinetti, "Futurist Speech to the English (1910)," 59–61 in *Marinetti: Selected Writings*, ed. Flint, 64.

48. Umberto Boccioni et al., "Manifesto of the Futurist Painters 1910," 24–26 in *Futurist Manifestoes*, ed. Apollonio, 26, 27.

49. Marinetti et al., "The Futurist Cinema 1916," 207–18 in *Futurist Manifestoes*, ed. Apollonio, 207.

50. Juvenal, *IVNII IVVENALIS SATVRAE*, Liber IV, Satura 10, line 356. Latin text based on Bucheler, 1983, at The Latin Library Web Page, http://www.thelatinlibrary.com/juvenal.html.

51. Marinetti, "Geometric and Mechanical Splendour and the Numerical Sensibility 1914," 154–59 in *Futurist Manifestoes*, ed. Apollonio, 154.

52. Marinetti, "Futurist Speech to the English (1910)," 59–61 in *Marinetti: Selected Writings*, ed. Flint, 61.

53. Marinetti, "Destruction of Syntax—Imagination without Strings—Words-in-Freedom 1913," 95–106 in *Futurist Manifestos*, ed. Apollonio, 96, 97.

54. Marinetti, "Electrical War (A Futurist Vision-Hypothesis), from "War, the World's Only Hygiene, 1911–1915," 104–8 in *Marinetti: Selected Writings*, ed. Flint, 106.

55. This is perhaps an allusion to Apollinaire's collection of poems, *Alcools* (1913), which experimented with punctuation and combined modern images, including fragments of overheard conversation, with classical poetic forms. And alcohol, of course, is a stimulant only in transient moments.

56. M. Perloff, *The Futurist Moment. Avant-Garde, Avant Guerre, and the Language of Rupture* (Chicago: University of Chicago Press, 1986), 48–49.

57. A letter from the Italian Futurist Severini to Raffaele Carrieri, an art historian, suggests that the idea of collage was first suggested by Apollinaire to Picasso, then to Severini himself in 1912; and that Severini communicated the idea to Boccioni and the latter to Carrà, with the result that Futurist experiments in collage began in 1913 (White, J. J., *Literary Futurism: Aspects of the First Avant Garde* (Oxford: Clarendon Press, 1990), 75).

58. Marinetti, "Technical Manifesto of Futurist Literature (1912)," 84–89 in *Marinetti: Selected Writings*, ed. Flint, 87.

59. Marinetti, "Destruction of Syntax—Imagination without Strings—Words-in-Freedom 1913," 95–106 in *Futurist Manifestos*, ed. Apollonio, 100.

60. Marinetti, "Geometric and Mechanical Splendour and the Numerical Sensibility 1914," 97–103 in *Marinetti: Selected Writings*, ed. Flint, 98.

61. Marinetti, "Dynamic and Synoptic Declamation (1916)," 142–47 in *Marinetti: Selected Writings*, ed. Flint, 143.

62. Richard Aldington et al., "The Futurist Manifesto," in Letters to the Editor, *Observer*, June 14, 1914.

63. Quoted in Walsh, *C. R. W. Nevinson*, 88.

64. Walsh, C. R. W. Nevinson, 63, 71, 72.

65. Lewis, "Marinetti Man of the Week" (New Weekly, May 14, 1914), 328.

66. Ibid., 329.

67. Walsh, *C. R. W. Nevinson*, 72.

68. Ibid., 87–88.

69. J. L. Austin, "Performative Utterances," 1430–42 in *The Norton Anthology of Theory and Criticism*, gen. ed., Vincent B. Leitch (New York: W. W. Norton, 2001).

70. Brookfarmer, "All Cackle . . . ," 154.

71. Ibid.

72. Richard Aldington et al., "The Futurist Manifesto."

73. "Futurist Squabbles. English Artists' Counterblast to Signor Marinetti" (*Daily Express*, London, June 11, 1914).

74. "Futurists and the Past," *Times*, Thursday, June 11, 1914.

75. C. R. W. Nevinson, "The Futurist Manifesto."

76. Wees, *Vorticism*, 159.

77. For an overview of the history and politics of the journal, see the chapter on "Lacerba" in Tisdall and Bozzolla, *Futurism*, 165–76.

78. *Blast*, no. 1, 1914, 30–43.

79. Ibid., 144.

80. Benjamin, "The Work of Art in the Age of Mechanical Reproduction" in *Illuminations*, trans. Harry Zohn, ed. Hannah Arendt (New York: Schocken Books, 1969), 224.

81. Ibid., 241.

82. Ibid., 234.

83. *American Heritage Dictionary of the English Language*, 4th ed. (Boston: Houghton Mifflin, 2000).

84. Somigli, *Towards a Theory . . .* , 4, 6.

85. Ibid., 7–8.

86. Ibid., 64–65, 75

87. Perloff, "Violence and Precision: The Manifesto as Art Form," in *The Futurist Moment*, 110.

88. Ibid., 90.

89. Benjamin, "The Work of Art . . . ," 234.

90. Perloff, "Violence and Precision: The Manifesto as Art Form," in *The Futurist Moment*, 81–82.

91. Quoted in Perloff, 81, and in slightly different translation in Somigli, *Towards a Theory . . .* , 84

92. Poggioli, *The Theory of the Avant-Garde*, 73–74.

93. Ibid., 25–26.

94. Ibid., 68–69.

95. Ibid., 223.

96. Ibid., 72.

97. Ibid., 223.

98. Ibid., 67–68.

Artists as Activists: C. R. W. Nevinson and Wyndham Lewis

Paul Edwards

WAS IT MORE THAN A COINCIDENCE THAT C. R. W. Nevinson and Wyndham Lewis both issued autobiographies in 1937? It may well be that Lewis was prompted to write his *Blasting and Bombardiering* by the example of Nevinson's *Paint and Prejudice*, the first installment of which appeared in the *Sunday Dispatch* in April of that year (Lewis's book was not published until October).[1] It would be fitting if it was indeed Nevinson who gave Lewis the idea (both of writing an autobiography and of providing it with an aggressively alliterative title), for it would point to a recurrent feature of their relationship and reputations: the way in which many of Nevinson's gestures have been eclipsed by the bigger explosions that Lewis detonated in their aftermath. Although by 1913 Lewis was already an established force in the avant-garde some time before Nevinson began to attract attention, in some ways it began like this as well. Nevinson was the inventor of the title of the magazine that was to be the vehicle of Vorticism, *Blast*, and he also had closer connections with F. T. Marinetti and the Futurist painters than Lewis did. It was Nevinson who first showed how the geometric vocabulary of the new painting could be adapted to the subject matter of war in the trenches, nearly three years before Lewis produced his first drawings as a war artist. The title of Lewis's 1919 exhibition of his own war art, "Guns," recalls that of Nevinson's show of the previous year, "War." Both of these artists cultivated the popular press and controversy, Nevinson with even more dedication than Lewis, for Lewis could communicate with his public through books and pamphlets. Both were prepared to comment for the press on such topics as women's fashion, with Lewis this time preceding Nevinson's 1923 comments with his "The Long and the Short of It" for the *Evening Standard*.[2] On any occasion where either of them felt aggrieved, their first instinct was to make as public a protest as possible; and again Nevinson's protest over the "censorship" of his war painting *Paths of Glory* could be seen as providing a model for the storm of publicity Lewis whipped up when his 1938 portrait of T. S. Eliot was rejected by the Royal Academy.

The 1937 autobiographies also share several features, the most important of which is that they cannot be relied on as records of fact, even though accurate facts can certainly be found in them. They are both, in Ian Jeffrey's phrase about *Paint and Prejudice*, "more work than source."[3] If both these books are summative efforts, neither attempts the self-analysis that is often associated with the genre of autobiography, though some of Nevinson's remarks about his childhood at least gesture toward that. They are summations, rather, of twenty-five years in the lives of deliberately constructed public personae. Since these personae are to some extent political (deployed both in the politics of art and the larger arena of "real" politics), the need for summation is tinged in both cases with an acknowledgment of failure, for it is in failure that all political careers end.[4] By 1937 it was clear to both writers that an era had ended, and that their recent influence on their time had been minimal: Lewis's constant warnings in the weeklies and in pamphlet volumes about the dangers of a repeated war were futile, and Nevinson's grandiose paintings of the 1930s depicting the recidivist violence of human culture, along with his almost hysterical *Exodus A.D.* "warning to civilians" about the threat caused by the armaments trade and by aerial bombardment, had been no more effective.[5]

It is not my intention to shift the critical balance between these two artists, or to assign priority to one or the other in each of the phases of their work and artistic strategy, but it should be recognized that in some cases priority should be assigned to Nevinson. It is the shared dislocation within a culture unsympathetic to modernism that seems to me most fruitful in discussing them alongside each other. However priority is decided, it seems to me that only in his war paintings does Nevinson begin to approach equality with Lewis's achievement as a painter (or writer) responding to the culture of their time.[6] Wyndham Lewis was a major artist and writer who, after a brilliant beginning as a leader of the avant-garde, never really found a place in British culture and so made a career out of being an outsider and "Enemy"; C. R. W. Nevinson, on the other hand, was a lesser artist who, after a brilliant beginning as a follower of Futurism and a war artist, likewise became dislocated from the cultural mainstream and sustained his career through publicizing his "outsider" status. "Eccentricity" (think of Stanley Spencer or William Roberts) was indeed the characteristic mode for artistic survival of British painters in the first half of the last century, caught between the restrictive formal and cultural aesthetic of Bloomsbury and the conservatism of the more lucrative side of the trade, represented by the Royal Academy. Both Lewis and Nevinson aspired, not to eccentricity, but to centrality in their culture; by altering that culture, however, not by conforming to it. This is why their careers are so littered with resentments, self-aggrandizing publicity, and intemperate attacks on their times. It is also why there is an aura of underachievement surrounding both these artists—most drastically around Nevinson, whose work simply declined in quality and interest, but also around Lewis, who never wrote the central masterpiece that would lead to recognition as the equal of Joyce, Pound, and Eliot, and never painted enough or with sufficient confidence to fulfill his promise as the leader of England's avant-garde. These may seem harsh judgments, but an essential component of them is an appreciation of the actual achievements of these artists—the unforgettable power of Nevinson's stark representations of war, the imaginative intelligence of Lewis's brilliant polemics and manifestos in *Blast*—and of what those achievements had promised.

Lewis famously described his own sense of underachievement by ascribing it to a cultural failure in Britain, brought about by the First World War. Implicitly it was a failure to recognize his own centrality. In *Blasting and Bombardiering*, he asserted of himself (and his fellow members of the avant-garde), "we are the first men of a Future that has not materialized."[7] Lewis's capitalization of "Future" is a tacit acknowledgment of what elsewhere in his autobiography he somewhat obscures, that, from 1910 on, his whole conception of the purpose of being an artist was radically influenced by Marinetti, the founder of Futurism. In fact both painters can be thought of as "school of Marinetti," since both took their conception of the artist from his example as the impresario of Futurism before the First World War. Marinetti's conception of the artist was quintessentially avant-garde: the objective of art is not merely to reflect its time, but to change it. For the Futurists, this entailed a breaking down of the barriers between art and life. Such a deliberate violation of the concept of the aesthetic as a privileged enclosure has been taken to be the defining feature of the avant-garde, distinguishing it from a mere Modernism which would leave that enclosure intact, no matter how much disruption takes place within its boundaries. Whether this theoretical distinction between avant-garde and modernist practices can ultimately be justified is not my concern here. It seems more useful to note that the critical problems of definition reflect actual dilemmas and conflicts that painters like Lewis and Nevinson needed to negotiate in their activities as advanced painters in England. Following Marinetti they took it for granted that the objective of the artist should be to have a direct effect on the life of his time. But neither painter altogether took the step of negating the aesthetic itself as a necessary part of implementing this strategy; art itself would not change its condition, even if artworks themselves would enter public culture surrounded by as much pugnacious publicity as possible. Both Lewis and Nevinson produced easel pictures, drawings, and watercolors, and many of Nevinson's most impressive works are lithographs and mezzotints of a "traditional" character.

Nevinson was Lewis's junior by six years, but in the period of Futurist incursion onto the British scene, Nevinson had a position of equality with him. His father's acquaintanceship with Marinetti and background in journalism and his own recent acquaintance with Severini in Paris gave him an entrée to the Futurist circle; what he perceived as Lewis's resentment of this position would lead to one of those rebuffs that punctuate Nevinson's career (such as Carrington's preference for Mark Gertler, and Tonks's shameful subsequent advice that he give up painting). As with Lewis's break with Roger Fry and the Omega Workshops in October 1913, in the break from Marinetti and Futurism it is difficult to separate the pretext (affronts that Lewis publicly and loudly declared to be insupportable) from the matters of artistic principle that underlay the schism. In the separation from Fry the public cause was Fry's alleged misappropriation of a commission from the Ideal Home Exhibition,[8] but the more fundamental dispute was over the relationship of the aesthetic with the public realm. Fry conceived this relationship broadly in line with the arts and crafts movement, and deprecated content of public significance in high art. Lewis had evidently been present at the Lyceum Club in April 1910 when Marinetti gave his "Futurist Speech to the English" (echoes of it can be discerned in an essay, "Our Wild Body," that Lewis published on May 5 in the *New Age*) and had already allied himself more closely to Marinetti's activist position on the relation between the aesthetic and public realms. His exhibits in the "Second Post-Impressionist Exhibition" in October 1912 showed him absorbing the formal lessons of Futurist painting, if not yet their commitment to a "modern" subject matter, in his pictures.[9] Accordingly, along with Nevinson he organized a dinner for Marinetti on November 18, 1913, and until June of the next year seemed happy to be associated in the public mind with Futurism. When the break with

Marinetti came, Nevinson quite probably knew it was on the way, and precipitated it by issuing "Vital English Art" with Marinetti from the "unauthorised" address of Lewis's Rebel Art Centre. The name "Vorticism" had already been chosen to indicate the separateness of the new English avant-garde from its main progenitor, but Nevinson decided not to join the secession.

In *Blast* Lewis now distinguished his version of the avant-garde from Marinetti's in the same way that he had previously distinguished it from Fry's. He was confident that in Vorticist abstraction, through which he had completely dissociated the elements of painting from their customary signifying function, he had invented a mode that answered the Futurist ambition of creating a new sense of contemporary life without recourse to illustrating modernity through subjects like cars—for if Lewis had publicly repudiated Fry, in practice he agreed that paintings needed to make their meanings through their form. The function of form was to create meaning, however; it was not simply there for aesthetic contemplation. The problem with Fry was that he was not enough like Marinetti, but the problem with Marinetti was that he was not enough like Fry; though of the two, Lewis definitely felt more at home with (and owed more to) the Italian. The Vorticists' noisy repudiation of the "Vital English Art" manifesto left Nevinson somewhat in the role of scapegoat, though it may have looked to him that in remaining loyal to Futurism he would ultimately be on the winning side—for art politics at this time was conceived in terms of winners and losers. "Vital English Art" is not one of the most impressive of Futurist manifestos, however, and it certainly does not bear comparison with the exuberant playfulness of the manifestos in *Blast*.

Vorticism distinguished itself from Futurism mainly through its disparagement, not of the subject matter of Futurist art (though Lewis did criticize some Futurist paintings for their illustrative approach to it), but of the Romantic and naively celebratory attitude it attributed to Futurist engagement with that subject matter. Lewis's Vorticist works, such as *Composition* [1913 (fig. 5)], accept fully the Futurist premise that machinery transforms human experience and perception: the mechanomorphic dancing couple are barely distinguishable from the vertiginous and oppressive structure in which they are set. This is not a "state of mind" picture, or a synthesis of impressions, since its violation of normal visual convention is not to be assigned to some hypothetical spectator-participant in the scene. Insofar as this is a representational drawing (and for Lewis all visual elements of a painting can be read as representing something)[10] it works metaphorically as a statement: this is what modernity makes of humans. Not that the painting insists on a representational reading; it is also simply what Lewis later called Vorticist abstractions, a set of "blocks and lines of various dimensions" that have been pushed around and arranged according to a "mental-emotive impulse" the artist recognizes as significant.[11] Either way, the resulting image is deliberately deficient in Futurist gaiety. Whether such differences in mood and conception of the function of pictorial elements would make the schism from Futurism inevitable is another matter. It is not as if the styles and objectives of such painters as Russolo, Boccioni, and Severini are indistinguishable; had he wished, Lewis could have exhibited—at least in England—under the banner of Futurism. Whether he could be confident that Marinetti would grant him anything like equality with the Italian painters on the international stage is far more doubtful, however. More important, Nevinson's account suggests that Marinetti may have treated Lewis as no more than Nevinson's equal (or not even that), and this would have been galling to him.[12] For Lewis was by now a mature painter, having arrived at maturity in 1912 at the age of thirty, an age that Nevinson would not reach until 1919.

Given his comparative youth, it is no criticism of Nevinson to point out that well into 1913 his own work was entirely triangulated by the Slade, the New English Art Club, and Camden Town (especially as represented by Spencer Gore).[13] It is difficult to guess what lies behind Nevinson's claim that (in 1913) the work of Picasso was well known to him and that Picasso was "still swayed by Toulouse Lautrec and was only just leaving his blue period," but the apprenticeship implied by the statement (Nevinson in touch from the beginning) in fact never took place. It was probably through contact with Severini and a rapid assimilation that Nevinson became a "Futurist" painter overnight. If anyone was "still swayed by Toulouse Lautrec" at this period it was Nevinson himself, for he brings out a sinister but somewhat fin de siècle air of corruption in his own representation of dance (*Dance Hall Scene*, [1913 (fig. 6)]). The spectator is not so much absorbed into the scene as held at a distance from it; it represents other people's hysteria. It established the mode of modernism with which Nevinson would work when he wished to make his most serious statements about modernity—a visual phantasmagoria. It also shows the aesthetic problem that would dog him in this mode: the need to choose what convention of representation would integrate into the larger psychological (or allegorical) structure governing the work as a whole. This was a problem certainly shared by Lewis at this time, when meaning, and hence subject

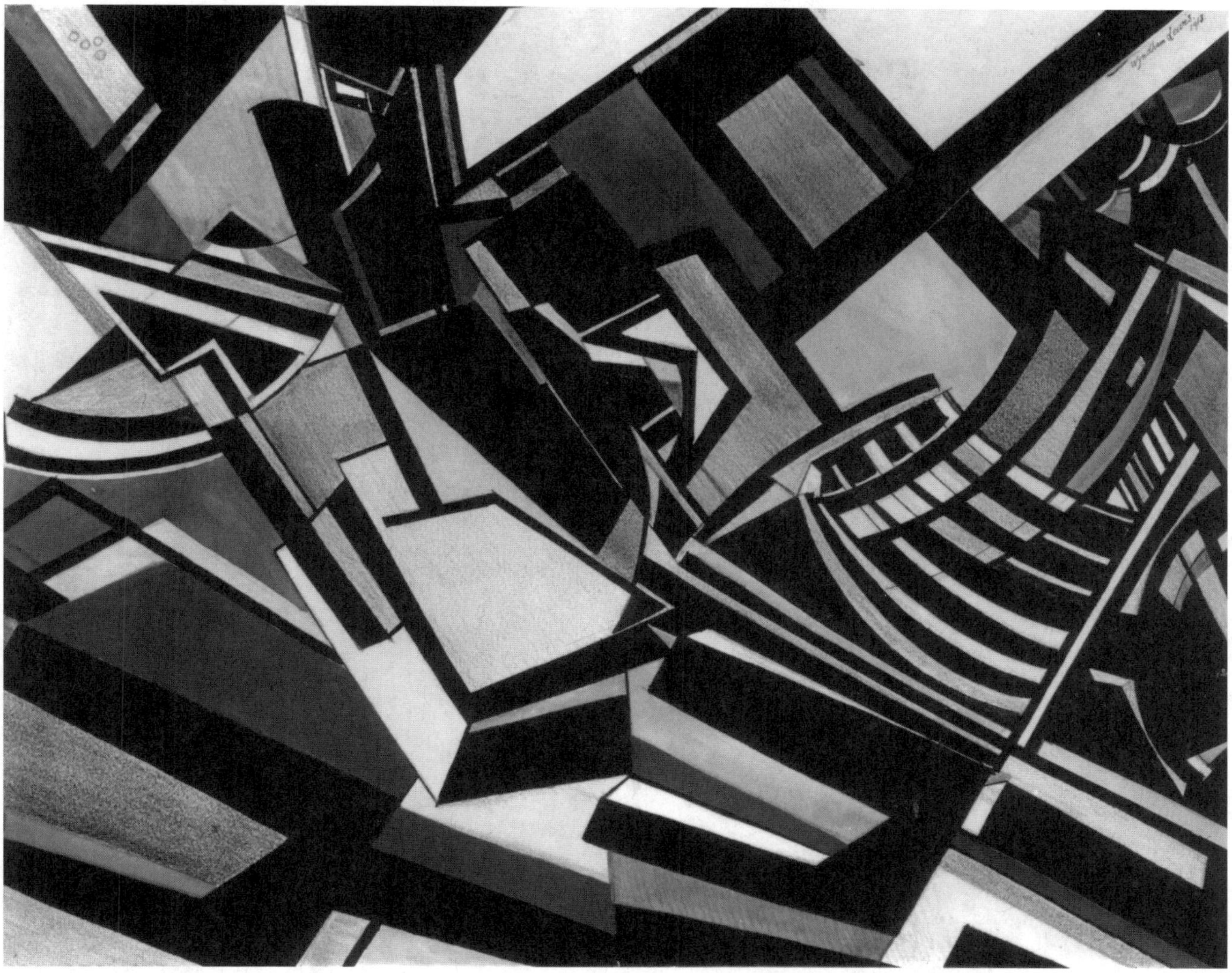

5. Wyndham Lewis, *Composition*, 1913. Pencil, pen and ink, watercolor, collage, 34 × 26.5. Tate Gallery, London.

matter, were crucial. His major surviving Vorticist canvas, *The Crowd* (1915) stylizes its little matchstick figures but places them within a geometric matrix that "represents" an urban environment only metaphorically. In the sketched *Dance Hall Scene* (it has traces of squaring up), the caricatural representational detail, though it weakens the image aesthetically, is primarily responsible for its air of menace. Nevinson's Futurist canvases *Le Vieux Port* (dated 1910 [1914?]) and *The Arrival* (1914) overcome this aesthetic problem and encapsulate with real charm the Vorticist desire to celebrate the "great ports" and seafaring, even though Nevinson refuses the austerity of Vorticist abstraction. But they do so at the cost of a meaning beyond pleasure in the represented scene.

By 1915, in the new context of a literal threat to survival posed by the First World War, Nevinson was admitted back into the avant-garde grouping; his *On the Way to the Trenches* (a black ink drawing from or woodcut of *Returning to the Trenches*) was reproduced in the second issue of *Blast*, while the original painting was awarded tactful praise in Lewis's review of the London Group in the same issue: "his *Marching Soldiers* have a hurried and harassed melancholy and chilliness that is well seen."[14] He goes on to praise *Searchlights*[15] as "perhaps, too, the best he has painted." Nevinson was also invited to show at the Vorticist exhibition in 1915, and was expected by Lewis to contribute an open letter to *Blast* itself.[16]

Nevinson had by now experienced the war at first hand and begun painting those war paintings for which he is best remembered. Owing to ill health, Lewis was not to enlist until 1916 and did not reach the front until June of 1917. As a first lieutenant in a heavy artillery battery in the second half of that year Lewis's experience differed considerably from Nevinson's. Nevinson was never a combatant, though he

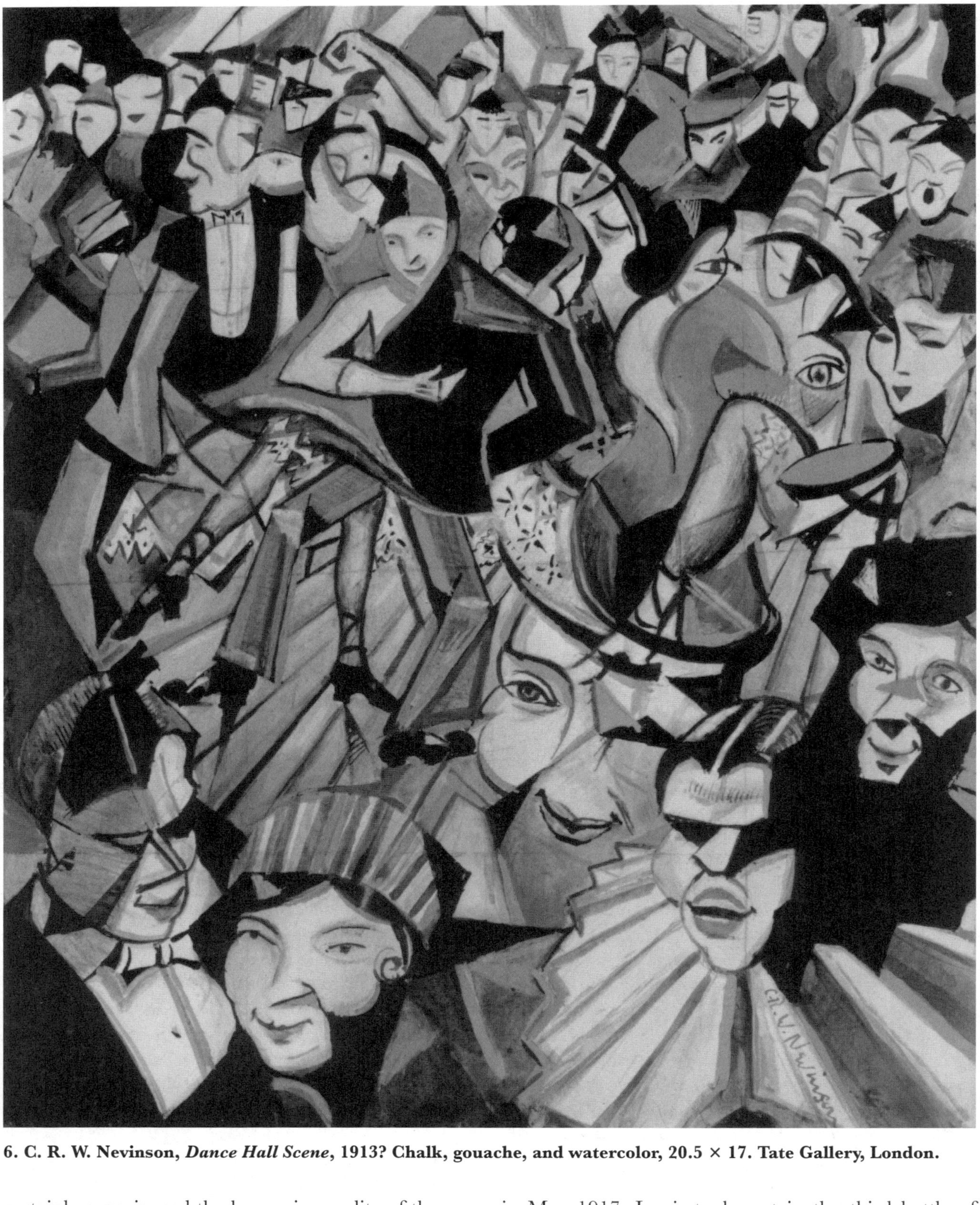

6. C. R. W. Nevinson, *Dance Hall Scene*, 1913? Chalk, gouache, and watercolor, 20.5 × 17. Tate Gallery, London.

certainly experienced the harrowing reality of the war in as distressing a form as Lewis did, particularly in his work in an ambulance unit and later as a private in the RAMC. He became an official war artist in May 1917. Lewis took part in the third battle of Ypres, becoming an official war artist in December. Whereas Nevinson's paintings, despite well-publicized controversy, were looked on relatively favorably by the

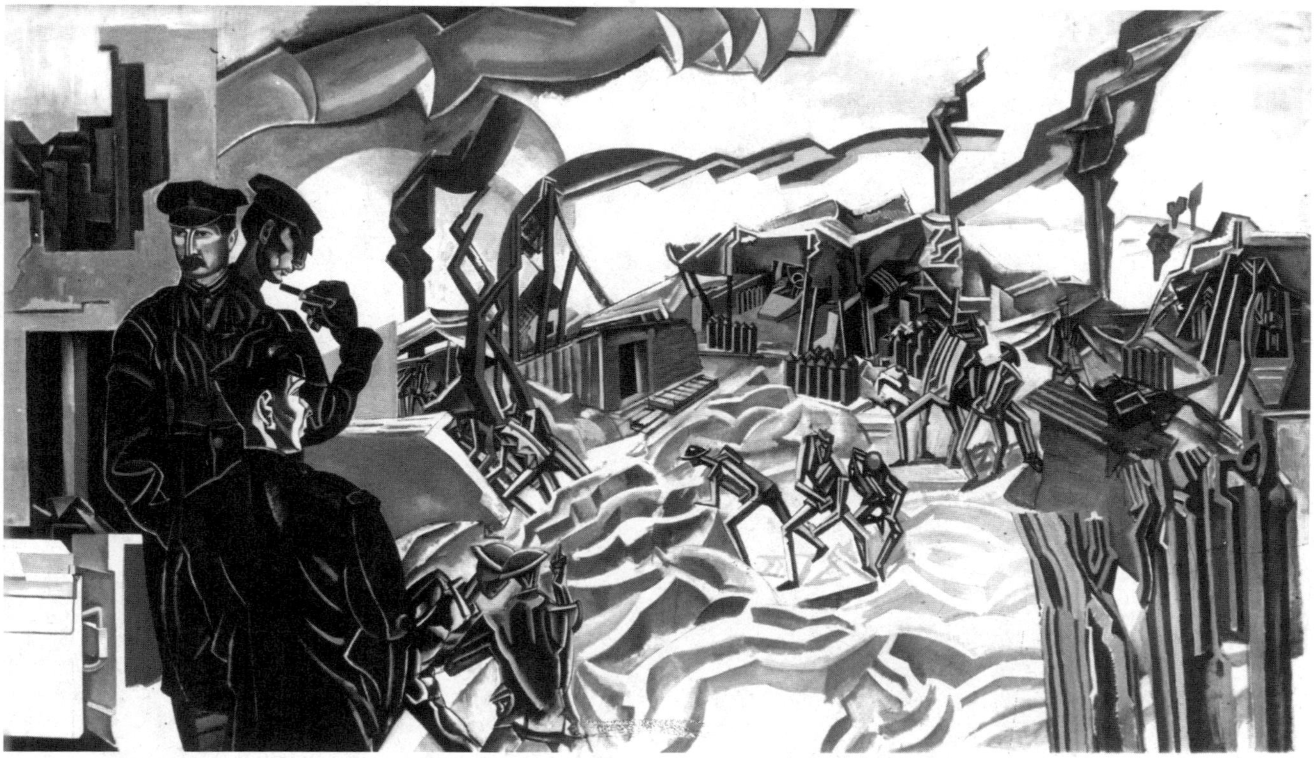

7. Wyndham Lewis, *A Battery Shelled*, 1919. Oil on canvas, 182.7 × 317.7. Imperial War Museum.

committee, so that many of his works are in the Imperial War Museum, Lewis's were not, and only two were added to the collection: his commissioned painting *A Battery Shelled* [1919 (fig. 7)], and the colored drawing, *Battery Position in a Wood* (1918), which was donated by Muirhead Bone rather than purchased for the scheme. Nevinson certainly seems to have had more commitment to painting the war than Lewis did, even though his commitment, as so often with Nevinson, has a lingering odor of opportunistic careerism. Nevinson's war art goes through several phases, while Lewis's only had time for one, but, especially in commissioned work, for both painters the need to produce representational images exacerbated the aesthetic dilemma concerning conventions of representation outlined above. Nevinson's Futurism had, anyway, not long survived his experience of the human cost of war; most importantly it did not survive in his conception of organizing visual images (the early *Returning to the Trenches* and *Bursting Shell* of 1915 excepted). As official painters of the war they were both now organizing their pictures as representations of real space, rather than as psychological, metaphorical, or decorative space (the two-dimensional space of the picture plane). The result is a kind of aesthetic compromise: an overlay of stylization on a naturalistic scene. It could be argued that for both artists this gave rise to a crisis whose full effects were not felt until after the war itself was over.

As far as the war art itself is concerned the question must be whether the quasi-cubist stylization itself has a function beyond rhetorical resistance to complete assimilation to "official" conceptions of the artist's role. In the case of Nevinson there can be little doubt that his radical simplifications and stylization of forms gave his painting a real power to concentrate particular moods. *French Troops Resting* [1916 (fig. 8)], a multifaceted pyramid of sharp blue and brown wedges and segments, brilliantly conveys the fatigued disenchantment of the figures that it comprises, while it hints also at a steely determination that would have made this an acceptable image at the time. The graphic simplification and geometrification of forms in *On the Road to Ypres* also enables Nevinson to present two moods with great force: again, a relentless determination that has subdued the individual to an unflinching purpose, and combined with that a sense of gothic horror at the hooded figures driving their carts on toward a harvest of death. *La Mitrailleuse* (1915), his most celebrated image, uses its stylistic reductiveness and concentration as a metaphor for an equivalent reduction and concentration in the men manning the machine gun. What Nevinson must have found, however, was that this style might also effect a

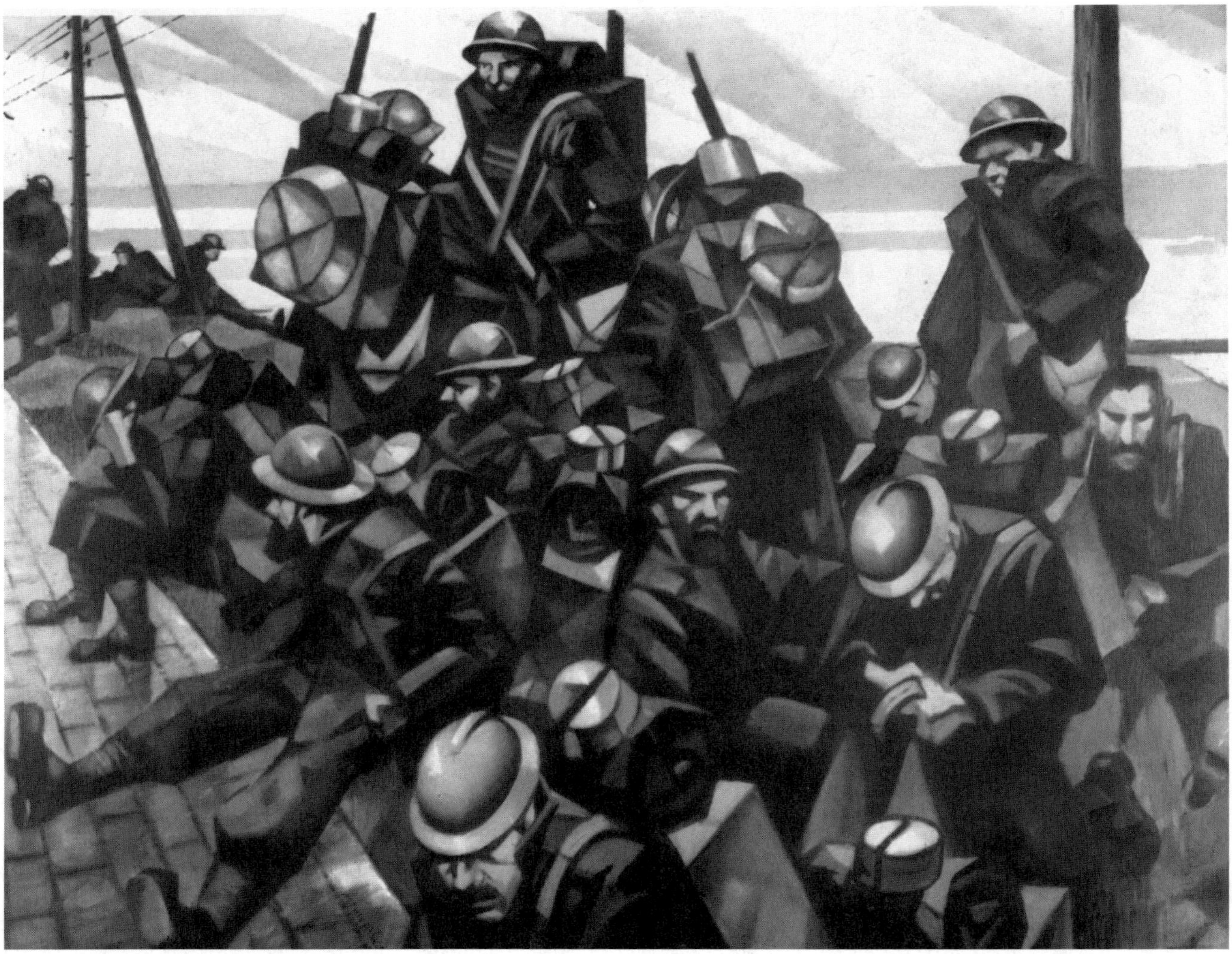

8. C. R. W. Nevinson, *French Troops Resting*, 1916. Oil on canvas, 71.1 × 91.4. Imperial War Museum.

damaging reduction. *La Patrie* (1916) does not do justice to the truly traumatic effect on Nevinson of the neglected, gangrenous, and dying wounded in "the shambles" at the railway goods yard in Dunkirk (we should remember that the primary meaning of "shambles" is a slaughterhouse or meat market). It is a dark and in some ways disturbing painting, but again the stylization conveys grim stoicism more than horror, just as the graphic simplification of *Night Arrivals* (1915) a representation of unloading ambulances, conveys calm efficiency. When Nevinson engages with the more fundamental horror and indignity of war, as in another representation of the shambles [*The Doctor*, 1916 (fig. 9)] he reverts to a much less stylized form of naturalism; only the face of the man wounded in the head having his injury inspected by the doctor is nonnaturalistic, almost reverting to the type of caricature seen in *Dance Hall Scene*, and as in that work the effect produced is closer to alienation from the victim than empathy with him.

It has been speculated (and was raised as a possibility at the time) that Nevinson's adoption of naturalism as a commissioned war artist reflected a desire not to alienate the authorities.[17] There is no doubt something in this, but it also seems that Nevinson was no longer content to mask the reductiveness of war by filtering it through his own abstracting stylizations. The *Flooded Trench on the Yser* (1916) is an aesthetically pleasing simplification of a scene in something of the style of a Japanese print; in contrast, *The Road from Arras to Bapaume* (1917) and *After a Push* (1917) owe their desolate simplification not to "aesthetic" choices, but entirely to the effects of continual bombardment on the landscapes they depict. *Paths of Glory* (1917), which employs a loose impressionistic form of naturalism to convey the indignity of death in battle, is hardly the painting of a timid man hoping to ingratiate himself with the authorities. We may now realize that the problem with Nevinson's naturalism is that as painting it is completely

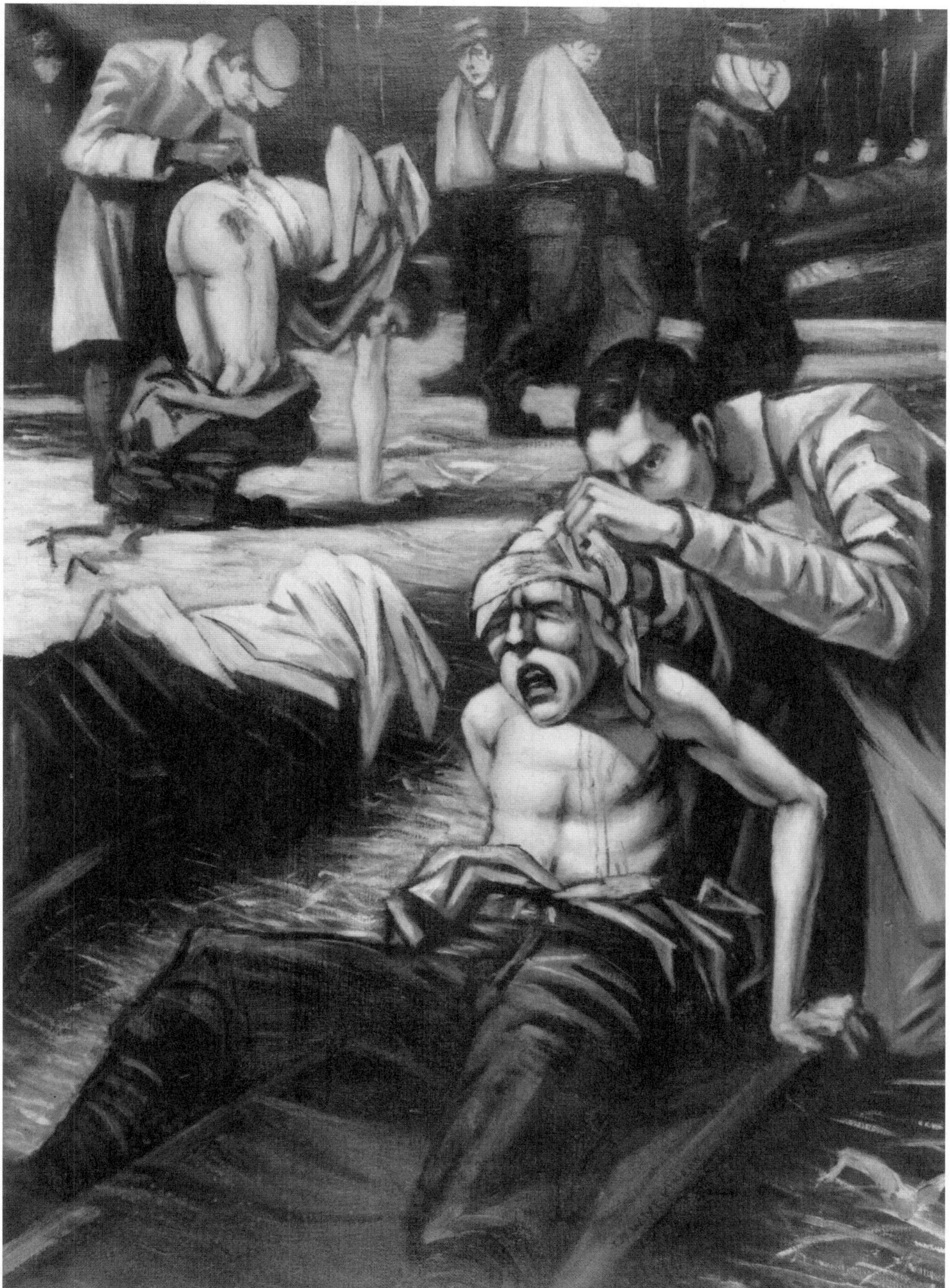

9. C. R. W. Nevinson, *The Doctor*, 1916. Oil on canvas, 57.1 × 41.2. Imperial War Museum.

uninteresting, but for him it must have seemed an extension of the means at his disposal to convey truth; his stylization had allowed only a restricted truth to emerge. Humanly, there is nothing discreditable at all about his large painting for the planned memorial chapel, *Harvest of Battle* (1919). It illustrates the horror of such battles as Passchaendale on a scale in every respect greater than he could achieve in *Paths of Glory*, but at the same time tries to find some redemptive shared humanity in the straggling line of mixed German and British wounded picking their way through the quagmire, their enmity forgotten. But this humanity has been achieved by Nevinson at the cost of the bold architectonics and structural simplification of the first phase of his war paintings. Relying on naturalism, it is a painting without vitality, exhibiting sympathy but failing to evoke empathy with its lifeless figures.

Most of Wyndham Lewis's war art consists of ink drawings heightened with colored chalks and washes, mainly designed as a series of images depicting the life of the heavy gunners, from installation of the howitzers in gun pits to combat itself. The stylization of the drawings can be read as metaphorical, like Nevinson's: war reduces men to machines. The equivalent in Lewis's work to *Harvest of Battle* is *A Battery Shelled* (1919), also commissioned for the planned memorial chapel. It is a heavily stylized representation of a battery under fire, with small insect-like men scuttling for cover, watched by three much larger, apparently detached gunners in the left foreground. As I have argued elsewhere, Lewis's painting can be read as a meditation on the same dilemma that split Nevinson's work into "modern" and naturalistic, the human implications of the choice between abstraction and empathy, and it is above all the presence of the three surrogate spectators between the imagined viewer and the scurrying soldiers that gives the painting this dimension of self-reflexivity. Looking like a representation from the standpoint of a Nietzschean superman of men reduced by war to mechanism, it also deconstructs its own apparent indifference to the human consequences of bombardment. The painting has been endlessly debated,[18] and though it may be a far more complex statement about war than anything Nevinson produced, it is not necessarily as resolved and satisfying an image as some of Nevinson's earlier paintings. Indeed for some critics (notably Richard Cork in his earlier writings on the painting) its self-reflexivity was symptomatic of a loss of direction in Lewis's art that would not be recovered. And Osbert Sitwell's 1925 denigration of the painting in comparison to Nevinson's war work still deserves a hearing. For Sitwell, Nevinson "was the first—and to many remains the only—artist able, by his allied qualities of eye and mind, to translate modern warfare into terms of veracity and art." Unlike Lewis (unnamed by Sitwell but clearly his target here), Nevinson managed not to "reduce warfare to an abstract and rather unmeaning arrangement of planes and cones, tokens of men and guns, transmuted into one indistinguishable mass, beneath smoke that creaked through the air, as if cut out from flat yellow cardboard and sent whirling up by a hurricane. . . . But in Mr Nevinson's pictures we are given the whole business of modern warfare."[19]

Supposing this to be true, the real problem for the painter returning to normal work after the war, and raised in the war work, remained. (It has been excellently discussed in David Peters Corbett's study of English painting of the period).[20] There were several aspects to it. First, the attitude of the public: a time of reconstruction demanded something less "frivolous" than the antics, schisms, and novelties of the prewar period. Secondly, "cubism" and geometrical abstraction were associated with the depiction of war, and found their symptomatic but temporary justification only in that. These were not simply external pressures on painters like Lewis and Nevinson, but arose to some extent out of the artistic choices they themselves had made in their war art. Instead of being the vehicle of a complete rethinking of the epistemology of painting, cubism and abstraction had become a stylization of scenes conceived fundamentally naturalistically. For both painters the subject and meaning of a painting was of fundamental importance. Bloomsbury painting on the other hand elected to paint subjects (still lives, interiors) that a spectator would "see past" so that no distraction from a modern "form" would occur. When subject becomes important because of the critical ambitions of the painter, the danger is that stylization becomes a variable manner, chosen for its appropriateness for particular types of statement.

This, as is well-known, is precisely the trap into which Nevinson fell; indeed, after denouncing Bloomsbury formalism he proclaimed his own new approach:

> Since my last exhibition I have experimented with various styles of painting: I wished to create a distinct method in harmony with each new picture. I do not believe the same technique can be used to express a quiet static moonlight night, the dynamic force of a bomber and the restless rhythm of mechanical transport. Many painters today try to find some particular style of mannerism, and when found they never vary it, hoping always to hall-mark

> their canvases and deceive the public (the Intellectuals especially) into the idea they have individuality. The truth is that the personality of a painter—if he has any personality of course—enables him to stand the test of any technical method.[21]

As Peters Corbett points out, in practice this strategy, whatever might have been made of it at this particular moment, was in practice vitiated by a fundamental bad faith in modernity itself on Nevinson's part. Modern life is now for him a recrudescence of the sinister hysteria that threatens the spectator of the *Dance Hall Scene*, and "modern" style only appears in his satirical depictions of such entertainments (such as *The Shimmy Shake*, or *Music Hall Patriotism*).[22] The "critique" that Nevinson makes is appropriately caricatural and appeals simply to popular prejudice. The "War-Profiteers" of the painting of that title (1917) are predatory females haunting a smoke-filled and dimly lit club (though the fur collar and facial features of the figure on the left of the painting associate her indirectly with the public image of the archetypal Jewish armaments profiteer).[23] Characteristically, when Nevinson wishes to appeal to a more humane set of emotions, as in *He Gained a Fortune but Gave a Son* (1918) he reverts to the transparency of naturalism. The association of stylization with a hostility to modernity is confirmed by Nevinson's contrasting images of the New York elevated railway. The impressionistic *Third Avenue, Elevated Railway* (1920) simply records the imposition of a structure of shadow on the sunny roadway and contrasts it with the dissolving effect of sunlight on the bustling crowd on the pavement: in this case a purely visual truth. *The Soul of a Soulless City* (1920) by contrast wishes to make the critical point given explicitly in its title. Here the "cubist" overlapping and compression of the skyscrapers signifies an inhuman, oppressive emptiness.

At first glance it seems that Wyndham Lewis is locked into the same logic that governs Nevinson's practice:

> If your subject-matter is your breakfast table, then, whatever you do to it, your picture should still remain structurally true to—be in some intimate and direct manner the pictorial equivalent of—that. The cups and coffee-pot, bread and plates, should not plastically usurp the character of the objects of a cobbler's shop, a scene in the Sierras, or a garden fête. In many cases in the pictures of Picasso, Gris, or Braque, this transformation has happened. A man with a mandoline becomes a group of buildings, and so forth.[24]

And although in his *Blast* days Lewis had been critical of what he saw as "cubing" onto a naturalistic representation,[25] his own painting after the war, in such works as the lost 1919 *Ezra Pound* or even the grotesque and expressionistic *Praxitella* (1921), could be described as applying the vocabulary of a modern style to a naturalistically conceived idea of the picture (ignoring, or at most simply alluding to, the grammar of modernism) in a way that is not in principle so different from Nevinson's, or from the principle of stylization that underlies Art Deco. What "saves" Lewis's paintings is the sheer extremity of the images he produces by this method (*Praxitella* and *A Reading of Ovid* [1921] are cases in point), and the fact that their mode of engagement with larger social and cultural issues is beyond Nevinson's ability.[26] Lewis's work could even be taken as confirming that assertion of Nevinson's that "the personality of a painter—if he has any personality of course—enables him to stand the test of any technical method," a test that Nevinson's own work fails. But, despite Lewis's frequently rebarbative individualism, certainly at this time he would not have wished to seek a justification for his practice in this idea.

But Lewis's theoretical link between a range of appropriate styles for a range of different subjects was more apparent than real, for at the same time he was demanding the establishment of a definite and single style rather than individualistic stylistic eclecticism: "How we *need* and can *use* this freedom that we have is to invent a mode that will answer to the mass sensibility of our time with one voice, not with a hundred voices. We want to construct hardily and profoundly without a hard-dying autocratic convention to dog us and interfere with our proceedings. But we want *one* mode. For there is only one mode for any one time, and all the other modes are for other times."[27] Insofar as Lewis's work of the immediate postwar period gives a guide to his conception of this mode, we can say that there is a deliberate restriction of the visual association of pictorial elements to those that are common to an urban, machine-dominated environment: line suggesting the tenseness of arcs of sprung metal, uniform application of mechanically graduated color rather than the virtuosity of "painterly" touch, and so on. Above all, these pictorial elements are deployed as a language from which the images, whether close to, or remote from nature, are frankly and synthetically constructed or generated. This applies equally to such imaginative "abstract" work as *Figures* (1921) and to the avowedly figurative *Seated Figure* (1921). Naturally, Lewis had to submit himself to a period of disciplined work in order to achieve mastery of this mode, and to that extent it is certainly his individual style. But, regardless of its adequacy, it had the potential to be the "one mode" of English modernism in the twenties, and its characteristic forms actually do recur time and again in the work of McKnight Kauffer, Edward Wadsworth, Frank Dobson, and others—even in Paul Nash, though not in the work of Nevinson.

This is not the place for a full analysis of why this modernism did not establish itself in the twenties. But both Nevinson and, eventually, Lewis chose a variety of individualism. In Nevinson's case his success as an artist in the war immediately after his "expulsion" from the ranks of the English avant-garde would have convinced him of the wisdom of this course. But he was also under nervous strain as a result of his wartime experience. His identity as an "individual" was the willed complement of a personality in danger of disintegration, a threatened incoherence that is the counterpart of the stylistic eclecticism of the post-war paintings: "My health started playing me up again and my nerves were all awry. I was overwhelmed by a feeling of futility that dried up my creative urge. The black pessimism to which I am always liable engulfed me now. No longer did I associate with any artists, and I avoided every sort of intellectual contact."[28] Lewis, while apparently committing himself to a group effort, nevertheless actually found working with others almost impossible. How symptomatic it is that his contribution to the "Group X" exhibition should have been four self-portraits![29] Lewis, too, was psychologically affected by the First World War, as he half confesses in his later retrospection on his work (mainly literary) of the twenties: "for some time I was very sore and that soreness increased, if anything, during the immediately ensuing years. The sentimental side of me suffered (I think now) more deeply than it should."[30]

Lewis and Nevinson (who, it seems, were no longer in contact) became a kind of mutual antithesis: Lewis, "the Enemy," suppressing his sentimental side in favor of the ruthless intellectual dissection of his culture in a series of critical polemics aspiring to diagnose the cultural crisis that forced him to spend his time polemicizing instead of painting or writing fiction; Nevinson on the contrary retreating to his sentimental side to produce nostalgic views of the English countryside and romantically atmospheric mezzotints from a chintz-furnished motor caravan—an ambulance in which he himself was the wounded patient. If the twenties are the years of failure in English modernism, the modernism that failed was the activist version taught to Lewis and Nevinson the other side of the great divide of the First World War. Lewis's work of the twenties is far from negligible—indeed his literary polemics transpose Marinettian ambition from the arena of an avant-garde that has "failed" to another which Lewis hoped, to some extent vainly, to create single-handedly through the sheer force of a multiple persona that would stand in for a missing group of supporters and collaborators.[31]

With Lewis the result of the "failure" of his polemical activism was the eventual narrowing down of any route to "success" (but what would have counted as success?) and its confinement to a political activism on behalf of a force that he hoped would prevent a repetition of the terrible war that caused the failure of the avant-garde in the first place. *Hitler* (1931), a sympathetic exposition of the rising movement of National Socialism, signaled the nadir of Lewis's career and an almost complete surrender to the irrational on Lewis's part.[32] It was not, fortunately, a permanent surrender, and in many ways the thirties see a reconnection in Lewis's work, particularly in his painting, with the revived current of modernism in England. If cultural crisis now preoccupied him (as it did), in his art at least he was able to stand back and attempt a less polemical engagement with the currents of history, instead of frantically attempting a one-man campaign to change their direction. And in Nevinson's work of the late twenties and thirties we see a parallel attempt to engage with these currents through painting, journalism, and fiction.

Both Lewis and Nevinson attempt to provide a historic perspective to their visual statements about Europe in the thirties: Lewis's *The Surrender of Barcelona* [1936–37 (fig. 10)], like several of his other paintings of the period, depicts a moment of historical transition in the past that appears to "rhyme" with a contemporary event, the connection here being between the 1472 victory of Ferdinand and Isabella at Barcelona and the contemporary Spanish Civil War. This is only part of a yet longer cycle involving European military adventurism hinted at in other of Lewis's thirties paintings. Precisely what these paintings mean politically, and how closely they should be read in the light of Lewis's sympathies for Fascist dictatorships in the thirties is not easy to decide. It is likely that he wished them to present historical cycles but not to enforce any partisan attitude toward them. By 1939 *The Surrender of Barcelona* had taken on an elegiac quality for Lewis in the light of his increasing understanding of the inhumanity of the regimes he had supported. In his 1939 volume *Wyndham Lewis the Artist* he prints a short lament for the extinction of the Spanish Republic and the suppression of the vital and creative artistic tradition of Barcelona. In 1937, when Lewis's sympathy for the Falangist side was clear

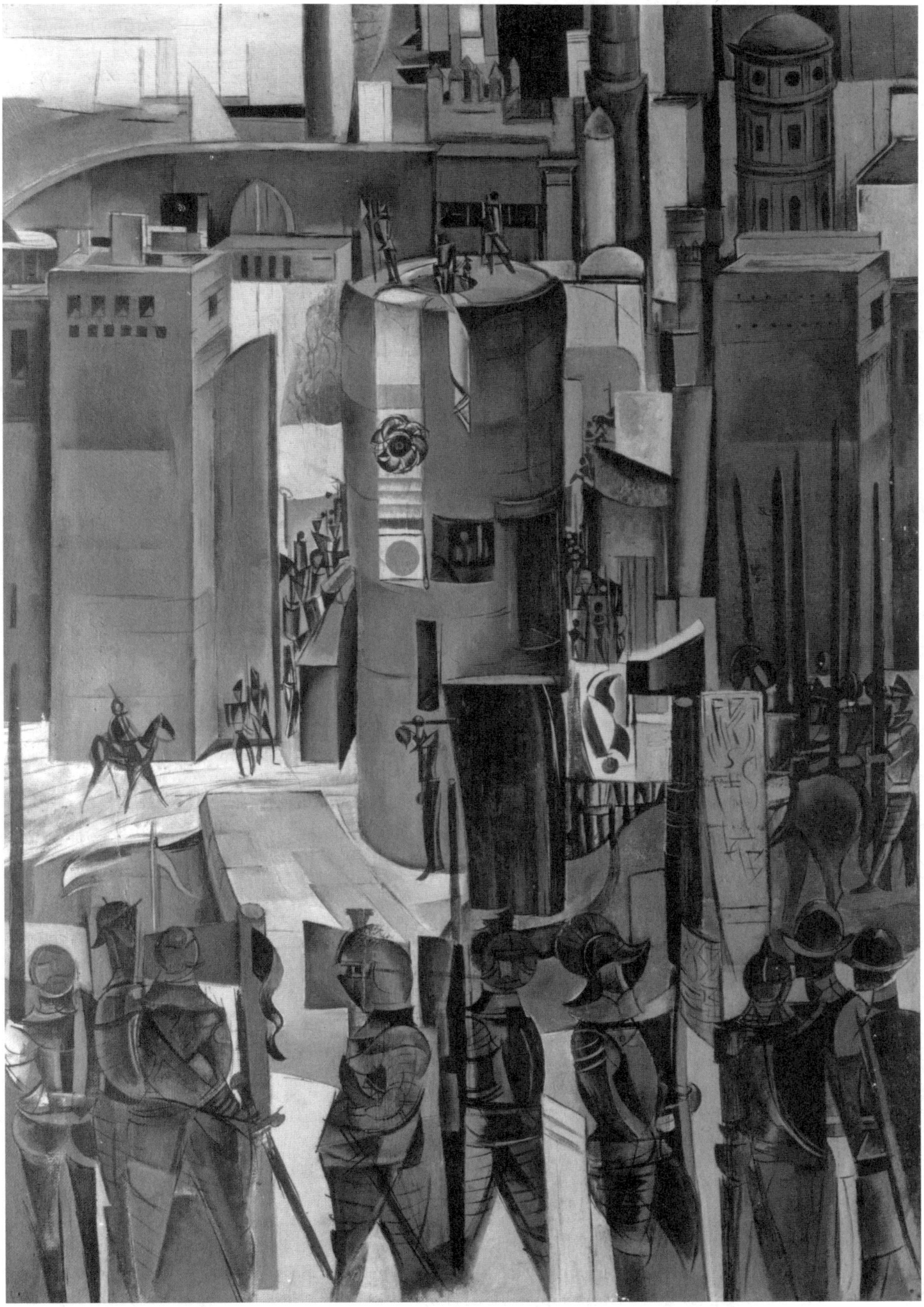

10. Wyndham Lewis, *The Surrender of Barcelona*, 1936–37. Oil on canvas, 84 × 59.5. Tate Gallery, London.

from his pamphleteering (when the painting had been exhibited as *The Siege of Barcelona*), a quite different reading would have been more probable.[33] Such "rhymes" in history echo the organization of Ezra Pound's *Cantos*, in which a transcendent "natural" foundation for cyclical repetitions of history is revealed through pagan epiphanies of goddesses and nature spirits. Where Lewis differs fundamentally, however, is in his conviction that Europe should no longer be governed by a "historical unconscious" that submitted it to such repetitions; he has no time, either, for a naturalistic pagan polytheism (even a metaphorical one).

Nevinson's own grandiose pictorial statements about European history are decried as some of his least successful work. But whatever artistic faults they may be felt to have are probably the consequence of Nevinson's desperate sincerity. The sincerity of a confused man is usually disastrous (Lewis's *Hitler* being an obvious example). Nevinson, however, whatever the confusion of his beliefs and emotions, did not express fascist sympathies. By the 1930s Nevinson's original Futurist method of organizing paintings through formal disruptions that were to be assigned to psychology (which I have suggested appears in his work as a kind of phantasmagoria) has become a rationale for a loose disposition of emblems around the picture surface in an indeterminate space. Thus the *Self-Portrait of the Artist, with his Wife* reproduced in *Nash's Magazine* in January 1934 assembles, like souvenirs around its naturalist portrayal of the two heads, brushes, canvas, telephone, a cat, marching men and bayonets, a luxury liner, and a bat (to represent Nevinson's awareness of his own eccentricity). This quasi-modernist organization of (often semitransparent) emblems within the picture is used in Nevinson's grand statement paintings of the early thirties. *Pan Triumphant* [c. 1934 (fig. 11)] is an arrangement of a transatlantic liner with tiny passengers boarding, girders, skyscrapers, two naked male and female figures, the open sea, and a traffic-filled New York street. Dominating all is a term of Pan. Like Lewis, Nevinson is attempting to show an ahistoric, immemorial dimension to contemporary history, in this case both parading the phenomena of modernity (here transatlantic travel to the city of the future, New York) but, like Pound, also asserting a mythical dimension that transcends both past and future.

It is fairly obvious that such paintings as *Pan Triumphant*, *The Twentieth Century* (1932–35) and *The Unending Cult of Human Sacrifice* (ca. 1934) are not going to be admitted to the canon of major British paintings. But it is worth pointing out that Nevinson does achieve in them something of the openness to interpretation and partial emancipation from the immediate that I have noticed in Lewis's history painting of the thirties, even if the cloudy and indefinite arrangement of his various motifs is the concomitant of an equivalent intellectual vagueness. Certainly a degree of detachment is discernible if we compare them with Nevinson's utterances and writings of the period, in which specifics were perforce made clearer, notably his own fear and confusion. *Exodus A.D.: A Warning to Civilians*, the novel Nevinson wrote in collaboration with Princess Troubetzkoy, has a plot that disintegrates, like the England it describes. It is an almost hysterical assemblage of all the elements of modernity that caused Nevinson to suffer nervous stress and had been manifested in his response to the First World War and its aftermath: the decadence of nightclubs and complacency of society people, the danger of "profiteers" (armament manufacturers) who operated behind tariff walls at the expense of the majority, the rat-like swarming of the majority itself when roused, the danger of death raining down from the air, and the gas that causes a panic from which there is no recovery. The "warning" is that from one air raid on London there will ensue a total collapse of all civilization and humanity.[34]

In an article in 1936, Nevinson explained that there was no hope for European peace, "nation state worship is only in its infancy, and that the creed of State and nothing but the State, is the new religion, whether called Soviet, Fascist or Socialist." He reaffirms the absolute centrality of the arts, particularly architecture, but only as the means by which gas-proof "citadels" may be constructed to protect the population from air raids: "I would like to see the Court, the War Office, the Admiralty, the Foreign Office, and the Bank of England moved to Ottawa . . . until these citadels are built."[35] In retrospect it is difficult to consider the man who expressed these views and conceived some of the wilder scenes of *Exodus* as entirely sane. But, as with Lewis's polemics of the period, there was a rational core to this obsession. For both artists a repetition of what they had seen and experienced in the First World War was to be avoided at any cost: from having welcomed the future in 1914, they now reached the point of casting themselves in the role of Cassandra, pointlessly warning the public of what the new future they had identified might bring.

Exodus confirms the phantasmagoria (of a particular paranoid type) as the method through which modernity is best to be revealed. The outbreak of war is virtually causeless (the death of a Zaharoff-like armaments king), and collapse is immediate and unstoppable. In a dream, the hero finds himself dead before the throne of God. The description of God ("almost naked, with

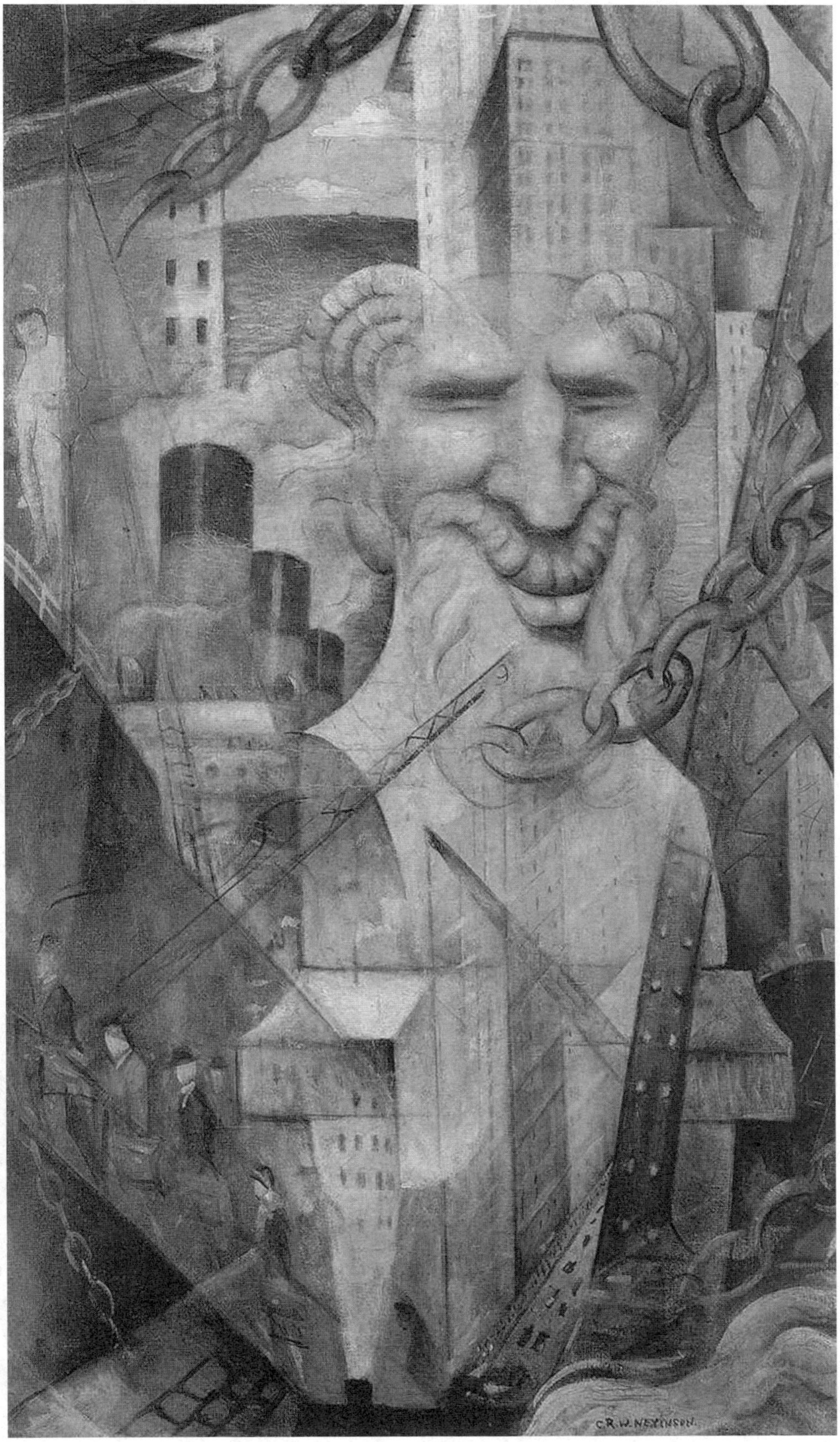

11. C. R. W. Nevinson, *Pan Triumphant*, ca. 1934. Oil on canvas, 127 × 77.5.

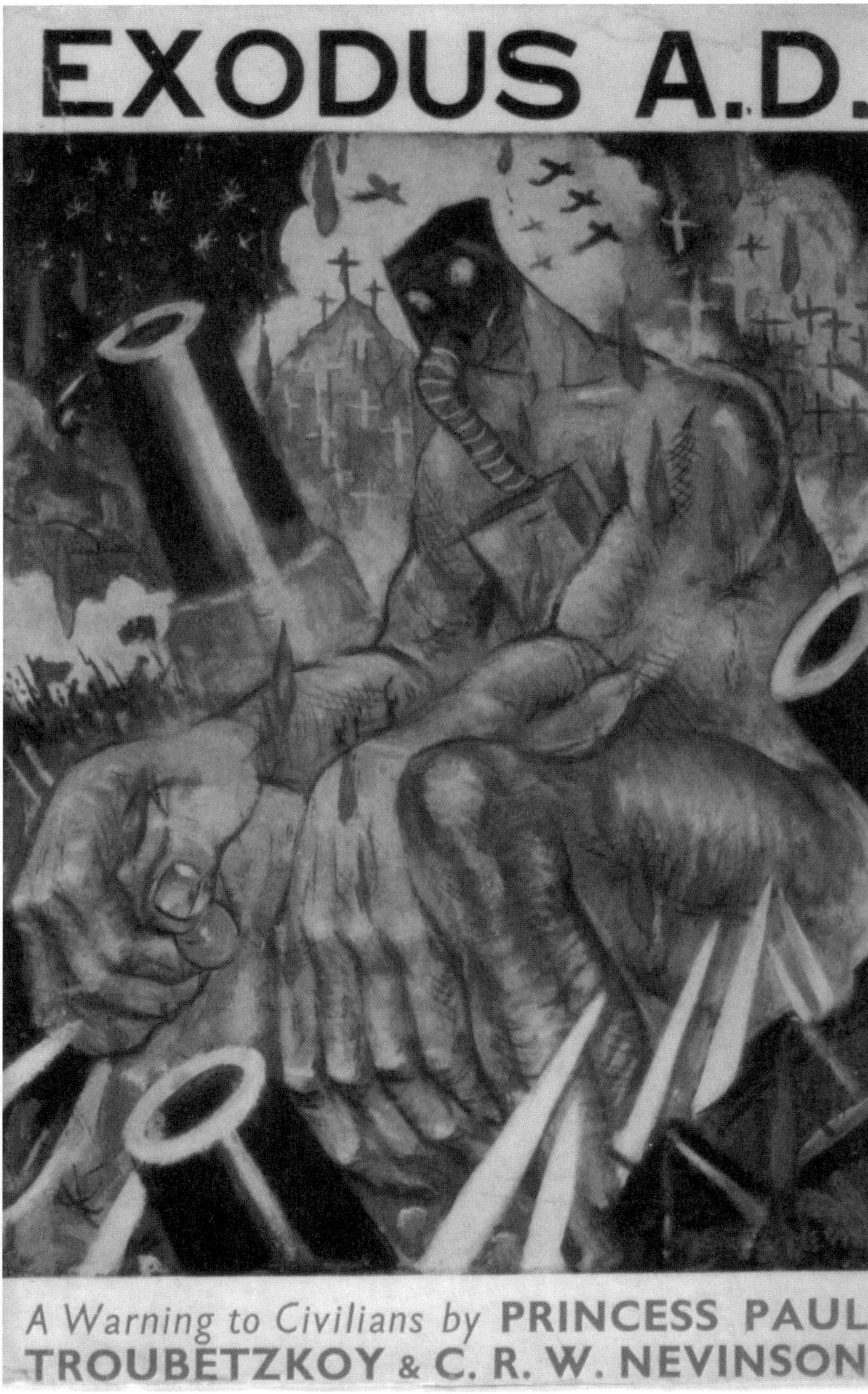

12. Dust wrapper illustration from *Exodus A.D., 1927*. Cambridge University Library.

great knotted arms hanging limply at His sides," peering through "wicked slits of a mask-like covering which protruded in a snout")[36] and the surrounding scene that he contemplates, is an exposition of the allegory sketched in the crude and garish version of Nevinson's *Homo Sapiens* reproduced on the cover, in which a gas-masked figure of God as Rodin's *Thinker* with gold coins dropping from his clenched hand is surrounded by emblems of crosses, gun barrels, dripping blood, and howling mobs (fig. 12). The epiphany of this God is intended to endow a transcendent dimension to the "modern" scene. In another dream, apparently the antithesis of this one, the idyll of the English countryside is evoked as a possible escape from this horrific modernity. The hero's beloved and he escape to her parents' farm from the universal hunger and destruction. But there is no escape, as there had seemed to be for Nevinson in his motor-caravan and in his "timeless" depictions of the English countryside. Her father and brother have become violent and predatory, and refuge is now impossible to find in rural life. Besides, it is only a dream, and she awakes alone in a ruined house in the suburbs. The wartime trauma that haunted Nevinson had returned as nightmare.

By the time these two artists wrote their autobiographies, then, it was as would-be activists who now realized their positions as outsiders with no prospect of influencing the events that had already shaped their time. Both autobiographies gesture at "warning" about the future, but the mood of both of them is nostalgic. The great strength of both of them is their anecdotes (in Lewis's case extended into vivid scenes of great artfulness, as in the famous account of his first meeting with James Joyce). Lewis consciously indulges in his realization that he is already building myths about his fellow men of 1914: "Even, people may ask themselves if such creatures ever in fact existed, or did not rather belong to the family of the phoenix, or if dragon-blood did not flow in their veins."[37] And, compared with the paranoid hysteria of his work of the thirties, Nevinson's autobiography also has a mellow clubmanesque tone.

This then was an ending: Lewis left the scene for the new world, to return to yet another fresh start. Nevinson, unluckier, would be prevented by his stroke from renewing himself as an artist. In histories of art Lewis has overshadowed his junior, but both faced similar artistic dilemmas, and the successes and failures of both men can be understood more fully when they are seen alongside each other, for both exemplify the fate of the English avant-garde in the first half of the twentieth century.

Notes

1. C. R. W. Nevinson, *Paint and Prejudice* (London: Methuen, 1937); Wyndham Lewis, *Blasting and Bombardiering* (London: Eyre & Spottiswoode, 1937).

2. *Evening Standard*, April 28, 1922.

3. Ian Jeffrey, "C. R. W. Nevinson: Artist Celebrity," in *C. R. W. Nevinson, 1889–1946: Retrospective Exhibition of Paintings, Drawings and Prints* (exhibition catalog; Cambridge: Kettle's Yard Gallery, n.d. [1988]), 60.

4. Neither of their careers actually ended in 1937, though Nevinson had only five more years before a stroke effectively put an end to his; Lewis, on the other hand, with his impressive ability to reinvent himself, after returning from his wartime "exile" in North America (where his lack of public success had consigned him to a more private role), renewed his public persona through a second autobiography very different from his first (*Rude Assignment: A Narrative of my Career Up-to-Date* [London: Hutchinson, n.d. (1950)]) and continued as a novelist, art critic, and literary critic, concluding his career with an appropriately controversial retrospective at the Tate in 1956, "Wyndham Lewis and Vorticism."

5. Princess Paul Troubetzkoy and C. R. W. Nevinson, *Exodus A.D.: A Warning to Civilians* (London: Hutchinson, n.d [1934]).

6. This is not to denigrate Nevinson's achievement as a printmaker; but his prints are not the vehicle of cultural comment.

7. *Blasting and Bombardiering*, 258.

8. For the documents relating to this break, see Quentin Bell and Stephen Chaplin, "The Ideal Home Rumpus," *Apollo* 80, no. 32 (October 1964): 284–91, and "Rumpus Revived," *Apollo* 83, no. 47 (January 1966): 78. Bell's and Chaplin's interpretation of the evidence, exonerating Fry from any impropriety, has been disputed most comprehensively by Jeffrey Meyers in *The Enemy: A Biography of Wyndham Lewis* (London: Routledge, 1980), 40–48.

9. The most "Futurist" of Lewis's works in the exhibition was the "Act I" watercolor from his *Timon* portfolio: *A Masque of Timon*. *Mother and Child* showed the influence of Boccioni's portraits of his mother (notably the study for *Empty and Full Abstracts of a Head* (1912), while *Creation* (a visual record of which has only recently been recovered) was clearly built on the Futurist premise that the force and energy of figures and machines in motion are best depicted through a breaking down of the integrity of the "material" bodies from which they emerge. See Paul Edwards, "Wyndham Lewis at the Second Post-Impressionist Exhibition: Reproductions of Three Lost Works," *Wyndham Lewis Annual* 9–10 (2002–3): 73–79.

10. "If a man is not representing people is he not representing clouds? If he is not representing clouds, is he not representing masses of bottles. . . . Or is he not representing in his most seemingly abstract paintings, mixtures of these, or of something else? Always REPRESENTING, at all events." Wyndham Lewis, "A Review of Contemporary Art" (1915), *Wyndham Lewis on Art*, ed. C. J. Fox and Walter Michel (London: Thames & Hudson, 1969), 68. The statement did not imply that representation was the primary mode through which painting creates meaning.

11. Wyndham Lewis, letter to Charles Handley-Read, September 2, 1949, *The Letters of Wyndham Lewis*, ed. W. K. Rose (London: Methuen, 1963), 504–5.

12. See Nevinson's account of Lewis's resentment of Marinetti's friendliness with him: *Paint and Prejudice*, 57.

13. For Gore's presence in Nevinson's work, see *The Railway Bridge, Charenton* (1911: Manchester City Art Gallery) and *St Ouen—Women Gardening* (n.d.—1913–14? private collection).

14. "The London Group," *Wyndham Lewis on Art*, 86.

15. Perhaps *The First Searchlights at Charing Cross* (1914; Leeds City Art Gallery), which, like his other searchlight paintings, reconciles Whistler with Vorticist geometric severity.

16. See "The London Group," 88.

17. See Jonathan Black, "A Curious, Cold Intensity: C. R. W. Nevinson as a War Artist, 1914–1918," Richard Ingleby et al., *C. R. W. Nevinson: The Twentieth Century* (exhibition catalog, London: Merrell Holberton in association with the Imperial War Museum, 1999), 34.

18. For my reading of the painting and a list of other discussions of it, see Paul Edwards, *Wyndham Lewis: Painter and Writer* (New Haven, CT: Yale University Press, 2000), 209–14 and 557–58, note 10.

19. Osbert Sitwell, *C. R. W. Nevinson* (London: Ernest Benn, 1925), 23, 24.

20. David Peters Corbett, *The Modernity of English Art, 1914–30* (Manchester, UK: Manchester University Press, 1997).

21. Preface for 1918 Leicester Galleries exhibition, quoted in *Paint and Prejudice*, 109.

22. See *The Modernity of English Art*, 152–57.

23. In the drawing from the painting, *War Profiteers* (1917; private collection) a seemingly arbitrary overlay of "cubist" disruption "confirms" the caricatural diagnosis of corruption. As the catalog entry in *C. R. W. Nevinson: The Twentieth Century* explains, "Nevinson appears to be exploiting a rich seam of public opinion" (120).

24. Wyndham Lewis, "Prevalent Design" (1919), repr., *Wyndham Lewis on Art*, 126–27.

25. "This deadness in Picasso, is partly due to the naturalistic method, of cubing on a posed model." "A Review of Contemporary Art," *Wyndham Lewis on Art*, 70.

26. For the significance of *A Reading of Ovid* see David Peters Corbett, " 'Grief with a Yard-Wide Grin': War and Wyndham Lewis's Tyros," in *Wyndham Lewis and the Art of Modern War*, ed. David Peters Corbett (Cambridge: Cambridge University Press, 1998), 119–21; for that of *Praxitella*, see Paul Edwards, "Wyndham Lewis and the *Rappel à l'ordre*: Classicism and Significant Form, 1919–21," in *The Geographies of Englishness: Landscape and the National Past 1880–1940*, ed. David Peters Corbett, Ysanne Holt, and Fiona Russell (New Haven, CT: Yale University Press, 2002), 162–63.

27. Wyndham Lewis, *The Caliph's Design: Architects! Where is your Vortex?* (1919), repr., *Wyndham Lewis on Art*, 164.

28. *Paint and Prejudice*, 154.

29. See Nigel Vaux Halliday, "The Identity of Wyndham Lewis's Painting at Group X," *Burlington Magazine* 1009 (April 1987): 245–47.

30. Wyndham Lewis, *Rude Assignment*, 184.

31. For a (sympathetic) reading of Lewis's work as an expression of paranoia, see David Trotter, *Paranoid Modernism: Literary Experiment, Psychosis, and the Professionalization of English Society* (Oxford: Oxford University Press, 2001).

32. For an analysis of this collapse, see Paul Edwards, *Wyndham Lewis: Painter and Writer*, 383–87.

33. Wyndham Lewis, *Wyndham Lewis the Artist: From "Blast" to Burlington House*, 19. See Andrew Causey, "Wyndham Lewis and History Painting in the later 1930s," in *Wyndham Lewis and the Art of War*, ed. David Peters Corbett, 155–80, and Paul Edwards, *Wyndham Lewis: Painter and Writer*, 428–31.

34. See note 4.

35. C. R. W. Nevinson, "What Next? No. V: Art in a Bellicose World," *Morning Post*, June 12, 1936.

36. *Exodus*, 145.

37. *Blasting and Bombardiering*, 257.

"A Veiled and Virgin Shore": C. R. W. Nevinson and the (end of an) American Dream

Michael J. K. Walsh

> An artist cannot be too aggressive. As I have often said, an artist should be a bellicose Jesus Christ: a man convinced of his mission and unashamed, with a song to sing, impossible to repress, and determined to be heard.

C.R.W. NEVINSON CATEGORICALLY STATED IN HIS autobiography *Paint and Prejudice* that the end of the Great War had brought with it the end of his war painting. The conflict over, his name made, and his place in the history of art assured, he now looked for alternatives to the subject matter that had brought this success but with which the public was now exhausted, if not repulsed. This was indeed a new challenge: what to do in a postwar world that wanted to hear no more of the four years of carnage that had just passed, and yet remain artistically loyal to his prewar, and war, modernist beliefs? Accordingly, Nevinson went in search of a positive modernity; a modern society that did not automatically associate development and invention with the devastation of Flanders and Picardy; somewhere that radicalism in thought, philosophy, and art could yet be associated with humanism and symbolize an intact, healthy, and progressive society. In short, somewhere that had not directly experienced the trauma of the war and that still looked to the future with excitement, pride, and optimism, very much as he had done in London in the months and years leading up to 1914. The answer clearly lay in New York City, untouched by war, imbued with a form of modern primitivism, and devoid of European cultural baggage, which had been described by Goethe as "vain and useless memories."[1] The destination was, as Barbara Haskell put it, "made for a new artistic language, barely intelligible to those invested in the sameness of the Old World."[2]

For C. R. W. Nevinson a fresh start was required in a dynamic, to say nothing of wealthy, environment where his name was well-known, but where his public was unfamiliar with his arguments and his enemies back in London. Besides, London and Paris would take quite some time to recover from the ordeal and subsequent stasis that both had just been through and to regain the momentum of their halcyon days, as Ezra Pound, T. S. Eliot, and Wyndham Lewis were discovering with their latest, not-yet-aborted X Group experiment. The London Group, alongside the New English Art Club, had almost completed its shift to the conservative "right," while Bloomsbury's dogged insistence on formalism, Nevinson believed, meant that art would have to be rescued from "the aphasia of an immoral *aesthesis*."[3] The Seven and Five Society was not even trying to disguise its contempt for the modernist experiments of the prewar, though Nevinson might have appreciated their call for individualism and their search for a positive modernity in the postwar world. London, in short, was not ready to move forward, even if Nevinson was. As he had embraced Futurism and then the war head-on, now he would turn to the New World for inspiration while the old world laboriously recovered from the latest bloody and destructive page if its history.

New York, on the other hand, boasted a youthful exuberance and confidence in which modern art must surely thrive—a relative tabula rasa with which Europe could not, at this time, compete. It would be erroneous, however, to assume that this was merely a wartime, or postwar, consequence of European crisis or that it was immune to many of the conservative Victorian ideologies so familiar in the old world.[4] But for sure there was a popular, ultramodern, forward-looking, niche not dissimilar to the one Nevinson had so neatly carved out back in London just before, and during, the war years. This was a chance to redefine both himself and his art, his image and his modernist beliefs, in a new environment where the momentum of his fame would carry him, while simultaneously liberating him from all previous, and now damaging, associations. Besides, *les transatlantiques* were becoming the set to know and *americanisme* appeared, in the postwar world, to be emerging as a viable alternative to Paris for bohemian chic.

As it happens Nevinson was no stranger to America and Americans. During his student days he had been aware of the great number of American artists studying in Paris and London and had come to respect both Wyndham Lewis (born in Canada) and Ezra Pound. He had submitted two paintings for inclusion in the Armory Show in New York City in 1913, but these had been rejected.[5] Undaunted, he had used American themes and names for some of his most daring Futurist compositions such as *Waiting for the Robert E. Lee* (named after a popular ragtime tune by Lewis F. Muir) and the sculpture *Une Americaine*. At the outbreak of war in 1914, Nevinson had been invited by agent Arthur Pond to tour the United States lecturing on Futurism, supporting the lonesome pronouncements of André Tridon who had been fighting for an American Futurism since 1911, but the invitation was turned down.[6] During the war years too, contact with the "new world" was not entirely severed as he had become friends with Joseph Pennell and this had brought him into contact with reproductions of some of America's most dynamic artists and photographers whose work he would otherwise have been very unlikely to see. By the war's end he would have been familiar with the images of Alden Weir, George Bellows, Childe Hassam, Paul Strand, Alfred Stieglitz, and Alvin Langdon Coburn (a signatory of the second Vorticist Manifesto 1915), among others. The decision to go there as soon as the war ended was very clearly neither impulsive, nor spontaneous, but logical.

But if England's most celebrated artist was to turn away from "the old country" it was not to be done with a whimper, and in no way was it to be seen as the defensive action of an artist caught in a retreating tide of popularity, or worse, scuttling away from reemerging, would-be competitors. Accordingly, he ensured that press reports were making their way across the Atlantic, preparing the route for a celebrity visit and a welcome that he believed an artist of his stature deserved. In London too, a going away dinner was held in his honor at the Café Royal, organized by Grant Richards and chaired by Walter Sickert, at which about sixty people were present.[7] His father's diary entry reads: "Then Richard spoke and read a long defensive offensive as to his position in art against narrow cliques + little sets who try to scorn and reject him as successful. Many of the words & illustrations were daring and violent: but the general effect fine and powerful."[8]

The press reported more fully on his "fiery and warlike response" saying that it was worthy of Marinetti himself, in which he proclaimed absolute freedom from all groups and ideologies, against which he was happy to declare war if they would not respect his autonomy. Other papers published a summary of his speech or extracts, which reported his attack on the Bloomsburies as "little Revolutionary groups in art which call themselves free, yet tyrannise their members into one formulated expression and turn themselves into narrow little academic societies."[9] Interestingly, one notable report in London stated "I see that a farewell dinner is to be given to Mr Nevinson before his departure to New York. I wonder whether he is going to be feasted by his erstwhile colleagues of the advance guard in art, or by his future fellow-members of the Royal Academy."[10] Though tongue-in-cheek, Nevinson would have noted how notoriety had brought with it implications of conservatism in the extreme so that, in effect, he was stylistically adrift at the time of his departure from Southampton dock.

Years later Nevinson wrote of his first impressions of this electric, yet human world, which was brilliant and alluring in all its modernity, and at the same time sinister and unconquered: "Then came New York. It was a wonderful morning, with some of the skyline in the mist and the higher towers jutting out of it in clear silhouette. Much as I love Venice, I was overjoyed by that glimpse of beauty New York gave me as we made our way up from Staten Island to the docks."[11] In the first of a series of lengthy articles devoted to his work, the New York-based *Evening Post* presented a generous two-page spread that let the artist speak for himself. Here he got to work in recreating the modern master, though decided to place the emphasis on his military and "unaffiliated" pedigree, rather than positioning himself too firmly in any camp—either to the "radical left" or to the "conservative right." Instead he turned to the identity of the patriot, the youthful rebel, the lone intellectual, the victimized genius, and the artist who had turned down a captaincy in the British army for the benefits of access that only a freelance could have. America's introduction was to the daring artist who had had his vehicle blown up on the front line as he drove it; to the survivor of an attack on a balloon in which he was sketching high above the western front; to the heroic individual who had dragged back the body of a comrade in arms from no-man's-land; and to the patriot who had done almost two years unbroken service as a motor mechanic. Betrayed only by his health, the fabrication continued, he had convalesced, then returned immediately to service so that by the war's end he could say he had been at Ypres at the beginning, had flown over Cambrai at the dawn of the great offensive in 1917, and had witnessed the German collapse at St. Quentin in 1918. There was no greater miracle, he could declare, than his own survival. In another article later in the month Nevinson was described as an artist who, in the front line of the great offensives, "hunted at night" and received numerous "invitations to commit suicide."[12] His legend introduced, he signed off at the end of the article by pricking the American conscience, blaming them for not having seen this artistic opportunity and, even now, for failing to acknowledge the genius of their own John Singer Sargent and his masterpiece *Gassed.* Indeed Eugene Gallatin (who in the same year wrote *Art and the Great War* in which Nevinson was championed) had reprimanded the American artistic community for precisely the same thing in a lecture at the College Art Association, saying that even the Australians had not failed to materialize on the opportunity.[13] Nevinson was quick to talk of ambitious schemes to bring the Canadian and British memorial exhibitions to New York, which he envisaged would require the use of Madison Square Garden, such would be the enormity of the show.[14] As a rearguard action, principally in case America was suffering the same anti-modernist tendency that was now rife in England, Nevinson also made sure that his painting, and his artistic stance, was modified to that of a "practical modernist."[15] And perhaps this was not a bad strategy as the *New York City Herald* ran an article which declared that, whatever his prewar allegiances, he had now "recovered from Futurism."[16] Safe, perhaps, but hardly the image required to thrust him to the fore of the New York experiment he was now proposing to lead. Nonetheless, the press could applaud the man, replete with Mons Star on lapel, and declare: "There is no other living artist who is so equipped as he is to show the inhabitants of this city what an interesting place they are living in."[17] The self-portrait presented was that of an interesting and eye-catching survivor; the sort who might now, relieved of the onerous baggage of conflict, thrive in the modern marvel of Manhattan.

In fact, the American press gushed a little too much and in so doing may have catalyzed the first antagonisms between himself and the New York, and former European, modernists who would soon be his outright enemies. Speaking of him and his work in the same breath as Holbein, Hokusai, Courbet, and Whistler, the admiring editor of the *Sun* got to work placing him on a pedestal that contemplated possible failure only through the ignorance of the public.[18] Others positioned him in a politically dangerous association with Bolshevik Europe[19] simply on the grounds that it represented the sort of dynamism that would attract a man of his standing, especially here in Trotsky's "city of prose and fantasy."[20] This comparison, at the time of the Red Scare and the Palmer raids, was far from helpful. When Hamilton Easter Field (with whom he had dinner at the Bankers Club on the top floor of the Equitable Building) concluded his article with the statement "Nevinson is a master" there could have been little doubt that the red (though not politically) carpet had been rolled out and that Nevinson had only to turn up to ensure that the next stage of his career was off to the kind of dynamic start to which he had become accustomed.[21]

But the New York avant-garde did not require the paternal guidance of this young and eye-catching Englishman, who seemed only to mimic the earlier pronouncements of European émigrés. Francis Picabia, they recalled, had "discovered" their city in 1913 and declared "Your New York is the cubist, the futurist, city. It expresses in its architecture its life, its spirit, the modern thought. . . ."[22] Nevinson's "discovery," therefore, was really no discovery at all in their opinion, but the act of a charlatan riding in on the European coattails of the real pioneers such as Marcel Duchamp, Albert Gleizes, and Elie Nadelman, who had already reinvented their bohemia in the Hotel Breevort in Greenwich Village (from 1915), and been afforded their deserved welcome by the American artistic elites such as the Arsenbergs, Dreiers, and Stettheimers. The Society of Independent Artists, 291 and the *Societe Anonyme* were already flourishing thanks, in Apollinaire's opinion, to the "missionaries" who had dared to cross the Atlantic long before Nevinson. But somehow their imperial, perhaps aloof, attitude had been tolerated and even welcomed as an education, not least as these foreigners had chosen to live in the city that was becoming the focus of their work. Nevinson's attitude did not follow suit. Neither did he appear to wish to learn anything from the city and its inhabitants, coming across instead as the altruistic missionary in the midst of an uncultured mob.

Nevinson liked to speak for himself too, and in an interview in the *New York Times Magazine* he got off to a positive start, reiterating the distance between himself and the macabre, and from the war in which a hundred thousand American "doughboys" had died. He declared, "Having lived among scrap heaps, having seen miles of destruction day after day, month after month, year after year, they are longing for a complete change. We artists are sick of destruction in art. We want construction." He emphasized this hatred of the negative consequences of modernity, saying "the effect of the war has been to create among artists an extraordinary longing to get static again. Having been dynamic since 1912 they are now utterly tired of chaos."[23] Besides, he did not want to be seen as cashing in on, or benefiting inappropriately from, what in the end was the tragedy of others less fortunate than himself, and on a war that many Americans had yet to be convinced had been their war at all. But if the implication augured the end of the artist's extreme modernist vocabulary and with it the war subject, it did not however, in his view, mean the end of the experimentation with modernity on the whole. On the contrary he was returning to the basic modernist ideology of industry, invention, the city, and joy-in-the-modern, which had been expostulated during the radical prewar days. His attitudes now echoed the words of Marcel Duchamp, who had declared from his new home in New York City, "if only America would realise that the art of Europe is dead—and that America is the country of the art of the future."[24] Nevinson might even have shared the sentiments of Alfred Stieglitz too, who famously described the new modernity as "America without that damned French flavor!"[25]

Then, through a series of very high-profile speeches, he made a fatal error. Whereas Eugene Gallatin had talked Nevinson up at the College Art Association in May 1919, the Englishman himself got to work later in the week at the American Federation of Artists, then later at the Society of Independent Artists at the Waldorf-Astoria where over two hundred artists were present. The latter had as members, and some of whom may therefore have been present: John Sloan (President), Robert Henri, Marcel Duchamp, Man Ray, George Bellows, and Joseph Stella, to name but a few from the pantheon of American art. Perhaps remembering the manner in which his old mentor Marinetti had come to London before the war, or perhaps riding on the back of his own polemical outbursts during the war years, Nevinson surprisingly, and unnecessarily, went on the attack. The outrageous sentiments were repeated and intensified in a further lecture delivered at the Kevorkian Gallery (40 West Fifty-Seventh Street) entitled "Art as a National Asset" where reporters had gathered, determined not to be caught off guard again. Here Nevinson not only read the old Futurist Manifesto, but reiterated what had previously been leaked to the press, stating that Americans were "splendid painters, but no artists." He distanced his audience further by saying that "It was with horror that I found artists in America a thing apart and of little importance" and then finally, plunged the knife with "The impression I have thus far gained of the American public is one of mental sterility."[26] Comments like this had been made before, not least in Duchamp and Roche's publication *Blind Man*, which had chided "For the average New Yorker art is only a thing of the past. Is New York afraid? Does New York not dare to take new responsibilities in Art? Where art is concerned is New York satisfied to be like a provincial town?"[27] But Duchamp had, at least, just suffered the humiliation of having *Fountain* rejected from a juryless exhibition and was, as a resident of the city, to some extent qualified to make such an assertion. But for Nevinson, recently arrived and an outsider, to throw down the gauntlet in true Marinettian manner from his bastion in the National Arts Club was arrogant, and ill informed, in the extreme.[28] Little wonder James Montgomery Flagg could write in the *Pittsburgh Gazette* "Don't you think your remarks were at least tactless and at most gratuitously insulting?"[29] Scarcely in the United States a week Nevinson was snatching defeat from the jaws of victory as his path to celebrity and prosperity had seemed virtually assured. Letters in his defense by painter and modern art collector Eugene Gallatin could not stop the rot and the positive impact of his earlier work was now being undone before his highly publicized Keppels show had even opened.[30] Neither could a series of hasty press reports (closely linked to his father's literary friends in the city) redress the balance, even when their adjectives to describe him, and by implication his attacks, turned to innocence as opposed to maliciousness, particularly when he was described as being availed with a "virgin mind and a boyish enthusiasm."[31] Almost two decades later, and by then an outspoken anti-American, he griped in his autobiography "Americans have no sense of humour, and as I was later to find out they took this Shavian joke in dead earnest." He further remarked, "Never had I come across so few intellectual people, yet that tiny minority was more first-rate than any circle I have discovered in Europe."[32]

Horace Brodzky, Joseph Pennell, and Charles Lewis Hind were all exempt from the sweeping criticism. So too John Quinn was an exception and a man with whom Nevinson said he enjoyed passing time on his visit. As he had been one of Nevinson's earliest patrons he was accepted as a man of learning and of taste, especially as his private collection included Picasso, Derain, Matisse, Kandinsky, Yeats, Gertler, and John. Had Nevinson known the contents of a recently discovered letter from Quinn to old enemy Wyndham Lewis back in London, he may not have been so comfortable. The letter confirmed that Nevinson had come to visit, but cast a slightly different light on the experience. In it Quinn said that Nevinson had stayed for a few hours, talked a good deal about himself, and had not really seen much of the collection. He observed, "I do not really think that he does have a feeling for the best art." He then went on to say that he had shown him a couple of late Matisse paintings and a few by Walt Kuhn, but that he had not shown any particular interest or appreciation of them. The letter then got down to the crux of the matter saying, "He seems to realize that the war and the post-bellum art exhibitions have given him a real chance. I have the feeling that he knows that he has not the real stuff but that he wants to cash-in and make big sales now while there is a market for war stuff." He also could not help but comment upon the onslaught in the press and the legend Nevinson was building around his own name: "he told about making sketches while sitting on the side of a flying machine, with the shells bursting all around. The damned thing was nauseating and the conceit of it was most amusing . . . Nevinson's vanity was really bad taste." Finally Quinn got down to it saying "America did not 'swell' Nevinson as an advanced artist" and claimed that it was only the sort of people who collected the works of Whistler, Strang, Lavery, and Sargent who may have been guilty. The real artists "sized him up very quickly as a journalist and a self-exploiter."[33] There would have been those back in London who would have readily agreed.

Eugene Gallatin was another such exception to the scythe-like sweep Nevinson had made of New York art personalities. He became a friend and confidant, writing letters to the press, supervising at least one exhibition in absentia and composing influential articles defending his English friend long after the latter had returned to London.[34] He also wrote the introduction for the exhibition at Keppel's entitled "Etchings and Lithographs by C. R. W. Nevinson," which promoted Nevinson as one of Britain's "most vigorous and original painters," while stating, rather hypothetically, that no American, not even John Marin, could have painted the way he had done on the western front.[35] The style of the work, seen throughout the forty-one works exhibited, was described as "a compromise between Futurism and illustration," but once again included the key Futurist words "dynamic," "synthesis," and "abstraction." More than anything it was "free from all music-hall and journalistic heroics," which may have been a swing at Charles Demuth, Stuart Davis, and Marsden Hartley. First and foremost his work aimed to harness the energy of youth, freedom, and the benefits of industry and efficiency to an art that could yet be devoid of tradition and irrelevant European taste. Indeed the show did demonstrate a profound diversity of images, from the first year of the conflict through to the last, utilizing both "freelance" and "official" styles. Strong pieces such as *Returning to the Trenches* and *Flooded Trench on the Yser* were offset against literary pieces such as *That Cursed Wood*.[36] Aviation themes, and even some non-war subjects such as *Wet Evening, Oxford Street*, were also hung.[37] The autonomy and diversity that he had fought so hard for was certainly on display at the show that introduced him to the United States, and the actual images were well received. The controversy that he, not his art, had created, however, led to a destructive and unnecessary storm that would rage long after his departure.

At the end of his visit Horace Brodzky, resident in New York and a mutual friend through the late Gaudier-Brzeska, advised him "You've made good here, and they seem to like you. Beat it and get away with it, and don't come back. I know these New Yorkers."[38] Nevinson obliged and sailed on the *Aquatania* following "probably the most extraordinary month ever lived by an artist."[39] Later, a journalist for an English paper could report, "Anyway, if he could hear the things they say about him now he would not be so keen to come back in the autumn as he was when he left America the day after that speech was made."[40]

Nevinson returned home to find that his infant son, whom he had never known, had died in his absence. Neither did he find any reprieve from his enemies in London and later recorded "Still the intelligentsia were showing me every form of hostility and contempt, and when I returned to London I found social life impossible. Everywhere I went I was wounded or driven to fury through some cheap insult from some superior Bloomsbury or an aesthetic bohemian."[41]

More importantly, it was becoming painfully clear that while he found himself still to the fore in any discussion concerning war and the depiction of it, he had slipped very much to the periphery of discussions on the future of art in postwar Britain. Little wonder then his attention soon turned back across the Atlantic where, by now, he must have been regretting the nature of the first impressions he had created. Guaranteed press coverage in the United States with every utterance he would now make as a result of his infamy, he realized the need to undo the damage, redress the balance, and get to work actually producing some paintings that might, in themselves, silence the critics. He had, after all, only introduced New York to the old Nevinson—the war painter. Now, full of inspiration, memories, experiences, and presumably sketchbooks, he could tackle what very few other British artists had ever attempted.[42] There was still time to put things right as he had not directly competed with American artists nor tried to beat them at their own game in anything other than rhetoric. First he attempted to cool the situation, or avert further disaster, by gradually renaming some of his more high-profile work to take the sting out of the anti-American comments he had previously confidently made. Slowly but surely the acerbic insinuations inherent in compositions such as *War Profiteers* were diluted with altered names as bland as *Two Women*. By doing so, he deflected the implication that Americans got rich by sitting on the fence until the penultimate year of the war to Spain and the

Spanish who had not got involved at all. Little did his public realize that he had attempted to move to Spain in 1917 to avoid a most unwelcome return to the western front. *Broadway Patriotism* was also renamed *Team Work of the Cabaret* neutralizing an otherwise harmless piece and returning this picture to a safer time when the public had welcomed the dance hall scenes of himself and Severini.[43] He also leaned on Gallatin again to try and redress the deteriorating situation with Montgomery Flagg sending a letter to the former saying, "He absolutely misquotes me & on this misquotation attacks me. If you happen to know the gentleman I shall be very glad if you will give him a slightly different opinion of me & inform him that I am not the type of man to gratuitously insult Americans, especially after the amazing kindness I received in New York & that I know my manners quite as well as he does."[44] Nevinson would have been aware that he had made a mistake, though it is entirely consistent with his character that he would have felt this as part of a persecution campaign whereby he was being unjustly treated.

Fresh reports and interviews in Boston and in New York City on the artist's possible return upped the ante in the press, reiterating his old attitude, "I am Nevinson and you can all go to blazes."[45] Talking in his absence they advised the American public to watch out for a man who, whatever medium he worked in, was clear-eyed, cynical, sensitive to beauty, sensitive to humor, and already a legend for a good reason in Europe. Like him or loathe him, he would be back, only this time armed with images of New York.

On top of everything else, new problems were arising with the touring exhibition organized by the Worcester Art Museum, Massachusetts, in conjunction with the British Ministry of Information. Here, a very large collection of British war art, already assembled and on show, was booked for the next two years to travel around the United States, and this included some key paintings by Nevinson, which he now realized he needed if he were ever to get back to New York to create a powerful exhibition. Like Sir William Orpen, he requested them to be pulled off the tour, but this was refused. Raymond Wyer who had organized the American tour, argued quite reasonably that Detroit, Boston, Cincinnati, Chicago, Cleveland, and Buffalo had all been promised the full catalog, and that to take out key pieces would dilute the overall effect. Nevinson was less than sympathetic and demanded them through the solicitors Rosenberg & Ball of Broadway. He wrote to Gallatin, "Who ever signed this contract (if it exists) had no right to sign away my property—as definitively stated by H.M. Government when sent to N.Y.—& I refuse to be bound by a contract I never was party to. If the Worcester Art Galleries still have the audacity to stick to my work I shall have to come to America earlier than I intended, find the show & cut out my property from their frames as all my pictures and prints were my personal property & for sale."[46] In the end the show was closed down early anyway and returned to the United Kingdom, except for Nevinson's work, which was sent directly to New York City in time for his opening. But the artist observed the temperature rising among artists and critics alike and wrote "they are just beginning to find their jaundiced spittle, I expect to be drenched soon."[47]

Conveniently, at the same time, Nevinson's father was in New York, assessing the damage done by the Kervorkian speech and the Worcester Galleries debacle, and analyzing the deteriorating climate for his son's return. At the Bourgeois Galleries where the second show was to take place, he also saw the work of Joseph Stella and pitched the degree of modernist, even Futurist, vision that New York seemed to be accepting. He saw too the work of another painter by the name of Alfred Wolmark whom he perceived as being a "serious rival to Rich. espec. in his imaginative pictures of N. York."[48] In haste he wrote to his son, who was sufficiently confident to blast Wolmark, ironically, for possessing "ignorance, arrogance and egoticism."[49] On his departure from the United States, Henry Nevinson wrote, "Good-bye to frequent and well appointed bathrooms, glory of the plumber's art!" Though innocuous in intent, his son would soon pilfer, then modify, this simple statement to imply that the American idea of art was a "well appointed bathroom" with their Raphael being a plumber. Perhaps Nevinson was trying to move closer to Marcel Duchamp, who had exhibited *Fountain* (a urinal) in 1917, and in so doing brought plumbing and art into an uncomfortable coexistence, but if this is what he was aiming for, few got the point.

And here, once again, Nevinson made a fateful strategic error. Why take images of New York to New York? Why believe that a brief European glance at New York, superficial to those who lived there, would appeal to those who daily scratched beneath the impressive veneer? Would not the whole point of painting this marvel of modernity be to show it to those for whom it would be a novelty and the source of awe and intrigue? No wonder he described the whole idea in a letter to Gallatin as "a horrible gamble."[50] Perhaps the most worrying trait of all, however, in the months leading up to the second visit to the United States was that his work was being described by those who got early glimpses of it as mild and insipid, employing none of the vision and vocabulary that had propelled him into the spotlight in the first place. Even his staunchest ally, his father, noted with concern that the images of the stock exchange were far from dynamic, and now, increasingly so, bearing slightly aggressive or condescending titles again such as *Dollar Worshippers*. Interestingly, his Futurist masterpiece of 1914, *The Arrival*, updated with the addition of the words "New York," made another appearance, six years after it had been painted. This had been, and seemingly still was, Nevinson at his most radical, and only served to identify how far behind the New York artists he had already slipped.[51] An image that may have been iconic in prewar London was barely noticeable in postwar New York.

Just before his departure he opened his studios at 9 Robert Street, London, to the public in a preview of what was to be taken to the United States. H. G. Wells, William Rothenstein, and Violet Tree were typical of the celebrity presence, and journalists from both sides of the Atlantic proliferated. They reported that the show was "Skyscraper Art by a Champion"[52] while Nevinson proclaimed again that the skyscraper itself was America's contribution to art. He had staked £1000 on the venture, which at that point represented everything he had, but this time it was to be a catastrophic loss.

The American papers were full of Nevinson's visit from before he left the shores of Britain, and read by the American public which braced itself for the second coming of this great, though abrasive, artist. Nevinson started well, claiming that "Today New York for the artist is the most fascinating city in the world. She is like a young woman, splendid in the unconscious strength of her compelling beauty. Cold and hard, perhaps, but only as youth always is. She doesn't sooth the nerves: she stimulates to action. Her abounding vitality is a constant challenge." So far so good. New York he believed was the rightful heir to Venice as the world's most beautiful, dynamic, and technically bewildering city. The skyscraper would also be described as "the most vivid art works of the day," being the epitome of utility, efficiency, man's achievement, and the spirit of the age. Then, as always, in praising someone or something, he felt the need to put others, by comparison, down. This time Paris was called the "grande marquise" who had learned the hollowness of laughter from bitter experience, while London was "a sensible old housewife who goes to bed early [and] has few aspirations."[53] Likewise, the actual appearance of New York (unlike Washington, which he described as purely imitative of Europe) made London appear in its dotage and Paris, by comparison, dull. The "stormy petrel," as he was described in a South Carolina paper, was back, only this time saying what his audience wanted to hear.

His exhibition, entitled "The Old World and the New," opened at Bourgeois Galleries, 668 Fifth Avenue, on November 4, 1920, and was introduced by Charles Lewis Hind, who had been carefully guided in what he was to write by Nevinson himself. He had been warned to reiterate the familiar call to be disassociated from "any possible clique, school, ist, ism, post, neo, pro, anit, academic, un-academic, conventional or unconventional" and this was firmly in keeping with what Robert Coady had preached several years before when he had despaired "Our new men are the 'ismists' who are more interested in theories than art. None of this is American; none of it has come from the soil."[54] Nevinson, like Coady, was pleading for individuality and subjectivity to triumph over everything else, and backed this up by saying that the subject should always dictate the method; "I maintain it is impossible to use the same means to express the flesh of a woman and the ferro-concrete of a sky-scraper." Individuality and self-critical introspection, he maintained, made artistic survival possible, and was certainly preferable to an unflinching adherence to formalism. Art was once again referred to as "virile" as he put down, one last time, the "slimy" salon and academies of old Europe.[55] Lewis Hind therefore could sign off the "Introduction" of sixty-seven oil paintings and thirty-one prints with confidence, "It is something, at the age of thirty one, to be among the most discussed, most successful, most promising, most admired and most hated British artists."[56] The gallery-goer might then have flicked to the back of the catalog to read the artist's own contribution entitled "My Art Creed." Here old arguments resurfaced in new clothes in a statement which was signed "Nevinson—living artist. Devoted to art, past and present, alive to contemporary civilization and barbarity." Nothing in this would have met the slightest resistance from the New York avant-garde, though there were surely some serious doubts that his work could live up to such proclamations and hype.

For a moment American critics seemed to be falling for Nevinson for exactly the same reasons the British had in 1916; namely his moderate approach (in painting if not in words), which was being received as the "sanest modernism."[57] In the *Evening Post* he was heralded as "a man with an idea . . . an artist of a new generation" though it ought to be mentioned that this was in an error-ridden article that praised Roger Fry as the head of the prewar Futurist movement in London; which accredited Nevinson with starting the Rebel Arts Centre with a certain N. Windham (*sic*) Lewis and highlighted that the only artist he had not fallen out with was a M. Matise Severini. Regardless, the writer enjoyed the idea that Americans had created "the mother of all art" in terms of high-rise architecture, stripped of aesthetic and retrospective devices such as Gothic detailing, and Nevinson was happy to play along. Versatility, variety, and adaptability seemed to be adjectives applied to his work in place of alternatives which might have talked of inconsistency or artistic meandering in pursuit of public acclaim. More serious and specialized journals expressed a note of concern, however, and demonstrated that they were not blinded with the high-publicity declarations of the new arrival. Instead they warned "his admirers should sound a note of caution, for it must be confessed that despite this versatility and undoubted ability, the present display gives somewhat an impression of a youthful ardor still floundering around and groping, if forcibly, for a more safe and surer pathway to success." The article finished on a grave note reiterating the charge that had dogged Nevinson for years when it read "but in the writer's humble opinion, he has yet to find himself."[58]

In late November 1920, Nevinson was asked to speak at the National Arts Club Grille with Frank Dilnot (editor of the *London Globe*) on their experiences in Czechoslovakia. In small print after Nevinson's name the invitation also said "and possibly of America." No one would have forgotten the stir he had caused on his first visit through his outrageous and discourteous remarks, and this would have attracted the critics and the would-be detractors who must surely have been waiting in the wings to get the story, if not revenge. Perhaps the bristles had begun to show in a review of the artist's work in the *Tribune*, which finished by picking up Lewis Hind's introduction that said he was also among the "most hated" artists in Britain today. Dismissively they trivialized that assertion with the line "for there is nothing really serious enough to inspire hard feelings"—a barbed remark, well camouflaged in mild compliments.[59] The *Nation* too talked about "a boyish swagger and eagerness to be understood" which was not an unpleasant or aggressive observation, but hardly displayed reverence.[60]

Nevinson's America, on display at the gallery, represented the urban modernity of F. Scott Fitzgerald, the flapper, and the speakeasy. He had made no effort to embrace or address the rural or the poor; the revival of the Ku Klux Klan; the Red Scare; the myopia of the Scopes Trial; the prohibition of alcohol or the hideousness of immigration and tariff laws. He had paid no attention to the political isolationism that led to the League of Nations starting life without the United States, nor concerned himself with the abuse of capitalism that saw so much of the nation's wealth find its way into the pockets of so few of its citizens. His was the world of jazz, of the city, and of the liberated, and voting, femme fatale, and "It" girl. His was the intoxicated, youthful, and wealthy white America, so prevalent on the cinema screens and on electronic advertisement hoardings which boosted commercialism and consumerism, and took joy in doing so. And his was the modern appearance of New York City, from the streets, from the Hudson River, from the rooftops, and from the pedestrian's perspective.

But this had been done before and many of Nevinson's images from New York City gravitated directly toward those already known at that time. Karl Struss had created powerful images from under the Brooklyn Bridge, while Joseph Stella had said of it, "It impressed me as the shrine containing all the efforts of the new civilization of AMERICA—the eloquent meeting of all forces arising in a superb assertion of their powers, in APOTHEOSIS."[61]

Nevinson made this modern icon the focus of one of his most dynamic and impressive prints *Looking Through Brooklyn Bridge*, but he should have made no claim to being either the first or the best at doing so. Other views of the city from the Hudson, as seen in Nevinson's *New York by Night*, harped back to Edward Willis Redfield's *Brooklyn Bridge at Night* (1909), or to Jonas Lie's *Paths of Gold* (1915); and scenes from the bars and the clubs had more than a hint of George Luks in them from almost two decades before. Jospeph Stella had talked about "your temples dedicated to commerce" and had tackled "The White Way" as a subject, which Nevinson aped with compositions bearing identical names. Charles Sheeler had made much of aerial perspectives from the top of skyscrapers, as Nevinson would do, and John Marin had captured the sheer dynamism of the city, which Nevinson hardly even attempted. In fact, Nevinson seemed to have returned to an urban theme, employing a technique last seen almost a decade before in his Slade days, and had virtually erased the legacy of prewar and war modernism from his palette entirely.

Frank Rutter argued that the acerbic insinuations had not entirely disappeared either in works such as *The Temples of New York*, where the spire of Trinity Church was dwarfed by the newly emerging skyscrapers at the head of Wall Street, mirroring the spiritual decline and the rise of the dollar worshipper. Nevinson's comment on the material and financial values of modern America, which had benefited so considerably from the Great War, were also echoed in *The Statue of Liberty* (viewed from the top of the New York Railroad Club which was, in turn, replaced by the Twin Towers of the World Trade Center) where the subject was almost completely out of sight. This beacon of light for millions, for the "huddled masses," was now almost entirely obscured with modern architecture that symbolized capitalism and that offered little or no liberty for communists, Catholics, immigrants, or African Americans.

Perhaps his own isolation was augured in the unpeopled cityscape *New York—An Abstraction*, which in itself had structural similarities to Stella's *The Voice of the City of New York Interpreted; The Skyscraper* or Stieglitz's photograph *The Hand of Man*. The title would soon be changed, in the wake of his New World defeat, to *Soul of a Soulless City*, whereby the literary sentiment in the title was borrowed from Marx who wrote of "the opium of the masses, the heart of a heartless world, soul of soulless conditions."[62] He later maintained in his autobiography that the classic film *Metropolis* had been inspired by this work, even if he mistakenly claimed that the film had been directed by Stromberg. His images are also more than coincidentally similar to stills from *Manhatta*, a film made in 1920 by Paul Strand and Charles Sheeler.

It was not long before Nevinson accepted that he was not going to make any significant impact in postwar New York City and admitted that the position of prominence afforded him by the war in London was not going to be recaptured here in the New World. Of course he glossed over it in his autobiography almost two decades later, and admitted that the whole second show had been a flop, due to other people, unfortunate circumstances, and bad luck. The trouble had started, he wrote, in the Café Royal in London, where somebody claiming to be him had given a full interview to an American journalist for the price of a dinner. The fraud had said some lively things that had traveled across the Atlantic before him and so hostility awaited him from the moment he arrived. Secondly, an elevator boy in New York, charged with the job of stamping and posting the invitations to the show, had stolen the cash and binned the invitations resulting in an "absolutely empty private view."[63] And lastly, and with typical Nevinsonian pomp, he said the real problem lay in the jealousy of the New York artists, who were galled that this Englishman was not only the first, but the best, artist to tackle the wonder of *their* city.

In reality Nevinson probably suffered from a variety of events. Perhaps he was caught in the brief downturn in the US economy "due to the strange, panicky, neurasthenic condition of last year's wealthy Americans, who, not content with the gold of Europe on their shoulders, still whined of poverty in their concrete palaces."[64] He might have gotten the idea from John Quinn, who had written to him, and sympathetically this time, offering his condolences saying "You, unluckily, have against your exhibition what is almost a panic in the country, at least a panic in the stock market and also in the commodity market . . . It may be [a] consolation to you that you have been, more or less, a pioneer or prospector, in holding your exhibition here and pioneers and prospectors do not always strike it rich first time."[65] Another possibility is that Nevinson had become caught up in the anti-Britishness which was brewing in the East Coast cities of the United States in response to Lloyd George's handling of the Irish bid for independence at, and after, Versailles. Or, perhaps, the art simply was not good enough, and had been outplayed by a New York avant-garde that felt had nothing to learn from him, and as a result of his arrogance did not feel inclined to humor him. The end of the American experiment was wound up in his autobiography with the statement, "I was treated as though I had some form of infectious disease" and so left for England "second class, with Italian emigrants, wounded, disappointed, insulted."[66]

But it was not in Nevinson's character to take this lying down. Instead he embarked on a lifetime of derogatory comments about the United States, its inhabitants and the total inability of art to survive there. In fact he had got to work on burning his bridges immediately after his arrival back in London, and his first target was the editor of the *Sun*.

> Dear Old Mr McBride
>
> Since my return to civilization, I have received a cutting about my show in New York written by you. I write to thank you for carefully avoiding any mention of criticism of my paintings and for merely confining yourself to a peevish outburst against an unclaimed and unfounded ambition for world fame. I admit I have exhibited in the Holy City of God's own country but I can assure you it was only at the invitation of dealers & not even they or wild horses would drag me over there again to be insulted by yapping chauvinists & bragging boosters.
>
> I admit in my case I unknowingly infuriated the "citizens" because I had painted the holy city & American painters hardly at all. No wonder Whistler, Sargent, Abbey, Shannan, Epstein etc prefer London & we do not insult painters *because* they came from other cities—God what a people. However, I can assure you I do not seek world fame I merely wish to paint a good picture (& sell if possible) but I would sooner show my pictures to the Sahara desert or the restless waves of the Atlantic than again to the neurotic, jaded inhabitants of your so-called "young country"
>
> Good bye "Old Man"
>
> Yours sincerely
>
> Young Nevinson[67]

Frank Rutter was also perplexed at the failure as he felt that the reason Nevinson would be attracted to, then inspired by, New York City was because he was only capable of painting that which he hated. Just as the war had brought out the best in him, so too, might America and Americans, with their love of money and their lack of respect for tradition.[68] It was not to be. Nevinson didn't let up and continued publicly "I hate the mob and most of all our present day Americanised 'Civilisation,'"[69] before diagnosing America as suffering from an "Uplift of Orgy and Optimism," in which they believed their shallow advances, not least the prohibition of alcohol, to be on a similar scale in its contribution to the development of Western civilization, as the death of Socrates and the crucifixion on Jesus Christ. Worse still, Nevinson claimed, they had now fouled up Paris with their "American bar tenders, banjo syncopators, and other Negroid noises," though London mercifully had, to this point, been spared. He capped it all off by saying that the art buyers might as well hang a cheque on their wall, as money, not taste, was their only concern, before twisting the knife with "Don't you worry, the Americans like being kicked. That's how they are going to learn in the end."[70] Of course the American press hit back, now with the gloves off, saying "Mr C. R. W. Nevinson reminds us of many things, particularly of the cuckoo—the bird that doesn't lay its own eggs."[71] Having suggested that plagiarism was his major metier, they then compared him to a honey bee swarming around taking honey from all the open flowers, before accidentally flying into a bottle where everyone could have a good laugh at it buzzing around and getting nowhere.

By the 1930s the architecture of New York was still visible in his work, but now in another role, located at the heart of the apocalyptic scenes of *Pan Triumphant* and *The Twentieth Century* that could warn only of doom for Western civilization at the hands, among other things, of Americanization.

When asked by the *Daily Sketch* whether or not he might, in the future, go to America again, he replied "Never in all my life. I couldn't stand it. They have no idea about what art means.[72] Little had changed since 1912 when, as a student in Paris, he had written Dora Carrington "Curse America! Christopher Columbus convinces me of the power of the devil."[73] He wound up his reminiscences on the whole experiment in 1930 saying "I have been an immense success there in my time and I have also known great failure—chiefly because I have been too popular, and I was young, and it was seen to that I had a good snubbing by chauvinist artists who had started a movement of American Art for the American People—and to hell with the condescending Englishman."[74] That does not alter the fact that Nevinson had been soundly drummed out of New York City before the Roaring Twenties had really started. However, with large collections in New York now vying to own and display his work (the Metropolitan Museum of Art alone had ten by the year 2000), and his images commanding ever increasing prices in Manhattan auction rooms, it seems that bygones may at last be bygones.

Notes

"A Veiled and Virgin Shore" from R. W. Gilder, *The Poems of Richard Watson Gilder* (Boston, 1908), 201.

"An Artist's War Cry," *Observer*, April 13, 1919, Tate Gallery Archive (hereafter: T.G.A.).

1. S. Bing, *Artistic America, Tiffany Glass and Art Nouveau* (Paris, 1896; repr., Cambridge, MA: Riverside Press, 1970), 186.
2. B. Haskell, *The American Century* (New York: W. W. Norton, 1999), 9.
3. M. Hall, "Modernism, Militarism and Masculinity: British Modern Art Discourses and Official War Art During the First World War" (PhD diss., State University of New York at Binghampton, 1994), 731.
4. "Le Futurisme et la Presse internationale," *Poesia* 5, nos. 3–6 (April–July 1909): 24.
5. The two paintings were *Gasometers* and *Bradford Scene.*
6. See: John Oliver Hand, "Futurism in America: 1909–14," *Art Journal* 41, no. 4 (Winter 1981): 337–42.
7. The dinner was arranged for 7:15 PM on April 11, at the Café Royal. On the committee were: The Right Hon. Lord Henry Cavendish-Bentick, M.P., Mr. H. Chadwick Moore (Hon. Secretary), Mr. Grant Richards, Mr. Walter Sickert (Chairman) and Mr. Charles Sims, R.A. (the latter did not attend).
8. Henry Woodd Nevinson Journals, Bodleian Library, Oxford University (hereafter: H. W. N. Journals) e.621/1, April 11, 1919.
9. "Hansoms, Pictures, Books, Plays," *Bristol Times & Mirror*, April 16, 1919. T.G.A.
10. "A Nevinson Dinner," *Daily Mirror*, March 15, 1919, T.G.A.
11. C. R. W. Nevinson, *Paint and Prejudice* (London: Metheun, 1937), 130.
12. *Evening Post*, May 31, 1919.
13. This lecture entitled "Pictorial Records of the Great War" was delivered on May 13 and says more or less what Nevinson said. It is difficult to know who was aping whom.
14. This was reported on in the *Daily Express*, May 21, 1919, and originated in an interview given in New York on May 19. T.G.A.
15. "C. R. W. Nevinson: Practical Modernist" *Christian Science Monitor* (n.d.)
16. *New York City Herald*, May 25, 1919.
17. "Mr Nevinson, British Artist, Thinks New York is too Modest," *Herald*, May 18, 1919.
18. *Sun*, May 18, 1919. Henry McBride commented, "We too have cubists, clever as he, but we haven't a public as clever as his to be amused by them."
19. This was the work of Helen Bullitt Lowry in the *Evening Post*, May 24, 1919.
20. Cited in C. Stanstell, *American Moderns: Bohemian New York and the Creation of a New Century* (New York: Metropolitan Books, 2000), 36.

21. Hamilton Easter Field, *Eagle*, May 25, 1919.

22. Cited in Chloe Johnson, "C. R. W. Nevinson: The Soul of a Soulless City," *British Art in Focus* (London: Tate Publishing, 2001), 4.

23. *New York Times Magazine*, May 25, 1919, 13.

24. Cited in Chloe Johnson, "C. R. W. Nevinson: The Soul of a Soulless City," 5.

25. W. Corn, *The Great American Thing* (Berkeley and Los Angeles: University of California Press, 1999), 3.

26. Lisa Messinger suggested that this speech was also delivered on May 29, 1919, at the Kelekian Gallery (40 West Fifty-Seventh Street; Dikran Kelekian) in "Nevinson in New York": A lecture delivered at the Yale Center for British Art, March 1, 2000.

27. *Blind Man: Independent's Number*, April 10, 1917.

28. From the National Arts Club, he was known to have sent notes to key figures in New York society to meet and discuss art with him. An undated letter to Dr Rabin for example, from this address, suggested meeting to walk around the city at night, to talk, sketch and experience the modern wonder which was New York. C. R. W. Nevinson to Dr. Herman Theodore Radin, Herman T. Radin Letters, N17 Frames 531–33. Archives of American Art. Smithsonian Institution. Washington, D.C.

29. *Pittsburgh Gazette*, June 23, 1919.

30. His work was concurrently showing in California (Official British War Lithographs), at the Anderson Galleries, New York (Canadian War memorial Show), and in an enormous traveling exhibition of British war painting organized by the Worcester Art Museum, Massachusetts. The latter exhibition, organized by Raymond Wyer, director of the Worcester Art Museum, was a traveling show of 241 works by Orpen, Rothenstein, Bone, Clausen, Brangwyn, Lavery, Nash, Lewis, Epstein, John, Kennington, Roberts, and others.

31. *Christian Science Monitor*, June 9, 1919.

32. C. R. W. Nevinson *Paint and Prejudice*, 136

33. John Quinn to Wyndham Lewis, dated June 16, 1919, Letter Box 21, New York Public Library (hereafter: NYPL). Thanks to Jonathan Black for finding and sharing this letter with me.

34. Gallatin also organized an exhibition of Nevinson's engravings at the Jesup Memorial Library, Bar Harbor, Maine, in August 1919.

35. A. E. Gallatin, introduction to *Etchings and Lithographs by C. R. W. Nevinson* (New York: Keppel, 1919).

36. The literary reference is to a poem entitled "Died of Wounds" by Siegfried Sassoon, which describes Delville Wood.

37. The latter would also be known as *Broadway in the Rain.*

38. C. R. W. Nevinson, *Paint and Prejudice*, 135.

39. Ibid., 137.

40. "Notes From New York," *Evening Standard and St. James Gazette*, July 3, 1919. T.G.A.

41. C. R. W. Nevinson, *Paint and Prejudice*, 142.

42. Lisa Messinger has also suggested that Nevinson used other photographic compositions, especially those of Emil Otto Hoppé, and suggests that original compositional ideas, such as looking through Brooklyn Bridge, might find their origin there. "Nevinson in New York" (unpublished lecture at the Imperial War Museum, November 1999).

43. See M. Walsh, "Vital English Art: Futurism and the Vortex of London 1910–14," *Apollo*, February 2005, 64–71.

44. C. R. W. Nevinson to Albert Eugene Gallatin, Gallatin Papers, Reels 507, 508, and 1293. New York Historical Society, Manuscript Division. Copies at Archives of American Art, Smithsonian Institution, Washington, D.C. (hereafter: Smithsonian-Gallatin).

45. Nevinson employed a press cuttings agency, Henry Romeike Inc, at 106–110 Seventh Ave, New York City, to collect all news releases containing his name.

46. C. R. W. Nevinson to Albert Eugene Gallatin, August 4, 1919 (Smithsonian-Gallatin). A further letter to Gallatin show that the Worcester Art Galleries affair still was not resolved by the end of February 1920. Richard had tried to get the government to intervene, but to no avail. C. R. W. Nevinson to A. E. Gallatin, February 29, 1920 (Smithsonian-Gallatin).

47. Ibid.

48. H. W. N. Journals, e.621/3 April 24, 1920.

49. Ibid., May 24.

50. C. R. W. Nevinson to A. E. Gallatin, February 29, 1920 (Smithsonian-Gallatin).

51. The Italian Futurists had had their own major show (albeit in San Francisco) in 1915.

52. "Nevinson for New York," *Daily Express*, September 16, 1920.

53. "Some Famous Figures in the Foreign News," *Union*, Springfield, Massachusetts, October 31, 1920. T.G.A.

54. From a letter from Robert Coady to Jean Crotti, published in *Soil*, December 1916, 32.

55. C. R. W. Nevinson, "My Art Creed," *The Old World and the New* (Bourgeois Galleries, November 10–December 4, 1920).

56. C. Lewis Hind, "An Appreciation," *The Old World and the New* (Bourgeois Galeries, November 10–December 4, 1920).

57. "Sane Modernism," *Tribune*, November 14, 1920.

58. "Nevinson—a Painter who is Developing," *American Art News*, November 20, 1920.

59. "C. R. W. Nevinson's New York Show," *Tribune*, November 14, 1920.

60. "Art: C. R. W. Nevinson," *Nation*, December 8, 1920.

61. J. Stella, "The Brooklyn Bridge," *Transitions* (published privately, 1929), 86.

62. K. Marx, *Towards a Critique of Hegel's Philosophy of Right: An Introduction* (1844). Cited in Chloe Johnson, "C. R. W. Nevinson: The Soul of a Soulless City," 4.

63. C. R. W. Nevinson, *Paint and Prejudice*, 151.

64. Gresty, H. *C. R. W. Nevinson: Retrospective Exhibition of Paintings, Drawings and Prints* (Kettle's Yard Gallery, Cambridge, 1988), 38

65. John Quinn to C. R. W. Nevinson, November 23, 1920 (NYPL).

66. C. R. W. Nevinson, *Paint and Prejudice*, 152.

67. C. R. W. Nevinson to Old Mr McBride. December 6, 1920. Beinecke Rare Book and Manuscript Library, Yale University.

68. F. Rutter, *Art in My Time* (London: Rich & Cowan, 1933), 169.

69. C. R. W. Nevinson, *John O'London's Weekly*, 1922. T.G.A.

70. "Nevinson with a Horsewhip," *Daily Express*, September 9, 1921.

71. *American Art News*, October 29, 1921.

72. *Daily Sketch*, February 16, 1927.

73. Nevinson to Carrington, July 24, 1912. Harry Ranson Humanities Research Center, Univeristy of Texas at Austin.

74. "Wild Parties in Three Countries: America," *Graphic*, May 17, 1930.

C. R. W. Nevinson and Fiction: A Survey

Christopher Martin

Nevinson caused a sensation with his one-man exhibition of war paintings in 1916. The images presented the modern age's first industrialized war, often in a bold modernistic style derived from Futurism, and the pictures all sold. Highly visible through press attention and frequenting such fashionable venues as the Café Royal, the artist himself became iconic. A previously unexamined aspect of Nevinson's art is how his iconic status led him to figure as a model for fictional characters, and as a contemporary reference, significantly in an early draft of T. S. Eliot's *The Waste Land*, to producing artwork specifically for writers, as well as to producing much journalism on a variety of subjects, and a novel. What follows is a survey of Nevinson's relationship to literature, represented by a remarkably diverse list of authors, and how it interrelates with his art and journalism, from the middle of the First World War onward.

Nevinson's parents, Henry and Margaret, were authors and campaigning journalists. Henry was a war correspondent, writing for many papers, including the *Manchester Guardian*, the *Daily Chronicle*, and the *Nation*, the latter two under H. W. Massingham. Margaret wrote for *Fortnightly Review*, the *English Review*, the *Vote*, and the *National Review*. Through his parents, Nevinson became friends with such key literary figures as George Bernard Shaw and H. G. Wells. His father put Nevinson in touch with artists, writers, and people of influence, such as the Futurist leader F. T. Marinetti, Muirhead Bone (who helped decide his training in art, which led to his attending the Slade with many of the outstanding British artists of his time), and General Sir Ian Hamilton (who wrote the preface to the catalog of Nevinson's 1916 exhibition of war pictures). Parental celebrity, particularly Henry's, enabled Nevinson's own to burgeon rapidly, eclipsing that of his contemporaries, and bringing him into contact with writers who attended his exhibitions (i.e., George Bernard Shaw, Joseph Conrad, John Galsworthy, and John Masefield at the 1916 show); bought his pictures (i.e., H. G. Wells, Arnold Bennett, Sinclair Lewis, Osbert Sitwell, Alec Waugh, A. P. Herbert, St. John Ervine, Gilbert Frankau); commissioned artwork for their novels from him (i.e., Ronald Firbank, Ethel Mannin); or sat for portraits (Sinclair Lewis, Arthur Machen, Edith Sitwell, and the journalists Hannen Swaffer, Sisley Huddleston, and Nevinson's father, Henry). Writers also used him. In fictional incarnations he was art student, celebrity artist famed for his depictions of warfare, Parisian bohemian, or London *bon viveur*.

Nevinson is mentioned only briefly in his father's autobiographies, mainly recording how unhappy he was at Uppingham School. Henry gives Richard's war art a footnote, but uses three of Richard's paintings to illustrate his third volume of memoirs, and sixteen of his son's pictures as an accompaniment to his book about England, *Rough Islanders*.[1] He was clearly proud of Richard's work, but did not mention how he took every opportunity to further his son's career, or his anguish at Richard's travails in pursuing art. Margaret, his mother, recalled seeing many signs of Richard's artistic ability from his early childhood on, and that he had "his own tastes and pursuits from the cradle—machinery, carpentering, electricity, drawing and painting, deft of finger, full of mechanical skill."[2] His love of machines found expression later in *Vital English Art*, the Futurist manifesto he wrote with F. T. Marinetti ("Hurrah for motors! Hurrah for speed!"); his war pictures of motor transports, ambulances, the then-new tank, and planes (the Making Aircraft set of six lithographs, his postwar *From the Paris Plane*); and the various forms of transport he used, from motorbike to customized motor caravan.[3] Margaret, too, was proud of Richard's success in art, and noted how leading collections in America and Europe held examples of his work. She also told how many young artists used to come to their house during Richard's time at the Slade, including "John Curry [sic] . . . the Spencers, Wyndham Lewis, Gertler, Allinson, Ethelbert White . . . the Nashes, the Carlines, McKnight-Kauffer, Gaudier-Brzeska . . . Nina Hamnett, and afterwards, John, Sickert, Epstein, Ginner . . . Robert Bevan and Harold Gilman."[4] Many young soldiers, interested in Richard's pictures, visited too, including the war poets Siegfried Sassoon, Robert Nichols, and Osbert and Sacheverell Sitwell, adding literary connections to Richard's many artistic ones. His drypoint of a devastated forest, *That Cursed Wood*, takes its title from a line in Sassoon's poem "At Carnoy." In Margaret's story "He Would be a Soldier," she used the name of Richard's childhood secret society for that of the character Tim who became "captain of the Manboya-gang . . . The rules and rites of this society were reported to be very severe . . . the secrets were guarded as jealously as the freemasons."[5] As with Richard's society, there were signings in blood. His mother's writing, both fact and fiction, showed Nevinson displaying an early predilection for belonging to an exclusive group, to being an insider in art and society, from Wyndham Lewis's Rebel Art Centre, through the Savage and Arts clubs, to the Royal Academy.

Nevinson's entrée into fiction came about through friendship with Mark Gertler, when in 1916 Gilbert Cannan's novel *Mendel*, drawn from Gertler's early life, was published.[6] The eponymous artist Mendel Kuhler is based on Gertler, a poor Jewish youth from the East End, and his fellow student at Detmold (the Slade) Humphrey Mitchell, on Nevinson. His parents are also depicted, as well as Slade students Dora Carrington, Dorothy Brett, John Currie, Dolly Henry (Currie's mistress), Edward Marsh, Augustus John, William Rothenstein, and Henry Tonks. Twenty-five years after leaving the Slade, Nevinson recalled in *Paint and Prejudice*: "I formed a real friendship with Gertler, who was the genius of the place and besides that the most serious, single-minded artist I have ever come across . . . and . . . being what . . . John called a man cursed with an educational tendency, I was delighted to be able to help Gertler . . . to the wider culture that had been possible for me through my birth and environment."[7] The mentoring role was a singular one for Nevinson as, unlike his Slade contemporaries Paul Nash, David Bomberg, and William Roberts, he never engaged in formally teaching art. As well as the different testimonies of *Mendel* and *Paint and Prejudice*, and letters, the closeness of Nevinson and Gertler's friendship is emphasized in the well-known photograph of the Slade picnic of 1912 (fig. 4), where Nevinson and Gertler sit side-by-side, with Carrington sitting apart from them, and also in John Currie's tempera painting of that year *Some Later Primitives and Mme Tisceron*. In the latter, the portrait heads of Nevinson and Gertler are side-by-side, with Currie himself looking on. After relations between them broke down, Currie took Nevinson's place as Gertler's best male friend at the Slade.

Gertler terminated his friendship with Nevinson, as both men were pursuing Carrington. She appears as "Morrison" in Cannan's book. In his autobiography, Nevinson refers only fleetingly to Carrington, without naming her, keeping any hint of Bloomsbury Group aestheticism firmly at a distance: "I coquetted with a girl with whom Gertler was violently in love. Poor girl, she killed herself on the death of Lytton Strachey years later."[8] Cannan suggests Nevinson's high regard for Gertler's talent, as Mitchell says of Mendel when introducing him to some of the other male students, "He is a genius," and Mitchell is said to have taken "a protective attitude towards him and defended him from the detestation which he aroused in the majority of his fellow students."[9] There is, however, some divergence between Mitchell and how Nevinson later portrays himself. In *Paint and Prejudice*, Nevinson drolly tells how a Slade model's child could have been fathered by him, or by any of seventeen other men, but in *Mendel* it is clearly Mitchell who makes Hetty Finch, Mendel's model, pregnant.[10] In the novel, Edgar Froitzheim (based on Tonks) takes a collection so the girl can go away to have her baby. Nevinson does not mention this, or that, to his shame, he could not afford to make a contribution. Similarly, the underlying rivalry and tension between father and son is explicit in the novel, whereas in the autobiography it is not. Mitchell says: "My father's a great man. Gawd! What can you do when your own father takes the shine out of you at every turn?"[11] Nevinson does not admit to feeling under his father's shadow, but neither does he give him credit for all the support he gave him, which may be a denial of rivalry. *Mendel*, though fiction, is an important source for Mark Gertler and the artistic milieu of London before the First World War, because Gertler confided in Cannan, who used much of Gertler's conversation verbatim. Gertler was put into other novels, such as Aldous Huxley's *Crome Yellow*. As Sarah MacDougall notes, "Gertler's life and personality made irresistible copy."[12] As did Nevinson's.

In 1917, H. G. Wells's documentary book *War and the Future: Italy, France and Britain at War* appeared, in which he showed an awareness of Nevinson's ability to depict the hardware of industrial warfare. "Only Mr C. R. W. Nevinson could do justice to the interior of a Tank. You see a hand gripping something; you see the eyes and forehead of an engineer's face; you perceive that an overall bluishness beyond the engine is the back of another man."[13] Such a description could almost fit the hard lines depicting French soldiers, both living and dead, crammed around the machine-gun in its pit (another confined space) in Nevinson's painting *La Mitrailleuse*, his most-reproduced war image, and one also existing as both pastel and ink drawings. That picture's enduring power is attested to by John Malcolm, writing seventy-six years after Wells, in his novel *The Burning Ground*. He concludes his description of *La Mitrailleuse*: "Nothing is soft or rounded; the images could be those of men trapped in a submarine's engine-room just before the explosion of a fatal depth charge outside."[14] Another writer of Wells's generation was evidently moved by Nevinson's incisive, mechanistic portrayal of frontline soldiers under pressure. Arnold Bennett acquired the ink drawing (as well *La Patrie*). It is a key image in the artist's early cubo-futurist phase of representing war.

The success of Nevinson's show of war pictures at the Leicester Galleries in 1916 was, in terms of sales and press coverage, immense, and consolidated by a second show there in 1918. An exhibition of etchings and lithographs at Keppel's in New York the following year launched him in America, succeeded by a much bigger show at the city's Bourgeois Galleries in 1920, where he appeared less a fashionable avant-garde artist and more of a celebrity one. His cultivation of newspapermen, his writing background, and his early experimenting with journalism, helped the transition. Nevinson would turn from writing about art to such topics as "Gay London: why not? Cheery vision of a famous painter" and "Why not medieval fashions?" and be chosen to judge a beauty contest.[15] He would be invited to premieres, literary luncheons, sent to Czechoslovakia as a cultural ambassador, become a public speaker, and be famed for the studio parties to which he and his wife Kathleen drew other celebrities.

W. Somerset Maugham was a celebrity-writer whom Nevinson "always noticed like many others . . . is the one man admired by all authors," and one of his early posters was for a Maugham play.[16] His poster designs numbered little more than a dozen in total, but began strikingly in 1918 with his Vorticist-derived poster for his own "War" exhibition at the Leicester Galleries. A large part of the design is taken up with the jagged outline of a mass of pure red bayonets. Nevinson had the inverted compliment paid him of it being copied for a poster promoting war bonds: "Now back the bayonets with your war savings certificates."[17] He reprised the typography for his "Peace" exhibition poster the following year. In both posters, the name Nevinson looms large above the image. The self-publicist in him was here equal to the artist. The first poster advertised a collection of war pictures, the genre with which he made his name. The second suggested pictures associated with peace. Nevinson wished to show his versatility by using a different technique for each different subject. It was an exhibition of mixed pictures, which drew mixed reviews, but it did prove his independence. His evident adaptability would serve him well in accepting off-beat assignments from literary quarters. For his posters, Nevinson worked in bold designs and flat coloring, with the results produced through large-format lithographs.

In 1920 Nevinson produced his poster, commissioned by the actress Viola Tree, for Maugham's play *The Unknown*, in which her mother Lady Maud Tree had a part. It was based on Maugham's own 1901 novel *The Hero*, and concerned a soldier's loss of faith. It attacked patriotism, and generally shocked audiences when a widow who had lost her only son in the war, cried out in despair, "And who will forgive God?" Nevinson's poster featured a sexually ambiguous figure on a cross, assailed by exploding bombs. The *Glasgow Evening Times* found the poster "a beautiful study in orange and blue, with the figure of Christ, black and impressive, dominating all in the background."[18] Nevertheless, the London Underground banned it, stating that "as it is held to be the figure of a nude woman, we consider it utterly unsuitable for theatrical advertisement."[19] Nevinson, seemingly surprised by the company's attitude, defended himself thus, without reference to sex: "I simply meant to represent the truth that Faith will in the end triumph over any form of scientific reasoning or doubts. It is, in fact, a piece of symbolism."[20] Nevinson, as a friend of Maugham's, must have felt confident in the poster, which was also staunchly defended by Violet Tree and displayed at the Lyric theater while the play was running. Ten years later, another theatrical venture linked Nevinson with the first television broadcast in Britain. He drew the "scenery," of "the boldest and simplest nature," on "thick pieces of mill-board," for an experimentally televised one-act play by Luigi Pirandello, *The Man With the Flower in His Mouth (L'uomo dal fiore in bocca)*.[21] The "black and white drawings" were "placed on the stand . . . the 'scene shifting' being performed by removing one drawing and exposing the next underneath."[22] The play was produced by Nevinson's friend, the writer and radio and television producer Lance Sieveking.

As T. S. Eliot was completing his seminal modernist poem *The Waste Land* in 1921, he was ready to acknowledge, within it, Nevinson's celebrity. In an early draft, Eliot put Nevinson's name at the center of these two verses:

> He, the young man carbuncular, will stare
> Boldly about, in "London's one café,"
> And he will tell her, with a casual air,
> Grandly, "I have been with Nevinson today"
>
> Or else a cheap house agent's clerk, who flits
> Daily, from flat to flat, with old bold stare;
> One of the low on whom assurance sits
> As a silk hat on a Bradford millionaire.[23]

"London's one café" is the Café Royal, "a forum for writers, a meeting place for artists" and the most high-profile of Nevinson's haunts.[24] Here Eliot could have met the artist, as well as, among others, Walter

Sickert, Augustus John, William Rothenstein, Wilson Steer, Jacob Epstein, William Roberts, Henri Gaudier-Brzeska, and Wyndham Lewis. Eliot and Nevinson were connected through Lewis's Vorticist journal *Blast*. They both had work in the second and final issue: Eliot with two poems, and Nevinson with a woodcut version of *Returning to the Trenches*. Eliot may well have appreciated the connection between Nevinson the war painter and the Café Royal, as the masses of war dead figure in *The Waste Land*, and Nevinson had painted them in his Passchaendale picture *Harvest of Battle*. Here, the wasteland of the battlefield prefigured Eliot's urban one which, in fractured images, reflected the spiritual and emotional breaking-up of Western civilization after the First World War.

The sense of disdain provoked by the adjective *carbuncular* gives the boast of being with Nevinson a dubious cachet, reinforced by the succeeding lines on the house agent's clerk who, like the "young man carbuncular," is possessed of a "bold stare," and is "one of the low." The former Vorticist Ezra Pound suggested Eliot conflate the two verses surrounding "Nevinson," into four lines of a longer verse, leaving out "Nevinson," which Eliot did, when publishing in 1922. That verse became a section of the poem's third part, "The Fire Sermon":

> He, the young man carbuncular, arrives,
> A small house agent's clerk, with one bold stare,
> One of the low on whom assurance sits
> As silk on a Bradford millionaire.[25]

B. C. Southam points out, "The Fire Sermon was preached by Buddha against the fires of lust, anger, envy and other passions that consume men."[26] Envy and pride are implied in the young man carbuncular's staring "boldly about" of the early version, and in the "one bold stare" of the final version. Eliot juxtaposes images of fire with water, a sign of regeneration: the River Thames and London are strong threads through the poem. The inclusion of Nevinson would have added some resonance, for they were his subjects, too. He knew the capital well from boyhood: "Instead of playing cricket or football I spent my time in exploring London, and my knowledge for a boy of my age became encyclopaedic."[27] With the passage containing the lines

> The barges drift
> With the turning tide
> Red sails
> Wide

Eliot evokes a Nevinsonian image, such as his 1920 watercolor *London Bridges* that, like "The Fire Sermon," features the church of St Magnus Martyr.[28] Another aspect of the poem is the grim urban environment which is also present, whether Nevinson influenced Eliot or not, in such early paintings as *The Towing Path, Camden Town*, and *Allotments, East Ham*.

The second issue of *Blast* appeared in 1915, when Nevinson was already somewhat distanced from Lewis and Vorticism. By 1922, though Lewis distrusted Nevinson ("always a dark horse," and "an interloper and a heretic"), Pound was slightly ambivalent toward his pictures, mocking his changes of style and calling *Harvest of Battle* "a bad painting," yet finding it "an excellent record of war."[29] It is most likely Pound suggested cutting Nevinson from *The Waste Land* to make a tighter, more intense poem, but also to remove an anomaly, the only reference to a real life contemporary personage, which would give the name Nevinson enormous prominence and importance, if left in.

It was at the Café Royal that Grant Richards, publisher of two books of Nevinson war pictures, introduced the artist to the eccentric novelist Ronald Firbank.[30] Nevinson subsequently designed the book jacket, reproducing his frontispiece illustration, for Firbank's *The Flower Beneath the Foot* which appeared, financed by the author himself, in 1923.[31] His picture is a portrait of the heroine Laura Lita Carmen Etoile de Nazianzi, whose last name means Star of Bethlehem, the flowered lily that features in a border around the picture, and also in the chaplet Laura wears. She appears as a nun, her face both icon and mask, prefiguring by three years the artist's pastel portrait of the poet Edith Sitwell, Madonna-like with black veil and headdress. Nevinson's design for the book appeared in blue and white in the first, Grant Richards, edition, and in tan and white in the first American edition.[32] He also designed the endpapers for Firbank's *Sorrow in Sunlight*, published in 1924 and the first U.K. edition of *Prancing Nigger*.[33] These are in sepia, but Nevinson also executed a large, square, colorful painting of the same scene of luxuriant tropical vegetation. The novella is a Jazz Age fantasy set on the West Indian island of Tacarigua. Nevinson enjoyed the writer's comic storytelling, evident in his own patois, in place names like Mediavilla and Cuna-Cuna, and characters called Miami and Bamboo.

The American novelist Sinclair Lewis was friendly with both Henry Nevinson and his son, and had acted as Henry's guide in Washington, D.C. In June 1921, Lewis gave public talks in London, and Henry, Richard, and Kathleen attended a tea party in Lewis's honor, at Henry's favorite restaurant The Ivy.[34] Lewis purchased Richard's painting *Looking through Brooklyn Bridge*, and in April 1924 wrote to *his* father saying that he was having his portrait done by Nevinson, "one of the best painters in England; fortunately, it was to be done in pastels and would only require two afternoons for sittings."[35] While this was a relief for Lewis, Nevinson recalled him as "the strangest literary man I have known. He was restless, clownish, and intense as only Americans can be, and he prowled round my studio incapable of sitting still, while all the time he poured out the most remarkable monologue of love and hate, shrewdness and sentimentality, that it can have been the lot of any portrait painter to hear. He used to leave me with a sense of exhaustion and elation I have never known any other human capable of producing."[36]

In 1925, Lewis followed the great success of his satirical novels of everyday life in America, *Main Street* and *Babbitt*, with *Arrowsmith*. In that novel, Lewis achieves what Eliot might have done more obliquely, using Nevinson's name, a detail amid a myriad of others, to denote sophistication. Martin Arrowsmith, the doctor hero, altruistic in struggling to pursue science at the expense of not having a fashionable, lucrative practice, and missing out on a wide experience of culture, listens to his assistant Gustav Sondelius holding forth: "For hours Sondelius talked, of Shanghai and epistemology and the painting of Nevinson."[37] The references in Lewis's novel and Eliot's discarded lines are about conspicuous sophistication, and possible sources of envy. In the former, Nevinson's painting is part of the recreational life of a "brilliant" doctor, while in the latter being with Nevinson himself is an ambitious clerk's boast.[38]

As well as registering, as the type of a fashionable modern artist, with such serious writers as Eliot and Sinclair Lewis, who were both awarded the Nobel Prize, Nevinson also made an impression on Agatha Christie. More of an entertainer than a high artist, albeit the most famous detective writer of the twentieth century, she was noted for her ingenious plots. Her 1939 thriller *Murder is Easy* features a reference to Nevinson's pastel *An Inexperienced Witch*: "Her black hair was blown off her head by the sudden gust and Luke was reminded of a picture he had once seen—Nevinson's 'Witch'. The long pale delicate face, the black hair flying up to the stars."[39] The picture, in which the hapless witch, sans clothing, is being swept off her broom, was shown in Nevinson's 1919 "Peace" exhibition, in which he showed himself as successful, in monetary and attendance terms, as with war subjects. Through the best-selling Christie's being struck with it, the picture and its artist became more a part of the ethos of popular fiction, thus continuing a trend in his work developed from the postwar years onward. One example is the appropriation of his painting *The Arrival* for the cover of Elizabeth Gill's 1933 thriller set aboard a liner *Crime de Luxe*. Other examples would be Nevinson's own novel *Exodus A.D.*, published the following year and, some sixty years later, John Malcolm's thriller *The Burning Ground*.[40] The latter is one of a series of novels featuring art investigator Tim Simpson. A First World War Nevinson picture features in the plot and, despite some mistitling, a number of his war images from that period are described in detail.

In 1926, Ethel Mannin's first successful, and perhaps (as she thought) best, novel *Sounding Brass* was published sporting a jacket by Nevinson.[41] It was fluent, caught the spirit of the time, and satirized the advertising world. "'I decided,' Mannin wrote later, 'that as the book was a satire on a facet of modern life, it ought to have an extremely modern jacket. I asked my publishers if they would approach Nevinson, as the most essentially modern artist I could think of in this country.'" His black-and-white design for the front cover showed a stylized Piccadilly Circus at night: the figure of Eros surrounded by neon lettering, isolated globes of light from which rays explode (echoes of a Futurist preoccupation, and a common feature of Nevinson's work, as in the war pictures *Exploding Shell* and *A Star Shell*), and the lit buses carrying silhouetted passengers. It is reminiscent of Nevinson's lithograph *Sur La Terrasse, Parnasse*, though on the book jacket the lit letters are more dominant, the ubiquitous advertisements inverting night, turning it into day. Despite Nevinson's fitting book jacket, Mannin, in her book of memoirs *Confessions and Impressions*, referred to his "slightly contemptuous manner and outbreaks of bitterness, and his rather sardonic smile." He was "touchy." She had compared him, in appearance, to the noted advertising man Sir Charles Higham, but Nevinson felt insulted to be bracketed with a "self-interested showman." He was displeased with the chapter on him, and it did not appear in Mannin's revised edition.[42]

In 1926, Nevinson also produced a Holbeinesque portrait drawing in pencil of his friend, the Paris-based author and journalist Sisley Huddleston (fig. 13), and used the latter's studio as a basis for his large painting *A Studio in Montparnasse*, striking for the sight, at its center, of a female nude and a cat, at a tall window, exposed to a vista of buildings rising up to the skyline, framed with them, between tall curtains. The following year, Nevinson's friend H. G. Wells presented the picture to the Tate Gallery, and immediately Huddleston "wrote to the Press protesting . . . as there was a nude in the studio," and he was European editor of the *Christian Science Monitor*.[43] The Tate accused Nevinson of a publicity stunt, but he claimed that when he put a nude into the

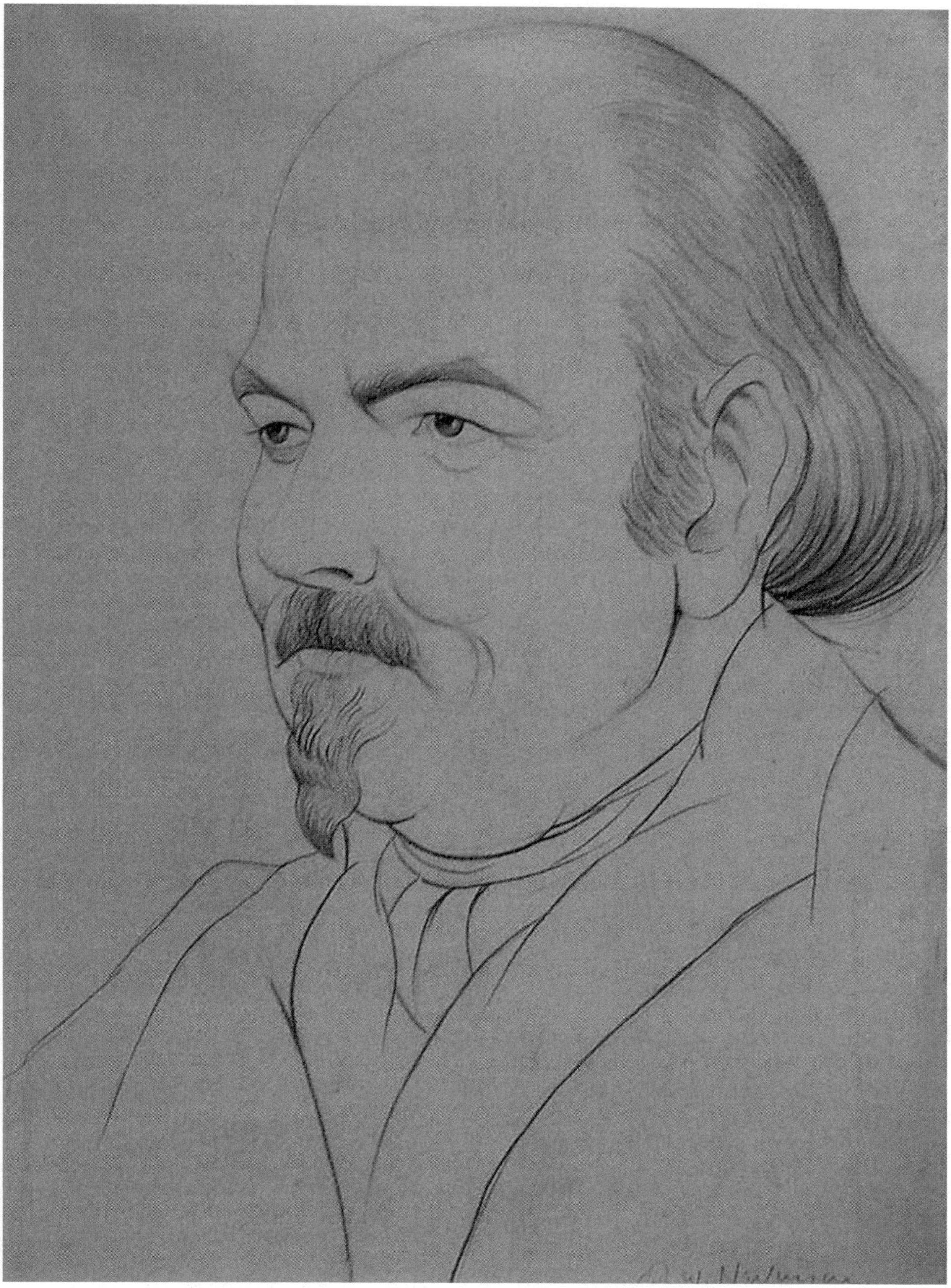

13. C. R. W. Nevinson, *Portrait of Sisley Huddleston*, 1927. Pencil on paper. Private collection.

picture he was "only thinking of the design."[44] In that year, too, Huddleston, in his novel of bohemian Paris *Mr Paname*, gave the artist a mien allying him with the god Pan, when depicting La Coupole, the celebrated Montparnasse café frequented by artists and writers: "Well-known men, like Augustus John, with his beautiful head, and Nevinson, of the faun's face, were sometimes to be seen; the Coupole was the rendezvous of all American or English artists passing through Paris."[45] Huddleston evidently thought highly of Nevinson's work, choosing two of the artist's finest large Paris paintings, *Sur La Terrasse, Montparnasse* and *Henri IV, l'Ile de Paris* to head the list of illustrations for his book of reminiscences *Back to Montparnasse*.[46]

The novelist Henry Williamson came to a party of Nevinson's at Steele's Studios in 1928. The Nevinsons were renowned for their studio parties in the 1920s and 1930s. Many celebrities attended: writers such as H. G. Wells, Sinclair Lewis, the Sitwells, Arnold Bennett, Michael Arlen, Ronald Firbank, and Lance Sieveking; actors such as Noël Coward, Diana Wynyard, and Constance Collier; music people such as Constant Lambert, Mark Hambourg, Josef Holbrooke, and Gracie Fields; artists such as Augustus John, Jacob Epstein, Alfred Munnings, William Orpen, Ethelbert White, and Barney Seale; the Countess of Drogheda and "a host of lords and ladies."[47] A similar mix of celebrities and prominent figures attended his private view parties at the Leicester Galleries. Many years later, Henry Williamson would write a fictional account of a Nevinson studio party. He and the artist, two men deeply affected by their experience of the First World War, became friends. When Williamson's *After Ten Years* (recounting his revisiting the battlefields of Flanders) was reprinted in 1929 as *The Wet Flanders Plain*, he dedicated it to Nevinson.[48] Their friendship, however, foundered on the publication in 1933 of Williamson's novel *The Gold Falcon*, in which Nevinson is portrayed as the artist Channerson (the name a conflation of Nevinson's surname and his nickname "Chips," which came from his love of carpentry). Nevinson was mortified by the suggestion that his art had shown a loss in value: "Channerson's war pictures were immortal; they could still be bought at sales for a few guineas."[49] For the implied slight, Nevinson threatened Williamson with "libel in trade."[50] Nevinson may have fed this part of the fiction himself, as he was usually defensive about the quality of his pictures, particularly of war, claiming his works were underpriced.

Despite Nevinson decisively dissociating himself from Williamson, the latter still referred to an ink drawing version (which he owned) of the artist's war painting *A Group of Soldiers*, in a semiautobiographical fragment of his 1934 anthology *The Linhay on the Downs*:

> the tall soldier . . . is the sensitive type of citizen-soldier who bears the war on his shoulders, but who will do what he is told to the end; and who knows, without bitterness, but with a certain irony, that he is doomed.
>
> Not the sort of picture that would be appraised for its patriotism during a war . . .[51]

The painting version had, in fact, initially been censored on the grounds that "the Germans will seize upon the picture as evidence of British degeneration."[52] Williamson kept the drawing in his writing hut, and used it to illustrate the back of the book jacket of *A Test to Destruction* in 1960, from his fifteen-novel sequence *A Chronicle of Ancient Sunlight*, a semiautobiographical narrative reflecting Britain's social history from the 1880s to the 1950s, noted for its realistic depiction of trench warfare.[53] Even though Nevinson had fallen out with him, and was now dead, Williamson put Channerson/Nevinson into two subsequent volumes of the series. The first, *The Power of the Dead*, from 1963, features a chapter entitled "Bottle Party," which gives a flavor of Nevinson's famous studio parties: "So this was postwar London semi-Bohemian society—face after face familiar from newspaper and magazine." The host is portrayed as outwardly genial, but barely concealing darker emotions: "Across the hot and crowded room came Channerson's hearty laughter. Phillip [Williamson's hero] turned slowly to observe him. Channerson was about thirty-six, with prematurely grey hair above eyes which remained hard during his laughter. The laughter sounded hollow, behind the eyes which had looked at him at the door had been caution, irony, even despair." Williamson does strike a sympathetic note, however, in having Phillip say: "I suppose Channerson has had a fairly grim time. Most people loathed his paintings of war—or did when he first painted them" to which Archie Plugg replies: "He suffers from a simply frightful persecution complex, I'm told. On three occasions when he drove Tony to London, he stopped his car outside the Slade and cursed Tonks." Channerson is imbued with Nevinson's extreme sensitivity to criticism of his work. By Williamson's fictional account, he still smarted from Tonks's undermining his self-confidence as a student, over a decade after the event.[54]

Henry Tonks, in Nevinson's time assistant professor at the Slade, was a former surgeon who specialized in teaching anatomical drawing. Nevinson's apparent bumptiousness may have set off an enmity between the two men. According to fellow student Paul Nash, "Tonks . . . disliked self-satisfied young men" but Nevinson was also sensitive, and would have been initially unnerved by Tonks, whom another student, Edward Wadsworth, found "rude and arrogant."[55] According to Nevinson, Tonks, in the course of doing his rounds, "managed to shatter my self-confidence, and I was wringing wet by the time he went on to Stanley Spencer."[56] Tonks warned students to stay away from the 1912 Second Post-Impressionist Exhibition so they "did not risk contamination."[57] It may well be that Nevinson showed too much of a leaning toward advanced art, and away from Tonks's classicism. He was an admirer of the Camden Town Group, was pleased to be encouraged by Walter Sickert, had met Wyndham Lewis, and was exhibiting and selling pictures, influenced by Impressionism, while still a student. "It seemed I was making progress," he later recalled, "Then Tonks advised me to abandon art as a career."[58] This checked him only temporarily. The two men had contact again, when Tonks was involved in the hanging of the 1919 Nation's War Paintings and Drawings exhibition at the Royal Academy. Nevinson felt his work was not just badly hung, but purposely so. Tonks had made the hang with Muirhead Bone and others, but he received the brunt of Nevinson's wrath. Henry Nevinson recorded that Bone "said he knew there is a violent set against Richard among a clique of artists: they call him bumptious, etc.," and some days later: "Richard . . . almost insane with rage against the Hanging Comm[ittee], Tonks and other enemies."[59] Nevinson later recalled that "Tonks . . . as he wrote and told me, had always disliked my work almost as much as he disliked me."[60] The father, while allowing that *Harvest of Battle* had been disadvantageously hung, "not in the big room," noted with satisfaction that it "attracted far more interest" than "most other big pictures" there, and "the biggest crowd."[61] As Nevinson recalled, "Tonks had asked members of the Press not to mention my name," but the press came and got his version of the affair, and dramatically publicized his paintings.[62] Later, it was alleged Tonks was also behind a petition to remove Nevinson's *La Mitrailleuse* from the Tate. Over the years Nevinson was to credit him with prejudice, malice, and envy. His father confided in his diary some time after the Royal Academy affair that Richard was "still haunted by persecution mania."[63]

In the subsequent novel by Williamson featuring Channerson/Nevinson, *The Phoenix Generation*, Channerson's fame is described as "fugacious," suggesting that Nevinson was past the peak of his celebrity and his artistry on his second trip to New York:

"Channerson . . . began to speak of his reception in New York on his second visit to that city, when he found that he was already forgotten. 'They drop you as completely as they take you up when the newspaper reporters push past you at Ellis Island, seeking the latest "celebrity" ', he said, ironically, 'But then the Americans are the only nation in history to have achieved decadence without civilization', and his hearty laughter broke out as his eyes roved around the table."[64] The laughter is Channerson/Nevinson's defense against exclusion from the American art world. In reality, Nevinson had antagonized Americans by claiming that nobody had depicted the beauty of New York before him, ignoring the achievements of such native artists as Joseph Stella, Max Weber, John Marin, and Edward Hopper, and the photographers Vorticist Alvin Langdon Coburn and Paul Strand; and by claiming, at a dinner given in his honor, "that America had painters but no artists."[65]

In 1934, the year after Williamson's *The Gold Falcon*, Nevinson collaborated with the popular novelist Princess Paul Troubetzkoy (author of two earlier novels, *Storm Tarn* and *Gallow's Seed*, and wife of the Russian American society sculptor Prince Paul Troubetzkoy) on an apocalyptic novel *Exodus A.D.: A Warning to Civilians*. Written in a popular style, it is complementary to H. G. Wells's speculative science fiction novel *The Shape of Things to Come*.[66] Wells analyzes world development, projects his story 180 years into the future, and shows not just the disintegration of a civilization but also its rebirth. *Exodus A.D.* is bleaker: Britain is unexpectedly attacked from the air by an unknown enemy delivering gas and bubonic plague, causing an exodus in which more people die than are killed by enemy action, because there is no system of underground shelters for them. At the end, the hero and heroine are barely alive, and there is no hopeful vision beyond the ruins. The overlapping worlds of modern warfare, journalism, and smart society are depicted with images redolent of Nevinson's past, and certain of his paintings. The novel is infused with fears arising from the sociopolitical situation. Following the Wall Street Crash in 1929, there was a world recession, industrial production fell substantially in Britain and, particularly, Germany, though Russia doubled its production, and there was high unemployment across Europe in the early 1930s. Liberalist governments collapsed, there was a widespread fear of communist revolution, and a rise in dictatorship, particularly with Hitler and Mussolini. German nationalism was exaggerated by the Depression. The nation was rearming, and investing massively in building gas-proof air-raid shelters. Many nations signed the

Chemical Weapons Convention to ban the use of such weapons, but Japan and Britain started biological warfare programs, in 1932 and 1934 respectively.

Richard Harden, the journalist hero of *Exodus A.D.*, and Nevinson's namesake, has some of his characteristics: "Richard . . . had a better understanding of the population of East London than most," while the artist claimed "Whitechapel had no terrors for me."[67] Both are, also, opinionated, and happy to express their ideas at length. Harden shares his surname with a family in Troubetzkoy's previous novel *Gallow's Seed.*[68] Rosalind, the heroine, a gossip columnist, echoes photographs of a blonde, slim, and youthful Princess Paul Troubetzkoy in the society pages of magazines of the time. Richard, in discussing the arms race, links Germany with Japan (which had invaded Manchuria in 1930), as two powers building up to war capability. Like Winston Churchill, who had Germany in mind, in speeches of the 1930s, he speaks of "this menace of attack from the air, which everlastingly hangs over our heads."[69] In the year of *Exodus A.D.*'s publication, the British government reacted to a perceived threat of such an attack by relocating its gunpowder factories in Kent, away from their proximity to London, to Scotland. The country would start investing in air-raid shelters the following year.

Planes feature a lot in Nevinson's novel. He had been up in planes and balloons during the First World War, and saw Dunkirk then, "one of the first towns to suffer aerial bombardment, and I was one of the first men to see a child who had been killed by it . . . the small body . . . a symbol of all that was to come."[70] Nevinson painted the child, calling his picture *A Taube*, meaning a "dove" and also, ironically, the name of Germany's staple military plane in the early part of the war. He had experienced, too, being fired on by an enemy plane, while up in a sausage balloon. In the novel he depicts a more modern invasion from the air with a Futurist sense of the beauty of the machine in flight: "High up . . . gleamed the blue of the sunny, summer sky . . . But across it, slowly, steadily, came the spreading formation of death-dealing, drilled grace."[71] This also reflects something of the balletic, but powerful and minatory, plane in flight painted by the second wave Italian Futurist Tato in his *Aeropainting no. 3* (1932). In both cases, airpower is suggestive of Fascism.

Nevinson's earliest images of planes were influenced by Italian Futurism. He exhibited his wood sculpture *Aerroplane* in June 1914, just before the First World War, and the war paintings *Pursuing a Taube* and *Before the Storm*, in 1915 and 1916 respectively. Later, he would say: "I still think my aeroplane pictures are the finest work I have done."[72] He would have meant those early pictures in which planes are central. In his apocalyptic pictures of the 1930s they are more emblematic, signs of advanced civilization. Rosalind is, however, briefly reassured by the appearance of the auto-giro, precursor of the helicopter, and a novelty when the book was written. She "could not remember when she had not heard it crossing above the sky, morning and night, watching the traffic, wirelessing its reports."[73] In Aldous Huxley's much more overtly futuristic novel *Brave New World* (1932), the auto-giro is the favored mode of private transport. In the First World War, with long-range artillery and fighter planes, the enemy became much less visible. As planes became faster and higher flying in the succeeding decades, they would become even less visible, as reflected in *Exodus A.D.*, in which the unseen enemy strikes with impunity.

The fear of poison gas was commonly reflected in interwar culture, in such works as Vicki Baum's novel *Grand Hotel (Menschen in Hotel)* (1929), in which a character has been hideously scarred by mustard gas in the Great War; G. W. Pabst's film *Kameradschaft* (1933), featuring a gas explosion in a mine; William Cameron Menzies's film *Things to Come* (1935) (from H. G. Wells's novel) with an aerial gas attack; and Ernst Krenek's opera *Der Diktator* (1926), in which a character blinded by poison gas sings about an attack, and the resulting disfiguration. Nevinson's awareness of gas in warfare probably dated back to his experience of Ypres, when the Germans had used it for the first time. In *Exodus A.D.,* Richard expounds on his ideas about war: "in the last war . . . They were getting some pretty little samples of gas bomb . . . ready" which would be delivered by air, and London would be much more under threat.[74]

In the 1930s, Nevinson also wrote journalistically voicing his ideas on planning, housing, the slums, political leadership, and his own worldview ("If I were Mr Lansbury," "A call for a leader: people tired of claptrap cynicism," "Thus would I rebuild London: an artist's solution to the slum problem," and "C. R. W. Nevinson re-plans our seaside," followed a few years later by "Vision of an artist: C. R. W. Nevinson re-plans the Empire"). In his essay "The Arts within this Bellicose Civilization," contributed to the book *The Seven Pillars of Fire* in 1936, a year after the Italians had used aerial mustard gas attacks against the Ethiopians, Nevinson showed his ongoing concern, in a Wellsian manner, for how cities were unprepared for that type of warfare: "Cities . . . should have buildings erected which are capable of preserving a gassed people within the cities . . . Reservoirs of food could be kept within these buildings, water supply and sewage should be made bomb-proof."[75]

In Nevinson's novel, his thinking about planning and civil defense finds its voice in Sir Thomas Grange who, claiming to be as visionary as H. G. Wells, would have citadels underground, and connected by Tube railways: "it would have been utterly, completely safe! Gas couldn't have penetrated to it, because gas lies on the ground . . . it can't descend unless there's suction. There would be no suction."[76] When gas seeps out in London, Richard asks himself: "What was the purpose of gas? To destroy the civil population—to attack it to run in panic, to destroy itself, and in its headlong directionless blundering prevent its machinery of defence from usefulness."[77] The use of gas as a weapon takes on a chilling aspect in the light of the Nazi gas chambers of the early 1940s.

In the First World War, of those killed in attacks by airships and planes in Britain, half were in London. Searchlights were a major part of defense, and Nevinson painted them in four graceful and evocative pictures: *The First Searchlights at Charing Cross*, *Searchlights*, *Among the Searchlights of London*, and *Piccadilly at Night.*[78] In *Exodus A.D.*, besides the exodus itself, searchlights are the spectacular signs of war: "Searchlights tore across the sky like the prolonged flashing of titanic lightning, flickered and swung." Planes caught by searchlights in the unfamiliar context of war appear surreal: "across the sky she saw a wheeling squadron, flashing through the arc of a searchlight, which picked them up, dropped them swiftly as if in terror that they should be noticed. They had . . . looked like fish darting through a haunted river, as the wings of the planes gleamed silver, turned to shadow and were gone." Richard finds the searchlights a gentle, reassuring presence: "He could see nothing in the sky beyond the quivering rays of the searchlights, caressing the clouds, with delicate gleaming tendrils." The beauty of the beams in motion is caught, too: "Dappling the sky with sprayed pools of light, more and more raying arms swung, circling, crossing each other like the weaving ribbons of a maypole," an image reminiscent of the paintings *The Searchlights at Charing Cross* and *Searchlights*, which show the deterrent beams converging.[79]

As a Futurist, Nevinson himself had initially looked on war in 1914 with excitement, stirred by Marinetti, whose manifesto of 1909 declared, "We will glorify war—the world's only hygiene—militarism, patriotism, the destructive gesture of freedom-bringers, beautiful ideas worth dying for."[80] Italian Futurists had got themselves jailed for incitement to join in hostilities. When war came, however, Nevinson declined any soldiering role but was persuaded by his father to join, with him, the Friends' Ambulance Unit. By early 1915, he was saying, "Unlike my Italian friends, I do not glory in war for its own sake, nor can I accept their doctrine that war is the only health-giver," while claiming it was a "violent incentive to Futurism."[81] In *Exodus A.D.*, Grant Oliphant encounters the surfacing of war fever among workers in his office:

> a dozen typists, wild-eyed, dishevelled, working with frantic haste . . .
>
> "What on earth is this all about—" Oliphant stared, rooted at the door in astonishment.
>
> "It's war!" one of the girls screamed at him. "Haven't you heard—we're at war! Report to the front room—"
>
> "War?"
>
> "Get on—" the girl screamed hysterically. "I've got to get this stuff done—they'll be over in minutes they say—isn't it exciting?"[82]

Much of the rest of book, however, shows war as gruesome and grim. Although the book warned of a war worse than the First World War, Nevinson supported the forces in the Second World War, being in favor of moblizing the under-50s, and having artists drawn from them to publicize Britain's war effort. He himself served briefly as a stretcher bearer, and sold paintings in aid of the Red Cross.

Exodus A.D. contains many images of dying and death. As a war artist, Nevinson defiantly showed corpses of soldiers in paintings such as *Paths of Glory*, *La Patrie*, and *Harvest of Battle*. In the novel, the casualties of the war are, usually, ordinary people, civilians, some overwhelmed by the panicking, prefiguring images in the film *Things to Come*, and recalling Wells's *War of the Worlds*: "The whole population of the great six-million city was stirring, slipping, running; presently it would be pouring *en masse* northward."[83] Richard feels, uneasily, a part of the exodus herd, trampling people underfoot: "He felt his feet tread upon a giving substance, but his brain refused to think what that substance might be." As on a battlefield, Rosalind sees bodies piled into basement areas: "Human flesh filled them to the brim, pressure had packed body upon body." Earlier, she had felt isolated in her fifth-floor flat, especially as she could not see the pigeons, and feared the gas had risen high enough to kill them. Rosalind considers how much death there must be around her, and how all meet "the levelling quality of disaster—death!" whether "those engaged in serving their pleasure . . . from kitchen and scullery" or "those of another class, revelling in night clubs." Nevinson had satirized the latter in his paintings *War Profiteers* and *Broadway Patriotism*, in which the spots and shafts of light reveal, like searchlights, an enemy on the home front: those who have done materially well from the war.[84]

In the novel, Nevinson satirizes the rich, the powerful, and the ambitious. Lord Ragner, proprietor of the *Morning Star*, panics at his arms shares plummeting, due to the outbreak of war: "I saw myself bankrupt. Millions of pounds' worth of armament stocks for sale and the brokers marking them down-down-down." Bankruptcy was a real threat following the Wall Street Crash, and hyperinflation in Germany. Ragner points out that the country is vulnerable because of a dock strike. Britain's General Strike was a fairly recent memory. Mordaunt the editor tries to reassure him: "We've pointed out repeatedly that compromise must be reached or the supplies of food in the country will be exhausted by tomorrow." Such a situation existed with the U-boat campaign in the First World War, and would be repeated in the Second, with the Battle of the North Atlantic. The war thwarts ambition, too, where it had promised to fulfill it. Oliphant, Sir Thomas Grange's secretary, is sorely disappointed in his employer, who is overcome with despair. He had expected Sir Thomas to be given the Ministry again, and he would have been promoted, too. As Oliphant tells himself, "There's nothing like a war for opportunity."[85] Nevinson's own reputation was made from war art, and he illustrates that opportunism, ironically, in his painting of a war armaments tycoon *He Gained a Fortune, but He Gave a Son* and in his Passchaendale painting *Glittering Prizes,* in which, originally, wounded soldiers retreat to the dressing station "between a 'holy grail' of champagne glasses and crossed cigars," which Nevinson later painted out.[86] Rosalind is socially ambitious, seeing the eligible Oliphant as "a rung in the ladder to the dizzy social heights." At the Florentine Temple, a new nightclub she is reviewing, Rosalind reflects on the clientele: "This is a section of London-life which it seems to anyone serious so utterly useless, so utterly futile, except that I suppose it keeps a certain amount of money in circulation." Though affecting scorn for London high life, she enjoys "the sight of the luxurious waste of money." The "gay noisiness of a city's playtime" contrasts with the devastation about to be unleashed.[87]

When war comes, from the air, it is to a London teeming and vulnerable, whose routine is reflected in Nevinson's 1930 *Among the Nerves of the World*, one of the most reproduced of all his paintings. It depicts Fleet Street, famed as the home of numerous newspapers, and dubbed "The Street of Adventure" by the novelist and war correspondent Philip Gibbs.[88] In an explosive composition, a network of wires, offices, signs, trains, and buses illustrates the shrinking world and the growing speed with which news was traveling in the modern age. In the novel, news of war is relayed via the press's "colossal machinery which was steadily printing the miles of paper, which would be ready for publication within another hour." News of war causes confusion: "If it's true why don't they tell us where to go?" asks someone, to which another voice suggests, "To the Tubes—to the Tubes—," a throwback to where people found refuge in the previous war, as the Nevinsons had, but the Tubes are closed, a situation occurring for real at the start of the Blitz.[89]

Richard imagines London firebombed: "One [firebomb], he reflected, could destroy Fleet Street from end to end within minutes. Fifty set London alight from end to end . . . London would burn—bitterly, steadily; as it had been in the Great Fire, so it would be again—there would be no more London!" The Houses of Parliament, which Nevinson had painted in *London Twilight from the Adelphi*, are "suddenly clothed in a garment of flame . . . A symbol of England. The core of her heart!"[90] As in Turner's two paintings of *The Burning of the Houses of Lords and Commons, October 16, 1834* (1835), England's symbolic heart is consumed by fire, a foretelling of the London Blitz, which Nevinson would mark with a painting of St. Paul's Cathedral engulfed in flames, *The Fire of London, 1940.*[91] That symbol of Britain's faith, with fire, has connotations of martyrdom. Much of *Exodus A.D.* is set along the Thames which, with its wharves, warehouses, bridges, barges, and landmark buildings, is much celebrated in Nevinson's paintings and prints, particularly in his monumental *London, Winter*. This is executed in charcoal, pencil, and tempera to give the view, looking over the river from the southern end of Waterloo Bridge toward St Paul's and the Shot Tower, the cast of the season at its darkest. A smaller, even darker, version also exists. The point of view emphasizes the river's width. Nevinson's 1928 painting *Blackfriars Bridge* also gives prominence to the Thames, framed by the busy urban roadways and a skyline of industrial chimneys. The scene in *London, Winter* of historic buildings, river, and barges, is both unified and brightened by ubiquitous white gulls. In his autobiography, Nevinson recalls seeing gulls around the river as a child: "The Thames froze over and I was taken to see the ox roasted near Waterloo Bridge. I remember being struck by the great number of seagulls near the Adelphi and being told that this was the first time they had come so far inland."[92] *Exodus A.D.* includes a scene on the same stretch of river, around Blackfriars Bridge (seen in the distance in *London, Winter*): Richard "saw against the grey-smudged skyline the Lever building, white and clear-etched, a civilized gesture of a world which the young man began to feel had utterly changed during the night. Yet, overhead, despite the smoke, the seagulls swooped and soared, flashing against the ships' rigging and funnels, in their eternal quest for refuse."[93] Through a range of Nevinson's artistic enterprises, gulls become emblems of continuity and survival.

Nevinson's apocalyptic painting *Ave Homo Sapiens*, "in part inspired the story" of *Exodus A.D.*, was used as the basis for the novel's artwork, and was one of a group of apocalyptic pictures he created in the early 1930s.[94] R. R. Tatlock wrote in the *Daily Telegraph*: "*Ave Homo Sapiens* . . . which depicts a "He-Man" encumbered with the paraphernalia of war behind a curtain composed of drops of blood, has little merit as an example of pictorial art. What value it has, is purely literary."[95] The Nietzschean overlord figure is God in the novel, when Richard dreams of himself dead: "God . . . peered through wicked slits of a mask-like covering which protruded in a snout . . . with great knotted arms . . . and His hands were vast . . . with clawing curved talons. From His curiously small head His body swelled vastly into hideous strength." Physically distorted, He is, to Richard's mind, spiritually distorted in his relish for human suffering, a militaristic reflection in an age of dictators. The image of God is a compelling one, that contrasts with a dream of Rosalind's alluding to providence: "the sky seemed like the mantle of Heavenly protection stretched across them for some inscrutable, but Almighty purpose." Aside from envisaging a monstrous God, Nevinson's painting reprises motifs from the First World War: bayonets, as in his War exhibition poster of 1918 and his painting and drypoint *A Dawn, 1914*, and howitzers, as in *Gun in Elevation*. In the background planes, flying above crosses on a mountainous slope, threaten, as in the novel, death and destruction.[96]

In Nevinson's painting *The Unending Cult of Human Sacrifice*, produced in the same year as *Exodus A.D.*, the crucified Christ, massed crosses, and prone bodies represent sacrifice. Their physical agony is echoed in *Exodus A.D.*, when Richard hears the sound of masses of people dying: "it was not human, yet it was the voice of humanity, despairing, casting its last imploring, its last imprecations at the inevitability of doom."[97] In contrast to the monstrous God of *Ave Homo Sapiens* who dominates suffering humanity, the sadly prayerful haloed saints and iconic figure of a Mater Dolorosa (Mother of Sorrow) represent a more human face overlooking marching soldiery, but make no apparent difference to centuries of conflict, symbolized by planes flying above horse-drawn chariot and knight in armor. Bayonets and howitzers are, again, repeated from Nevinson's First World War graphics and paintings. Patriotism, symbolized by flags, appears tied to religion, and equally encouraging of war. Nevinson, though the grandson of a clergyman, claimed that "religion has always left me untouched."[98] In his apocalyptic pictures, however, there are images suggesting the worship of art rather than God in *The Spirit of Progress*, symbolized by an elevated female torso, palette, and brushes, and the god Pan, the creative force connecting the psyche with nature, in *Pan Triumphant*. This painting can be linked to *The Twentieth Century* on account of its size, and to the other "apocalyptic" pictures, for its liners and skyscrapers, but it differs from them, in referencing neither war nor mob. A huge bust of Pan mounted on a pillar dominates the picture, bursting through chains, and linking liner and skyscrapers, signs of affluence and monetary power, and naked male and female figures separated by sea. Such a pillar is the focal point of a bacchanal revel in Arcadia in Nicolas Poussin's *The Triumph of Pan* (1636). The subject had personal importance for Nevinson. He also depicted such a statue of Pan in his 1934 canvas *My Garden*, and had shown a picture called *Pan* as early as 1919.

Bayonets and howitzers recur as powerful motifs in Nevinson's epic painting *The Twentieth Century*. He worked on it from 1932 to 1935, intending it as a cartoon for a mural to represent "the Clash between Thought, Mechanical Invention, Race Idolatory and the Regimentation of Youth," juxtaposing the achievements against the follies of modern civilization, and reflecting the rise of Hitler and Mussolini. Again, massed troops march under their flags, the Union Jack at the left edge of the canvas, a swastika at the right. Behind them are workers under a red banner, Nevinson's despised "mob" who appear in his 1919 lithograph *The Workers*, and are related to the striking dockers and panicking masses of *Exodus A.D.* Skyscrapers tower in the background, with massive girders representing engineering wonders, framing planes (not threatening as in *Exodus A.D.*) and an ocean liner, while a colossal naked male figure akin to Rodin's *Thinker* broods over the armies below.

In *Exodus A.D.*, the world is seen largely through the eyes of journalists out in the streets, not those of an artist in his studio. The woman's headless, legless torso "sprawling like a beast's carcass"[99] is an inversion of the traditional figurative artist's concerns symbolized by a cast of the female form in *The Spirit of Progress* and *Asters*. Other symbols of Nevinson's include the seagulls, signifying freedom, weaving together an image of boats, river, and city in *London, Winter*, adding interest to a flat landscape in *A River Winding Slowly Out to Sea* (1938) (after his dry point *Ebb Tide, Rye* of 1918) and the only signs of life in the harbor in *Crab-pots* (1944). In *Exodus A.D.*, pigeons are a sign of faithfulness and hope. Rosalind fears, when she cannot see them, that gas may have risen to the height of her flat, and is much relieved when "High above her came the faint echo of cooing."[100] Like the gulls, they are associated with freedom, for they can rise above earthbound messes, and like the bat in Nevinson's self-portrait, might signal the hope of rebirth. Nevinson's use of ocean liners starts with the semiabstract painting *The Arrival* (1914), in which simultaneity gives a sense of movement. Liner and quay reappear in *Pan Triumphant*, in which the funnels steam in harmony with curling waves. In this and other pictures of the period, *With Nothing to Lose—Not Even Chains*, *The Spirit of Progress*, and *The Twentieth Century*, a liner is linked with skyscrapers. Nevinson's skyscraper pictures start with buildings being shown from a variety of viewpoints, as in *The Statue of Liberty* (1921), and also stylization, as in *The Soul of a Soulless City* (1920), which serves as a template for later depictions, as in *The Twentieth Century* and *Pan Triumphant*, where the buildings are more featureless, impersonal, but reach into the clouds. There are no such buildings in *Exodus A.D.*, not even Rosalind's high flat in Piccadilly is comparable, rather there are landmarks such as the Houses of Parliament and the Albert Memorial, associated with traditions of British democracy and the monarchy. Planes as well as skyscrapers were objects of veneration for Futurists. In Nevinson's pictures, they became much less particular after *From the Paris Plane* (1929), his view through the wings of a Handley-Page W8, but he maintained an interest in flight, putting distant planes in to most of his apocalyptic images, and *Wanda* (1935), his portrait of Wanda Baillie-Hamilton, as well as three Spitfires, a vast expanse of tilted landscape beneath them, in his Second World War picture *The Return* (1942).

There was a small amount of press coverage of *Exodus A.D.* Among the minority of publications relating it to Nevinson's art was the *Manchester Evening News*, which said: "He can see ugliness and look it in the face."[101] They also found it "vividly written," as did others, and "a haunting picture of utter devastation and degradation." A common charge among reviews was unbelievability. For all its own sense of topicality, the novel did not make much impact, and Nevinson said later it was probably ahead of its time.

For Nevinson, the act of writing much journalism, some essays for books, then eventually a novel, may have been a welcome escape from the art world, where he was many times embattled. In *Who's Who*, he listed his recreations as motor-caravanning and journalism. Between the wars, Nevinson occasionally produced some of his best work, such as *Among the Nerves of the World* and *London, Winter*, and also many fine prints. He associated with writers, and produced a variety of graphics for books and posters. His journalism helped maintain his celebrity, and as a celebrity artist he fed the fiction of Henry Williamson and others. Fiction, in the form of *Exodus A.D.* enabled him to articulate some of his ideas about war and civilization: warnings of lack of defense and wartime shelter; war fever; the fight for survival leading to savagery; death the leveler of the classes; the awesome but deadly formations of enemy planes; and a London in ruins (as it is in *War of the Worlds*). The novel illustrates the fears that generated Nevinson's cycle of apocalyptic pictures. Like the fiction, these drew on images of the First World War, as well as attempting to warn of an immanent war. The novel is full of horrors, including a nightmare vision of a monster God, and the running down of civilization and human life itself.

As one of the greatest artists of the First World War, Nevinson diversified his activities after the war, became a celebrity, a pundit, and an iconic figure appropriated by some of the greatest, and some of the most successful, writers of the age. He enjoyed recounting stories associating himself with writers, such as James Joyce, Sinclair Lewis, H. G. Wells, Arnold Bennett, and Firbank, indicating perhaps a hankering for approval in his father's world. Through Eliot he was linked to a great modernist poem and, through Agatha Christie, to popular fiction. He derived as much pride in his involvement with writers overall, maybe, as from the Legion of Honor or Mons Star. To an artist attempting to work beyond war art, writers sometimes afforded an antidote. Well after producing his main body of war pictures, Nevinson used his experiences of warfare to produce a vivid novel of apocalypse, acting as a subtext for his art, particularly his own images of the time, and this reflected many of the anxieties and fears of the interwar years.

Notes

1. Henry W. Nevinson, *Last Changes, Last Chances* (London: Nisbet, 1928); *Rough Islanders or The Natives of England* (London: Routledge, 1930)

2. Margaret Wynne Nevinson, *Life's Fitful Fever* (London: Black, 1926), 119.

3. F. T. Marinetti and C. R. W. Nevinson, "Vital English Art: A Futurist Manifesto," *Observer*, June 7, 1914; reprinted in W. Hugh Higginbottom, *The Frightfulness of Modern Art* (London: Cecil Palmer, 1928), 130–31.

4. Ibid., 217–18.

5. Margaret Wynne Jones, *Fragments of Life: Tales and Sketches* (London: Allen & Unwin, 1922), 153–58, 154.

6. Gilbert Cannan, *Mendel: A Story of Youth* (London: T. Fisher Unwin, 1916)

7. C. R. W. Nevinson, *Paint and Prejudice* (London: Methuen, 1937), 25–26.

8. Ibid., 29.

9. Cannan, *Mendel*, 87, 58.

10. Nevinson, *Paint and Prejudice*, 29.

11. Cannan, *Mendel*, 87.

12. Sarah MacDougall, *Mark Gertler* (London: John Murray, 2002)

13. H. G. Wells, *War and the Future: Italy, France and Britain at War* (London: Cassell, 1917).

14. John Malcolm, *The Burning Ground* (London: HarperCollins, 1993), 84.

15. *Evening News*, August 29, 1921; *Daily Express*, March 1, 1930.

16. Nevinson, *Paint and Prejudice*, 180.

17. Steven Heller, "A Man Possessed: The Wolfson Collection," *Print* 48 no. 2 (March–April 1994): 87.

18. *Glasgow Evening Times*, September 28, 1920.

19. *Daily News and Leader*, September 28, 1920.

20. *Daily Herald*, September 28, 1920.

21. *Times*, July 15, 1930; *Manchester Guardian*, June 27, 1930; Luigi Pirandello, *The One-act Plays of Luigi Pirandello* (New York: Dutton, 1928)

22. *Graphic*, July 19, 1930, 1.

23. T. S. Eliot, *The Waste Land: A Facsimile and Transcript of the Original Drafts including the Annotations of Ezra Pound*, ed. Valerie Eliot (London: Faber, 1971), 33, 45.

24. Bernard Denvir in *The Café Royalists: An Exhibition of Café Royal Artists* (London: Parkin Gallery, 1972), [1]

25. T. S. Eliot, *The Waste Land* (New York: Boni & Liveright, 1922)

26. B. C. Southam, *A Student's Guide to the Selected Poems of T. S. Eliot* (London: Faber, 1974), 81.

27. Nevinson, *Paint and Prejudice*, 6.

28. Eliot, *The Waste Land.*

29. B. H. Diaz (Ezra Pound), "Art Notes," *New Age*, January 1, 1920 (TGA).

30. *Modern War: Paintings by C. R. W. Nevinson, with an Essay by P. G. Konody* (London: Grant Richards, 1917); *The Great War: Fourth Year, by C. R. W. Nevinson, with an Essay by J. E. Crawford Flitch* (London: Grant Richards, 1918)

31. Ronald Firbank, *The Flower Beneath the Foot* (London: Grant Richards, 1923)

32. Ronald Firbank, *The Flower Beneath the Foot* (New York: Brentano's, 1924)

33. Ronald Firbank, *Sorrow in Sunlight* (London: Brentano's, 1924); Ronald Firbank, *Prancing Nigger* (New York: Brentano's, 1924)

34. Henry W. Nevinson, journal, June 19–28, 1921, Henry Woodd Nevinson Papers, MS.Eng.e.621/4, Bodleian Library, Oxford University.

35. Mark Schorer, *Sinclair Lewis: An American Life* (London: Heinemann, 1961), 395.

36. Nevinson, *Paint and Prejudice*, 179–80.

37. Sinclair Lewis, *Martin Arrowsmith* (London: Cape, 1925), 400; published in United States as *Arrowsmith* (New York: Harcourt Brace, 1925)

38. Ibid., 400.

39. Agatha Christie, *Murder is Easy* (London: Collins, 1939), 32–33.

40. Princess Paul Troubetzkoy and C. R. W. Nevinson, *Exodus A.D.: A Warning to Civilians* (London: Hutchinson, 1934); Malcolm, passim.

41. Ethel Mannin, *Sounding Brass* (London: Jarrolds, 1926)

42. Ethel Mannin, *Confessions and Impressions* (London: Jarrolds, 1930), 197, 198.

43. Nevinson, *Paint and Prejudice*, 177.

44. Ibid., 178.

45. Sisley Huddleston, *Mr Paname: A Paris Fantasia* (New York: Doran, 1927), 197.

46. Sisley Huddleston, *Back to Montparnasse* (London: Harrap, 1931)

47. Nevinson, *Paint and Prejudice*, 164.

48. Henry Williamson, *The Wet Flanders Plain* (London: Faber, 1929)

49. Henry Williamson, *The Gold Falcon, or The Haggard of Love*, published anonymously (London: Faber, 1933), 5.

50. Anne Williamson, *Henry Williamson: Tarka and the Last Romantic* (Stroud, UK: Sutton, 1995), 156.

51. Henry Williamson, *The Linhay on the Downs and Other Adventures in the Old and the New World* (London: Faber, 1934), 168.

52. Alfred Yockney to C. F. G. Masterman, December 4, 1917, 226-A6-129, Imperial War Museum Archive, London.

53. Henry Williamson, *A Test to Destruction* (London: Macdonald, 1960).

54. Henry Williamson, *The Power of the Dead* (London: Macdonald, 1963), 208, 210.

55. Paul Nash, *Outline* (London: Faber, 1949), 89; Barbara Wadsworth, *Edward Wadsworth: A Painter's Life* (Salisbury, UK: Russell, 1989), 29.

56. Nevinson, *Paint and Prejudice*, 24.

57. Nash, *Outline*, 93.

58. Nevinson, *Paint and Prejudice*, 30.

59. Nevinson journal, December 10, 14, 1919, Henry Woodd Nevinson Papers, MS.Eng.misc.e.621/2.

60. Nevinson, *Paint and Prejudice*, 123.

61. Nevinson journal, December 12, 1919, Henry Woodd Nevinson Papers, MS.Eng.misc.e.621/2.

62. Nevinson, *Paint and Prejudice*, 124.

63. Nevinson journal, July 31, 1921, Henry Woodd Nevinson Papers, MS.Eng.misc.e.622/6.

64. Henry Williamson, *The Phoenix Generation* (London: Macdonald, 1965), 233.

65. "Nevinson Talks on Art," *New York Times*, May 30, 1919 (T.G.A. 7311.4–783)

66. H. G. Wells, *The Shape of Things to Come: The Ultimate Revolution* (London: Hutchinson, 1933)

67. Ibid., 55; Nevinson, *Paint and Prejudice*, 26.

68. Princess Paul Troubetzkoy, *Gallow's Seed* (London: Grayson & Grayson, 1934)

69. Troubetzkoy, *Exodus A.D.*, 30.

70. Nevinson, *Paint and Prejudice*, 76.

71. Troubetzkoy, *Exodus A.D.*, 155.

72. Nevinson, *Paint and Prejudice*, 96.

73. Troubetskoy, *Exodus A.D.*, 123.

74. Ibid., 30.

75. C. R. W. Nevinson, "The Arts in this Bellicose Civilization," in *The Seven Pillars of Fire: A Symposium by Dr Maude Royden, Dr L. P. Jacks, Prof. A. E. Richardson, The Marquis of Tavistock, C. R. W. Nevinson. Capt. Bernard Acworth and Sir E. Denison Ross* (London: Herbert Jenkins, 1936), 218.

76. Troubetzkoy, *Exodus A.D.*, 96.
77. Ibid., 103.
78. The painting *Searchlights* referred to here is in Manchester City Art Gallery.
79. Troubetzkoy, *Exodus A.D.*, 101, 118–19, 106.
80. F. T. Marinetti, "Futurist Manifesto," in *Futurism and Futurisms*, ed. Pontus Hulten (Milan: Bompiani, 1986), 514.
81. *Daily Express*, February 25, 1915.
82. Troubetzkoy, *Exodus A.D.*, 87.
83. H. G. Wells, *The War of the Worlds* (1898; repr., London: Heinemann, 1951), 81.
84. Troubetzkoy, *Exodus A.D.*, 101, 255, 213, 212.
85. Ibid., 66, 68, 162.
86. Nevinson, *Paint and Prejudice*, 157.
87. Troubetzkoy., *Exodus A.D.*, 50, 47, 50, 80.
88. Philip Gibbs, *The Street of Adventure* (London: Heinemann, 1909)
89. Troubetzkoy, *Exodus A.D.*, 54, 100.
90. Ibid., 105, 114.
91. The painting was reproduced in *Strand Magazine*, January 1942.
92. Nevinson, *Paint and Prejudice*, 2.
93. Troubetzkoy, *Exodus A.D.*, 136.
94. *Scotsman*, November 15, 1934.
95. R. R. Tatlock, *Daily Telegraph*, November 24, 1933.
96. Troubetzkoy, *Exodus A.D.*, 145, 272.
97. Ibid., 109.
98. Nevinson, *Paint and Prejudice*, 10.
99. Troubetzkoy, *Exodus A.D.*, 179.
100. Ibid., 240.
101. *Manchester Evening News*, December 8, 1934.

Beauty, Rhythm, Strength: C. R. W. Nevinson as a Printmaker, ca. 1916–32

Jonathan Black

C. R. W. NEVINSON MAY BE BETTER KNOWN TODAY as the sole English Futurist, or for his compelling and memorable art of the First World War.[1] However, in less than a decade after he first began to make prints in 1916, he was widely hailed as one of Britain's most consistently interesting and accomplished printmakers.[2] The best of the one hundred and fifty-five or so images Nevinson produced between 1916 and 1932 radiate a concentrated poster-like directness and immediacy, and justly stand comparison with the work of more established painter-printmakers such as Frank Brangwyn, Sir Muirhead Bone, James McBey, Harry Rushbury, and Sir David Young Cameron. Initially derived from his powerful images of the First World War, exhibited in 1916 and 1918, critics marked him out as extremely promising and, typically, the *Glasgow Herald* saw the prints he had produced as an official war artist as conveying an irrefutable "truth from the trenches . . . showing war as it is, divested of all sentimental and picturesque humbug."[3] His prints depicting New York, produced between 1919 and 1921, quickly led to his identification as one of the first chroniclers of urban Jazz Age excitement and dynamism, and so the *New York Evening World* could also describe Nevinson's images of the city as having captured "the Twentieth Century story of the sky-scraper."[4] Although stylistically less daring, his prints of the later 1920s depicting London, Paris, and the English countryside were greatly appreciated by contemporary critics and were much in demand by discerning collectors throughout Western Europe and North America.[5] However, toward the end of the decade, Nevinson suffered a series of debilitating illnesses and found it increasingly difficult to perform the physically demanding, labor intensive aspects of the printmaking process.[6] Consequently, his output rapidly diminished until he gave up entirely around 1932. This decision was probably influenced by the dire economic situation after the Wall Street crash, which had triggered the complete collapse of the hitherto commercially buoyant British contemporary print market, and by the fact he was developing a lucrative career as a provocatively opinionated newspaper columnist and pundit.

Before embarking on a discussion of the first prints he executed, all drypoints (please refer to the Glossary of Technical Terms at the end of this essay) related to images of the First World War that he had painted in oils during 1915–16, it would be useful to explore how and why Nevinson came to take up printmaking during the summer of 1916. He would have been familiar with drypoints and etchings from an early age. His father, Henry, was interested in prints and was friendly with a number of prominent and influential printmakers such as Muirhead Bone, Francis Dodd, and Professor Fred Brown of the Slade School of Art, where Nevinson himself studied between 1909 and 1912. In October 1910, for example, one finds H. W. Nevinson dining at the home of William Rothenstein alongside Dodd, Bone, the painter-etcher Augustus John, as well as his son's tutor at the Slade School of Art, Henry Tonks. Nevinson's father appears to have actively encouraged his son to take an interest in the medium and in February 1907 took him to an exhibition of Whistler's etchings at the Whitechapel Art Gallery,[7] and then in March 1909 to a lecture on Japanese printmaking given at the British Museum by Laurence Binyon, assistant keeper of Oriental Prints.[8] Two years later, in May 1911, Henry Nevinson took his son and his fellow student at the Slade School of Art, Mark Gertler, to the home of Professor Michael Sadler in Weybridge to look at the professor's extensive collection of German Expressionist paintings and prints.[9]

In his autobiography, admittedly written many years after the fact in 1937, Nevinson claimed that while he was studying at the St John's Wood School of Art (ca. 1907–8) the prolific etcher James Abbott McNeil Whistler was "one of my gods," while he also admired the celebrated woodcuts and copperplate engravings of Albrecht Dürer. Nevinson also noted that, while he was at St John's Wood, his work was praised by the eminent Scottish etcher Sir David Murray,[10] and further described his younger self, about to leave the Slade, as "obsessed by Goya, Daumier and Toulouse-Lautrec."[11] Attracted, perhaps, by their shared sharp caricatural approach to physiognomy, references to all three artists can be discerned in prints he produced throughout his career, such as the etching of *The Acrobat* (1923–24), which touches on the continuing fascination he felt for Degas's and Toulouse Lautrec's captivating images of the circus and of fearless trapeze artists. His large lithograph *Hans and Fritz* (1918) and the drypoints *Success* (ca. 1922) and *Any London Street* (ca. 1922), in their bitingly satirical approach to physiognomy, hark back not only to Goya and Daumier but also stand comparison with images of social satire produced at the same time in Weimar Germany by Otto Dix and Georg Grosz.

Early in May 1916, Henry Nevinson visited the painter-printmaker Alfred Hartley (1855–1933) at his home in St. Ives, Cornwall. According to Nevinson senior, Hartley showed him "his process of etching and aquatint," after which Henry bought some examples.[12] One can only presume that, on returning to London, Henry showed these examples to his son—who had recently been invalided out of the army and was now keen to prove his artistic versatility. Meanwhile, during the early summer of 1916, Nevinson Junior participated in the foundation of the Decorative Art Group, which contained a large contingent of printmakers including Carlo Norway (linocuts),[13] Frank Potter (an etcher), Nancy Smith (who produced lithographs for poster designs), and Ethelbert White (who had recently begun to experiment with woodcuts).[14]

Nevinson's first confident foray into printmaking comprised eleven drypoints, all executed between June and the middle of September 1916. They were included in his first solo show, which opened at the Leicester Galleries, in London, on September 26, 1916. All Nevinson's 1916 drypoints were derived from oils, pastels, and charcoal studies related to his searing experiences as an ambulance driver and male nurse with the Friends' Ambulance Unit (November–December 1914), and while serving as a Private in the Royal Army Medical Corps [RAMC] at the Third London General Military Hospital, Wandsworth (June 1915 to January 1916). Early in 1916 he was given an honorable discharge from the RAMC owing to "rheumatic fever," which had affected his heart.[15] His nerves would remain in a vulnerable state for the rest of the war and there is some evidence to suggest that Nevinson found that the particular form of highly disciplined yet compartmentalized concentration required by printmaking had a calming effect on him.[16] After leaving the RAMC, unable to afford a studio of his own, he lived and worked at the family home of 4 Downside Crescent, Belsize Park, and it is likely that all the 1916 drypoints were executed in one of the top-floor rooms there.

Nevinson's Leicester Galleries exhibition was a tremendous success with the public and the press, with the *Manchester Guardian* praising his paintings and prints for bringing home to an ignorant public "the black gloom, the horror, the feeling of despair . . . in this epoch of horror."[17] Several critics found themselves pleasantly surprised by his drypoints, for they discovered in them a technical virtuosity they did not readily discern in his handling of paint.[18] Indeed, the majority of those who commented on his prints felt that his drypoint versions of designs, initially executed in oils, were invariably more persuasive and compelling.[19] Paul Konody, for example, singled out the drypoints of *Returning to the Trenches* (one of the very few prints Nevinson executed in his robust cubo-futurist manner), *Troops Resting* [1916, 21.2 × 26.2 cm (fig. 14)], *Column on the March* [1916, 17.6 × 27.7 cm], and *Deserted Trench on the Yser* [1916, 15.4 × 19 cm] for special praise. He also correctly suspected that the composition for the grimly austere *Deserted Trench* was heavily informed by the artist's enthusiasm for the eighteenth- and nineteenth-century Japanese woodblock prints of Kitagawa Utamaro (1753–1806), Katsushika Hokusai (1760–1849), and Utagawa Hiroshige (1797–1858). Nevinson's stylized treatment of falling rain is decidedly reminiscent of Hiroshige in some of the color woodblock prints he executed in the early 1830s as part of his series *The Fifty-Three Post-Stations of the Tokaido* (1830–34). Konody was also struck by how the artist could suggest different moods in the same design depending on whether it was executed in oils, pastel, or drypoint. Invariably, the mood of the drypoint version was bleaker, implying those figures present were menaced by some dire peril. The oil of *On The Road To Ypres* (1916) suggested to him the purposeful bustle of transport and ammunition wagons. By contrast, in the print (1916, 12.5 × 22 cm), the dark areas created by the characteristic drypoint burr gave the impression that the wagons were moving in desperate haste, perhaps away from the advancing Germans, or from the prospect of coming under devastating enemy shell fire, since the position on the windswept road was so open and vulnerable. As for *Column on the March*, in the oil the line of French *poilu* conveyed a distinct impression of marching confidently and irrepressibly toward the firing line, whereas the soldiers in the drypoint version appeared to Konody to be recoiling away from battle in disheveled disarray.[20]

Nevinson was quick to appreciate the marketing potential offered by his widely praised drypoints. He produced *Twilight* (edition of seventy-five), first exhibited at the New English Art Club in November 1916, for example, to serve as a tool to market the luxury edition of *Modern War: Paintings by C. R. W. Nevinson* with twenty-five reproductions and a text by Paul Konody. The book

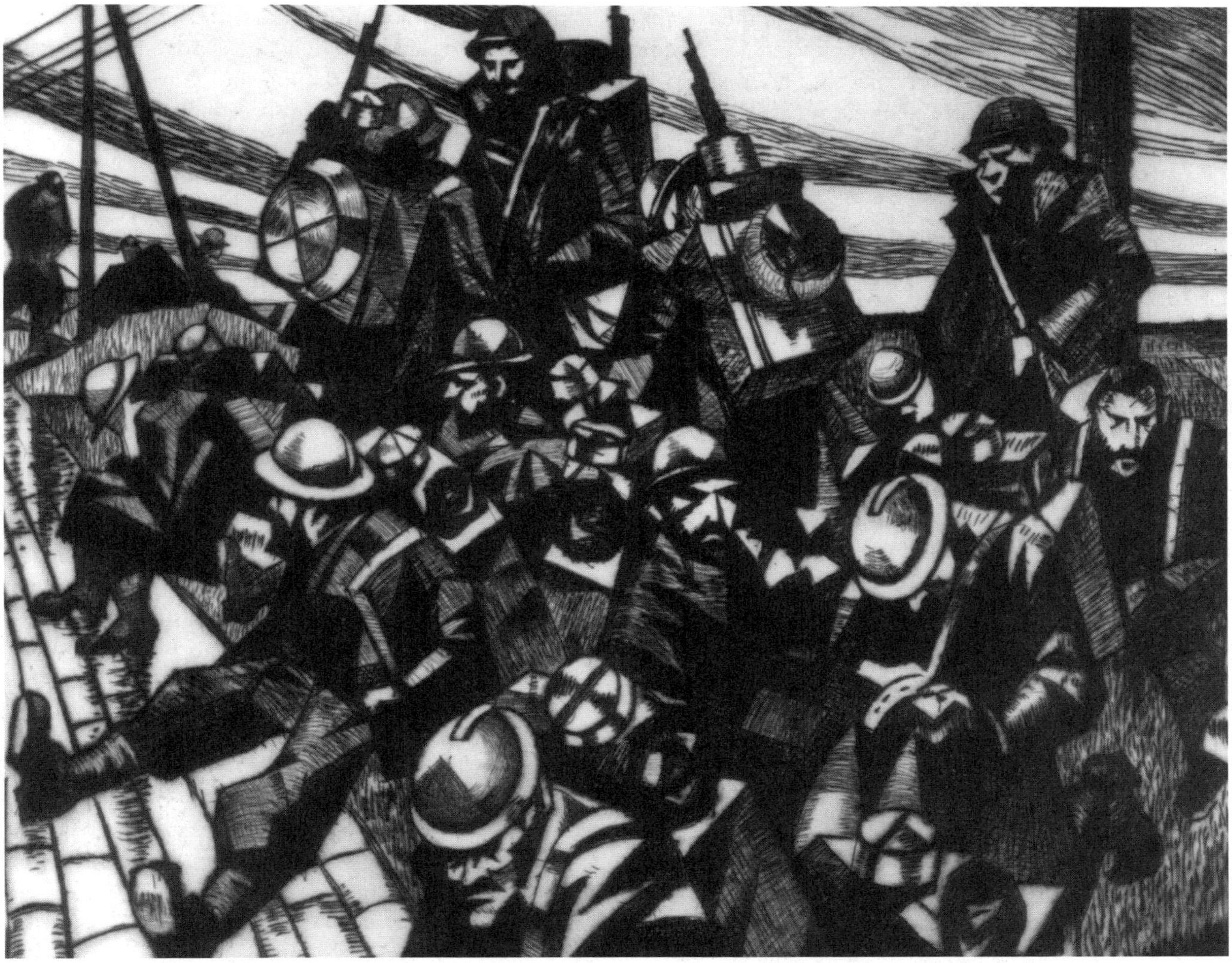

14. C. R. W. Nevinson, *Troops Resting*, 1916. Drypoint, 21.2 × 26.2 cm. By Kind Permission of the Fine Art Society PLC, London.

was published by Grant Richards in January 1917 with 1,125 standard copies priced at 10s 6d each, and 75, at 31s 6d, with the more expensive "luxury" edition signed by the artist and containing a signed print of *Twilight* described as "a hitherto unpublished etching."[21]

Towards the end of 1916 Nevinson began to experiment with both transfer lithography and with the more traditional approach, which required the artist to work directly on the lithographic stone with ink and/or charcoal stick. Nevinson's first three lithographs, *Dawn at Southwark* (1916, 34.3 × 44.8 cm, edition of 50), *La Villette* (1917, 38.5 × 30.3 cm, edition of 50) and *Loading the Ship* (1917, 43.2 × 33.8 cm, edition of 25) were exhibited at the Senefelder Club toward the end of January 1917.[22] Nevinson may have decided to take up lithography when he did as a result of contact with other members of the Decorative Art Group, such as Nancy Smith and Carlo Norway, or through Joseph Pennell, a champion of the medium, and especially of the transfer method.[23] In his autobiography, Nevinson later stated he had first studied lithography in about 1912 under Ernest Jackson (1872–1945) at the "London County Council School on Southampton Row."[24] Indeed, he paid Jackson an uncharacteristically handsome tribute: "Of all the men I have met, who deal with the teaching of art, he is the finest and most erudite: a technician and an artist."[25]

Jackson began to teach regularly at the Central School from 1906 onward, and two years later he and Joseph Pennell founded the Senefelder Club, dedicated to raising the profile of lithography in Great Britain. In 1909 the Club held its first exhibition at the Goupil Gallery, London, and by 1914 Pennell felt so optimistic about the future prospects of the medium in Britain he wrote, "The most brilliant of the younger men are all now making remarkable lithographs and they are being encouraged by collectors and dealers to do so as well as by publishers . . . there is a genuine renaissance of the art."[26] Pennell, in 1914, also noted the growing popularity of working directly on the stone with mezzotint rockers, penknives, scrapers, and roulettes as opposed to the transfer method he championed, and this became evident early in Nevinson's *Dawn at Southwark* (1916) and *La Villette* (1917). In 1919 Malcolm Salaman, an advocate of "experimental" British printmaking, confidently asserted that the most "genuine" lithographers preferred this.[27]

Nevinson's first efforts at the Senefelder Club in January 1917 were well received, and Oscar Drey in the *Westminster Gazette* hailed *Dawn at Southwark* as "the best English lithograph [made] in years."[28] Three months later he exhibited his first color lithograph *The Blue Wave* (1917, 34 × 42.5 cm) with the Friday Club, an image which again strongly suggests a considerable compositional debt to Japanese color woodblock printing and, in particular, Hokusai's *The Hollow of the Deep Sea Wave off Kanagawa* (part of the series *Thirty Six Views of Mount Fuji*, 1829–31). The influence is certain, though Nevinson's skill is such that his image is not overwhelmed by the presence of Hokusai and rather to be admired for the discipline with which he streamlined the minutiae of lavish detail—so evident in the work of the Japanese artist—to emphasize the crushingly concentrated power of the wave.

In May 1917, Nevinson was appointed an official war artist by the recently created Department of Information and asked to contribute six drawings, on the theme of *Making Aircraft*, to an ambitious series of sixty-six propaganda lithographs by eighteen artists under the collective title of *Britain's Efforts and Ideals*, the printing of which would be supervised by Ernest Jackson. Of the six drawings Nevinson produced, the two that most successfully translated into lithographs are *Making the Engine* (1917, 40.4 × 30.3 cm, edition of 200) and *Acetylene Welder* (1917, 40.4 × 30.3 cm, edition of 200). The other four images are *Assembling Parts* (1917, 40.3 × 31.8 cm), *In the Air* (1917, 40.3 × 31.8 cm), *Banking at 4,000 Feet* (1917, 40.2 × 30 cm), and *Swooping Down on a Taube* (1917, 40.2 × 30 cm). The *Britain's Efforts and Ideals* exhibition opened at the Fine Art Society, London, in July 1917. Though Nevinson was by far the youngest artist exhibiting, his *Making Aircraft* set was singled out for particular positive comment by Frank Rutter who wrote in the *Sunday Times* that Nevinson's depictions were "the most powerful and arresting of all the exhibits."[29] *Making the Engine* and *Acetylene Welder* confirmed Nevinson's status in the minds of many, as the war artist who possessed the ability to depict the reality of modern warfare based upon standardized mass production and rigorously organized industrial processes. At the same time *Banking at 4,000 Feet*, in the evocative detail of the artist's hand clutching at the side of his cockpit as the flimsy craft made the turn, convinced the authorities that Nevinson possessed the daredevil courage to be a successful war artist.[30] Accordingly, in early July 1917, Nevinson was sent to work in France as an official war artist for a month. He returned to London early in August 1917 and during the remainder of the year, at great speed, painted a series of war images in oil. Then, in less than two months, between late December 1917 and the middle of February 1918, he produced a torrent of some twenty-three prints, including many of his best, comprising fourteen lithographs, seven drypoints, and two woodcuts (his first foray into that particular medium). In December 1917, Nevinson wrote to C. F. G. Masterman, at the Ministry of Information, with a proposal to execute a wide-ranging "series of lithographs, etchings and woodcuts of the War with a view to getting exhibits of my work abroad and in the provincial towns of England, Scotland etc. (It is quite impossible nowadays to send paintings and drawings on voyages and also patrons object to loaning). Already my dealers can fix an exhibition of this kind in New York . . ."[31] The final comment suggests that he was already contemplating, some eighteen months before he eventually arrived there, a visit to the American city which would inspire some of the most scintillating examples of his printmaking prowess.

At the exhibition of Nevinson's official war art, held at the Leicester Galleries between March and April 1918, only six prints (all lithographs) were displayed without their "parent" image in oils. In a handful of cases the print seems to have been made first, with Nevinson painting the image on canvas some months after the print had first been displayed in public. Henceforth, the vast majority of Nevinson's print output would be reproductions of already extant designs; at the time and thereafter this was not interpreted as evidence of lack of skill or imagination on the part of the printmaker, rather, critics and collectors derived enjoyment from appreciating the subtle differences in emotional resonance between a design in oils and then its slightly later print version.[32] Some of the most haunting images Nevinson created both in print form and in oils, were of the pulverized, desecrated landscape of the western front, such as the lithographs *After a Push* (1918, 48.5 × 38 cm, edition of 25) and *The Road from Arras to Bapaume* (1918, 47.2 × 38.5 cm), and were as powerful and moving in their own way as anything produced by Paul Nash.

In his autobiography, Nevinson wrote that he returned to London, from a fortnight's holiday in Cornwall, to discover that "a bomb had fallen on the printing works where my lithographs were kept and that my stones were damaged. The reason for the extra ridge in *The Road from Arras to Bapaume* is because I had to put it in to cover the injury done to my original stone."[33] An entry in H. W. Nevinson's diary suggests that the lithographic stone was damaged during an air raid on the evening of January 27, 1918. The next day he noted that his son's lithographic printers in Holborn had been hit and "three of his stones [were] broken."[34] Nevinson's drypoints of the period, such as *Reclaimed Country* (1917, 20 × 14 cm), *Survivors at Arras* (1917, 28.5 × 23.4 cm), and *That Cursèd Wood* (1918, 25 × 34 .7 cm), also forcefully convey the devastation inflicted on town and country alike by unceasing shelling and by sustained unsparing aerial bombing.

Other lithographs and drypoints dealt with other aspects of life led by British soldiers at the front. The lithograph *Inside Brigade Headquarters* (1917, 35.4 × 25.4 cm) probably refers to an infantry brigade that was part of the Fourth Infantry Division with whom Nevinson stayed in July 1917. Comments Nevinson later made to a New York newspaper in May 1919 shed light on what he was seeking to convey in this image of peaceful bureaucratic life in a deep dugout: "Men were just creatures of routine. Everybody, from Generals to privates, was just a clerk . . . There is hardly any excitement in war. It is routine and dullness and greed . . . The charge gets written up and painted—not the tuning up of the great machine that is behind the charge."[35] *The Bomber* (1918, 28.6 × 22.3 cm) was one of Nevinson's few wartime prints (in this case a lithograph) to be executed in a quasi-Futurist style; a style the artist believed was suited to the subject matter, with Futurist lines of force conveying the force of the explosion that will inevitably follow once the grenade hurled by the British soldier has hit its target and detonated. Simultaneously, the staccato Futurist idiom supplies an unsparing indication of what havoc the grenade explosion, creating hundreds of whirling jagged fragments of steel, will inflict on the body of one of its victims.

Nevinson also memorably depicted ordinary British and German soldiers in his prints. The lithograph *Hans and Fritz* (1918, 47 × 34.5 cm) presents a surprisingly sympathetic image of two recently captured German prisoners and, as noted earlier, their faces are recorded in a blunt manner that anticipates Dix and Grosz, and harks back to the work of Goya, Daumier, and the French caricaturist Jean-Louis Forain (1852–1931). There is also something of a decidedly caricatural edge to Nevinson's representations of British soldiers such as the drypoints *A Group of Soldiers* (dated 1917, 35.5 × 25.5 cm) and *The Mule Team* (1917, 17.8 × 24.8 cm). The War Office in London was horrified by the oil painting of the former and, initially, wanted to prevent its public display on the grounds that it would be seized upon by the Germans "as evidence of British degeneration."[36] In the latter there is little to distinguish between the features of the British soldier and those of the transport mule he is riding. The men from the Royal Engineers attempting rather maladroitly to repair a broken telephone wire, in the drypoint of *Nerves of an Army* (1918, 20 × 14.2 cm, edition of 100), hardly strike one as adept professional technicians and therefore likely to make a good job of the task they are undertaking. Presumably, Nevinson thought highly of this print since it was used to market copies of *The Great War: Fourth Year by C. R. W. Nevinson*, text by J. E. Crawford Flitch and published by Grant Richards with twenty-four reproductions in September 1918. Nine hundred copies were produced at 15s each, while one hundred copies of the luxury edition (at 42s) were signed by the artist and contained a signed print of *Nerves of an Army*.[37]

One of Nevinson's most striking First World War lithographs is *Hauling Down an Observation Balloon at Night* (1918, 51.5 × 36.2 cm), an image probably inspired by a visit made in July 1917 to a Balloon unit at St. Nicholas, near Arras, commanded by Richmond Temple (1893–1958), a friend of the war poet Siegfried Sassoon. Here, Nevinson depicts a relatively novel piece of military equipment but in a manner that recalls the approach to figuration pursued by the sixteenth-century painter El Greco, whom he singled out for praise in an article in October 1919. In this he argued that El Greco had pioneered the "deliberate distortion of form either to overstate, for dramatic effect, or sometimes merely to create a unity, a cohesion of design, within the limits of the picture."[38] In April 1919, the notable American critic and collector Albert Eugene Gallatin described Nevinson's print as "a scene drawn in front of Arras of a balloon being put to roost after a night up spotting the flashes of enemy guns in order to observe their positions, often impossible to detect in daytime."[39]

A month later Nevinson told the *New York Times*, with palpably lip-smacking relish, that he went up in a balloon:

> during the great British attack on Greenland Hill near Arras. When we were some distance up the officer in charge shouted to me "Sit on the edge of the basket . . .

> we're going to be shot down" [by a marauding German fighter reported in their sector] . . . I strapped on my parachute and sat on the edge of the basket, while the German shells burst in the air above and below. "I'll tell you when to jump" said the officer in charge [presumably Richmond Temple]. Thank God he never did. If he had, I know I could not have found the courage to jump off the balloon into the air. But, all the time, I was making shorthand sketches . . .[40]

During January and February 1918 Nevinson produced two of only four woodcuts he would make throughout his printmaking career. It was a brief flicker of interest, possibly stimulated by awareness in 1918 of a series of eye-catching woodcuts by Edward Wadsworth depicting ships sporting "dazzle" camouflage with bold black and white stripes.[41] It is unfortunate that Nevinson produced so few woodcuts since the two he executed, *Ramming Home a Heavy Shell* (1918, 23 × 30.6 cm, edition of 12) and *MT* [*Motor Transport*] (1918, 21.7 × 28.5 cm, edition of 12) are both images infused with a direct and eye-catching vitality.

Nevinson appears to have found that the technical demands of printmaking had a beneficial and soothing affect on his severely strained and tattered nerves.[42] In January 1918, anxiety attacks, combining insomnia and something of a persecution complex, prompted him to consult the famous psychiatrist, Dr. Henry Head. Though he was finding it difficult to put brush to canvas, Nevinson was still keen to build on the favorable response given to the war prints he exhibited in March 1918. In June of that year, he wrote to C. F. G. Masterman reminding him of his print series idea "last Christmas . . . I rather fancy myself as an exponent of those mediums [etching and lithography]." Printmaking helped him to ward off "my fits of melancholy which end in sleeplessness."[43]

During the summer of 1918, without having received a positive reply to the offer he had made to Masterman, Nevinson decided to experiment with the print technique of mezzotint—widely regarded by his contemporaries as time-consuming and decidedly archaic. Mezzotints were damned by their association with countless prints of the eighteenth and early nineteenth centuries, reproducing portraits, genre scenes, and historical epics. The laborious work required with a rocker on the surface of the plate was regarded as toxic to the imagination in its repetitive tediousness. Nevinson made three mezzotints during 1918: *From an Office Window* [25.3 × 17.5 cm (fig. 15)], *Limehouse* (22.5 × 15 cm), and *Wind* (12.5 × 37.5 cm, edition of 25), and all were exhibited at the Keppel Gallery in New York during April and May 1919. All were derived from earlier oil paintings: *From an Office Window* was first exhibited with the Friday Club in April 1917, while *Limehouse* was related to a quasi-Futurist rendition of the Thames riverside painted ca. 1913 and the oil of *Wind* was exhibited with the New English Art Club in January 1918. *Limehouse* proved a particular success when it was exhibited in New York with one newspaper critic praising its dense, atmospheric evocation of "the murky Chinatown district of London"—an area rumored to be thick with opium dens and the depraved abodes of white slavers.[44]

It may not have been entirely coincidental that Nevinson began to exhibit mezzotints in the spring of 1919, as in April a central London gallery exhibited a large selection of the finest eighteenth-century British images in the same medium, and it is possible Nevinson, who had got wind of this, hoped the exhibition would stimulate a revival of interest in his own. The exhibition, at the Harvey Gallery, off St. James's Street, was well received and the *Times* thought it "one of the choicest artistic treats of the year."[45] The show did not, however, succeed in resuscitating a favorable perception on mezzotints in the country. In a sense Nevinson's fine work in the medium anticipated a revival that never actually came to pass. He would produce only two more, both impressive, in 1919–20: *The Roof Garden* [1919 (fig. 16)], first exhibited at his Peace show, held at the Leicester Galleries in October 1919; and the unfinished *New York Night*, first exhibited at the Alpine Club Gallery, London, in April 1921.

Following the end of the war Nevinson immediately made a deliberate attempt to further secure his reputation as a daring and inventive printmaker by exhibiting with the Senefelder Club, and in January 1919 he exhibited two of his largest ever prints, both lithographs, there: *Le Port* (1919, 50.7 × 38.8 cm, edition of 25) and *Wet Evening, Oxford Street* [1919, 74.2 × 48.5 cm, edition of 25 (fig. 17)]. The imagery of both touch on a renewed interest in the sights of the industrial and bustling commercial world, sights which had stimulated his imagination before the war. Some of the faces, for example, in the crowded foreground of *Wet Evening, Oxford Street* recall the ragtime dancers of *Waiting For The Robert E. Lee*, one of his first fully fledged Futurist works exhibited in London in October 1913 at the Post-Impressionists and Futurists show held at the Doré Galleries. At the same time, ever sensitive to developments and trends within the contemporary art world, the prominent positioning of the umbrellas in *Wet Evening, Oxford Street* refers to a resurgence of interest in the work of Pierre August Renoir who had recently died and whose striking early Impressionist canvas *Umbrellas*

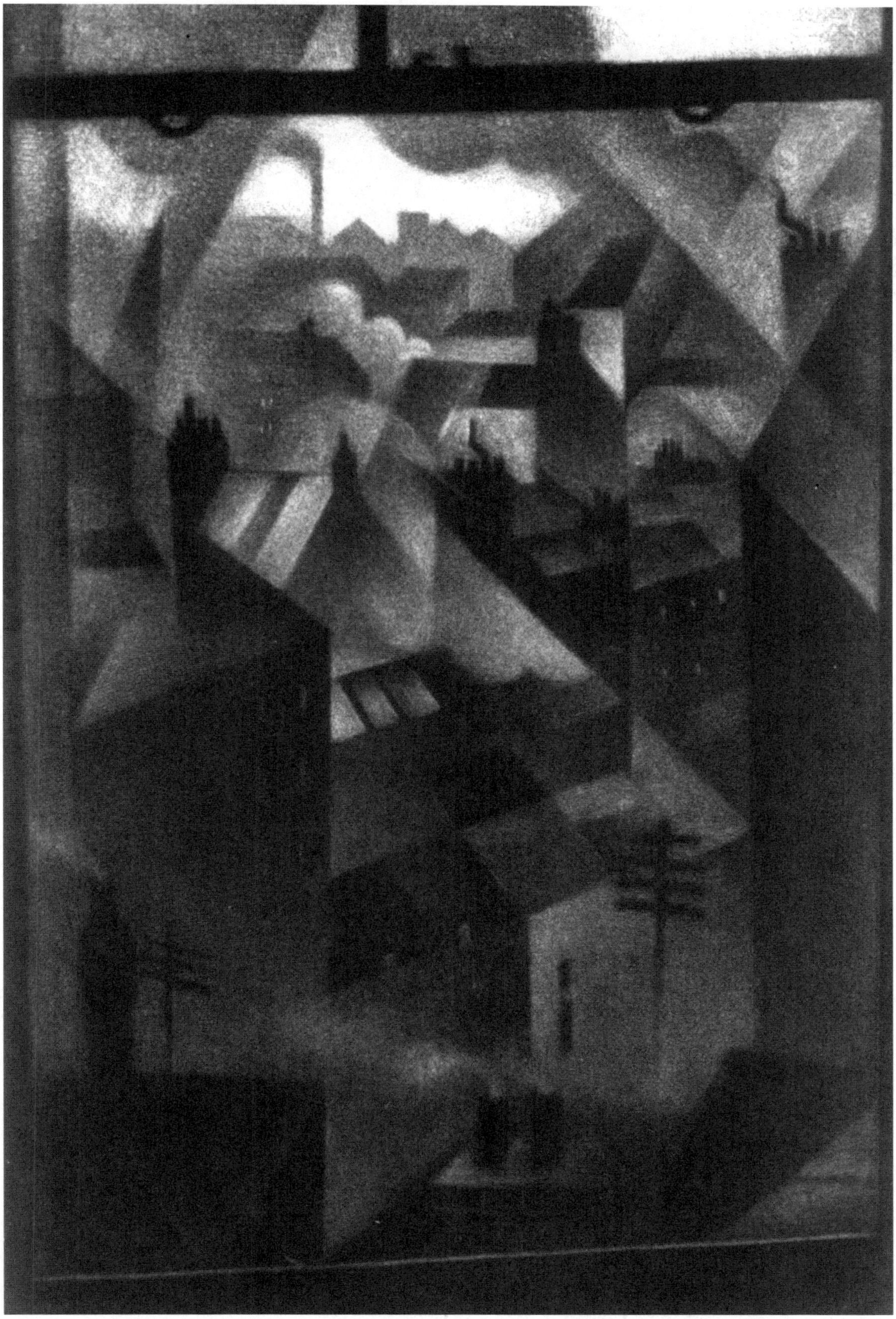

15. C. R. W. Nevinson, *From an Office Window*, 1918. Mezzotint, 25.3 × 17.5 cm. By Kind Permission of the Fine Art Society PLC, London.

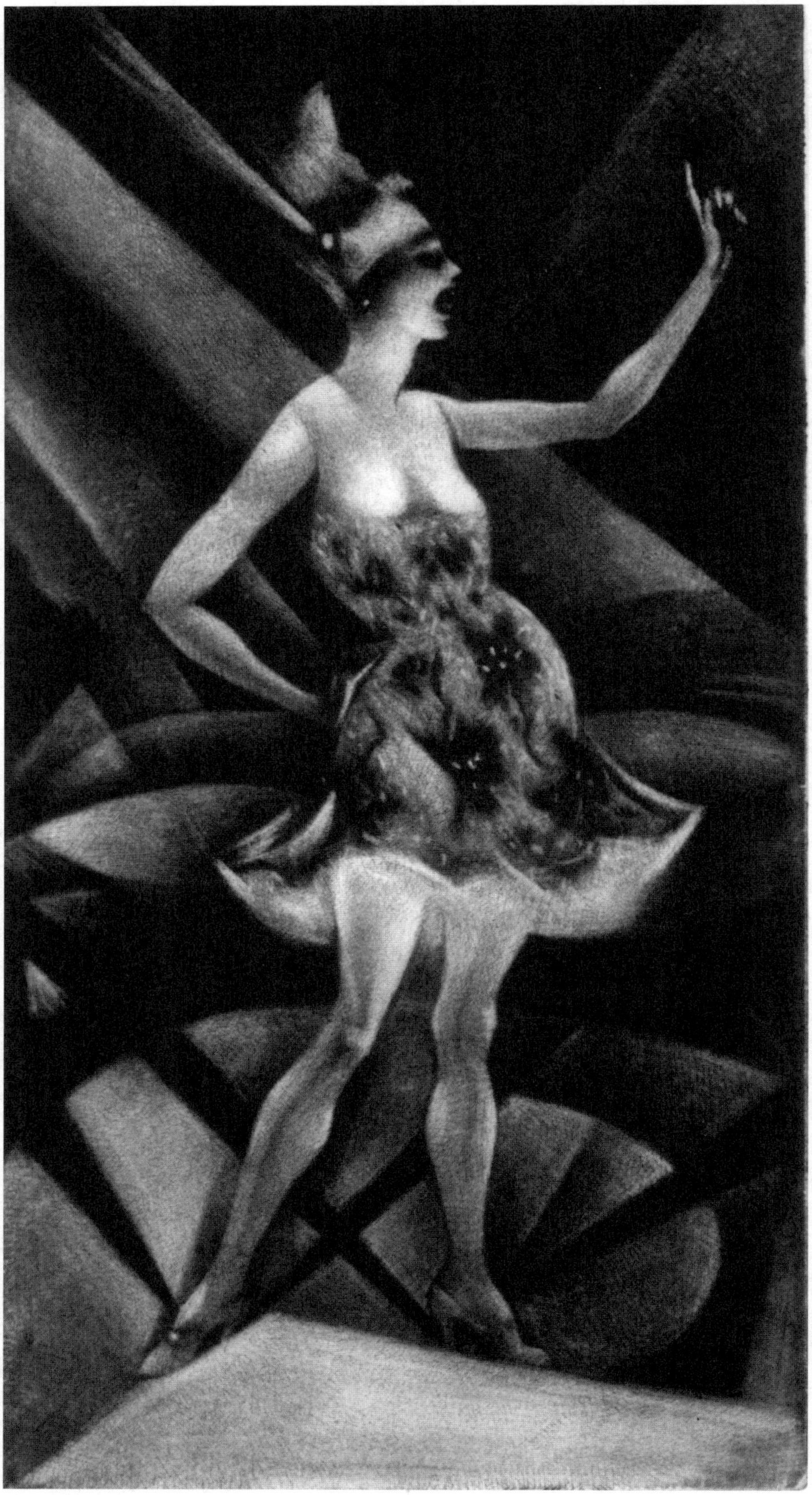

16. C. R. W. Nevinson, *The Roof Garden*, 1919. Mezzotint, 21.1 × 11.6 cm. By Kind Permission of the Fine Art Society PLC, London.

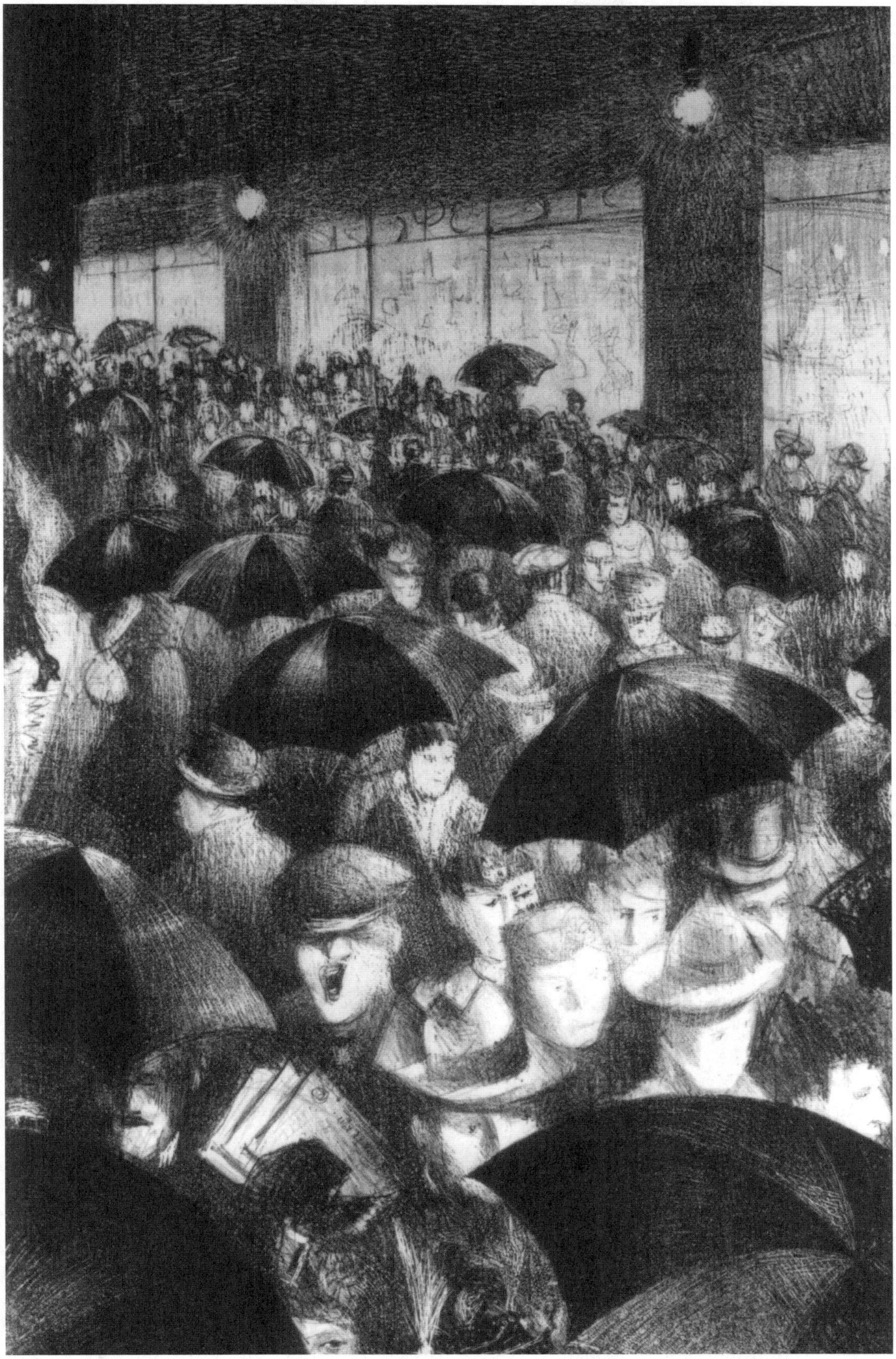

17. C. R. W. Nevinson, *Wet Evening, Oxford Street*, 1919. Lithograph, 74.2 × 48.5 cm. By Kind Permission of the Fine Art Society PLC, London.

in the Rain had just entered the collection of the National Gallery in London. The rehabilitation and favorable reassessment of Renoir became one of the strands constituting Jean Cocteau's so-called "rappel à l'ordre" movement in France. At the same time, true to the call he had made in March 1919 for artists to pay more attention to happenings on the streets of the nation's big cities, Nevinson later produced another large and imposing lithograph *The Workers* (1919, 51.5 × 35.3 cm, edition of 50) commenting upon a recent strike by the National Union of Railwaymen that had crippled the United Kingdom for the best part of ten days.[46] The lithograph caused a considerable stir when it was included in Nevinson's Peace Exhibition, which opened at the Leicester Galleries on October 25, 1919. The Quaker magazine *Ploughshare* (November 1919) thought *The Workers* "might well [depict] the beginning of a revolution,"[47] and two years later, in October 1922, Nevinson actually allowed the Labour Party to use the image as the basis for a general election poster.[48] However, by 1929, Nevinson was expressing a near pathological hatred for Socialists and Socialism in general, "naturally, as an artist, I loathe Socialists as I always give my best trying to construct and Socialists always destroy and take and take . . ."[49]

The prints at the Leicester Galleries, in October 1919, which attracted the most favorable attention, however, were those in which Nevinson depicted his reactions to the stimulus of New York, in which he had stayed for about three weeks in May 1919. Works such as the lithograph *Looking Down into Wall Street* (1919, 48.7 × 34.8 cm, edition of 25), the drypoint *The Temples of New York* (1919, 19.7 × 15.2 cm), the drypoint *Broadway Girls* (1919, 13.8 × 17.6 cm), and the mezzotint *The Roof Garden* (1919, mezzotint, 21.1 × 11.6 cm, edition of 50) powerfully conveyed Nevinson's fascination with the dizzying, neck-craning vertiginousness of the architecture and of the dynamic energy of its raucous and brassy nightlife. *The Roof Garden*, his last completed mezzotint, was derived from a pastel he sketched of a "flapper" glimpsed at the Roof Garden of the Waldorf-Astoria Hotel. The print supplies sterling proof of one of Nevinson's many strengths as an artist; the ability to capture a telling moment in time. This gaudy, tawdry harpy of the dance floor is the corporeal distillation and quintessence of New York in the Jazz Age, with flappers, bootleggers, and speakeasies, created by Nevinson at least three years before F. Scott Fitzgerald coined that evocative label. Her gesture could be a dance move or a summoning of her rumrunner escort to take her to one of Jay Gatsby's riotous parties.

During his short stay in New York Nevinson met the influential art critic of the *Christian Science Monitor*, Charles Lewis Hind, the British painter-printmaker Horace Brodzky (1885–1969), the important collectors John Quinn and Lillie Bliss (both of whom bought examples of Nevinson's prints), while Albert Gallatin introduced him to the American artist who had impressed Nevinson the most, the painter-printmaker George Bellows (1882–1925).[50] Nevinson later wrote that he greatly preferred Bellows's "lithographs to his paintings" while he also found him to be "a fine, open-minded, cultivated American."[51]

Evidently, Nevinson's prints exhibition at the Keppel Gallery was both a commercial and critical success. The day after the exhibition closed, the *New York Herald* commented: "It is to be hoped that Mr. Nevinson will make a set of lithographs of New York while he is here. There is no other living artist who is so equipped as he to show the inhabitants of this city what an interesting place in which they live."[52] Meanwhile, no less than the *New York Times* devoted a lengthy review to analyzing why Nevinson's lithographs of First World War subjects were so technically impressive: "The artist works directly on the stone . . . because he thus can put in his lights instead of leaving them out. When you draw with the black chalk alone all your marks are dark marks and the parts you wish to leave light you must leave untouched. But when you draw with both chalk and scraper you can scratch your lights with as nervous and positive touch as you have . . . perhaps the print becomes something of a mezzotint in the process."[53] The reviewer was struck by how many of the lithographs were distinguished by a combination of delicacy, sensitivity, "persuasive compositional rhythm," and solidity.[54] Nevinson, presumably, must have relished the challenge explicit in this article, which he no doubt avidly read since he had a clippings agency busily gathering every mention of his activities in the press.

Nevinson returned to London early in June 1919 to be informed of the recent death of his infant son, Anthony. In his memoirs, immediately after commenting upon this dreadful event, Nevinson wrote: "my time was spent in etching and I did practically no painting at all. I know of no job more engrossing and, to be frank, I think that is its danger."[55] By the last week of October 1919 he had four New York-inspired prints *Looking Down into Wall Street*, *The Temples of New York*, *Broadway Girls*, and *The Roof Garden*, as well as seven related works in other media (oils, pastel, and watercolor), on display at the Leicester Galleries. Toward the end of June 1919, Nevinson and his wife Kathleen had moved out of 4 Downside

Crescent (where they had been living since their marriage in November 1915) and into their first home—a flat on the Euston Road, London.[56] It was, presumably, in the Euston Road flat that Nevinson executed one of his most dazzling evocations of New York's electrically illuminated Broadway, the lithograph, *The Great White Way* (1920, 50.3 × 30.6 cm, edition of 25), which was first exhibited at the Senefelder Club in February 1920. A few months later, in July 1920, he exhibited the magisterial drypoint *Three AM: A Corner by Madison Square at Night* (also known as *2 AM New York* and as *Metropolis*) (1920, 25.1 × 17.4 cm, edition of 75) at Manchester City Art Gallery. The apartment blocks loom up impressively, and almost oppressively, lit by electric street lamps amid the darkness, and yet the image is infused by a lingering sense of forbidding urban loneliness and disquiet reminiscent of some of the etchings of New York scenes that Edward Hopper produced between about 1915 and 1922. It is not beyond the bounds of possibility that Bellows could have introduced him to the prints of his good friend Hopper. At the same time the image anticipates some of the striking sets present in Fritz Lang's classic 1926 cinematic science fiction distopia *Metropolis*.[57]

During the summer of 1920 Nevinson concentrated on producing scenes of New York in oils, watercolor, pastel, and gouache. Printmaking took a back seat for a while, perhaps, because he wanted to see which works proved most successful before determining which could be translated into print, and then what print medium would be apposite. By the middle of September some twenty works inspired by New York were on display at his Robert Street studio. At the time Nevinson ringingly told a journalist that "the most beautiful products of the modern world are a Rolls Royce car and a skyscraper. They have been built for strict utility, their lines are perfect . . . New York will be remembered for its introduction of the architecture of the skyscraper."[58] The paintings were eventually exhibited at the Bourgeois Galleries, on Fifth Avenue, for a month over November and December 1920, but on this occasion the critical reception given Nevinson's work was far less positive and enthusiastic and he only succeeded in selling two of the ninety-eight works on display.

On returning to London he produced a series of prints (mostly drypoints), after the oil paintings of New York he had exhibited at the Bourgeois Galleries, and in March 1921 H. W. Nevinson noted his son was hard at work on what he referred to as a series of "New York etchings" (these were actually drypoints as Nevinson did not take up etching with acid for the first time until early in 1922).[59] The majority of Nevinson's New York drypoints were exhibited at the Friday Club, in London, in April 1921 and then at the Keppel Gallery in New York in July of that same year, where, ironically, they attracted far more appreciative and admiring reviews than the original oils and watercolors had done at the Bourgeois Galleries during November and December 1920. The critic of the *New York Evening Globe*, for example, thought Nevinson handled with aplomb all the varying sights of the city from "Winter Garden girls, with their mobile shoulders, to . . . the deep shadows cast by tall metropolitan buildings and the dazzling electric lamps of Broadway."[60]

The print images of New York that Nevinson produced, between January and March 1921, suggest that his reaction to the city, and to the furious pace of American urban existence, had become a highly complex and ambivalent one. Some of the images are frankly admiring of the beauty and power of American engineering and architecture such as the drypoints *Looking Down on Down Town from the Railway Club* (1921, 19.7 × 13.3 cm), *Third Avenue* (also known as *Elevated Railway* and *Under the Elevated*) (1921, 19.7 × 15.2 cm, edition of 75), and the stunning *Looking Through Brooklyn Bridge* (1921, 23.5 × 17.5 cm)—the oil version of which was bought in 1921 by a new friend, the novelist and future Nobel Prize winner Sinclair Lewis. Others, such as the drypoint *New York Stock Exchange* (1921, 26 × 21.5 cm) respond to the commercial "boosterism" of the horn-rimmed spectacle-wearing, go-getting American businessman with a mildly satirical eye, while the drypoint *New York: An Abstraction* (later exhibited as *The Soul of a Soulless City*) (1921, 12.7 × 8.9 cm) forcefully emphasizes bleak urban alienation and loneliness. The unfinished mezzotint *New York Night* (1921, 20 × 14.9 cm) visually equates nocturnal Wall Street to a new Dantean circle of hell—a heart of all-consuming darkness driven by the drive for profit, material accumulation, and excess. It is not surprising that shortly thereafter he bemoaned what he clearly regarded as the pernicious growing influence of American culture on British society: "We are all becoming Americanised. You see it everywhere. America, America, American taste [and] combustion engines . . . creeping up, crowding out everything, hot baths and hotels . . . money for everything, except buying pictures. America, America, America!"[61]

The drypoints Nevinson had exhibited at the Alpine Club and Keppel Galleries in 1921 were both a critical and commercial success, though a solo show at the end of September 1921 at the Leicester Galleries proved a failure, despite his success in creating a furor in the press at the time of its opening. He had done this by launching himself as the "lone wolf" of the British art world, lambasting the influence of the Royal Academy, the New English Art Club, the London Group, Roger Fry and the Bloomsbury "coterie," as well as his old tutor, Henry Tonks, at the Slade School of Art.[62] Henry Nevinson noted how his son had suffered a heavy blow to his confidence and was declaring to anyone who would listen that he would from henceforth "paint only careful landscapes and portraits. He is thoroughly sick of the critics and yet he cannot forget them and is always angry and afraid . . . if he could only find his genius and imagination."[63] As always, however, Nevinson rallied; even if he had only sold twelve of the forty ones works on display at the Leicester Galleries.

It is logical to assume that Nevinson now decided he should apply himself to mastering his hand at etching, the most prestigious and lucrative of the print mediums between the wars, in an effort to simultaneously rescue his reputation and restore his failing finances.[64] Indeed, as early as February 1922, his father noted that Nevinson was trying to occupy his mind and focus his talent by doing just that.[65]

Many years later, Nevinson told Malcolm Salaman that he made his first etchings in 1922.[66] In his autobiography he gives the impression that it was Walter Richard Sickert, toward the end of the First World War, who "advised" him to try his hand at etching as it was "the easiest medium in the world." It is unclear whether Nevinson, in this account, sought to mock Sickert, or himself, or ridicule the high status enjoyed by etching as a medium. Sickert "explained" to Nevinson that all one did was to get a prepared plate on which your drawing has been photographed or if you preferred to be a purist, you merely whetted your pencil drawing, had it pressed and therefore reversed on the wax, and then kept the plate in your pocket and did a bit of drawing with a needle, while you were waiting for a girl. If you wanted your lines to be darker you cut into the copper, as the old masters did and dipped the plate in nitric acid as soon as you felt you had done enough.[67] Nevinson enigmatically concluded: "It was a thoroughly inaccurate description of etching but a very helpful one,"[68] and mentioned that "Hartley . . . and Strang" had also encouraged him to experiment with the medium. The former was no doubt Alfred Hartley, whom Nevinson's father had known since at least 1916. The latter could have been either William Strang (1859–1921) or his son the painter-etcher Ian (1886–1952). (Ian's younger brother, David, printed the majority of Nevinson's drypoints and etchings from the early 1920s onward.)[69] As far as one can tell, Nevinson did not take to carrying around a prepared copperplate, with ground pre-applied, "in his pocket" as Sickert advised, and in 1925 Nevinson emphatically told the printmaker Ernest Lumsden: "I never work on the spot. I can't compose out of doors."[70]

During 1922, Henry Nevinson noted his son had worked assiduously to produce a series of etchings depicting a variety of subject matters and was impressed by how quickly his son had grasped the essentials of working with acid and copperplate.[71] He was less enthralled by what he regarded as his son's often unadventurous and prosaic choice of subject matter; bland, topographic views of well-known Parisian tourist haunts such as *Statue at Versailles* (1922, 17.5 × 13.8 cm) and *Luxembourg Gardens* (1922, 18.6 × 30.2 cm), which he thought were not "worthy of him."[72] Some of the prints Nevinson produced in 1922, however, such as *Pont des Arts* (1922, 31.1 × 25.4 cm) and *Quartier Latin* (1922, 35.2 × 25.1 cm), are distinguished by their clarity and crisp simplicity of design. The latter, in particular, strikes one as imbued with the sort of enigmatic wistfulness Hopper brought to his scenes of New York streets from later in the 1920s. Despite the often tame nature of the subject matter, the great majority of the etchings Nevinson exhibited at the Leicester Galleries early in February 1923 were given an overwhelmingly positive critical reception. Paul Konody affirmed that the exhibition had bestowed upon Nevinson a "definite position among the leading figures in Modern Graphic Art," while he thought the atmospheric etched portrait of the recently deceased bohemian singer and painter *Geoffrey "Badger" Moody* (1922, 25.4 × 17.7 cm) was equal in skill and visual impact to any of the portrait etchings Augustus John had produced in the decade before the outbreak of the First World War.[73] Konody was equally taken, as were a number of other critics, with Nevinson's first attempts at pure landscape etchings such as *Romney Marsh* (1922, 28.9 × 45.2 cm, edition of 25) and *Sussex Downs* (1922, 28.2 × 45.8 cm), writing that such images would come as a surprise to those who assumed Nevinson was incapable of "appreciating the charm of rural life. In these plates he makes the etched line express a spaciousness, airiness and breeziness that are as a rule reserved for the experienced landscape painter's brush. They suggest physical well-being and happy communion with nature." Konody believed, as did H. Granville Fell writing a year later, that Nevinson deserved to be congratulated on his skillful ability to quote from landscape traditions of the past, represented by such hallowed artists as John Crome, John Constable, Thomas Gainsborough, and Rembrandt, without being merely derivative.[74] Both accurately assumed that Nevinson was wisely seeking to put some distance between himself and his reputation as a war artist and reposition himself as an artist who could work successfully in a wider spectrum of subject matter.

Meanwhile, Oscar Drey, writing for the *Evening News*, thought that although "opinions may vary as to Mr. Nevinson's position as a painter . . . there can be only one opinion about his etchings. They are straightforward, thoroughly competent, well-designed and . . . carry conviction." Moreover, Nevinson saw "in a personal way" but did not "deliberately set out to find the unusual . . . wherever he goes, he seizes the spirit of the place." Drey was particularly impressed by Nevinson's unsentimentally down-to-earth, and therefore credible, etchings of working-class London life such as *Any London Street* (1922, 13.8 × 17.4 cm), which did not attempt to patronize the inhabitants of the poor north London neighborhood near Nevinson's wartime studio on Robert Street.[75] In a lengthy article, the veteran art critic Frank Rutter, who had been commenting on the development of Nevinson's career since 1911, pondered the question of whether his etchings revealed him to be "A Great Artist." Rutter was impressed by his "power of design," the confident execution of the "carefully balanced arrangement" in many of his landscapes of the English countryside, with their wide open clear skies and the sensitivity and lightness of touch, and evident in drypoints such as *The Acrobat* (1922, 14 × 8.9 cm, edition of 40) and *The Connoisseur* (1922, 30.2 × 22.6 cm), which revealed the artist's continued respect for the achievements of the Impressionists. A work such as *Success* (1922, drypoint and etching, 20.3 × 15.2 cm), Rutter thought, revealed that the artist had in no way allowed his talent for biting satire to atrophy. Indeed, the vividness with which the desiccated monocle-wearing man about town and his puffed-up, overelaborately dressed paramour seated beside him in a theater box are realized in *Success*, strongly suggests that Nevinson was one of the few British artists with the ability to create work of comparable satirical power to the contemporary images produced by Otto Dix, Conrad Felixmüller, Rudolf Schlicter, and Georg Grosz of Weimar Republic's depraved and corrupt ruling classes. Rutter concluded that in his etchings, far more convincingly than in his oils, Nevinson had demonstrated that he possessed "two of the qualities of greatness, Vision and Design."[76]

Nevinson's decision to embrace etching, thus, paid off both critically and—what would have brought considerable relief—financially. Six months after the February 1923 exhibition, he boasted to the *Daily Graphic* that he had sold over £1,500 worth of etchings and that collectors from "London, America, Paris, Glasgow and Zurich [were] anxious to buy them."[77] His timing had also been impeccable for he was able to benefit considerably from the beginnings of a veritable "etchings boom" in Britain that would last until the effects of the Wall Street Crash began to tell on the British economy in 1930. In 1924 an article in the London *Times* declared: "There was a time when etchings appealed mainly to discerning collectors, people with money who could afford to buy freely of the masters who pleased their fancy . . . Now, however, demand has become more general and this change has led to a wider output and a greater range in treatment and subject . . . Etchings are now very popular among art-lovers of but limited means."[78] And heading the list of contemporary etchers (including James McBey, Gerald Leslie Brockhurst, and Harry Rushbury) whose works the *Times* urged its readers to seek out was Nevinson.[79] His position as a leading British etcher was further solidified by regular contributions to the prestigious annual exhibitions of *Masters of Modern Etching* held at the Leicester Galleries; by agreeing to be interviewed by Ernest Lumsden for his book *The Art of Etching* (published in 1925); and by the inclusion, from December 1923 onward, of an example of his etched work in *Fine Prints of the Year*—edited by Malcolm Salaman, who would publish a book devoted to Nevinson's prints in May 1932. Above all, Nevinson produced distinctive drypoints and etchings (his output of lithographs dwindled to virtually nothing after 1922 and he ceased to exhibit with the Senefelder Club) that made a virtue of their combined technical accomplishment and traditional subject matter, which the new breed of collectors identified by the *Times* actively wanted to buy.

For the next four years or so, Nevinson's print output decreased somewhat (to a total of twenty-eight) as he sought to avoid depressing his prices through overproduction, and while he also experienced ongoing problems with his health.[80] However, it was during this 1924–27 period that he produced his first aquatints such as his elysian evocation of idly punting on the river Thames at Thames Ditton, entitled *Sunday Evening* (25.1 × 35.4), and *From Waterloo Bridge—Sun Bursting Through Fog* (1924–27, drypoint and aquatint, 27.5 × 17.5 cm, edition of 40), in which he deftly referenced his admiration for views of the River Thames painted by French Impressionists such as Monet and Pissarro in the 1890s and early 1900s. Indeed, during the 1920s, Nevinson appears to have progressively fallen again under the spell of those French Impressionist artists whom he had worshipped as an art student at the Slade. In 1932 he was to plaintively ask, with regard to an exhibition of Impressionist work at the Royal Academy, "Can We Paint Like This Now? . . . can we attain the heights of Renoir, Monet, Manet, Pissarro, Cézanne and . . . Seurat . . . the finest flowers of Western Civilisation up to the present?"[81] It is clear, from the tenor of the article, that Nevinson feared the answer was a curt "no."

Traces of Monet and Pissarro, as well as of Whistler's etchings of the Thames riverside from the 1860s, are also evident in a series of smoke-blackened views of London's main transport artery winding through the "heart of Empire," such as *Blackfriars* (ca. 1926–27, 38.2 × 49.8 cm), and *Westminster from a Savoy Window* (ca. 1924–27, 28 × 35 cm). In the latter, the clouds of smoke from a steam locomotive on Charing Cross Railway Bridge are skillfully rendered, while the gathering gloom of dusk is pierced only by a scattering of electric lights, depicted in a manner that recalls Giacomo Balla's Futurist treatment of such details before the First World War. The print proved a particular favorite with the press and the public when it was exhibited, firstly in April 1927 at the Lefèvre Gallery and then in February 1932 with the National Society. In 1932 Sideny Dark, of the *Star*, wrote of *Westminster from a Savoy Window*, "Anyone who has an attachment to London cannot fail to pause before it . . . One man was seen to return three times to gaze on it once more."[82] *Waterloo Bridge from a Savoy Window* (ca. 1925–27, 27.5 × 35.2 cm) was another favorite with the public. Old Waterloo Bridge, demolished in 1938–39, appears several times in Nevinson's prints of the 1920s. In 1924 he was appalled by a proposal to have the bridge widened, describing it as "the most beautiful bridge in the world . . . Widen it and you destroy its proportion. Destroy its proportion and you destroy its beauty," a surprising attitude from an ex-Futurist who had once advocated that all that was traditional and hallowed in British society ought to be swept away.[83]

Stylistic fragments from Nevinson's Futurist past, however, are integrated into the backgrounds of two of his later symbolic etchings, *Conflict* (ca. 1926–27, 35.1 × 27.5 cm) and *Bacchus* (ca. 1926–27, 35.1 × 27.5 cm), to strengthen the impact of the overall design by providing a lively staccato pattern to highlight the wrestling and drunkenly dancing bodies. A stylized Futurist, or more accurately Art Deco, sunburst motif is deployed by Nevinson as a dramatic backdrop to his fine late etched portrait of the poet *Miss Edith Sitwell* (ca. 1926–27, 18.9 × 15.1 cm). The eminent yet eccentric female poet had never looked more enigmatic and sphinx-like.[84]

The majority of the aforementioned etchings and aquatints were exhibited for the first time in April 1927 at Alex Reid and Lefèvre's Gallery in London. It is evident from his scathing catalog polemic, entitled "An Apology—for my English name and descent," that Nevinson believed he had yet to be accorded the respect as a printmaker so freely given to Scottish contemporaries such as Muirhead Bone (1876–1953), David Young Cameron (1865–1943), and James McBey (1883–1959). At the beginning Nevinson declared: "Sometimes, how I wish as an etcher, I had been called MacNevin—every year, as the cost of living rises higher and higher, the more do I become convinced that there must be some Scottish blood within me. Many of my contemporaries, though far more gifted than myself, have also been handicapped by this well-known British prejudice against artists who are both English and professional." He mock-seriously proposed that in the nation's art schools the rising generation should receive as their first "art lesson" instruction on "how to adopt an exotic name and to cast away their English nationality, so that it may face the ghastly life of a modern artist without too great a handicap."[85] Though this sarcasm is amusing enough, Nevinson's determination to carp at extremely successful Scottish etchers, such as Bone and Cameron, suggests his frustration that he had not yet dethroned them as Britain's leading, most distinguished and most highly priced painter-printmakers. Still, the splenetic catalog preface was guaranteed to arouse the critics who, on the whole, were bemused as to why the artist should feel the need to traduce the reputations of contemporary printmakers when his own work was held in such high esteem and was much sought after.[86]

Three years later, at the Leicester Galleries in October 1930, Nevinson exhibited thirty-eight drypoints, etchings, and lithographs. This would be the last occasion on which an exhibition of his included a considerable number of prints; the majority had been exhibited at Lefèvre's in April 1927. Indeed, after 1927, Nevinson's print output declined markedly. The cause for this may largely lie in the fact that for the next four to five years he suffered from frequent periods of serious, sometimes life-threatening, illness. During the period 1928–32 the newspapers often contained notices that Nevinson was ill and in the hospital. In April 1928, for example, the *London Evening Standard* noted that he was suffering from pleurisy[87] while two years later the *Sunday Chronicle* informed its readers that the artist had been "seriously ill over the summer."[88]

The October 1930 exhibition constituted something of a swansong for Nevinson as a printmaker. Among the prints that had not been seen before there were many that were technically proficient, well-designed, and charming, but not terribly stimulating or visually intriguing, such as the etching *The Balcony, Dieppe* (ca. 1928–29, 17.4 × 13.8 cm, edition of 40) and the drypoint of *The Willows* (ca. 1928, 17.8 × 14 cm). However, the exhibition did include a handful of works in which one can detect flashes of the old wartime Nevinson; vivid, stimulating designs executed with brio and superb technical precision such as the drypoint *Westminster from the Savage Club, Adelphi* (ca. 1928–29, 28 × 35.5 cm) and one of his last lithographs *From a Paris Plane* (ca. 1930, 40.5 × 49 cm, edition of 25). The latter recalls some of his airborne themed First World War images as it balances an innocent delight in the possibilities of flight with the intoxicating strangeness of the myriad new vantage points offered from looking down through a window that is thousands of feet in the air. Another work that caught the imagination of the critics in 1930 was the drypoint *A Sinister Paris Night* (ca. 1928–29, 24.2 × 19 cm), in which the area of the plate within the lamp has been carefully and skillfully wiped clean to leave the paper a brilliant white. The image also harks back to the murky, mysterious nocturnal world of Nevinson's 1918 lithograph *Hauling Down an Observation Balloon at Night,* and further still to Nevinson's pre-1914 identification with the exploits of suave Parisian outlaws—*les Apaches*.[89]

Such a carefree and raffishly exiting milieu was very far removed from the state of things that prevailed at the time of the opening of the October 1930 exhibition. The Wall Street Crash of October 1929 quickly undermined the fragile British economy and triggered a complete collapse of the hitherto healthy market in the country for contemporary prints—especially etchings. In 1931, Nevinson produced a series of four etchings of the Seine entitled *Les Quais de Paris*. They are undoubtedly impressive from the point of view of technique and the draughtsmanship, skillfully simplifying hallowed landmarks such as the cathedral of Nôtre Dame into imposing, shadowy geometric blocks. The series received lavish praise from Malcolm Salaman in his book devoted to Nevinson's career as a printmaker published in May 1932.[90] However, there can be no denying that *Les Quais de Paris* series suggests a serious want of confidence on Nevinson's part, of wanting to play it safe, perhaps in the hope of appealing to a broader tourist-oriented market that was shrinking as travel abroad became increasingly more expensive. Indeed, a recurring criticism of some of the new prints exhibited in October 1930 was that the artist placed too high a premium on technique and was too in thrall to the example of the Impressionists at the expense of devising a strong imaginatively idiosyncratic design.[91] At the same time the drive for broad appeal and respectability rendered these scenes of Paris rather commonplace and lifeless when compared to similar views of the French capital painted by Monet and Pissarro from hotel windows in the more prosperous and settled years of the 1890s.

After 1932, Nevinson did not publish or exhibit any new prints, which suggests that this was the moment he decided to give up printmaking for good.[92] As mentioned previously, his poor health continued to trouble him,[93] and he was finding it increasingly difficult to operate the press he kept at his home on Haverstock Hill (it appears as an enigmatic cropped object in the background of his 1922 print *The Connoisseur* that appears on the dust jacket of this book). Presumably, the combination of poor health and the devastating effects of the worldwide "slump" on the contemporary market persuaded Nevinson that producing more prints was no longer an economically viable proposition. Perhaps he felt he no longer needed to zealously explore every avenue to earn a guinea, as by the early 1930s he was earning considerable sums from his regular journalism[94] and he was no longer the enfant terrible, "shocker of the suburbs,"[95] and "lone wolf" of the British art world. In March 1932, he was elected a member of the prestigious Royal Society of British Artists; he had already been welcomed back to the fold by the New English Art Club and he was also invited to exhibit with the Royal Institute of Oil Painters. Nevinson was turning respectable, noted those who had long followed his career. Indeed, one proof of that very respectability was the fact that Malcolm Salaman had devoted a volume of *The Modern Masters of Etching* to him in 1932. As the *Bystander* magazine wryly observed; who could have predicted that the "young Turk" of 1914 would find himself "lumped together with a lot of RA's [Royal Academicians], for in this series have previously figured Frank Brangwyn, Sir Frank Short, Sir David Young Cameron and . . . even Rembrandt."[96] As a printmaker Nevinson had very definitely "arrived," yet ironically it was at this very moment he decided to renounce printmaking once and for all. However, his prints continued to be enjoyed and appreciated, whenever they were exhibited thereafter, for their "exuberant variety, design, rhythm and magnificent strength,"[97] and it is for these recurring qualities that Nevinson deserves to be considered one of the major British printmaking talents of the twentieth century.[98]

Glossary of Printmaking Technical Terms

Aquatint
An intaglio etching process used to create a range of delicate tones. A finely powdered resin is distributed over the surface of the copperplate. Heat is used to fuse the resin to the surface of the plate and then acid etches through the fine grains of the resin dust.

Bite
The action of acid within an etching bath on the metal (usually copper) etching plate.

Burin
A cutting tool used for incising line on a copperplate to create a drypoint

Burr
The ridges of metal formed either side of an incision made with a drypoint burin, or needle or mezzotint rocker on a metal plate. When the plate is inked, ink will collect on the burr and will reproduce a thick, velvety back line on taking a print from the plate.

Drypoint
First introduced toward the end of the fifteenth century in Europe. The simplest intaglio technique in which a line is scratched in to the surface of the metal or zinc plate, not with acid but by the action of a sharp round-pointed burin.

Etching
First introduced in early sixteenth-century Europe. A demanding indirect intaglio technique in which the surface of the metal plate is first covered with an acid-resistant material known as the ground. A sharp small-headed etching needle is then used to incise design into the surface of the ground, exposing the metal beneath. Once immersed within an acid bath only those areas of the plate exposed by the action of the etching needle will be bitten into by the acid. On removal from the acid bath the ground is removed, the etched plate is inked and a print taken from its surface. The depth of the etched line is determined by the strength of the acid and the time the plate is left immersed in the acid bath.

Intaglio
A process in which the image to be printed is cut in to the surface on a metal (usually copper) plate either by a hand-held burin or using the effects of acid. The cut or etched line fills with ink on the plate being inked and the image is transferred to paper on the plate being run through a printing press.

Lithography
Devised by Alois Senefelder in the late eighteenth century. A process by which a print can be obtained from a drawing made in water-repellent, greasy ink or crayon on the surface of a dampened lithographic limestone block or zinc or aluminium plate. The stone is then thoroughly inked, and the design drawn on the surface of the stone will take up the ink, which will not adhere to those areas that have been dampened. The stone, or plate, is then run through a printing press and the design executed in ink or lithographic crayon will be reproduced on the paper. For this reason this process is also known as a "planographic" one, as the image is reproduced from the surface of the stone or plate.

Mezzotint
Became widespread during the eighteenth century. A form of intaglio printmaking in which a device called a rocker is used to pit the surface of the metal plate with minute indentations that will hold the printing ink. Areas on the plate, which will print as white, can be created by burnishing and rubbing so the indentations created by the rocker are smoothed away and can no longer carry ink. A physically demanding and labor-intensive technique.

Planographic
A form of printing in which the print is taken from a flat surface, such as a lithographic stone or zinc or aluminium plate.

Plate Wiping
When an etched or drypoint metal plate is inked, certain key areas can be wiped so that when the plate is printed the corresponding area appears on the print as white or as a more nuanced shade of the ink color.

Relief Printing
A process in which the image to be printed is created in relief as in the case of Wood and Linocuts in which the base material is the side grain of a piece of hardwood or linoleum respectively.

Resin
A finely grained substance that forms a porous film deposit on the surface of a metal plate and can be used as a ground for the aquatint process.

Rocker
A rounded steel tool so shaped that its teeth will penetrate and pit the surface of a metal plate. Primarily used to prepare the surface of copperplate to produce a mezzotint.

Roulette
A wheel-shaped instrument with teeth to make small perforations in the ground on a plate to be etched or on the plate surface of a drypoint.

Scraper
A tool used in wood engraving to remove large areas of wood from around the image to be printed. In the twentieth century increasingly used as an instrument to scrape away areas of lithographic crayon from the surface of the stone.

Transfer Lithography
A variation on more traditional forms of lithography in which a chalk or charcoal drawing on prepared paper is transferred to the surface of the lithographic stone or zinc plate either by tracing or by photography. The design is reinforced by greasy ink or crayon to take up ink while the dampened surface areas will not print ink.

Woodcut
One of the earlier forms of printmaking developed in Western Europe toward the end of the fifteenth century. The areas to

be inked and printed stand in relief from the surface of the side grain of a piece of hard wood such as poplar and pear. The areas that will be printed as white are cut away using a variety of knives and gouges.

Notes

1. Jonathan Black, "'A Curious Cold Intensity': C. R. W. Nevinson as a War Artist," in *C. R. W. Nevinson: The Twentieth Century*, ed. Julian Honer (London: Merrell Holberton, 1999); Michael J. K. Walsh, *C. R. W. Nevinson: This Cult of Violence* (London: Yale University Press, 2002).

2. Frank Rutter. *Some Contemporary* Artists (London: Leonard Parsons, 1922), 193–203; Osbert Sitwell. *Contemporary British Artists: C. R. W. Nevinson*, ed. Albert Rutherston (London: Ernest Benn, 1925), 29–30; Ernest Lumsden, *The Art of Etching* (London: Seeley, Service, 1925), 358.

3. *Glasgow Herald*, September 19, 1918, Nevinson Press Clippings, 7311.3A, Hyman Kreitman Research Centre, Tate Britain, London [henceforth: HKRC].

4. *New York Evening World*, July 27, 1921, Nevinson Press Clippings, 7311.4, HKRC.

5. *Manchester Guardian*, February 20, 1923, Nevinson Press Clippings, 7311.6B, HKRC; Malcolm C. Salaman. *Modern Masters of Etching: C. R. W. Nevinson* (London: Studio Publications, 1932), 4; Kenneth M. Guichard, *British Etchers: 1850–1940* (London: Robin Garton, 1977), 52.

6. Nevinson quoted in the *Daily Express*, September 6, 1932, Nevinson Press Cuttings, 7311.9, HKRC.

7. H. W. Nevinson Diaries, entry for February 23, 1907, MSS Eng. Misc. e.614/1, Department of Modern Manuscripts, Bodleian Library, University of Oxford [henceforth: BLUO.]

8. H. W. Nevinson Diaries, entry for March 24, 1909, MSS Eng. Misc. e.615/2, BLUO.

9. H. W. Nevinson Diaries, entry for May 21, 1911, MSS Eng. Misc. e. 616/3, BLUO.

10. C. R. W. Nevinson, *Paint and Prejudice: The Life of a Painter* (New York: Harcourt Brace, 1938), 25.

11. Ibid., 50.

12. H. W. Nevinson Diaries, entry for May 6, 1916, MSS Eng. Misc. e. 619/4, BLUO.

13. Norway later (ca. 1918) produced a striking linocut portrait of Nevinson that gives him the air of a villain from a German Expressionist film.

14. The Decorative Art Group had its inaugural exhibition at the Modern Gallery, Bond Street, London, in July 1916. On this occasion Nevinson did not exhibit any prints. *Sunday Times*, July 9, 1916, Nevinson Press Clippings, 7311.2B, HKRC.

15. C. R. W. Nevinson, *Paint and Prejudice*, 111.

16. H. W. Nevinson Diaries, April 29, 1917, MSS Eng. Misc. e.620/1, BLUO.

17. *Manchester Guardian*, September 27, 1916, Nevinson Press Clippings, 7311.2B, HKRC.

18. In 1925, discussing his technical approach to the drypoint, Nevinson told the leading etcher Ernest Lumsden that "My drypoints are invariably traced onto the surface of a smoky liquid ground, cut through with a ruby point and then the ground cleaned off. After that, the ordinary working of a drypoint [with a burin to create the burr] a well-polished plate and a dirty finger of oil and charcoal to study the lines." Ernest Lumsden. *The Art of Etching* (London: Seely, Service, 1925), 358.

19. *Nation*, September 30, 1916, 814.

20. *Observer*, October 1, 1916, Nevinson Press Clippings, 7311.2B, HKRC.

21. *Times Literary Supplement*, December 14, 1916, 789.

22. The private view of the exhibition took place at the Leicester Galleries on January 23, 1917.

23. Pennell had known H. W. Nevinson for many years.

24. C. R. W. Nevinson, *Paint and Prejudice*, 73.

25. Ibid.

26. Joseph Pennell and E. Robins Pennell, *Lithography and Lithographers* (London, 1915), 157–58.

27. Malcolm Salaman, *Modern Woodcuts and Lithographs* (London: A. & C. Black, 1919), 121.

28. *Westminster Gazette*, January 29, 1917, Nevinson Press Clippings, 7311.2B, HKRC.

29. *Sunday Times*, July 15, 1917, Nevinson Press Clippings, 7311.2C, HKRC.

30. C. F. G. Masterman, in charge of visual propaganda at the Department of Information, described Nevinson as a "desperate fellow and without fear" in a letter to the department's director the novelist John Buchan, May 18, 1917, Nevinson WWI File, 226-A6-1, Department of Art, Imperial War Museum, London [henceforth: IWM].

31. Nevinson to C. F. G. Masterman, December 30, 1917, Nevinson WWI File, 226-A6-1, IWM.

32. See comparisons made between the oil and print version of a Nevinson design made by Sidney Dark in the *Daily Express*, March 1918, Nevinson Press Cuttings, 7311. HKRC and later by Eric Newton in the *Observer*, September 11, 1932, Nevinson Press Cuttings, 7311.9, HKRC.

33. C. R. W. Nevinson, *Paint and Prejudice*, 153.

34. H. W. Nevinson Diaries, entry for January 28, 1918, MSS Eng. Misc. e. 620/3, BLUO. The impression of this print now in the collection of the British Museum, London, was donated by Nevinson only three weeks after the stone had been damaged during the bombing raid.

35. *New York Times*, May 25, 1919, p. 13.

36. Alfred Yockney to C. F. G. Masterman, December 4, 1917, Nevinson WWI File, 226-A6-1, IWM.

37. *Times Literary Supplement*, September 19, 1918, p. 439. The advertisement concluded that once all the copies of the "luxury" edition had been sold, the drypoint plate would be destroyed. It is not certain whether this did indeed take place.

38. *World*, October 4, 1919, Nevinson Press Cuttings, 7311.3-C, HKRC.

39. Albert Eugene Gallatin, *Etchings and Lithographs by C. R. W. Nevinson* (New York: Frederick J. Keppel Galleries, 1919), p. 10.

40. *New York Times*, May 24, 1919, p. 13.

41. For the most recent analysis of Wadsworth's "dazzle" woodcuts see Jeremy Greenwood and Richard Cork, *The Graphic Work of Edward Wadsworth* (London: Wood Lea Press, 2002).

42. H. W. Nevinson Diaries, January 21, 1918, MSS Eng. Misc. e.620/3, BLUO.

43. Nevinson to C. F. G. Masterman, June 22, 1918, Nevinson WWI File, 226-A6-1, IWM.

44. *Current Times*, August 1919, Nevinson Press Cuttings, 7311.4, HKRC.

45. *Times*, April 7, 1919, p. 16.

46. The National Railway Strike lasted from September 27

to October 6, 1919 and ended with Lloyd George's Coalition Government capitulating to the railwaymen's demands for better pay and conditions. Nevinson told the *Graphic* magazine that *the Workers* depicted "one of the great meetings held on Tower Hill during the Railway Strike." It is intriguing to note that Nevinson had painted a strike meeting at Tower Hill, London, as early as 1912.

47. *Ploughshare*, November 1919, Nevinson Press Cuttings, 7311.4, HKRC.

48. *New Labour Leader*, October 13, 1922, Nevinson Press Cuttings, 7311.6A, HKRC. This was the weekly journal of the Independent Labour Party and tellingly reproduced *The Workers* as *Revolution*.

49. Nevinson to E. W. Blackley, Curator of Art, Imperial War Museum, January 17, 1929, Nevinson WWI File, Part II, IWM.

50. C. R. W. Nevinson. *Paint and Prejudice*, 178.

51. Ibid., 180.

52. *New York Herald*, May 18, 1919, Nevinson Press Cuttings, 7311.4, HKRC.

53. *New York Times*, May 25, 1919, p. 11.

54. Ibid., p. 12.

55. C. R. W. Nevinson, *Paint and Prejudice*, 188.

56. H. W. Nevinson Diaries, entry for June 26, 1919, MSS Eng. Misc. e.621/1, BLUO.

57. It is possible that Schultze-Neudam, who designed the posters for the German release of *Metropolis*, was aware of Nevinson's prints of New York—images of which had been widely circulated in the German and French art press.

58. *Daily Mail*, September 17, 1920, Nevinson Press Cuttings, 7311.5A, HKRC.

59. H. W. Nevinson Diaries, entry for March 9, 1921, e.621/4, BLUO.

60. *New York Evening Globe*, July 27, 1921; see also the *San Francisco Post*, August 26, 1921, and the *New York Evening Post*, August 30, 1921, Nevinson Press Cuttings, 7311.4, HKRC.

61. *Daily News*, May 28, 1923, Nevinson Press Cuttings, 7311.6B, HKRC.

62. *Daily Express*, September 9, 1921, Nevinson Press Cuttings, 7311.5A, HKRC.

63. H. W. Nevinson Diaries, entry for April 12, 1922, MSS Eng. Misc. e.622/3, HKRC.

64. For the "print boom" in Britain between the wars see: Kenneth M. Guichard. *British Etchers 1850–1940* (London: Robin Garton Publications, 1977), 30; and Frances Carey, Anthony Griffiths, and Stephen Coppel, *Avant-Garde British Printmaking: 1914–1960* (London: British Museum Publications, 1990), 1–10.

65. H. W. Nevinson Diaries, entry for February 26, 1922, MSS Eng. Misc. e. 622/3, BLUO.

66. Malcolm C. Salaman, *Modern Masters of Etching* (London: Studio Publications, 1932), 7.

67. C. R. W. Nevinson. *Paint and Prejudice*, 151.

68. Ibid., 152

69. Ibid., 152–53.

70. E. S. Lumsden, *The Art of Etching* (London: Seeley, Service, 1925), 358.

71. H. W. Nevinson Diaries, entries for August 13, 1922, MSS Eng. Misc. e.622/3 and October 15, 1922, MSS Eng. Misc. e.622/5, BLUO.

72. H. W. Nevinson Diaries, entry for February 28, 1922, MSS Eng. Misc. e. 622/3, BLUO.

73. *Observer*, February 11, 1923, Nevinson Press Cuttings, 7311.6B, HKRC.

74. Ibid. and *The Queen*, March 26, 1924, Nevinson Press Cuttings, 7311.6C, HKRC.

75. *Evening News*, February 3, 1924, Nevinson Press Cuttings, 7311.6B, HKRC.

76. *John O'London's Weekly*, March 3, 1923, Nevinson Press Cuttings, 7311.6B, HKRC. Nevinson probably found Rutter's complement a double-edged one as *Vision and Design* was the title of a book on aesthetics published in 1920 by his bête noire Roger Fry. I am indebted to Michael Walsh for this observation.

77. *Daily Graphic*, September 11, 1923, Nevinson Press Cuttings, 7311.6B, HKRC.

78. *Times*, May 12, 1924, Nevinson Press Cuttings, 7311.6C, HKRC.

79. Ibid. It appears that Rushbury thought highly of Nevinson's prints and bought several of them during the 1920's. H. W. Nevinson Diaries, entry for September 18, 1927, MSS Eng. Misc. e.624/3, BLUO.

80. In February 1927, for instance, he was struck down by "shingles in the head," the effects of which may have been exacerbated by working with acid fumes produced during the etching process. H. W. Nevinson Diaries, entry for February 23, 1927, MSS Eng. Misc. e.624/2, BLUO.

81. *Daily Express*, February 17, 1932, Nevinson Press Cuttings, 7311.9, HKRC.

82. *Star*, February 10, 1932, Nevinson Press Cuttings, 7311.9, HKRC.

83. *Daily News*, April 1, 1924, Nevinson Press Cuttings, 7311.6C, HKRC.

84. Nevinson first met the Sitwells, Edith, Osbert, and Sacheverell, in 1917–18. Sir Osbert bought a number of Nevinson's paintings and prints and wrote the text for the volume of *Contemporary British Artists* devoted to Nevinson, which was published in 1925. He also wrote the preface for Nevinson's memorial exhibition in May 1947

85. C. R. W. Nevinson, *Watercolours, Drawings and Etchings by C. R. W. Nevinson* (London: Alex Reid & Lefèvre, 1927), 3–4.

86. *Westminster Gazette*, April 26, 1927, Nevinson Press Cuttings, 7311.7B, HKRC.

87. *London Evening Standard*, April 17, 1928, Nevinson Press Cuttings, 7311.7B, HKRC.

88. *Sunday Chronicle*, August 6, 1930, Nevinson Press Cuttings, 7311.8A, HKRC.

89. C. R. W. Nevinson, *Paint and Prejudice*, 88. Nevinson claimed he had been known in Paris, ca. 1912–14 as "l'apache qui rit."

90. Malcolm C. Salaman, *Modern Masters of Etching* (London, Studio Publications, 1932), 12.

91. *Scotsman*, October 11, 1930, Nevinson Press Clippings, 7311.7C, HKRC.

92. He did produce a drawing for one last transfer lithograph which was reproduced in the *Studio* magazine in April 1933. The design was a composite of elements present in his diluted Futurist works of the early 1930's such as *Self-Portrait: With Nothing To Lose* (1930) and *Pan Triumphant* (1931).

93. *Times*, February 25, 1932, reported that Nevinson was "seriously ill at home . . . suffering from influenza with complications." Nevinson Press Cuttings, 7311.9, HKRC.

94. Characteristic articles of the time include: "The Worst Women in the World and Alas! They're British!" and "Wives Don't Understand Their Husbands" in the *Sunday Chronicle*, February 23, 1930 and the *Daily Mail*, July 21, 1932 respectively. Nevinson Press Cuttings, 7311.8A and 7311.9, HKRC.

95. *Referee*, March 16, 1924, Nevinson Press Clippings, 7311.6C, HKRC.

96. *Bystander*, June 8, 1932, Nevinson Press Clippings, 7311.9, HKRC.

97. *Christian Science Monitor*, June 7, 1932, Nevinson Press Clippings, 7311.9, HKRC.

98. The verdict also of Frances Carey, Anthony Griffiths and Stephen Coppel, *Avant-Garde British Printmaking: 1914–1960* (London: British Museum Publications, 1990), 70; and Gordon Cooke, "C. R. W. Nevinson as a Printmaker," *C. R. W. Nevinson: The Twentieth Century*, ed. Julian Honer (London: Merrell Holberton), 70–75.

Denying the "Foe-to-graphic": C. R. W. Nevinson and Photography

Ben Jones

THE PERCEIVED BOUNDARIES BETWEEN PHOTOGraphy and fine art during the early modern period in Britain were drawn clearly along indexical lines—the lens recorded, the canvas interpreted. Since the last quarter of the nineteenth century, establishment voices had called into question the extent to which British painters were relying inappropriately on photography as a compositional aide-memoire. Although the use of the photograph as a compositional device was common practice and openly admitted by many of the defining artists of the early twentieth century—preeminently Walter Sickert—Nevinson consistently and vociferously denied any reliance on photography. While publicly he denounced it as inimical to the authenticity and originality of the true artist's vision, his own artistic output belied a working process which relied as much on the photograph as on pure imagination in the composition of his paintings.

We still know all too little about the way Nevinson really worked in the studio since few of his personal effects have survived and the main record of his working life is the public testimony of press cuttings compiled on his behalf but donated by the artist himself to the Tate Gallery Archive. Ever the self-propagandist, adverse reviews were often conveniently deselected to create an archival impression of universal press adulation for an artist of uniquely unimpeachable veracity who relied only on his extraordinary visual memory for inspiration. Surviving photographs from Nevinson's early career show an artist with an eye for self-presentation and the projection of frequently theatrical personae. Richard was always "absorbed in back-stage" according to his wife Kathleen, who wrote that being married to the artist was like having several different husbands: "the painter, writer, mechanic, carpenter and cook, thus solving the problem of women's promiscuity."[1]

At the Slade until 1912—where his own incorrigible promiscuity culminated in denied responsibility for the pregnancy of Leila, one of the life-class models—he inhabited the rôle of the swaggering *apache*. As the self-conscious bohemian in bowtie and Homburg hat, he was a leading member of the Slade student Coster Gang along with Mark Gertler, sometime friend and competitor for the affections of fellow student Dora Carrington. By day these young men were painting studiously Botticelliesque self-portraits, while by night their coster-mongering penchant was for roughing up passersby on the London streets around Fitzrovia which centered on the Roebuck public house. For a short time they sought to distinguish themselves from Roger Fry's Postimpressionist tendency by branding themselves "Neo-Primitives." But with the arrival in London of the Italian Futurists in 1912, Nevinson was soon to detach himself once again and reinvent his persona along more radical avant-garde lines.

By 1914, the Italians' thrill to the machine had forged a self-conscious visual recasting in Nevinson into the daring and debonaire *Automobilist (Machine Slave)*, this the title of a sculpture he submitted as a founding member of The London Group to their first display in March 1914 at Regent Street's Goupil Gallery (fig. 18). The bronze cast self-portrait and its charcoal counterpart (whereabouts of both unknown) present the artist in head-and-shoulder bust as inscrutably hard-edged; the visual embodiment of Futurist leader F. T. Marinetti's poems which celebrated thrusting *automobilista*. Dark pitted eyes are overshadowed by geometrically opaque goggles strapped around a peaked cap like the mechanized stand-ins for vision itself.

Only months before the commencement of the Great War we see Nevinson here projecting an artistic image of himself in self-styled avant-garde uniform; long leather trenchcoat, driver's gloves and goggles symbolically accelerating the progress of "Vitalism"[2] in art. The Futurists always wore suits, but in this early experimentation with dressing his own individual artistic persona, Nevinson prefigured his First World War service as a Red Cross ambulance driver. He commented later that "When war actually came, it found the modern artist equipped with a technique perfectly well able to express war."[3] One might add that when war came it found this particular artist already suitably costumed for it. As the critic Charles Lewis Hind put it, he was "all dressed up and nowhere to go. Then came the war: in the war he found himself."[4]

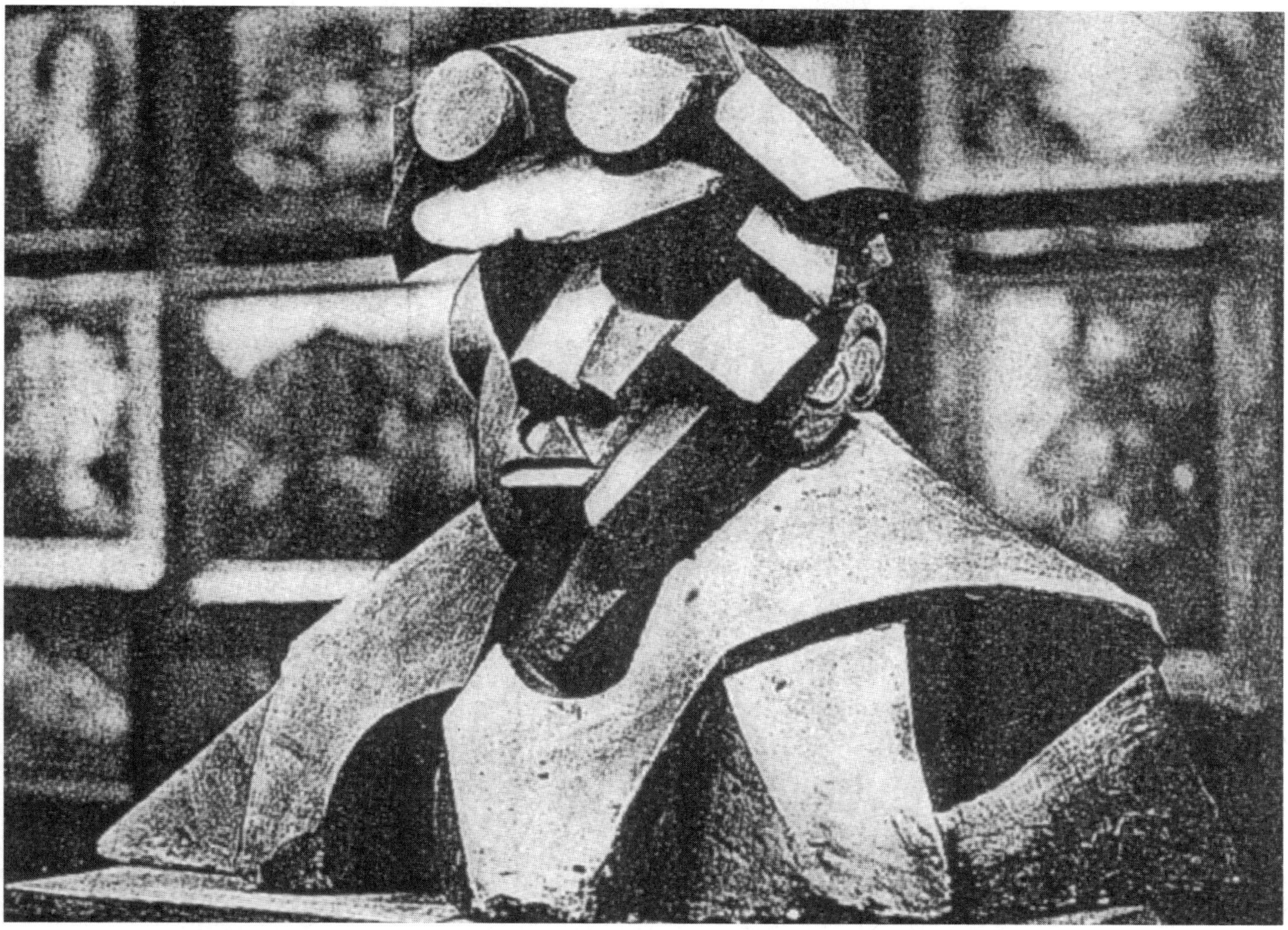

18. *Automobilist* (Machine Slave) (1914) bronze, whereabouts unknown.

In December 1914, Nevinson had a photographic *carte de visite* made that depicted him standing next to his "bus" in full chauffeur garb complete with Red Cross armband, his self-styled projection of military couture (fig. 19). He sent one of the cards to Marinetti, reporting proudly to the Futurist leader the damage that his ambulance had sustained following the impact of a "Boche" shell under the back axle. "Tout ça etait demoli" he scribbled dramatically over the image on the front of the card, an arrow pointing to the back wheel of a vehicle that ironically he would have driven for little more than a week in November 1914.[5] Yet, in the early part of the war at least, he continued to reinforce the visual representation of himself as the dynamic "Automobilist,"[6] and in this he appropriated two key visual sources.

In his painting *Motor Ambulance Driver* of 1916 (fig. 20), we are reminded immediately of his *Automobilist (Machine Slave)* sculpture of two years previously, as if the bust has been brought to life by powerful arms exaggeratedly elongated into heavy gloves. With one hand depicted as clamped to the steering wheel while the other hangs limply at his side—he had received an honorable discharge in January 1916 on the grounds of acute rheumatic fever, which particularly affected his control of his hands—the painting communicates an uneasy balance of control, a pictorial parallel perhaps for the battle Nevinson was having with the brush. *Motor Ambulance Driver* was probably a reworking of his 1913 painting *The Motorist* (destroyed) in which he had utilized real glass and a coat button. The compositional addition of the scarf, although not collaged on this occasion, serves to disguise the face and convey the chill of the winter air, but also recalls an Umberto Boccioni painting of 1904, *Speeding Car* (Automobile Club d'Italia), in which a motorist wrapped up in scarf and goggles tests the velocity of his machine against the natural speed of horses and hunting dogs. Nevinson references this proto-Futurist painting perhaps as a way of emphasizing by contrast the stillness of his own

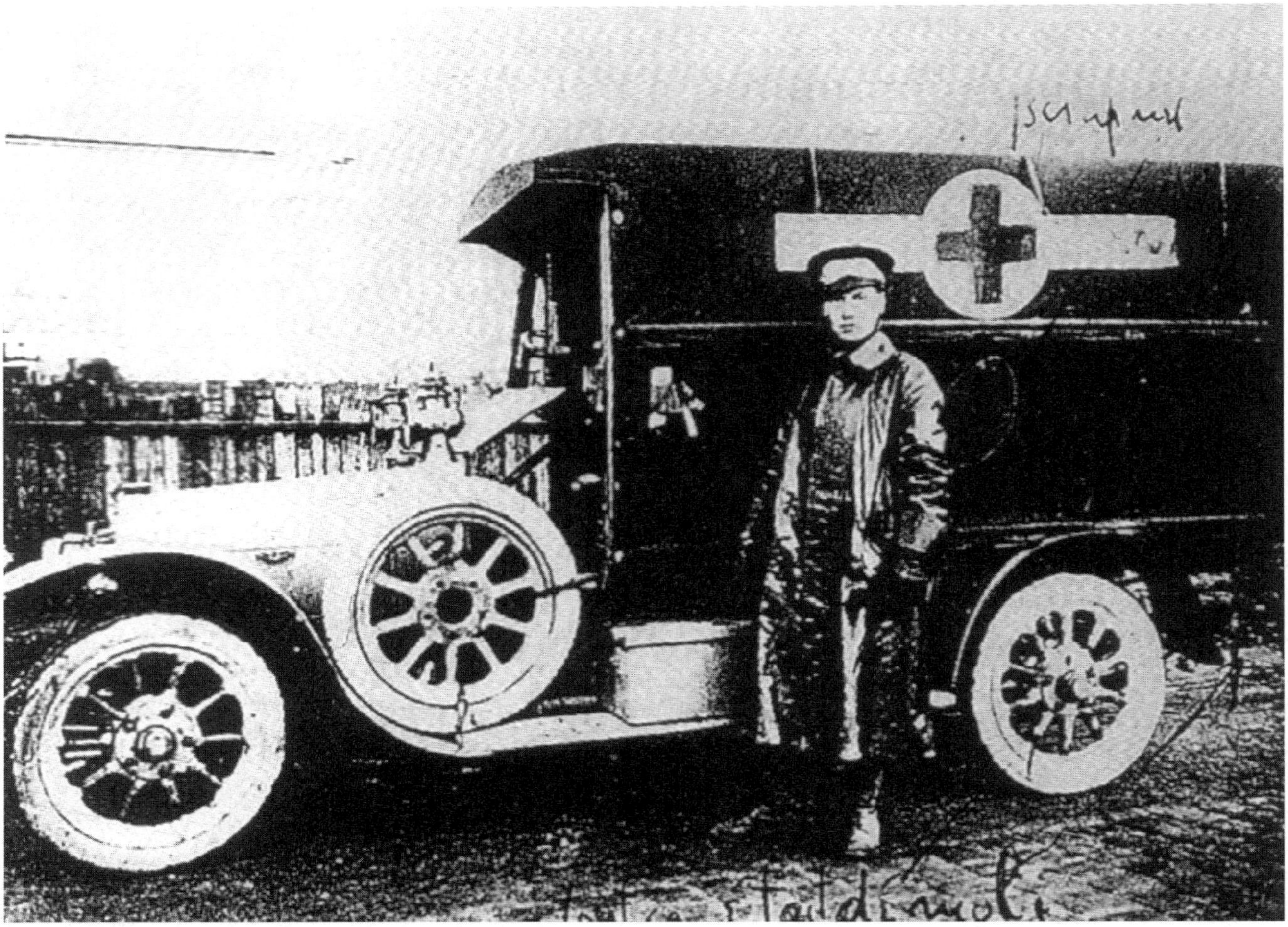

19. Nevinson postcard to Marinetti (December 1914), photograph Palazzo Grassi, Venice.

image, purged of all dynamism. At this midpoint of the war, which by August 1916 had seen 4.6 million lives lost in Europe, he and his friend Severini had rejected Futurism's celebration of brutal mechanistic imagery. In *Motor Ambulance Driver*, all vitalism and urgency has dissipated. With no horizon line visible beneath the blue expanse of sky, the car seems to float spatially above the ground and perhaps also, metaphorically, above the Futurist rhetoric that famously demoted the suffering of a human being to that of an electric light. Here, lamps are transmuted into the automobilist's goggles propped above his brow. In reflecting the light they become the car headlamps themselves, literally replacing the one cropped out of the painting's lower right. The work is clearly based on a photograph of the artist in civilian dress behind the wheel of his "Motor Caravan" in the Tate Gallery Archive (fig. 21). The composition is almost identical and tellingly the eyes and hands are the major stylistic areas of change, serving to exaggerate the artist's presence as masculinist mechanomorph. The disjunction between the documentary "truth" of Nevinson's rheumatically limp handhold on the steering wheel in the photograph, and the painted muscularity of mechanical grip once translated into paint, is striking.

But there is another, more personal visual influence on this pre–1916 self-fashioning: Richard's father Henry Woodd Nevinson who, in a photograph taken from his 1928 autobiography *Last Changes, Last Chances*, stands out as the only one among a group of fellow war correspondents self-consciously sporting goggles around his military cap (fig. 22). In Nevinson junior, we come across the goggles once again in Malcolm Arbuthnot's early 1917 photo-portraits of the artist for the *Third London General Hospital Gazette* (fig. 23), but here his noticeably lifeless fists support a face framed by leather trenchcoat and, once again, those disembodied eye pieces. Richard had recently begun sessions with a nerve specialist and his gaze here is glassy, uncertain, curiously effeminate—eyelids heavy with makeup like a

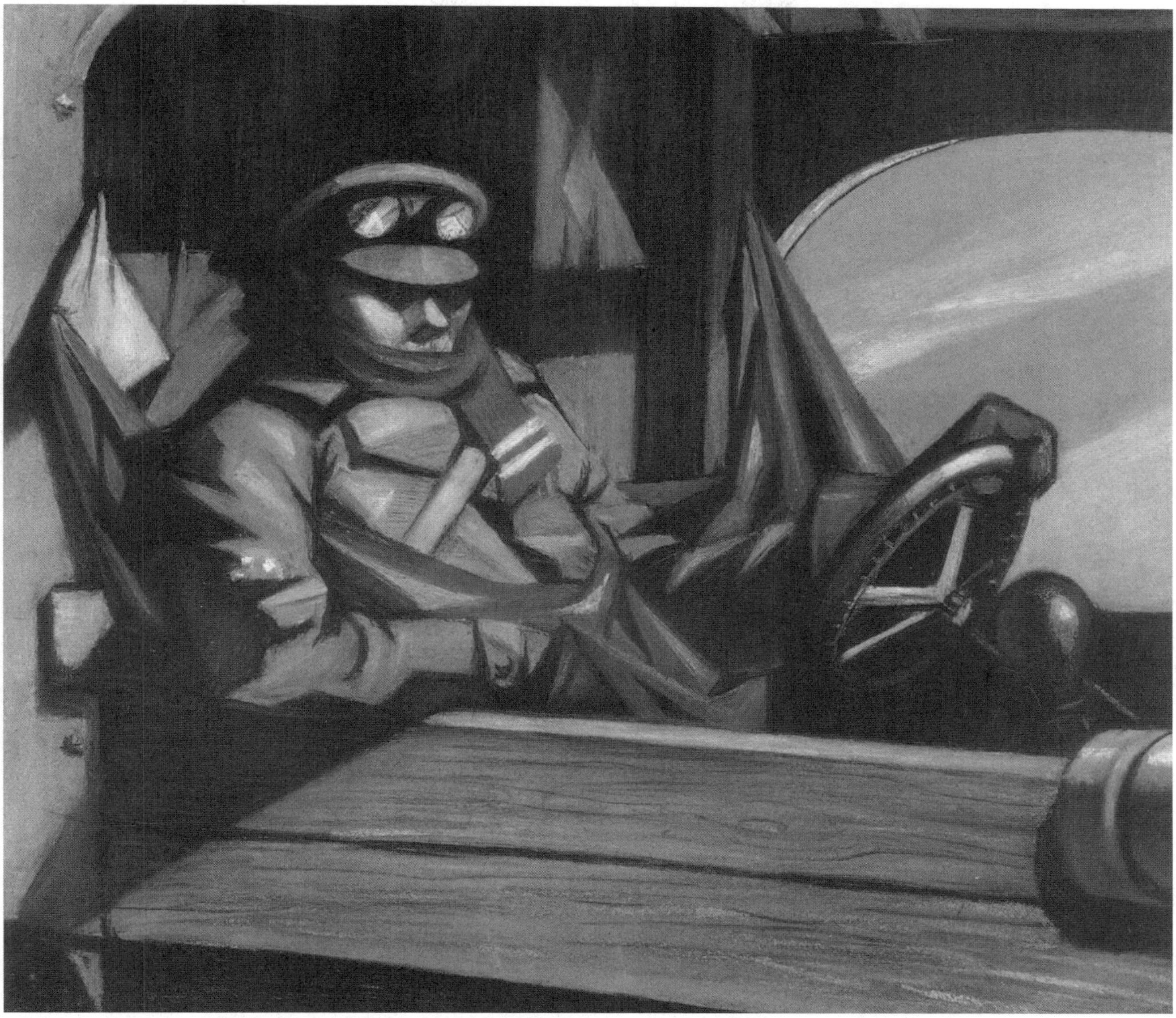

20. *Motor Ambulance Driver* (1916) pencil and pastel, 25.2 × 29.1 cm. Private collection.

milk-skinned Valentino. This image in particular contradicts his erstwhile exploitation of the photograph to communicate overweening self-confidence and avant-garde bravado.

Although he was only strictly a disciple of F. T. Marinetti for perhaps a year—exhibiting officially as a Futurist for the final time in the first and only Vorticist exhibition of June 1914—the Italians' avant-garde precepts glorifying originality and scorning imitation were never diluted in Nevinson. This though had an unfortunate and damaging tendency to manifest itself recurrently throughout his career as a thin-skinned defensiveness when discussing his work. Deeply embedded in Nevinson's psyche was the fear of his originality being questioned; it dogged his subconscious and made him hypersensitive to criticism and what he perceived as the insufficient recognition his work received.

In his own entry to the catalog for his debut one-man exhibition *Paintings and Drawings of War* at the Leicester Galleries in September 1916, Nevinson qualifies with "some exceptions" his preference "to give in my pictures an abstract, dynamic, and mental impression rather than a concrete, static, or optical [*sic*]."[7] One suspects that even at the time it was apparent to audiences of contemporary art that the exceptions were in fact overwhelming the rule. One of a number of key "exceptions" might in fact be *Motor Ambulance Driver*, not only due to the "optical" source material and effect already discussed but since it had a literally "concrete" counterpart in this solo display. *The Mechanic*, when set alongside

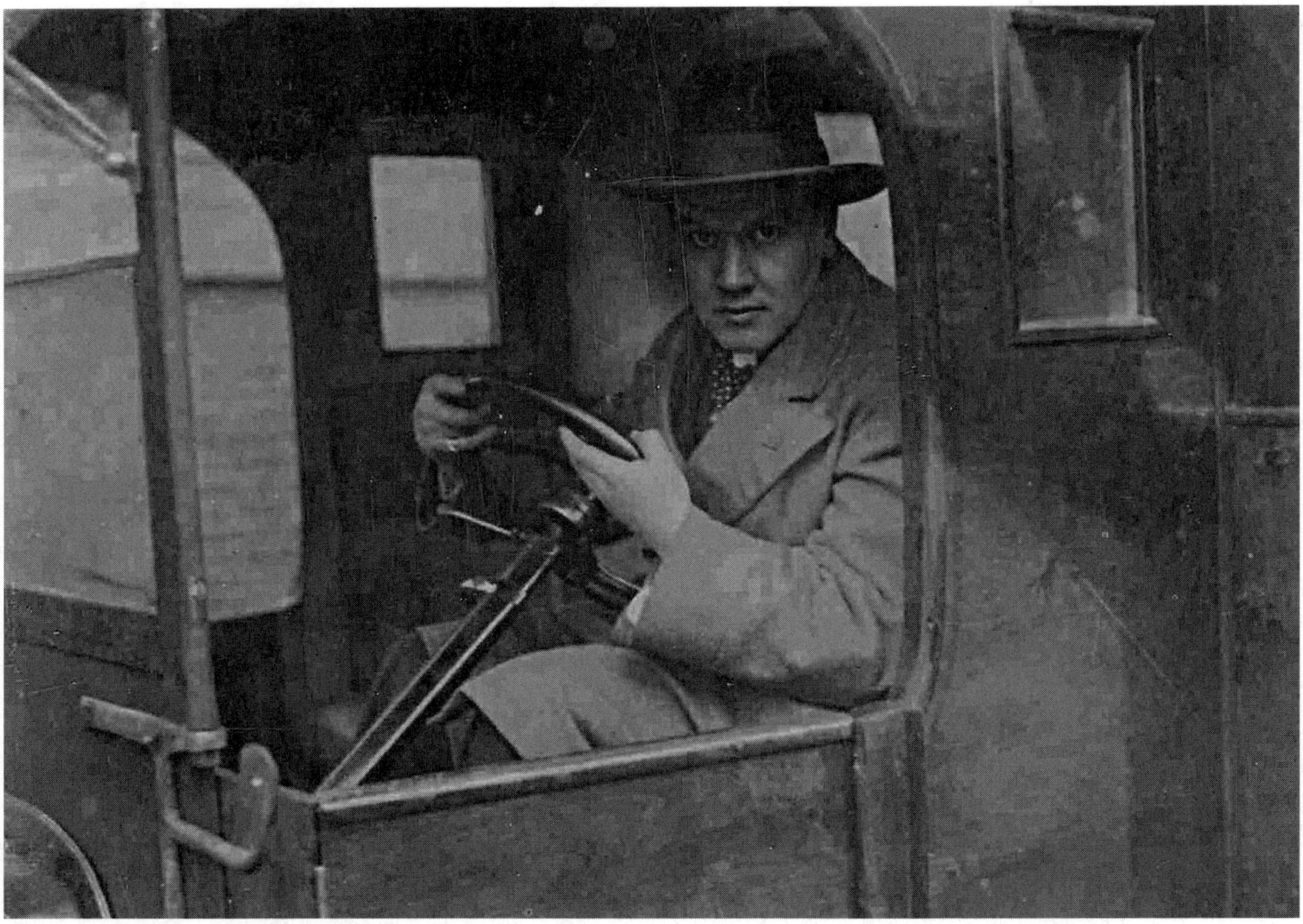

21. Nevinson at the wheel of his Motor Caravan, Tate Gallery Archive, London.

say Boccioni's sculptural advances in plastic dynamism such as *Development of a Bottle in Space* (1912, Kunsthaus Zurich), comes across as "static." The encroachment of the representational had taken effect much earlier in his career whether Nevinson recognized it or not. For modernist art historian Charles Harrison, Nevinson's skill for intensification over willful distortion is evidence that he was always more Camden Town than Futurist in his avant-garde instincts.[8] Certainly, once he had renounced Futurism around 1915, he only achieved the concise eloquence of abstraction on the rare occasions when his chattering urge to representation was successfully repressed. "I nearly always do work from memory,"[9] he wrote in July 1917 at a time when he had already been reliant on photography as a compositional aid for some time.

"Memory," said Henri Bergson, the French philosopher whose thinking was so influential on Boccioni's Technical Manifesto of Futurism, is "inseparable in practice from perception, imports the past into the present, contracts into a single intuition many moments of duration."[10] For Nevinson, in Bergsonian terms, this complex interface had broken down and a kind of shortcut had become necessary in the import of past experience to the present expression of it on canvas. In war photography, he found a suitable patch for his neurasthenically etiolated memory, although in his autobiography he insists that "Photographic art had never appealed to me and for years I did not attempt to paint pictures just like life."[11] But while Nevinson clearly eschewed anything like photo-realism—what he meant, I think, by the term "optical"—his painting was far more grounded in photography than he cared to admit.

La Mitrailleuse (fig. 24) is the earliest example I have discovered of a Nevinson painting that suggests a method of combining and masking a specific photographic source behind appropriations of key avant-garde imagery. Painted on honeymoon leave under stress collapse in November 1915, the painting is an unusual example within Nevinson's oeuvre of a direct and contemporaneous response to a specific news event.[12] Popular illustrated news tabloids such as the

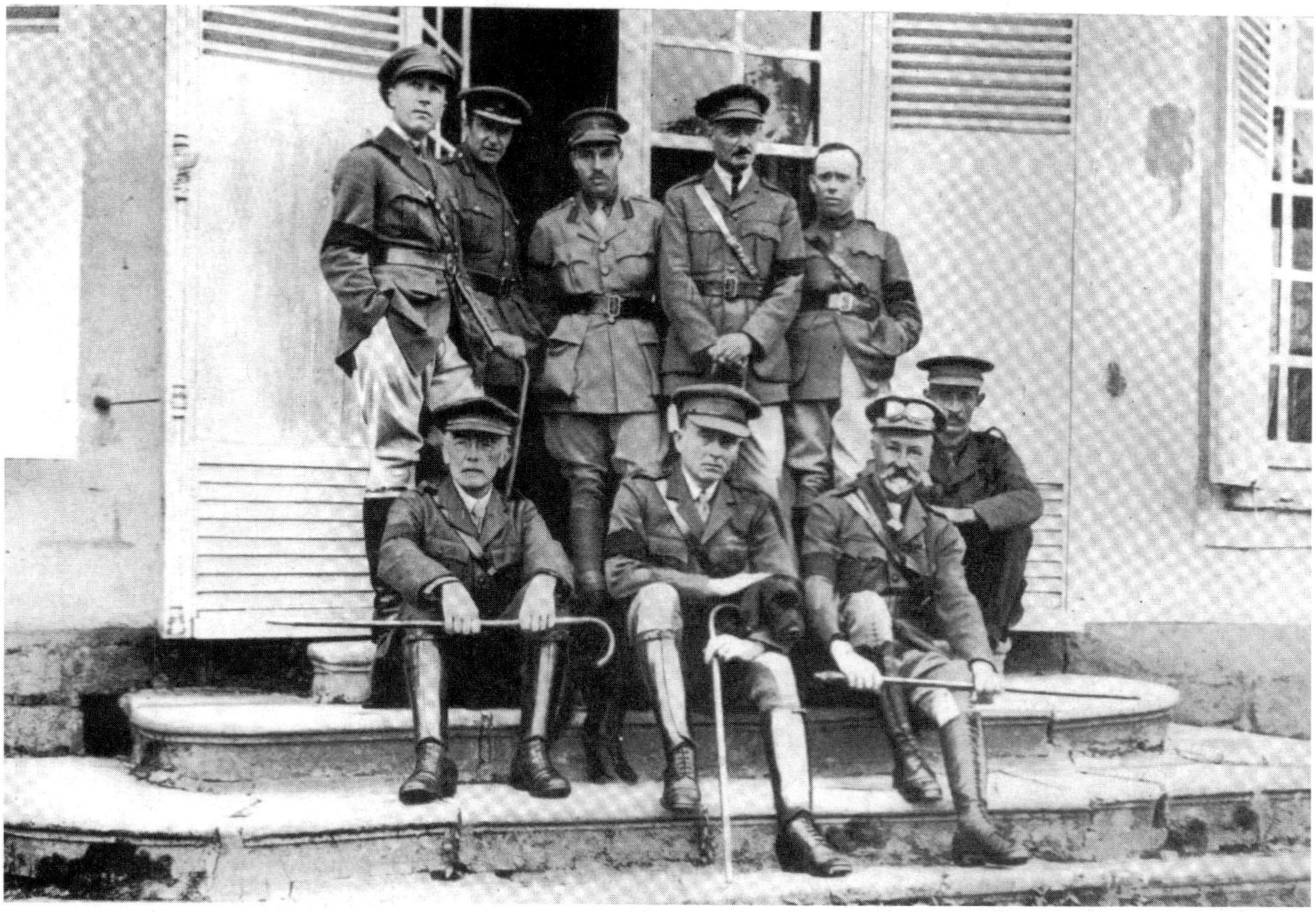

22. Some War Correspondents and Press Officers at Rollancourt (1918), photograph.

Daily Mirror, the *Sphere*, and the *Graphic* were reporting in November 1915 on the French troops' replacement of the peaked cap in the trenches with the distinctive *Casque Adrian* steel helmets. One headline read "The Armoured Man and The Armoured Trench" and using a French official war photograph depicted "French soldiers, wearing the new helmets, entering a captured German trench in the Sabot Wood."[13]

Since evidence of Nevinson's working and reading habits is limited to a handful of letters and the exhaustive cuttings albums which the artist paid for throughout his career, it is impossible to say with certainty which, if any, particular journals he subscribed to. But this premeditated act of self-presentation alone conveys the impression of a man who took a voracious interest in the press, just as one would expect for the son of such a famous international correspondent. His claims throughout his career that "I have no literary or journalistic tastes"[14] in particular come to seem at the very least disingenuous in the context of such comments as: "I had painted what I had seen without a thought for exhibition. To me the soldier was going to be dominated by the machine. Nobody thinks otherwise today, but because I was the first man to express this feeling on canvas I was treated as though I had committed a crime."[15] *La Mitrailleuse* is clearly a painting Nevinson cannot have based on direct observation, for although his Red Cross work was exclusively with French wounded, he had not been posted back to Belgium since returning to England with rheumatic fever in January 1915. By late June 1915, he was serving as an RAMC orderly with the Third London General in Wandsworth attending to neurasthenics—"some were mad, some were shell-shocked and some were nit-wits, I began to have an uneasy feeling that I was catching their complaint."[16] One can well imagine the artist leafing through copies of the illustrated press that would have been made available in the hospital to the recovering men.

Although the public had become used to daily photographic images in the press of troops marching or being transported up the line, nearly ten months of fighting elapsed before the first photograph was published of soldiers engaged in combat in the *Daily Sketch* of May 29, 1915.[17] Images the artist began to see, then, over

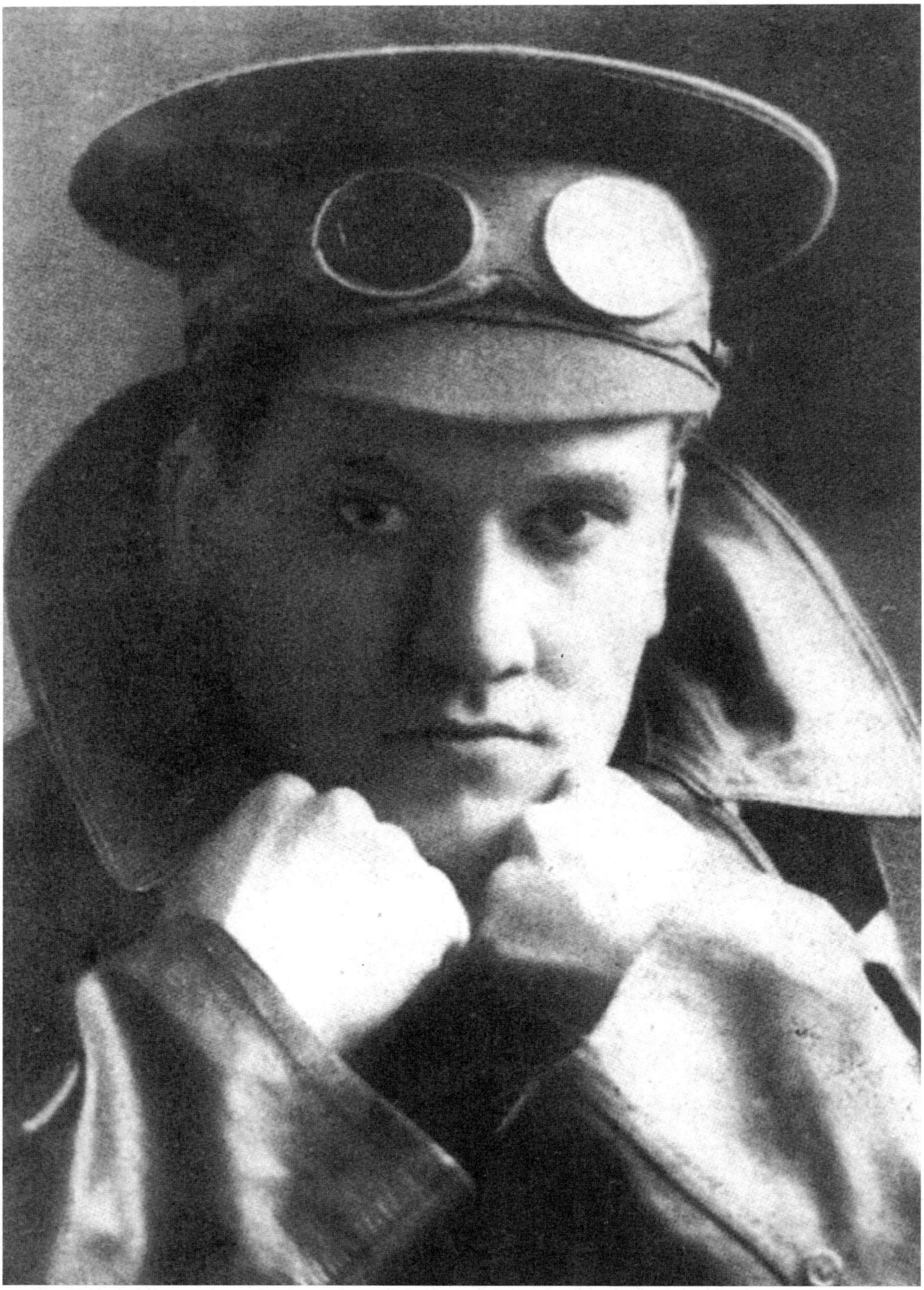

23. Photographic portrait of Nevinson by Malcolm Arbuthnot (March 1917).

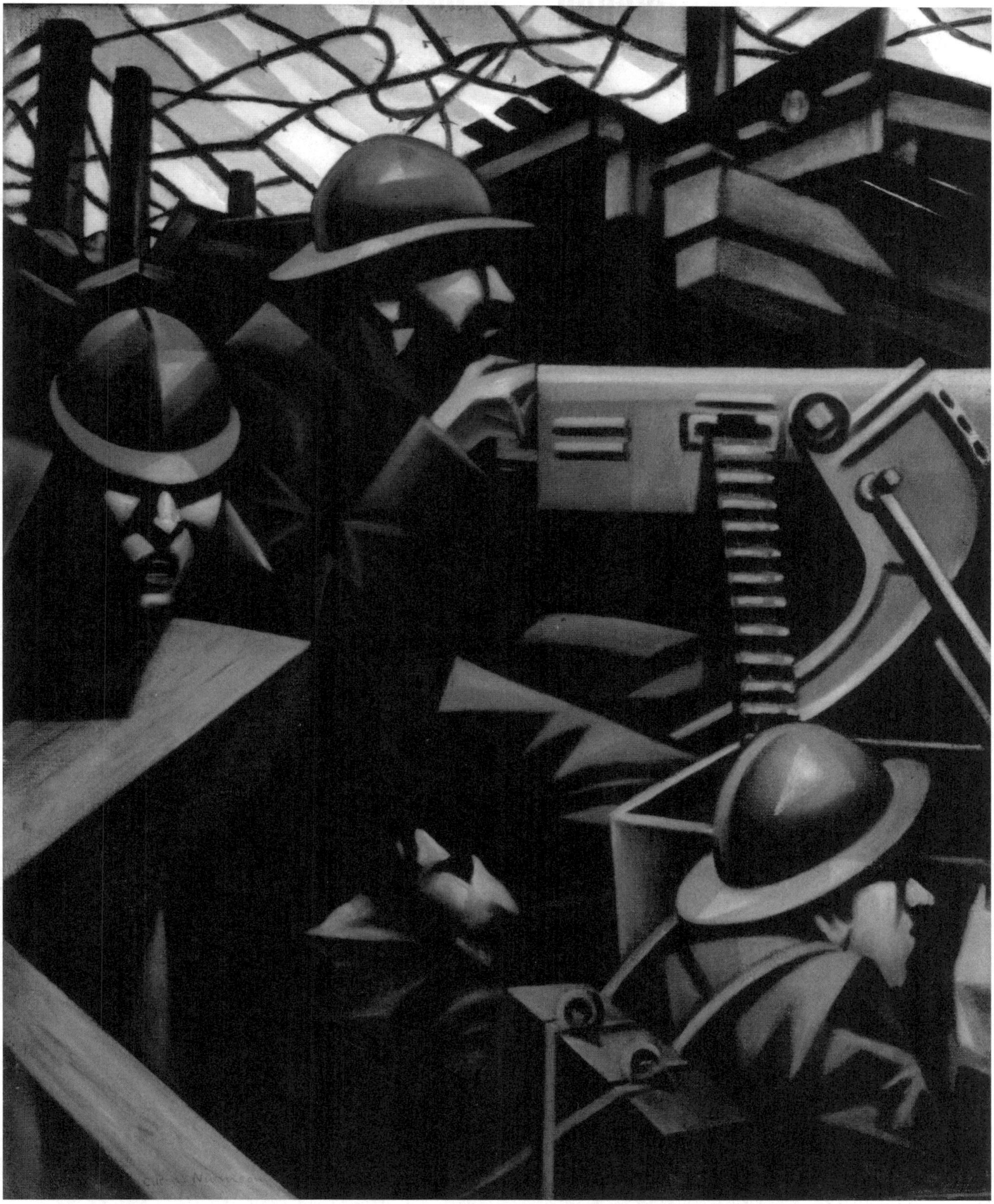

24. ***La Mitrailleuse*** **(1915), oil on canvas, 61 × 50.6 cm. Tate Gallery, London. Presented by the Contemporary Art Society 1917.**

the summer of 1915 of French soldiers in particular, would have rekindled the sensory oxymoron of suffering and excitement from his own physical experience of the battleground and trench systems around Ypres. An interesting visual reference point here is provided by the double-page spread in the *Sphere* titled "The Steel Helmet in Actual Use in the Trenches: The Disappearance of the Old French Cap." Dated November 20, 1915, it coincides so closely with the two-day period in which Nevinson returned from Ramsgate to paint that it would seem most likely that he would have had the article in mind as he made *La Mitrailleuse*. In the double-page spread, seven photographs investigate the average French soldier's daily life up and down the line, and two images in particular (fig. 25) focus on the moustachioed "Poilus," or "hairy ones" as they were known by the clean shaven English "Tommies." On the left, three soldiers engage with a Maxim machine gun. The figure on the left of the group bears a similarity to the main gunner in Nevinson's painting. An image of a different gun has obviously been sourced from elsewhere in addition to the gunner figure being dressed with full beard rather than moustache (perhaps literally to disguise the connection with this photograph) along with the minor adjustments of the arm position. This is a clear example of Nevinson patching over his visual memory with the most current press imagery. There is a link back to the clamped grip of the *Automobilist* of course, and this may also have a relevance to Nevinson's complaint at the time of his marriage that "my hands were in an appalling state, scarcely human."[18]

But for a painting that attracted such praise for its controlled density of emotional expression, *La Mitrailleuse* was far from original in its composition quite apart from its apparent photographic source. The huddled intensity of the gunners in Gino Severini's *Armoured Train* (1915, Richard S. Zeisler Collection) resonates through the painting, although any compositional borrowing from his Futurist friend belies Nevinson's challenge to Severini's implicit celebration of the war machine. By honing in on the pit-like trench Nevinson mediates the cold, unindividuated silence of Severini's soldiers into protest through the barking appeal made by the *poilu* on the left on behalf of his dying comrade at the foot of the picture. Considering the recent death of Vorticist Henri Gaudier-Brzeska,[19] his *A Mitrailleuse in Action* (1915, Modern Art Museum, Pompidou Center) offers up a more poignant context to *La Mitrailleuse*. One of the few of Gaudier-Brzeska's war works that survive, the drawing was posted back from Craonne and had been exhibited at the London Group exhibition of March 1915—scarcely two months before—alongside Nevinson's own work. The contrast in the handling of the key element in each picture reminds us of how far Nevinson's style compromised contemporary abstraction to intensify his message. Evidence of more traditional influences on this painting indicate Nevinson's increasingly illustrative urge.

Walter Sickert wrote that *La Mitrailleuse* "will probably remain the most authoritative and concentrated utterance on the war in the history of painting."[20] What is often overlooked is that in the same "Monthly Chronicle" column for *Burlington Magazine* three months earlier, Sickert had lamented "the somewhat theoretic simplification of [Nevinson's] war pieces"[21] when put alongside his output for the New English Art Club, which included Impressionistic paintings such as *Camden Town* (1912, Ashmolean Museum). The discrepancy in Sickert's criticism might be explained by his recognition in *La Mitrailleuse* of his own painting,[22] inspired by Belgian heroism in the defense of Liège in August 1914, *The Soldiers of King Albert the Ready* [1914, Graves Art Gallery (fig. 26)]. However different in their handling, the compositional similarities are striking: four soldiers engaged in battle, one in death-throes at the foot of the picture and guns pointing right.[23] A closer look through Sickert's work in Wendy Baron's monograph,[24] reveals precursors for the triangular eye and roughed-in face Nevinson developed as a facial shorthand. Since Sickert did not serve in the war, clearly his painting had to based on a secondhand image source. Sickert was consistently transparent regarding his use of newspaper photography as a compositional device in his art. Nevinson in stark contrast clearly felt threatened by the admission, feeling that it somehow undermined the audience's perception of the artist's originality. "An artist's business is to create, not to copy or abstract," he wrote in the preface to his March 1918 solo exhibition. Psychologically, one of the triggers to this anachronistic purism must have been the strictness of Slade tutor Henry Tonks for working "from the Life."[25]

La Mitrailleuse I suggest owes its intensity to the skillful synthesis of tabloid newspaper shots of the "Armoured Man" with a photo-by-proxy source in Sickert. Nevinson, though, would have been furious at the suggestion, despite being quick to pounce on anyone whom he suspected of "cribbing" from him.[26] In Quentin Bell's reminiscences of Sickert's advice to him, Bell recounted the words: "Look through old copies of the *Illustrated London News*, or *Punch*, or better still some paper like *Judy*, something the bloody critics will never have heard of. Find an engraving that you like, square it up, paint it in monochrome using white and ultramarine and then let it dry for two or three weeks."[27] Looking at *On the Road*

TRENCHES : The Disappearance of the Old French Cap.

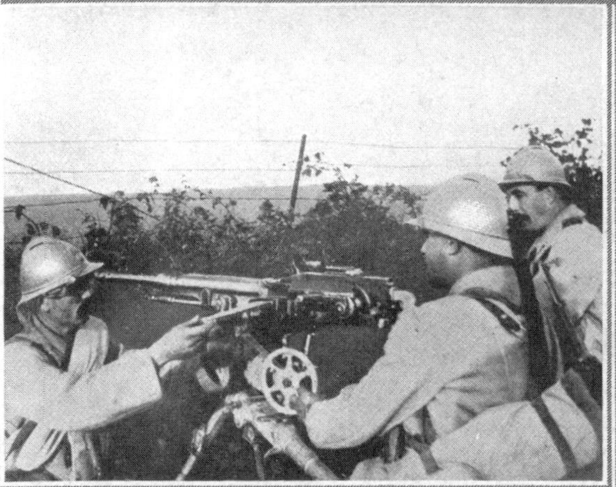

A French Maxim Gun Detachment in Action near Souchez

The ventilation slits at the top of the helmet are well shown in this view. They are placed at the side of the ridge running from front to back. The crest on the front of the helmet shows the regiment to which the wearer belongs

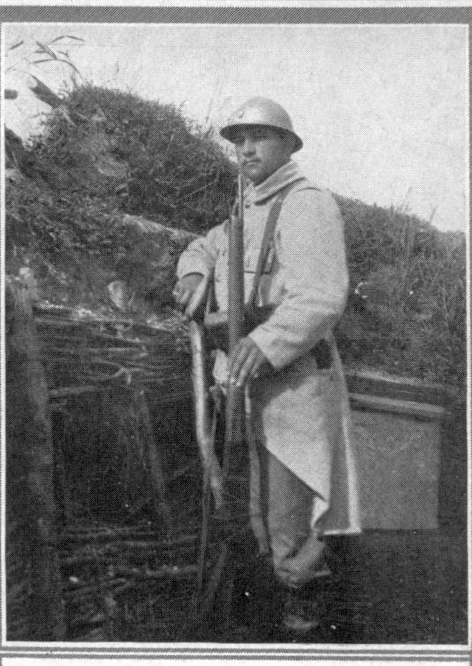

A French Sentry on Duty Wearing his New Steel Helmet

Mention has already been made of the helmet's proved utility; in this connection the following account—from *The Times*—should prove of interest. "I heard to-day," the writer states, "a story of how an unfortunate French officer was killed in circumstances which would probably have been obviated by a steel helmet. A duel was going on overhead between French and German airplanes, when this officer suddenly said to his companions that his nose was bleeding. His companions were chaffing him about his 'wound' when the officer pitched forward and fell dead. His body was carefully examined, and it was then found that a French bullet, obviously from the airplane gun, had penetrated the top of his skull, and come out through the bottom of his chin."

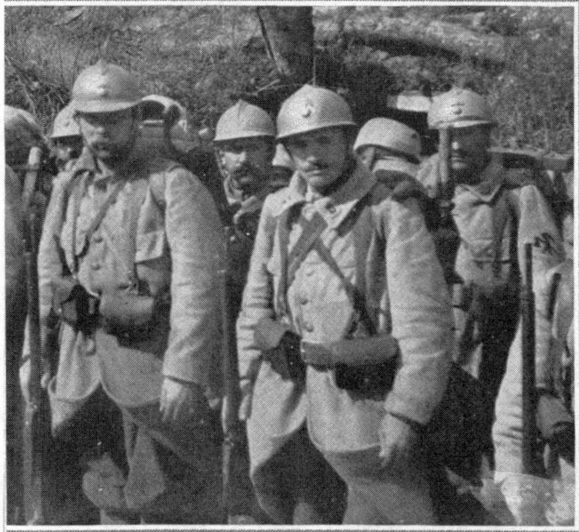

to Advance—the Men are Wearing their Helmets

The "Casque Adrian"—as the French call it in gratitude to its inventor—has apparently come to stay. Curious examples of the helmet's life-saving capabilities have already reached the French authorities from the front. In a war of trench fortifications it is the head more than any other part of the body which is liable to be hit by exploding shrapnel or by a sniper's bullets; the employment of the helmet reduces this mortality caused by head wounds very considerably, as figures given on another page indicate. There are now over 2½ million helmets actually in use.

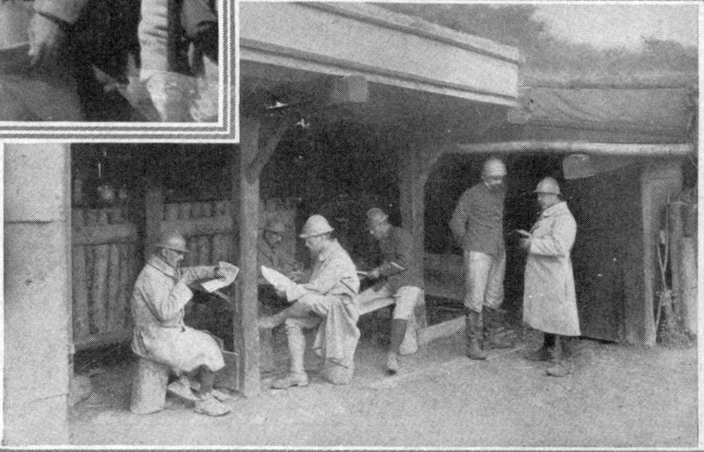

Helmet in the Trenches

In Champagne and Artois

French Soldiers Taking their Ease in a Well-constructed Dug-out

The men are comfortably seated in their protected dug-out, which boasts many articles of furniture not usually met with in the fighting lines. The substantial covering above their heads affords ample shelter from all but very heavy projectiles

25. ***The Sphere*, page 207 (November 20, 1915).**

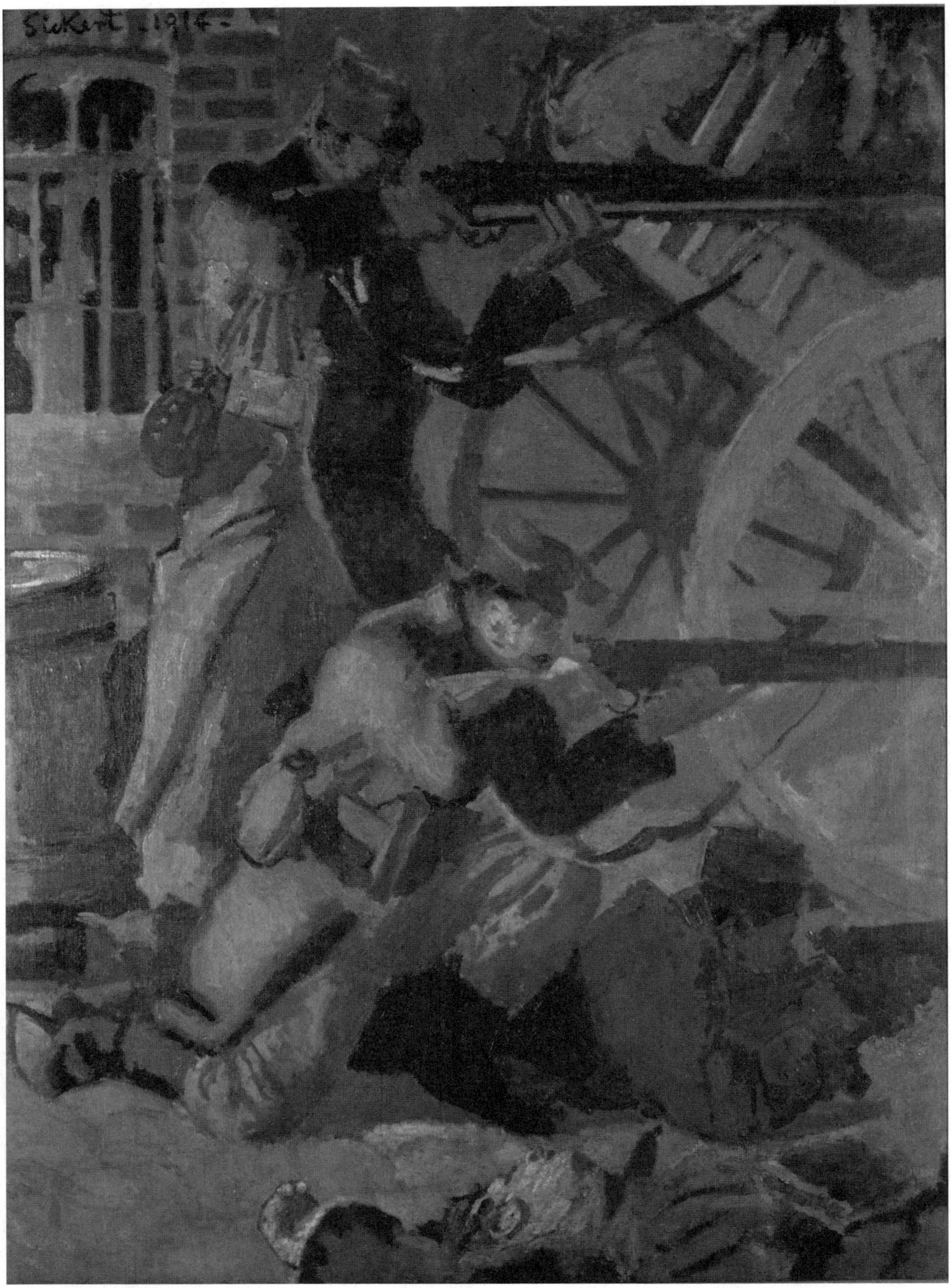

26. *The Soldiers of King Albert the Ready* by Walter Sickert (1914), oil on canvas, 199 × 153.8 cm. Sheffield Art Galleries and Museums Trust, UK / Bridgeman Art Library.

to Ypres [1916 (fig. 27)], there are signs that Nevinson adopted a similar technique. The photograph I present next to it is one of tens of thousands of documentary records roughly cataloged according to subject matter in the Imperial War Museum Photographic Archive (fig. 28).[28] Taken by John Warwick Brooke, the second official photographer to be employed by the Ministry of Information on the western front, it is the kind of image one can equally imagine being buried in a publication that was the military equivalent of Sickert's *Judy*. But often such photographs were reproduced in the more public arena of the illustrated presses such as the *Sphere*, the *Graphic*, and *War Illustrated*. Such publications had considerable readerships among soldiers and civilians alike.

If there be any doubt that Nevinson would have read the illustrated news, then it is dispelled by their interest in covering his work. For example, in the *Graphic* of March 2, 1918 (fig. 29), six of Nevinson's paintings were reproduced on one page under the heading "A New Way of Looking at the War: Mr. C. R. W. Nevinson's Pictures in the Leicester Galleries." The painting reproduced at the very bottom stands out due to its unusually elongated landscape format, which would have reminded the more visually alert readers of the *Graphic* of four wide-format photographs published only two months earlier (fig. 30), particularly the top one. Nevinson had received his first full-page reproduction of a painting in the *Graphic* as early as May 5, 1917. It depicted a soldier in the trenches scanning no-man's-land through the newly introduced optical device of the periscope. Spectatorship itself becomes the theme of the work here and this is picked up again by the *Graphic* a year later in an article entitled "The Trench From Different Points of View: The Battle of the War Artists: A Little Account of the Variety of Viewpoints"[29] in which Nevinson's painting of a Tommy using a trench periscope echoes the simplification of form in the Paul Nash set alongside it (fig. 31). These two examples of the avant-garde are placed below three official photographs in additional comparison to a conventional painted record of the war by academician James P. Beadle that is given prominence in the article.

To a large extent of course this was a commercial battle. An advertisement masquerading as an article in a September 1917 edition of the *Graphic* had declaimed as "The War's Greatest Pictures" *The Great Sacrifice* and *The Greater Reward* (fig. 32). These highly romanticized illustrations of toothsome, wounded Tommies by James Clark R.I. were sold as prints by mail order. The advert copy goes on to inform the reader that *The Great Sacrifice* "has been everywhere acknowledged to be the greatest of all the pictures inspired by the war."[30] One suspects that the readership such an advertisement was aimed at did not overlap with that of Sickert's in *Burlington*. In order to highlight the two contrasting visual languages within painting which claimed authenticity in recording the grim experiences of war and polarized "popular" and "avant-garde" notions of representation by September 1917, one need only contrast the Clark paintings with Nevinson's newest work *A Group of Soldiers* (fig. 33). The painting may appear to us today as rather banal and cartoonish, perhaps bearing too close a resemblance to the Bruce Bairnsfather caricaturing of the British Tommy in the "Ole Bill" cartoon series, as in this advertisement for the stage show carried by the *Graphic* on September 29, 1917 (fig. 34). For Nevinson, though, it was absolutely based on firsthand experience of contact with unidealizable men who were caught up in the horror of war and making the best of it: "This is the spirit I have expressed in my paintings. This is the Truth not romance."[31] The prosaic treatment was key to the overall effect of portraying the truth about soldiers who after the huge losses to the Allied armies by 1916 were mainly conscripts rather than volunteers. He took issue with Major Lee's argument that the British soldiers depicted were somehow "not sufficiently good-looking,"[32] and following the painting's censorship by Lee on the grounds of it portraying the Tommy as inept and unheroic, wrote in a fury again via Masterman at the Office of Information. "I will not paint 'castrated Lancelots' though I know this is how Tommies are usually presented in illustrated papers etc.—high-souled eunuchs looking mild-eyed, unable to melt butter on their tongues and mentally and physically incapable of killing a German. I refuse to insult the British army with such sentimental bilge."[33]

The "Battle of the War Artists," "viewpoints"—or perhaps more correctly of the "vision" they expressed to an increasingly visually sophisticated audience—dated back to spring 1916 when Ivor Nicholson's Office of Information at Wellington House was established and officially sanctioned images of fighting on the western front were first distributed. May 1916 was a pivotal point in the war—the early optimism for a swift British victory had been snuffed out—and coincided with the commission of Muirhead Bone as the first Official War Artist. "Bonehead Muir" as Nevinson contemptuously dubbed him was a safe, prosaic artist in midcareer. Made easily malleable by his employers at the propaganda office, he painted in what might be described as a third category outside the illustrative heroics of Clark and the emotional realism of Nevinson. He had not previously seen active service and

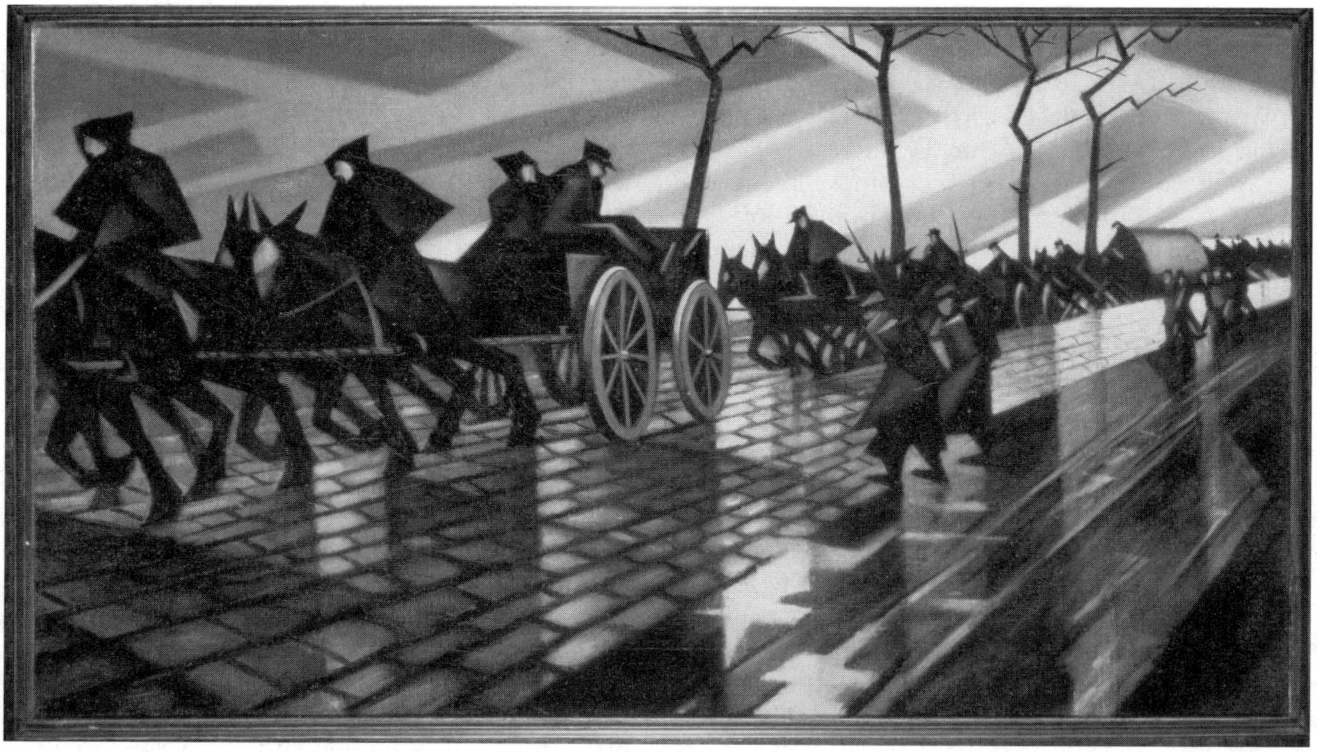

27. *On the Road to Ypres* (1916), oil on canvas, 49 × 90 cm. Private collection. Courtesy of The Fine Art Society, London / Bridgeman Art Library.

his hundreds of drawings and washes as Official War Artist—reproduced in a ten-part series of booklets[34]—were dominated by a viewpoint that was distant and detached, encompassing wide vistas of battlefield with all the panoramic compositional disinterest of a large-format glass plate camera set on a hilltop miles from the localized menace of the trenches.

The question of Bone's expressive limitations stood at the center of a debate starting in 1916, in the light of the propaganda office's control of pictorial dissemination, over whether official paintings were depicting war as it really was. Photography may originally have served as a touchstone for veracity, but its truthfulness became dubious following suspicions of manipulation and staging in the work of Ivor Castle. By comparison, war painting seemed to get much nearer the truth without having to rely on the realistic detail or cohesive narrative offered by the lens. In an article of 1916 entitled "Art and the Camera," John Salis reviewed an early exhibition of Canadian war photographers on painters' turf at the Grafton Galleries, comparing its impact with Nevinson's recent one-man show specifically in terms of a truthful portrayal of war. Photographs potentially undermine their own emotional impact, he argued, because of their tendency to bathos. The "robbed emotions" engendered in us by a posed photograph don't figure in front of a Nevinson painting, Salis argues, where we understand implicitly that the soldiers, imagined in the act of painting, concentrate the truth of remembered experience. "The non existence of his sufferers does not make it a forgery, for it is a synthesis. 'This is War, cries the camera, as I see it'. 'This is war, says Mr. Nevinson, as I understand it.' And herein lies the difference."[35] For a public who had been deprived of a meaningful visual record of the disastrous first two years of the war photographically, the heightened painted "truth" of Nevinson's (unofficial) work with its "efforts to show us something novel and strange"[36] had become the popular standard by which official war painting would be judged.

Subsequent reviews, which still appeared months after the Leicester Galleries exhibition, recycled what had become a familiar terminology of "truth" in describing Nevinson's work: "These pictures tell you more about the war as it actually *is* than any of the photographs and reproductions of drawings which fill the illustrated journals."[37] Resentful of the implicit swipes these articles made at official war artist Bone, C. E. Montague, the copywriter for the Office of Information, hit back: "And then it is hinted that we are all in league to hide from our friends at home some extreme, mysterious horror which is 'really' war, 'war as it is', something which,

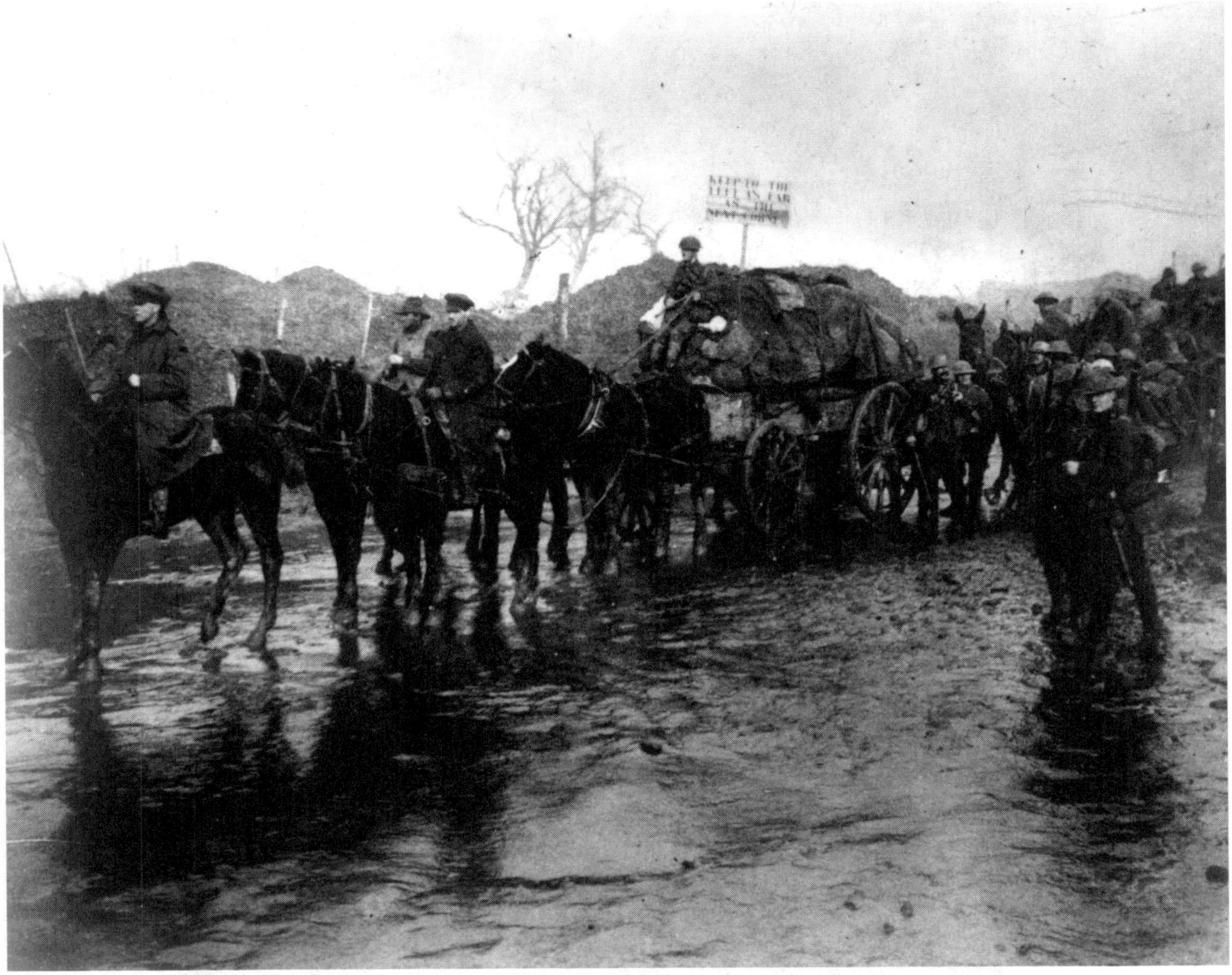

28. Ration wagons on the muddy road, Montauban, by John Warwick Brooke (November 1916), photograph, Imperial War Museum, London.

if it leaked out, would make the world lay down its arms on the spot, and the nations kiss and be friends."[38] Today, Bone is all too easily dismissed as "an artist who inclines to inform rather than suggest."[39] In his own era, for an artist to have his own work disparaged by his art historical contemporaries as "mere illustrated journalism"[40] was particularly insulting.

At the same time as self-consciously presenting himself as of "unjournalistic mind"[41]—usually by railing against what he saw as the effete literary pretensions of "the Bloomsburies"[42]—Nevinson liked to issue derogatory broadsides against photography. Sometimes he would use as a mouthpiece the friend employed to write the introduction to his latest catalog. With comments such as "The camera lacks the power of discrimination. It has, indeed, an infallible *flair* for the inessential"[43] he sought to denigrate the status of the photograph as work of art by arguing that artistic composition was anathema to the mechanical lens. For this painter, unlike those of Sickert's ilk, admitting to the use of photography in one's working practice tainted the artist's perceived originality, even genius. Yet there is strong evidence to suggest that Nevinson had an eye for the very uninflected limitations he criticized in photography, skillfully exploiting the surface dullness of these war images to express the disassociation brought on by firsthand experiences of war. Nevinson was using photographs to plug gaps in his supposedly formidable memory; he appropriated compositional ideas from photographs just as he copied from the French and Italian avant-garde in his juvenilia. In the figurative work he found so difficult there is evidence of him integrating ready-made stances and faces into his paintings.

A NEW WAY OF LOOKING AT THE WAR

MR. C. R. W. NEVINSON'S PICTURES IN THE LEICESTER GALLERIES

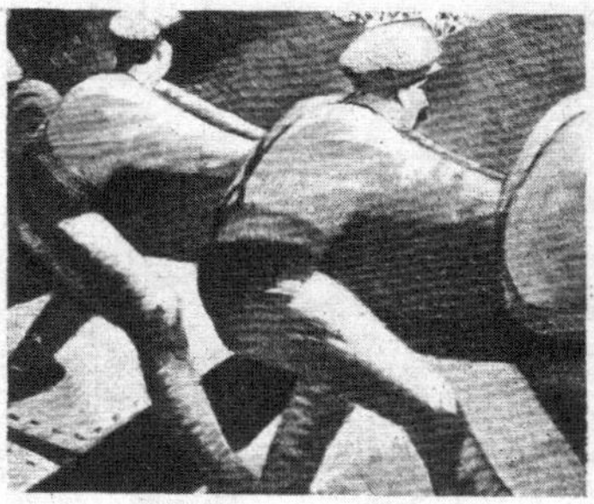

RAMMING HOME A HEAVY SHELL

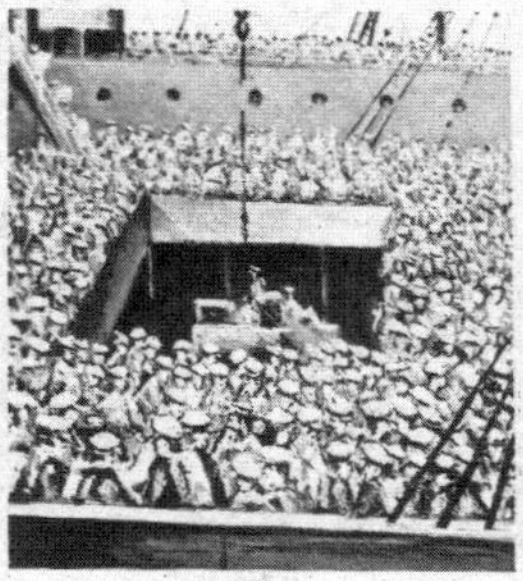

THE LEAVE BOAT FROM THE QUAY

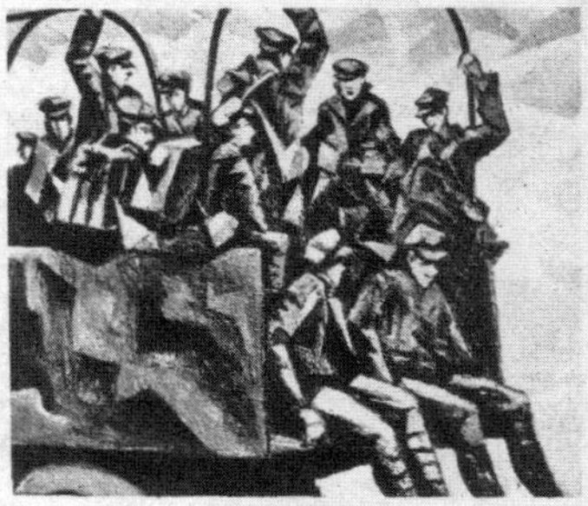

MOTOR TRANSPORT: A FULL LOAD

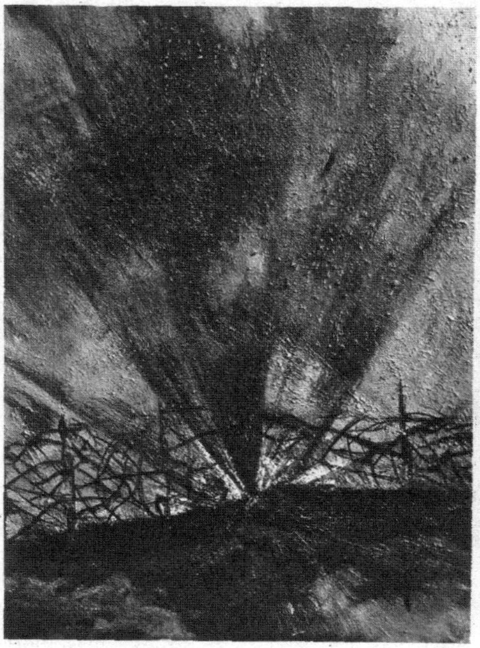

A SHELL BURSTING ON A HIGH-ROAD

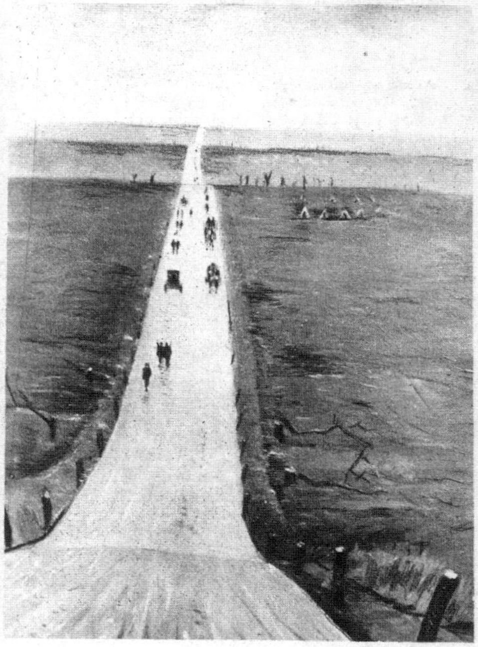

THE ROAD FROM ARRAS TO BAPAUME

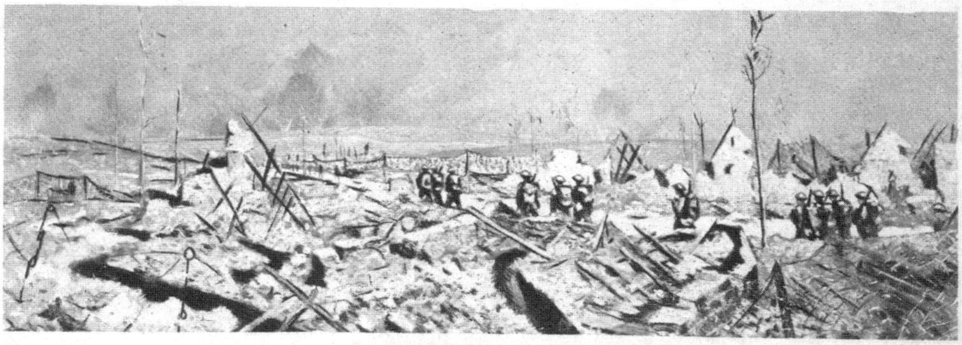

A RUINED HIGHWAY OF FRANCE, WITH BRITISH INFANTRY IN EXTENDED FORMATION

29. ***The Graphic*, page 269 (March 2, 1918).**

THE WESTERN FRONT FROM YPRES TO ARRAS

SOME OF WAR'S GRIM REALITIES

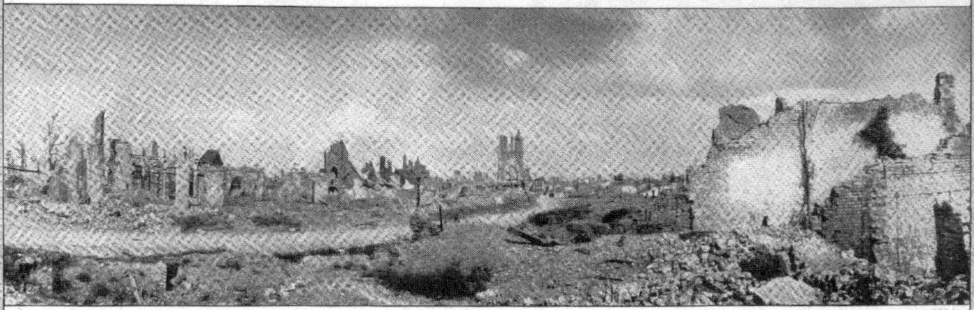

Official

THE WRECK OF YPRES, SHOWING ALL THAT REMAINS OF THE FAMOUS CLOTH HALL

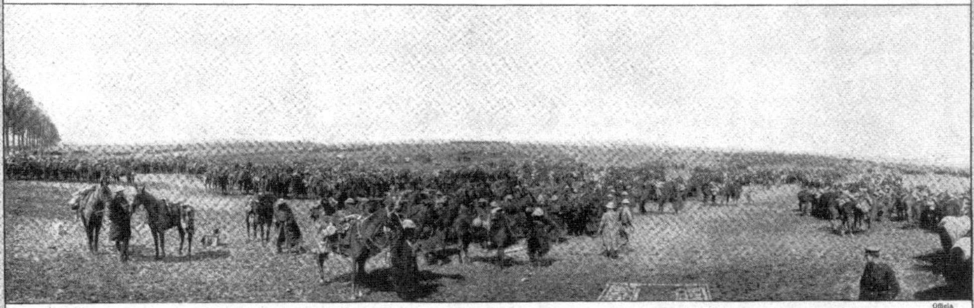

Official

OUR CAVALRY AWAITING THE ORDER TO "MOUNT": SCENE NEAR THE ST. POL-ARRAS ROAD

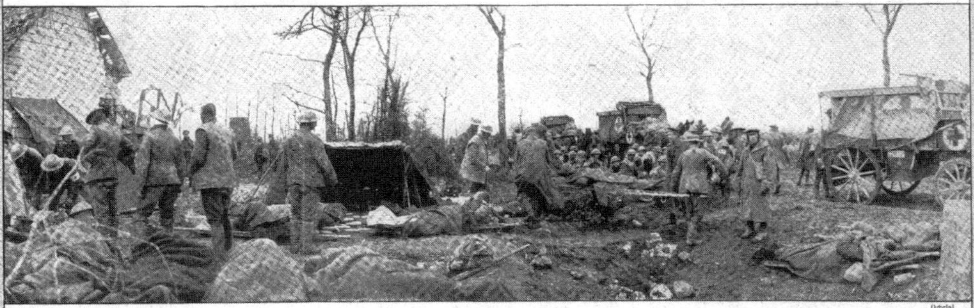

Official

AN ADVANCED DRESSING STATION IMMEDIATELY BEHIND THE LINE OF BATTLE: THE FIRST ARRIVALS

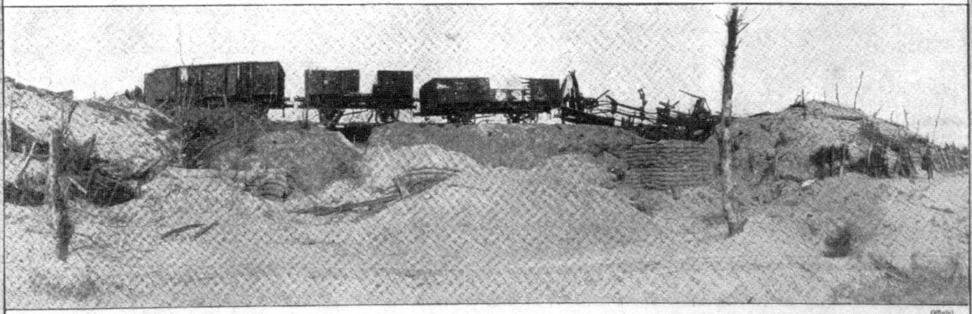

Official

WAR'S WRECKAGE: WHERE TRAINS RAN IN PEACE A BUTTRESSED PARAPET STRETCHES ACROSS NO MAN'S LAND

30. ***The Graphic*****, page 9 (January 5, 1918).**

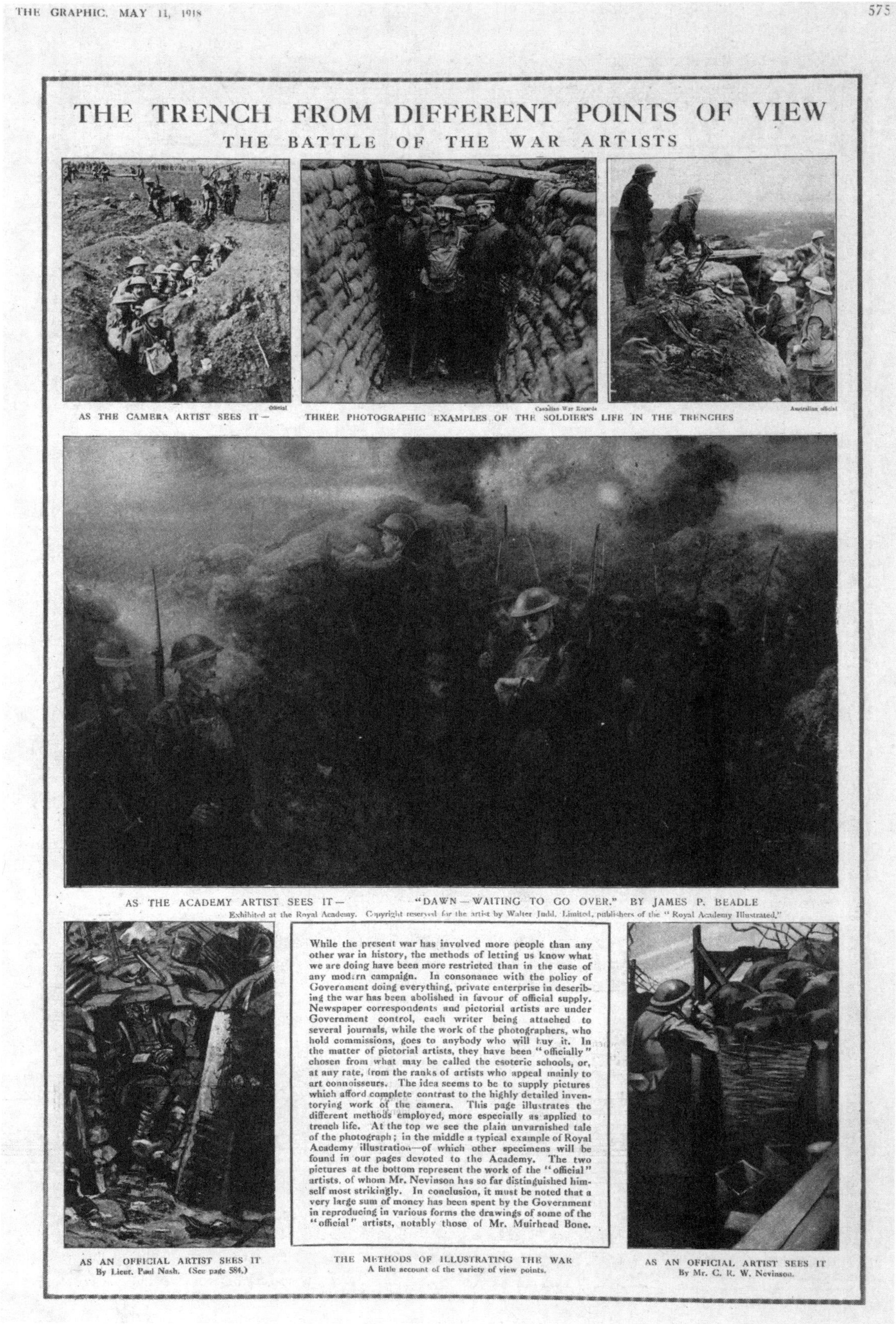

THE GRAPHIC, MAY 11, 1918 — 575

THE TRENCH FROM DIFFERENT POINTS OF VIEW

THE BATTLE OF THE WAR ARTISTS

Official — Canadian War Records — Australian official

AS THE CAMERA ARTIST SEES IT— THREE PHOTOGRAPHIC EXAMPLES OF THE SOLDIER'S LIFE IN THE TRENCHES

AS THE ACADEMY ARTIST SEES IT— "DAWN—WAITING TO GO OVER." BY JAMES P. BEADLE

Exhibited at the Royal Academy. Copyright reserved for the artist by Walter Judd, Limited, publishers of the "Royal Academy Illustrated."

While the present war has involved more people than any other war in history, the methods of letting us know what we are doing have been more restricted than in the case of any modern campaign. In consonance with the policy of Government doing everything, private enterprise in describing the war has been abolished in favour of official supply. Newspaper correspondents and pictorial artists are under Government control, each writer being attached to several journals, while the work of the photographers, who hold commissions, goes to anybody who will buy it. In the matter of pictorial artists, they have been "officially" chosen from what may be called the esoteric schools, or, at any rate, from the ranks of artists who appeal mainly to art connoisseurs. The idea seems to be to supply pictures which afford complete contrast to the highly detailed inventorying work of the camera. This page illustrates the different methods employed, more especially as applied to trench life. At the top we see the plain unvarnished tale of the photograph; in the middle a typical example of Royal Academy illustration—of which other specimens will be found in our pages devoted to the Academy. The two pictures at the bottom represent the work of the "official" artists, of whom Mr. Nevinson has so far distinguished himself most strikingly. In conclusion, it must be noted that a very large sum of money has been spent by the Government in reproducing in various forms the drawings of some of the "official" artists, notably those of Mr. Muirhead Bone.

AS AN OFFICIAL ARTIST SEES IT
By Lieut. Paul Nash. (See page 584.)

THE METHODS OF ILLUSTRATING THE WAR
A little account of the variety of view points.

AS AN OFFICIAL ARTIST SEES IT
By Mr. C. R. W. Nevinson.

31. ***The Graphic*, page 575 (May 11, 1918).**

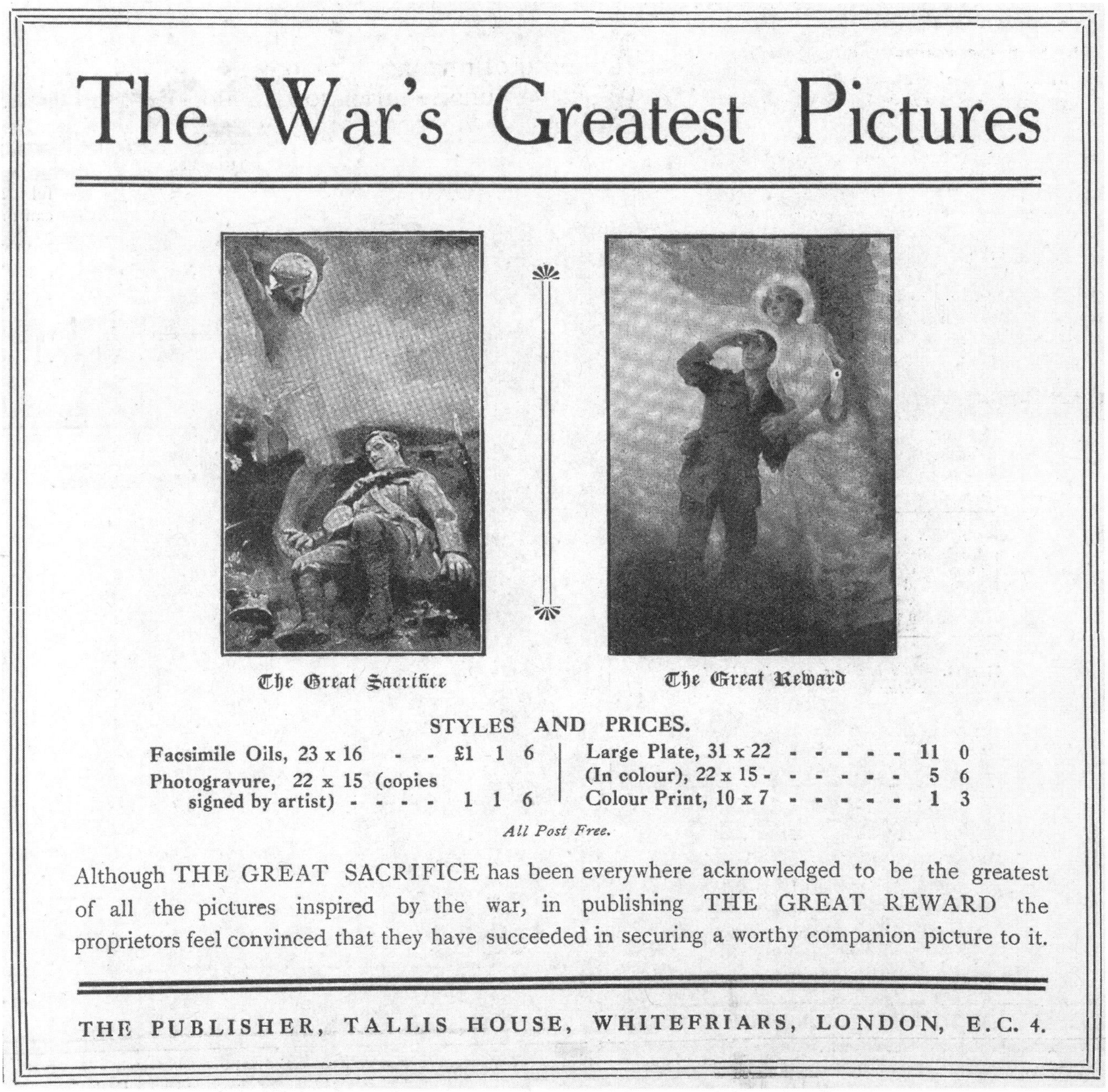

32. *The Graphic*, page 339 (September 15, 1917).

Leafing strategically through the illustrated press around dates at which we know Nevinson was creating key works can produce telling results. The grouping of soldiers in a photograph on the front cover of the *Sphere* of August 1917 (fig. 35),[44] for example, bears a strong resemblance to the Tommies of Nevinson's *A Group of Soldiers* painted at precisely the same time—the month of the artist's return from Passchaendale. In their ramshackle appearance and distinctly unmilitary bearing the men are recognizably the working man in uniform, far from the erstwhile Futurist idealization of man-as-machine as depicted in *La Mitrailleuse.* Although one could argue for the generic similarity of any number of photographs featuring a group of standing soldiers, on closer inspection of this particular image the figure on the extreme right is almost identical in pose and angle of head to the figure on the right of the painting, even down to the left hand in the pocket. Only his left foot is reworked in the lower half of the painting for greater compositional balance. In the photograph

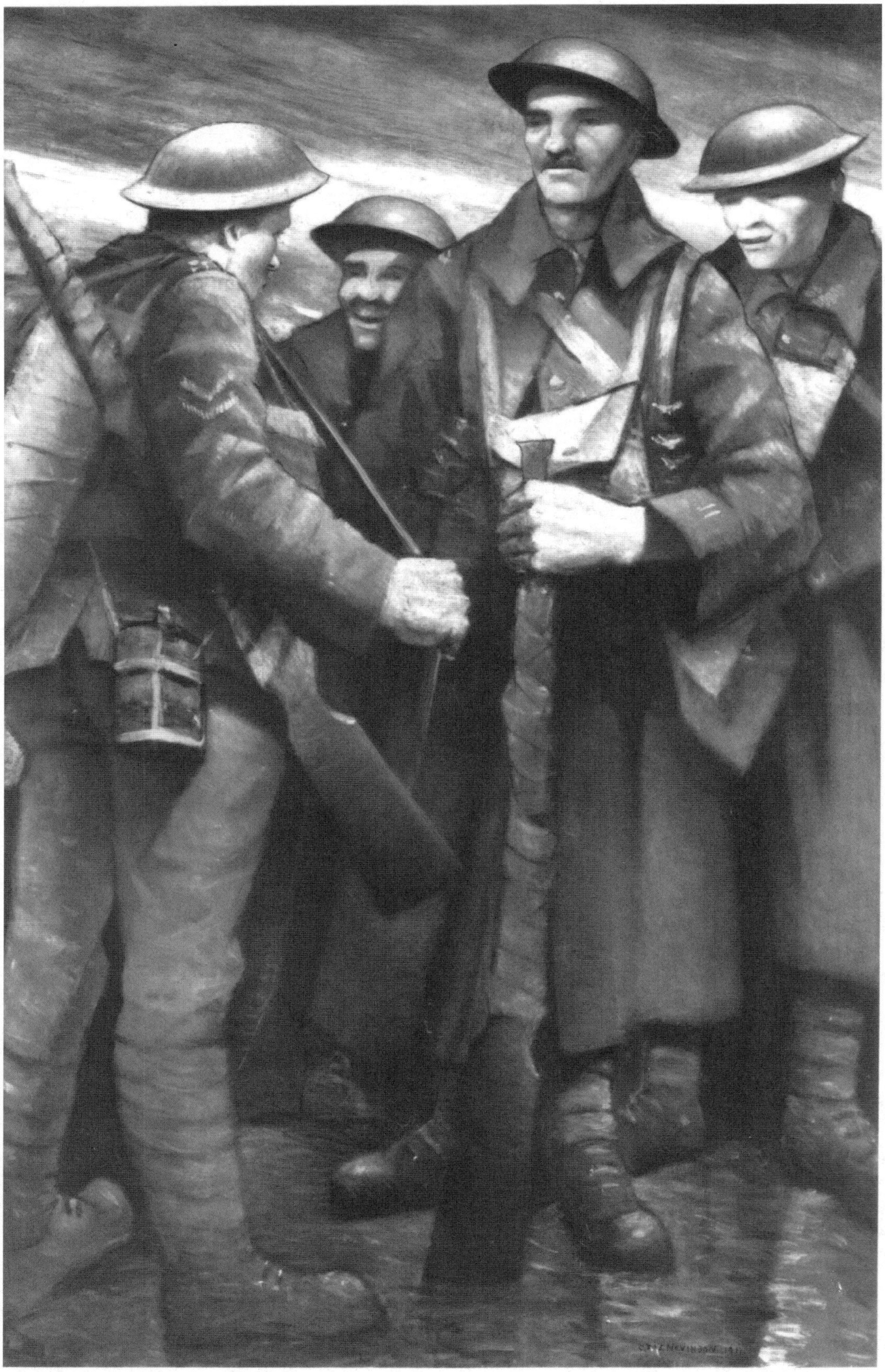

33. *A Group of Soldiers* (1917), oil on canvas, 91.4 × 60.9 cm. Imperial War Museum, London. Purchased from the Artist 1918.

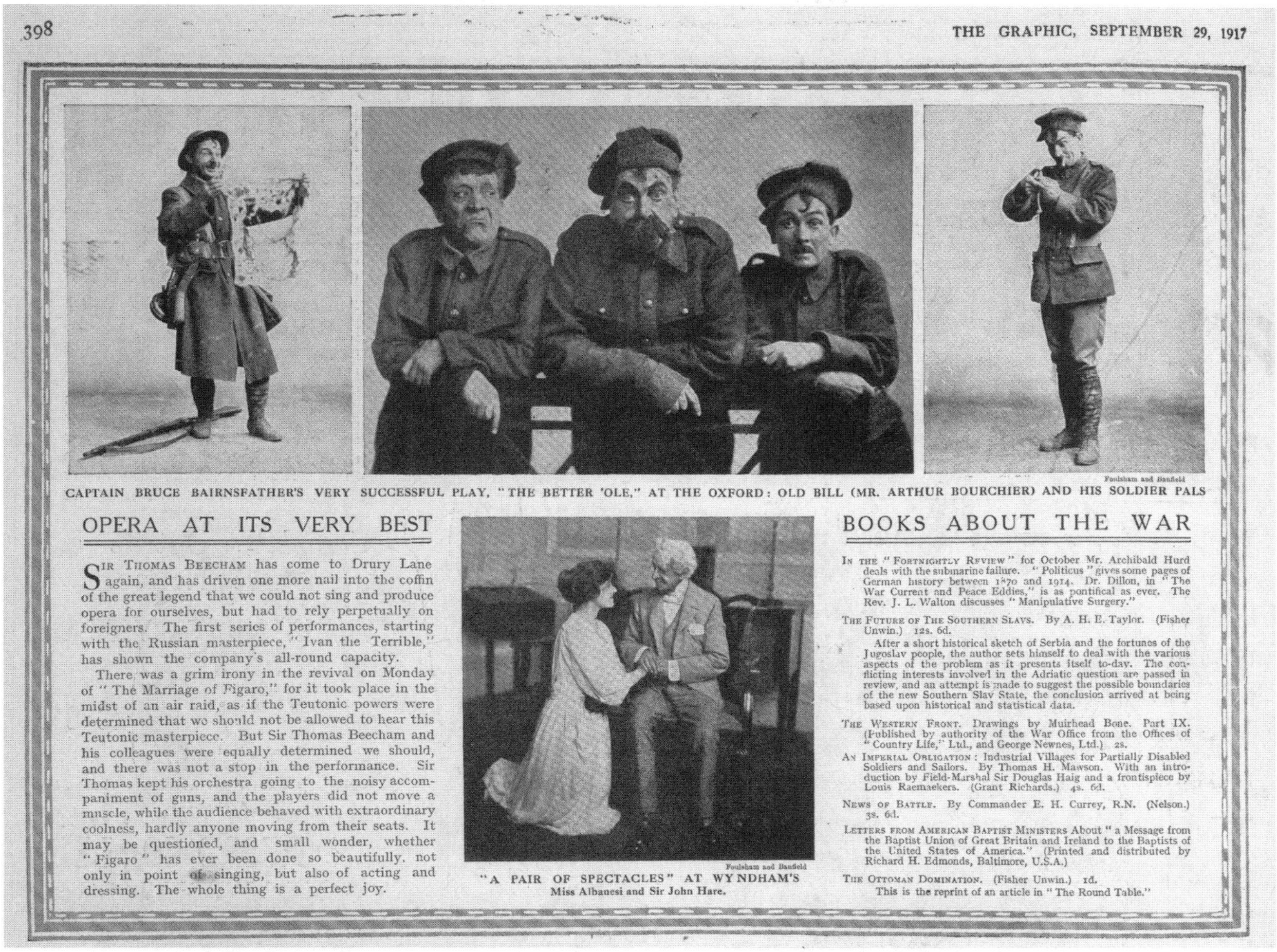

398 THE GRAPHIC, SEPTEMBER 29, 1917

Foulsham and Banfield

CAPTAIN BRUCE BAIRNSFATHER'S VERY SUCCESSFUL PLAY, "THE BETTER 'OLE," AT THE OXFORD: OLD BILL (MR. ARTHUR BOURCHIER) AND HIS SOLDIER PALS

OPERA AT ITS VERY BEST

Sir Thomas Beecham has come to Drury Lane again, and has driven one more nail into the coffin of the great legend that we could not sing and produce opera for ourselves, but had to rely perpetually on foreigners. The first series of performances, starting with the Russian masterpiece, "Ivan the Terrible," has shown the company's all-round capacity.

There was a grim irony in the revival on Monday of "The Marriage of Figaro," for it took place in the midst of an air raid, as if the Teutonic powers were determined that we should not be allowed to hear this Teutonic masterpiece. But Sir Thomas Beecham and his colleagues were equally determined we should, and there was not a stop in the performance. Sir Thomas kept his orchestra going to the noisy accompaniment of guns, and the players did not move a muscle, while the audience behaved with extraordinary coolness, hardly anyone moving from their seats. It may be questioned, and small wonder, whether "Figaro" has ever been done so beautifully, not only in point of singing, but also of acting and dressing. The whole thing is a perfect joy.

Foulsham and Banfield

"A PAIR OF SPECTACLES" AT WYNDHAM'S
Miss Albanesi and Sir John Hare.

BOOKS ABOUT THE WAR

In the "Fortnightly Review" for October Mr. Archibald Hurd deals with the submarine failure. "Politicus" gives some pages of German history between 1870 and 1914. Dr. Dillon, in "The War Current and Peace Eddies," is as pontifical as ever. The Rev. J. L. Walton discusses "Manipulative Surgery."

The Future of The Southern Slavs. By A. H. E. Taylor. (Fisher Unwin.) 12s. 6d.

After a short historical sketch of Serbia and the fortunes of the Jugoslav people, the author sets himself to deal with the various aspects of the problem as it presents itself to-day. The conflicting interests involved in the Adriatic question are passed in review, and an attempt is made to suggest the possible boundaries of the new Southern Slav State, the conclusion arrived at being based upon historical and statistical data.

The Western Front. Drawings by Muirhead Bone. Part IX. (Published by authority of the War Office from the Offices of "Country Life," Ltd., and George Newnes, Ltd.) 2s.

An Imperial Obligation: Industrial Villages for Partially Disabled Soldiers and Sailors. By Thomas H. Mawson. With an introduction by Field-Marshal Sir Douglas Haig and a frontispiece by Louis Raemaekers. (Grant Richards.) 4s. 6d.

News of Battle. By Commander E. H. Currey, R.N. (Nelson.) 3s. 6d.

Letters from American Baptist Ministers About "a Message from the Baptist Union of Great Britain and Ireland to the Baptists of the United States of America." (Printed and distributed by Richard H. Edmonds, Baltimore, U.S.A.)

The Ottoman Domination. (Fisher Unwin.) 1d.

This is the reprint of an article in "The Round Table."

34. *The Graphic*, page 398 (September 29, 1917).

(which is actually of Canadian soldiers), the rim of the metal hat shadows the eyes affording Nevinson the ready-made shorthand for facial representation, albeit noticeably less summary than that of *La Mitrailleuse* or *French Troops Resting*.

Alfred Yockney wrote to Nevinson on November 21, 1917 to inform him that *A Group of Soldiers* had not been passed by the censor Major Lee since he considered them "unworthy" of the British army. In a letter from Nevinson to Major Lee intercepted by the Information Office and marked "not sent" the artist is indignant at the censorship of his painting: "I might mention that all these four men in this particular picture were portraits, men I chose quite haphazard from the Tubes as they came from France on leave."[45] Nevinson claimed to have stood at Victoria Station, sketchbook in hand, but it would seem unlikely that any artist would have been able to capture effective individual facial likenesses of soldiers from crowds of men dispersing at speed. Indeed it was Nevinson's own view, expressed elsewhere, that "nature is far too confusing and anarchic to be merely copied on the spot."[46] Again, one is struck by the irony of Nevinson's indignance since at least one of the subjects for his painting was culled from a photograph, and a Canadian soldier at that.[47]

The point here of course is not that using photography as a reference should be considered inimical to painting per se, but that Nevinson should continue to take such a publicly polarized view on the medium's alleged lack of artistic insight while continuing to plunder photographic ideas in private. With comments such as "an artist's business is to create, not to copy or abstract,"[48] he unnecessarily increased the stakes of his disingenuousness being discovered. And yet, it was a risk which clearly paid off (no critic to my knowledge has ever drawn attention to it) and the evidence offers a fascinating insight into an artist at the height of his fame, yet losing his technical and imaginative powers.

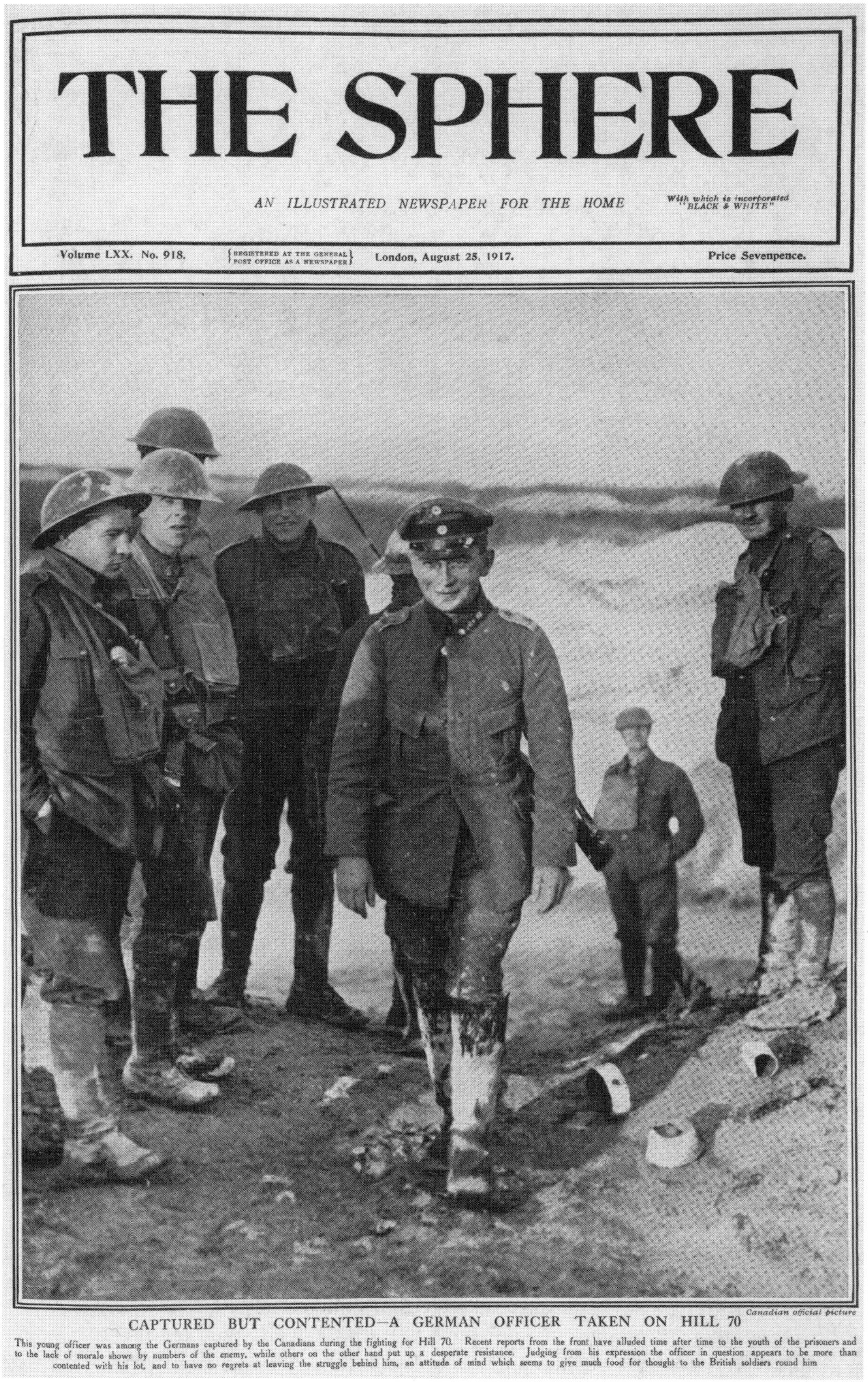

THE SPHERE

AN ILLUSTRATED NEWSPAPER FOR THE HOME *With which is incorporated "BLACK & WHITE"*

Volume LXX. No. 918. {REGISTERED AT THE GENERAL POST OFFICE AS A NEWSPAPER} London, August 25, 1917. Price Sevenpence.

Canadian official picture

CAPTURED BUT CONTENTED—A GERMAN OFFICER TAKEN ON HILL 70

This young officer was among the Germans captured by the Canadians during the fighting for Hill 70. Recent reports from the front have alluded time after time to the youth of the prisoners and to the lack of morale shown by numbers of the enemy, while others on the other hand put up a desperate resistance. Judging from his expression the officer in question appears to be more than contented with his lot, and to have no regrets at leaving the struggle behind him, an attitude of mind which seems to give much food for thought to the British soldiers round him

35. *The Sphere*, front page (August 25, 1917).

In October 1916, a few weeks after his debut solo exhibition Paintings and Drawings of War had opened at the Leicester Galleries, Nevinson was recuperating in Falmouth, resting the limp and stiff hands his rheumatic fever had caused. From here he wrote to artist friend William Rothenstein that "I intend to paint no more war pictures for some time. I hope to change my method of painting . . . I wish always to work within the limits of some self-imposed convention and a different one in relation to each new subject."[49] At the height of his fame, albeit embattled by nerve damage, we observe an artist keen to articulate himself afresh outside the parameters of war by discovering new pictorial resources. Nevinson seems to acknowledge that in the face of increasingly normative mechanical recordings of optical veracity offered by the camera, painting had to reassert its claim to truth through a kind of creative pragmatism to the requirements of individual subjects and settings. But although eclectic in subject matter, the work Nevinson produced over the following six months offers few examples of method and picture "in hard embrace, so close and tight that they seem to have become one"[50] that Charles Lewis Hind for one had found so impressive in his paintings of war.

The first new paintings Nevinson exhibited under his "self-imposed convention" were on show at the fifth London Group salon of November 1916 prior to which Sickert had urged him to accept the post of secretary as a mark of his rising notoriety. *A Music Hall* (whereabouts unknown) predictably attracted attention for its use of real lace and half an inch of projecting wood on which the "audience" was depicted, but such pseudo-Cubist punning must have come across as hackneyed and weakly self-referential. *Spiral Descent* was the first of a series[51] of highly aestheticized paintings of aeroplanes swooping elegantly through ethereal clouds in a sphere detached from the trenches of battle. Somewhat surprisingly, Nevinson felt in retrospect that these were his finest paintings, although this had more to do with the vertiginous new perspective they offered in 1916[52] and the reflected originality, not to mention bravery, they allowed Nevinson to claim. From a psychological standpoint they might appear to us more symptomatic of the disassociation and "impaired ideation" of shell shock, a term newly applied to war and first discussed in a 1915 analysis of the condition.[53] At the Sixth London Group of April 1917, the rudimentary *Halifax* and *White Horses* bespeak the numbing effects of his treatment by a nerve specialist since the New Year and must have seemed particularly dilute examples of the avant-garde in the vicinity of Slade colleague Mark Gertler's silent scream *Merry-Go-Round*. The deliberate lack of consistency in subject matter continued to belie a sameness in paint handling. For Nevinson, stylistic continuity was something he deliberately eschewed in intellectual terms—"only bad work goes on forever"[54]—but in practical terms could not seem to avoid. The pattern echoes contemporaneous psychological models of neurasthenia as a vicious circle under which the lowering of the neuron threshold due to exhaustion results in a greater sensitivity to stimuli and in turn further depletes neuron reserves.

Nevinson found that he was unable to adhere to what he said was a self-imposed convention not to paint war and from spring 1917 badgered various decision makers, notably Colonel John Buchan at the Office of Information, to consider him for the Official War Artist scheme.[55] Information Officer Charles Masterman expressed reservations by letter to Buchan concerning the psychological suitability of Nevinson "who as you know, is a desperate fellow and without fear, only anxious to crawl into the front line and draw things full of violence and terror."[56] But they underestimated Nevinson's own disconnectedness and exaggerated a waning thirst by this point in the war for making work that expressed direct experience. By June, Nevinson was making flights over London, developing new modes of spectatorship to realize in painted form. On July 6, 1917 he commenced a trial month as Official War Artist, unpaid and in the rank of private, stationed in the area of the Third Army between Dunkirk and Passchaendale. Once transferred to the Fourth Division and no longer restricted by being ferried every day by car—delivered near to the front at midday and picked up at four—Nevinson was able to work with the degree of freedom that allowed him to move within the machine of war recording and memorizing. Yet the paintings Nevinson produced disappointed his new employers and would justify the criticisms in a report to Masterman that "Nevinson seems to have restrained himself—sometimes to the point of dullness"[57]—a new sort of dullness that seemed to explain itself as a self-conscious reaction to his official status. Derrick went on to report on advising the painter that "his restrained, decorous, official self is valued rather less highly: instead of—as I think he fancied—more highly."[58] The official war works—including the trammeled spinal cord of *The Road from Arras to Bapaume* (1917) and *Survivors at Arras* (1917)—were not only restrained examples of a reversion to English landscape tradition, they largely de-emphasized the body and took a detached, panoramic view of the topography of war that was an unfortunate reminder of Muirhead Bone.

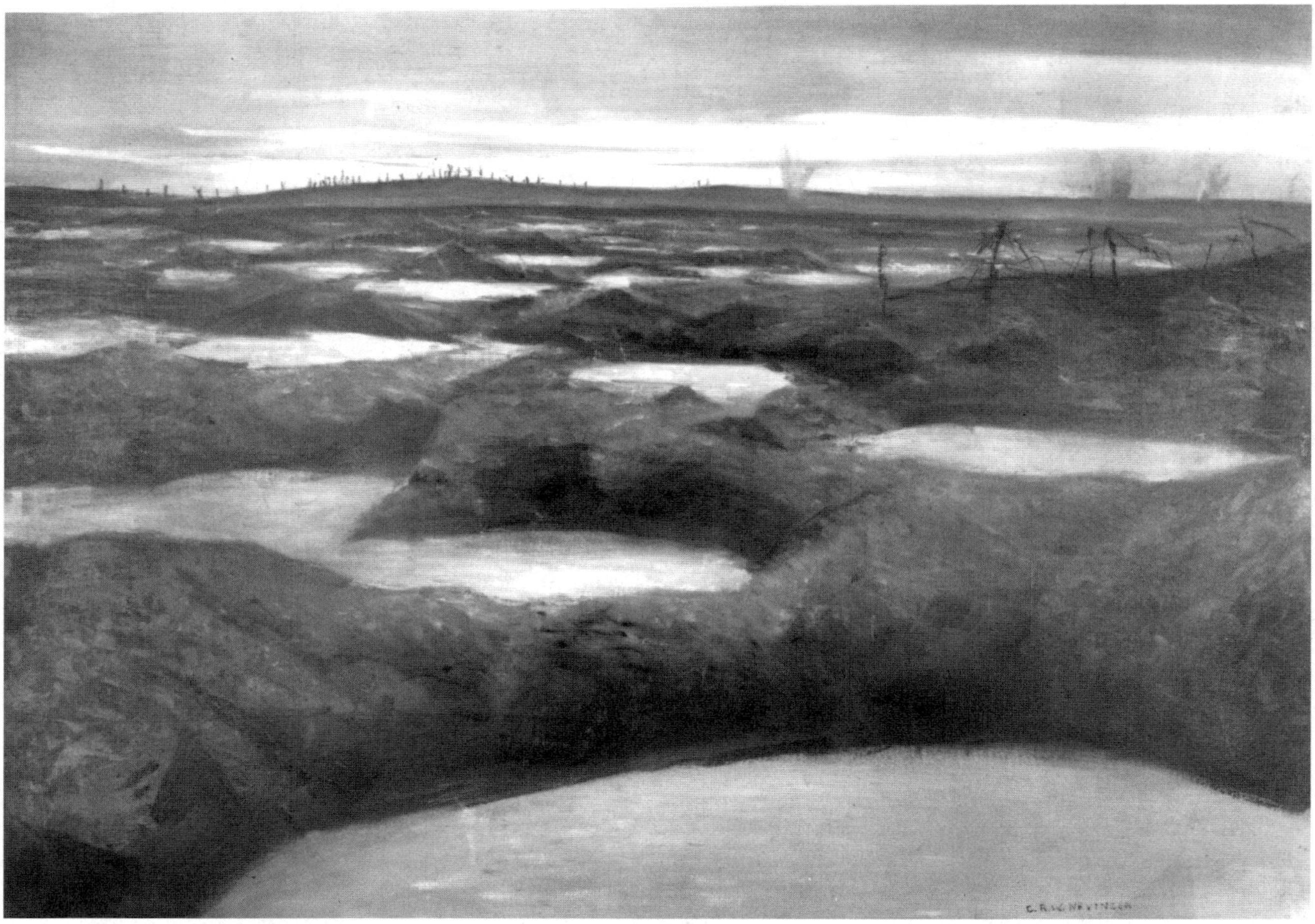

36. *After a Push* (1917), oil on canvas, 57.1 × 80 cm. Imperial War Museum, London. Purchased from the Artist 1918.

These works seem even more extraordinarily restrained if one believes Nevinson's recollection two years later of accepting a senior officer's "invitation to commit suicide" when a patrol he joined into no-man's-land came under heavy German artillery fire for over an hour. "After that I could paint just exactly what it feels like to lie in a shell-hole,"[59] he wrote, although in fact he had already done this in 1916 with the powerful *A Star Shell* (1916). Immediately prior to being sent back to London for rank insubordination by Major Lee on August 5, 1917, Nevinson had somehow managed to escape the parental clutch of his GHQ minder toward the end of his time in France and go AWOL in Ypres where he witnessed the enervating quagmires of Passchaendale only days before that most disastrous, decimating four-month campaign began. Looking again at the sixty works Nevinson produced as an "Official Artist on the Western Front" between his return home in August 1917 and his second one-man show of March 1918, the uninitiated viewer might be surprised to learn that the artist had spent four weeks in France getting as close as possible to mortal danger. The only resultant work that remotely conveys the intensity of this experience is *After a Push* [1917 (fig. 36)]. It is a painting that communicates disconnectedness and depersonalization, both of man from the theater of war and artist from faith in the authenticity of representation itself.

Nevinson had come back to a London beset by German bombing raids that became more concerted as the summer light ebbed away in the rented Robert Street studio off the Hampstead Road where Whistler and Sickert had worked before him. The explosions must have been an unnerving reminder of the shells at the front, where Nevinson confessed it had interfered with his work. "I find shelling most disconcerting for any actual drawing even when it is half a mile away,"[60] he had explained to Masterman in a letter from headquarters, and he must have felt the same disturbance on his return. As he considered how best to convey the complexity of the frontline operations he had witnessed—which stood in contrast to his rearguard Red Cross experiences of 1914–15—he must have been attentive to

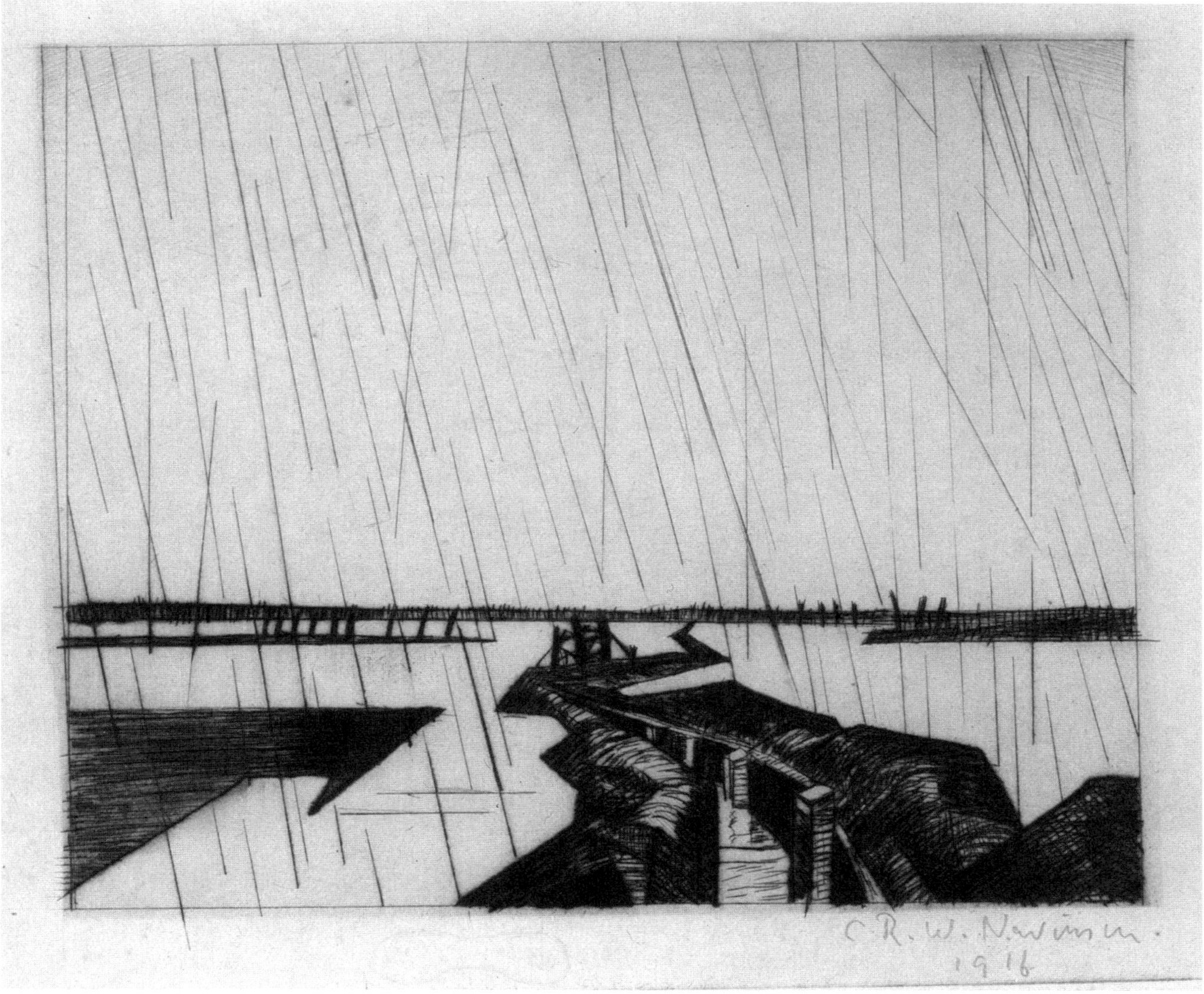

37. *Flooded Trench on the Yser* (1916) drypoint, 15.4 × 19 cm. Private Collection courtesy of The Fine Art Society, London / Bridgeman Art Library.

newspaper reports on the devastating losses at Passchaendale that he himself had only escaped by a matter of days. As a new painting formed itself in his mind he would have consulted the characteristic "scrappiness of my notes"[61] and attempted to summon up the powers of visual recall of which he made so much. In his introduction to the catalog of his 1918 solo exhibition in which the fruits of this period were eventually presented, he reasserted that "I relied chiefly on memory, a method I learnt as a student in Paris and for which I am ever grateful." On the contrary, he was struggling to remember with the clarity he once had. By this time, Nevinson would surely have recognized in himself the symptoms of Neurasthenia, which the eminent Dr. W. H. Rivers had recently designated as the second category of War Neurosis and diagnosed thus: "On the mental side there is usually depression, restlessness, irritability and enfeeblement of memory."[62] In Nevinson, this weakness of recall combined with inadequate sketches of the mud and the wet, meant that the painting appeared less and less an authentic observation or even sense impression than a copy of a photograph.

The following two-year comparison underlines the deterioration. Consider the concentrated pictorial impact in *Flooded Trench on the Yser* (fig. 37), from November 1915, painted immediately after *La Mitrailleuse*. This was hardened imagery carried back from the front imprisoned in his mind and all the more memorable for its formalized rigidification in the drypoint version of the original painting. This stands in stark contrast to the softening up of *After a Push* (of November 1917) to a far more traditional, even banal, mode of seeing. Not

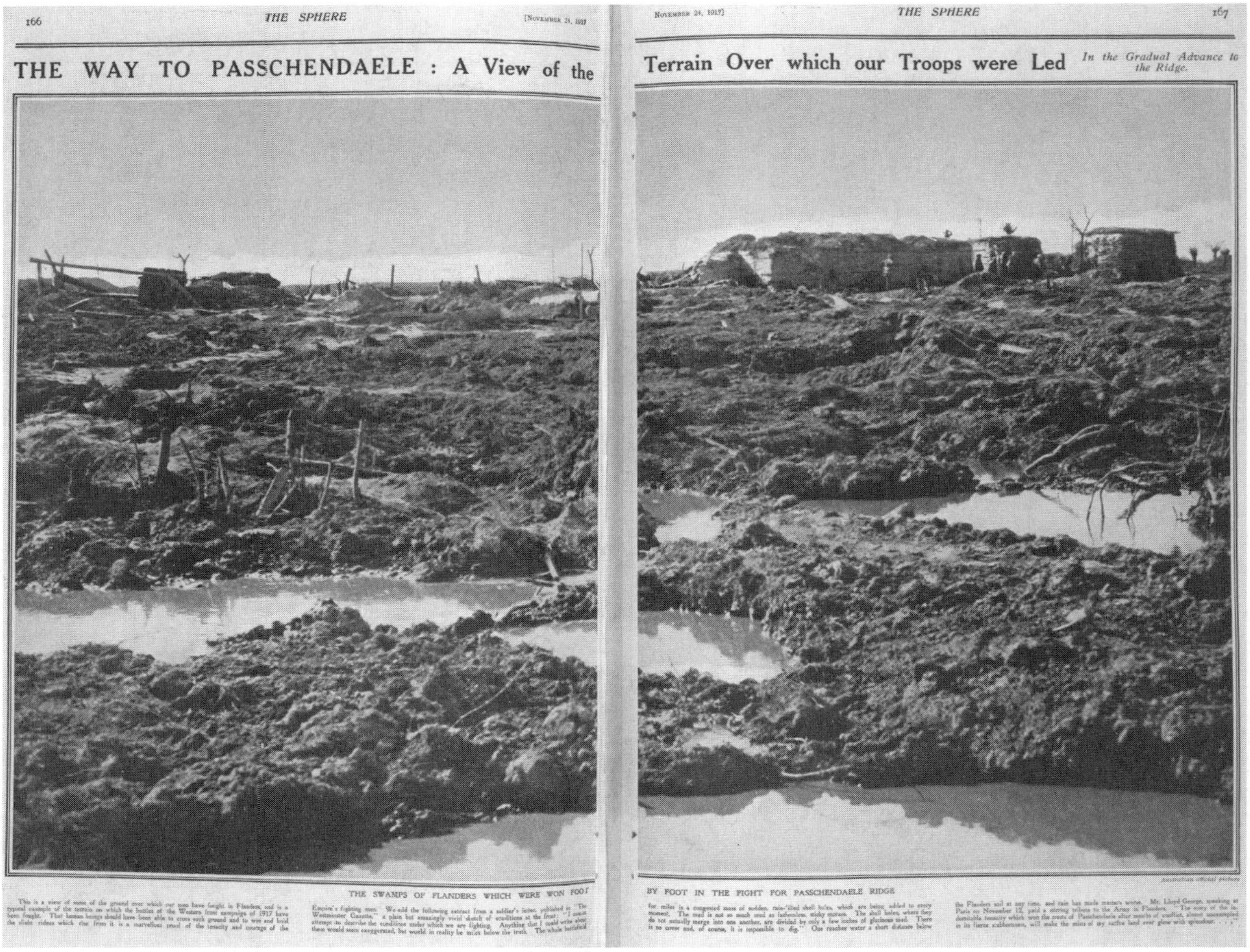

38. *The Sphere*, pages 166–67 (November 24, 1917).

coincidentally, perhaps, it transpires that the latter work was almost certainly based on a photograph.

After a Push was first seen in January 1918 in the prestigious first issue of a four-part publication entitled *British Artists at the Front.* The text alongside plate 13 encourages us to believe that the painting depicts "the aspect of wide tracts of country East and North-East of Ypres during the wet weather battles of October, 1917." We know, however, that Nevinson was forced to leave Passchaendale three months earlier and yet it was not entirely erroneous to claim this painting as an authentic record of the actual ground over which troops fought during October 1917. The *Sphere* carried a documentary image on November 24, 1917 (fig. 38) depicting the very mud troops waded through in their advance on Passchaendale Ridge. One is struck immediately by the almost identical configuration of the puddles in the lower half of the photograph as compared to the lower two-thirds of the painting. The interplay of soft mud and hard cropping at the edges of the *Sphere* image is a particularly effective photographic trait that Nevinson has elected not to conceal. Heightening further the risk of his appropriation being noticed, the date of publication for the photograph exactly coincides with the period during which Nevinson would have been painting *After a Push.*

Whereas in works from before his commission as an Official War Artist, such as *On the Road to Ypres* (1916), there was a tendency to disguise the influence of photography using the gauze of an angular avant-garde mode, in Nevinson's more fully representational paintings of 1917—the year when war photographs really flooded into the public consciousness[63]—there is a greater transparency, perhaps even suggesting a desire in the artist to be discovered. Wendy Baron, in her review of the 1999 retrospective at the Imperial War Museum, makes a keen observation concerning Nevinson's painting from memory. "When without further

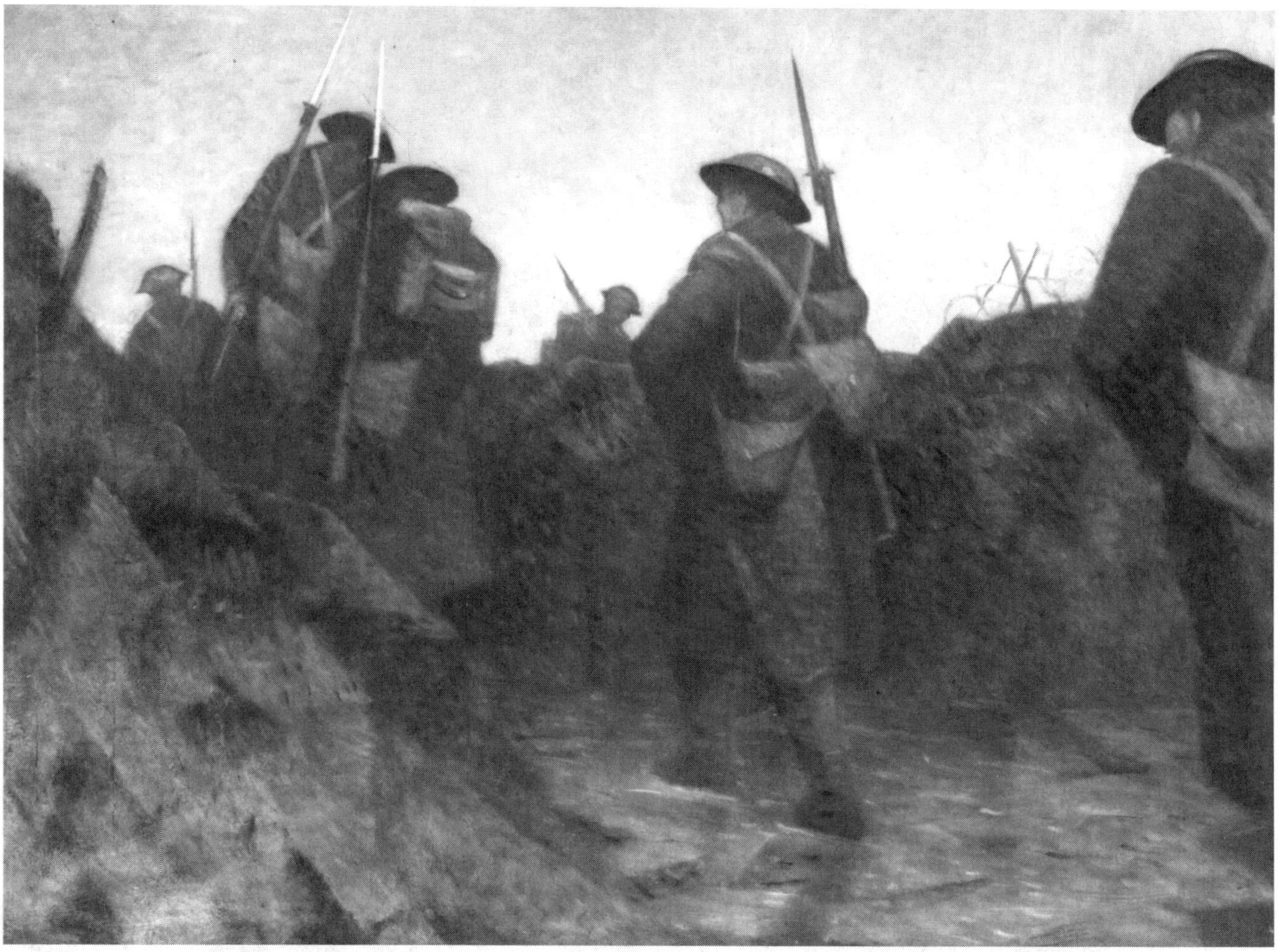

39. *Reliefs at Dawn* (1917), oil on canvas, 71.1 × 91.4 cm. Imperial War Museum, London. Purchased from the Artist 1918.

elaboration he trusted the image in his mind's eye, he recaptured both the formal and the emotional essence of what he had seen."[64] Nevinson rarely did trust that image; for him, photography expedited the recapture.

In *Reliefs at Dawn* [1917 (fig. 39)] we are presented with the most convincing example yet of Nevinson's use of a photographic compositional mnemonic. When positioned next to an unpublished photograph of soldiers passing up the line at Montauban discovered in the Imperial War Museum's Photographic Archive in London (fig. 40), the similitude is clear. The label attached to the photograph is unrevealing as to the nationality of the soldiers—and in this it is not unusual—but when compared to the image in the *Sphere* it seems likely that the image is again of Canadian troops, with whom Nevinson never directly served. In another apparently random connection, the Official War Photographer who took the image is John Warwick Brooke, whose work we have already come across in the photograph that seemed to echo through *On the Road to Ypres*. Brooke was the second official photographer on the western front and even though he was British, conceivably the photograph could have been displayed at the first exhibition of Canadian Official War Photography at the Grafton Gallery, which overlapped with the end of Nevinson's debut one-man exhibition only a stone's throw away at the Leicester Galleries. Apart from zooming in on the original image slightly to emphasize the melancholy of procession, Nevinson hardly bothers to alter the composition. Using a divisionist approach to technique, which makes it hard to distinguish between forms up close to the painting due to the close modulation in tone, he deadens the daylight contrast of the photograph by transposing the scene into the diffused half light of a dawn or dusk. The etiolated palette symbolizes the depersonalization of these men who are presented like solitary whispers in a landscape lulling them toward the muffled scream of battle prefigured in

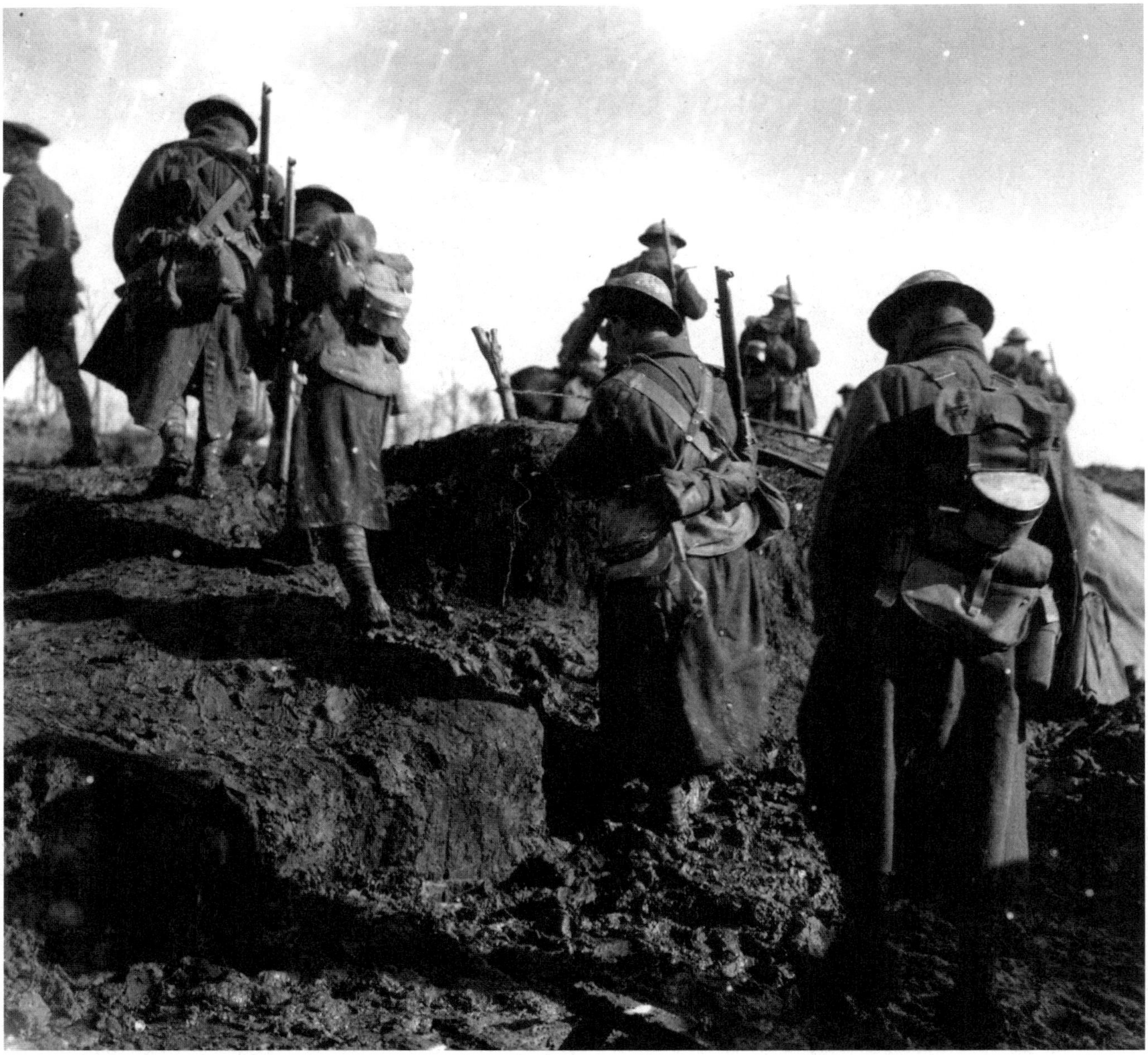

40. Men going up to the Trenches, Montauban by John Warwick Brooke (October 1916), photograph. Imperial War Museum, London.

the tangle of barbed wire and the unnoticed glint of the soldiers' bayonets.

This highly contrived and, one must admit, successful mimicking of memory seems to contradict Nevinson's 1918 assertion that "All of my work had to be done from rapid shorthand sketches made often under trying conditions." Commenting on *Reliefs at Dawn* in his book *The Great War Fourth Year 1918*, J. E. Crawford Flitch wrote that "what so many painters have attempted to do and failed—to find, not an accidental, but an authentic, and, as it were, collective gesture of war—Nevinson has succeeded in doing, almost, one feels, without knowing it." To disagree with Flitch, I would suggest that any authenticity the work might convey arises precisely out of the self-conscious appropriation of the photograph Nevinson refused to acknowledge. Is it possible that he had privileged access to Brooke's unpublished photographic records of war during meetings at the Office of Information or via his well-connected father?

Within a month of the British War Memorials Committee being set up, some sort of outside influence was brought to bear on H. W. Nevinson's son being chosen alongside the more established John Singer Sargent and Wyndham Lewis to paint a large-scale memorial work

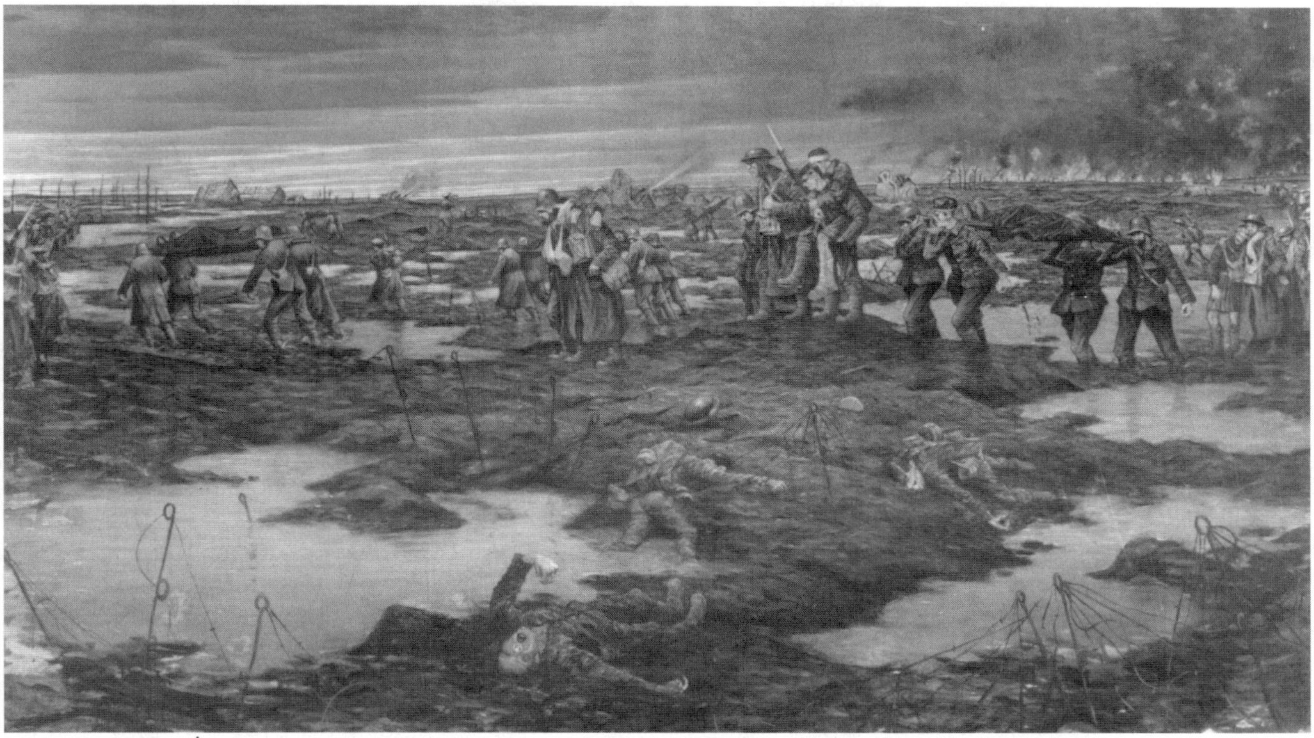

41. *The Harvest of Battle* (1919), oil on canvas, 182.8 × 317.5 cm. Imperial War Museum, London.

for the planned Hall of Remembrance in anticipation of the war's end, for he was not on the original shortlist. *The Harvest of Battle* [1919 (fig. 41)] was by far the biggest painting he attempted (at roughly six meters square), and one in which he was particularly keen to express his personal experiences of the conflict[65] in an attempt to make one last epic statement. It became a year's work, completed in early April 1919. Ironically, when the new Minister of Information Lord Beaverbrook received a letter from Henry Head warning of Nevinson's nerve damage and limited manual dexterity, Beaverbrook made the unexpected suggestion that Nevinson should produce smaller pictures which the Office of Information would then photograph and scale up into a larger composite which, when transferred to the canvas, the artist could simply paint over. One can only imagine the insult Nevinson would have inferred from the suggestion had it reached him, although it seems likely that he was thinking of Frank Hurley's newly impressive composite images on display in the Australian Battle Pictures exhibition at the Grafton Galleries in June 1918.

As proprietor of the *Daily Express*, Beaverbrook was well aware of current artistic developments in the field of photography. It was Hurley who introduced the public to the use of the composite negative in war photography, making hugely compelling pictures like *An Episode After the Battle of Zonnebeke, 1917–18* in which several dramatic moments are seamlessly collaged together in a concentrated experiential image "in order to convey accurate battle impressions."[66] Although paintings were also displayed at the Australian Battle Pictures exhibition, they were kept in a separate room and commanded far less public attention than the photographs. The Grafton Galleries had played host to a series of successful photography exhibitions, stretching back to the first Exhibition of Canadian Official War Photography in November 1916. Undoubtedly, Nevinson would have been one of the one hundred thousand visitors in July 1917 who attended the second Canadian exhibition to see the largest image of war yet produced. It was an enormous photograph, cinematic even by today's standards, of life-size Canadian troops engaged in the recent Vimy Ridge campaign.[67] It coincided with, and one can imagine overshadowed, Nevinson's new paintings of aircraft on display at the Fine Art Society's *Britain's Efforts and Ideals* exhibition.

On March 4, 1918, in what must have been seen by more traditional painters as the most direct attack on the history genre yet, the first color tinted photographs of war were displayed in an exhibition of British Official Photography. It claimed to have the biggest photograph in the world, a colored enlargement measuring twenty-two by sixteen and a half feet, made in two pieces in order to fit through the gallery doors. This time the exhibition clashed directly with Nevinson's Official War Artist display that had opened three days previously at the Leicester Galleries, six paintings from which as we saw earlier were reproduced in a full page in the *Graphic* under the title "A New Way of Looking at the War." A week later, the photographic exhibition received its own full page in the *Graphic* under the title "British Battles in Photography: The Camera as War Correspondent" (fig. 42).

Nevinson had perhaps second-guessed the press description of the photographs as "thrilling incidents"[68] by stage-managing his own shock event at his opening. He took it upon himself to display *Paths of Glory*—a painting showing two dead British soldiers face down in the mud which had been rejected by the censor—partially covered from bottom-left to top-right diagonal by a blue banner that read "Censored" in Nevinson's own hand. The issue was a recent censorship law dictating that images of identifiable dead Allied soldiers could no longer be displayed. A twofold irony, which made him apoplectic with anger, was that the Canadian photographs predated the censor's ruling and so could still go on view while Nevinson's later painting was banned. Nevinson had begun the argument with Masterman in December 1917 after his painting was censored: "Of course, it is natural that photographs of dead men should not be published broadcast, as it would possibly give offence to their relatives, though with customary lack of logic Canadians are allowed to exhibit to a London public photographs of actual corpses for propaganda. My picture happened to be a work of art (but unlike the other, not actual portraits) therefore I cannot see how it comes into this photographic category."[69] And yet the mode in which Nevinson decided to paint *The Harvest of Battle* could hardly reference the compositional density of contemporary war photography more clearly. Soldiers stream across the scarred landscape from right to left as in *The Taking of Vimy by the Canadians*. The ghoulish body in the central foreground, contorted into a Munch-like scream of rigor mortis bears comparison with the shocking photograph (fig. 43) by Frank Hurley, given prominence on the front page of the *Graphic* of June 1, 1918, at just the time that Nevinson would have begun to mark out his large canvas. In a final touch of ironic self-referentiality, our eye is led to the figure face down in mud just above, whose pose is a direct quote from his own *Paths of Glory*. In his autobiography, Nevinson looked back on this infamous work and averred "What I had painted in 'The Paths of Glory' (*sic*) was reality. I showed dead men caught in wire."[70] In *Harvest of Battle*, then, it is as if Nevinson implicitly parodies our expectation of the image to depict the "real" through the paradoxical pictorialization of painted-corpse-as-painting next to painted-corpse-as-photograph. In the artist's mind neither is "real" in the literal sense of course, but whereas photography freezes a moment of optical reality with an indexical charge, painting will always offer a greater, more enduring emotional truth through the synthesis of that real moment into the act of pictorialization.

Nearly twenty years later, Nevinson was compelled to revisit the theme in an essay entitled "The Arts Within This Bellicose Civilisation" (1936): "Deformation, and the exaggeration of form, which came about through the dullness that was obvious in photographic fact, has died because youth is slowly getting accustomed to, and unperturbed by, the invention of photography, and realizes that the intention of the mechanical lens, and the expression of the visual world through a human mental process translated by mental dexterity, are entirely different." We might even infer from this a retrospective admission in Nevinson that he was himself "perturbed" by photography and throughout the 1910s unable to separate the mechanical and the mental presentation of imagery even if he inwardly acknowledged its separate processing. It was in his aeropaintings above all that Nevinson claimed to have discovered and forged a truly unique visual language. But even here, the two visual languages remain in conflict. *Aerial View (From a Paris Plane)* [1919 (fig. 44)] had always seemed to be a title that rather contradicted its subject until a chance encounter with a temporally removed photograph provided a clue (fig. 45). Taken from the *Graphic* dated August 14, 1915, the photograph accompanied a report on the Dardanelles campaign. The distinctly un-Parisian coastal background of the Gallipoli peninsula bears a striking similarity to Nevinson's painting; each depicts a small harbor occupied by military vessels, three jetties projecting into the inlet in the same relative positions. The undulating shape of the distant coastline in each echoes that in the other. By contrast, in one of the main differences between painting and photograph, Nevinson chooses to push the inlet back into the picture plane by adding a river, partly to increase our sense of pictorial depth and partly, one suspects, to disguise the image source. The relative height above the ground of each viewpoint is only slightly different although he has made a significant adjustment to the structural detail of the aeroplane wing depicted in the foreground.

In relation to this particular alteration, it may have been another specifically photographic press image which provided a supplementary impetus to the work. In the same week that Nevinson returned home from New York the *Sphere*, dated June 14, 1919, happened

THE GRAPHIC, MARCH 9, 1918 293

BRITISH BATTLES IN PHOTOGRAPHY

THE CAMERA AS WAR CORRESPONDENT

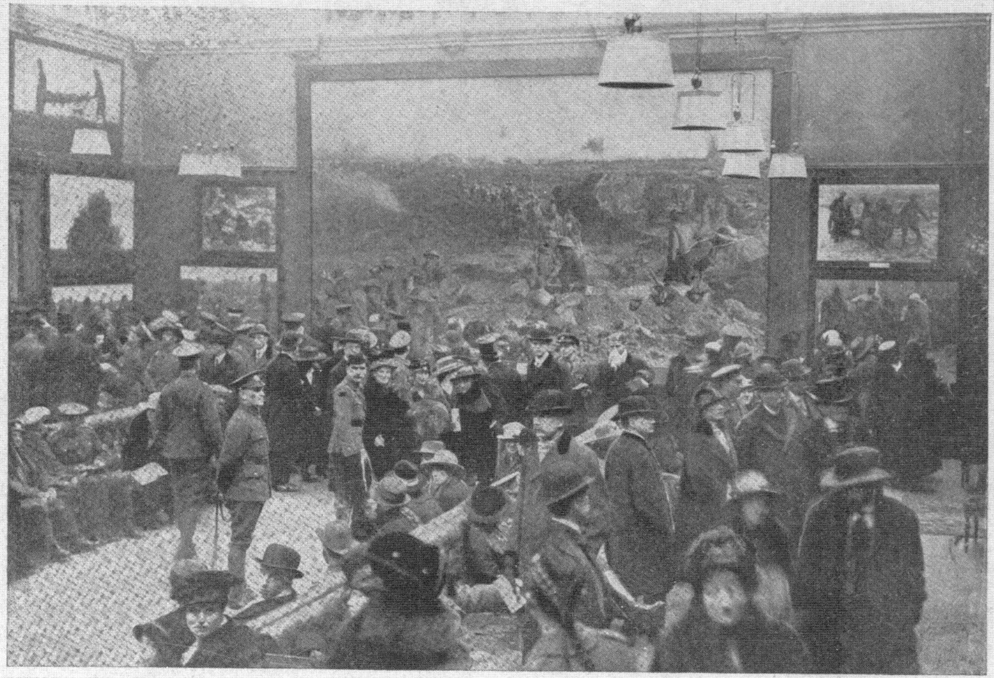

BEFORE A THRILLING INCIDENT; THE CROWD ON THE OPENING DAY OF THE COLOUR PHOTOGRAPHS AT THE GRAFTON GALLERIES

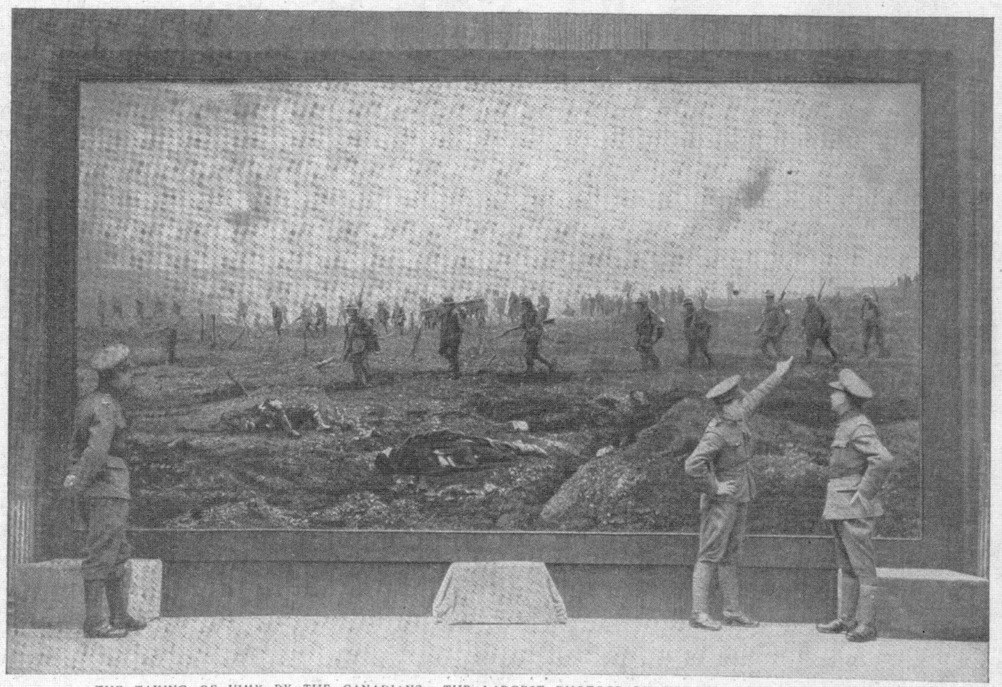

THE TAKING OF VIMY BY THE CANADIANS; THE LARGEST PHOTOGRAPH YET TAKEN DURING THE WAR

42. *The Graphic*, page 293 (March 9, 1918).

THE GRAPHIC

AN ILLUSTRATED WEEKLY NEWSPAPER

No. 2531. Vol. XCVII. *Registered as a Newspaper.*

SATURDAY, JUNE 1, 1918

PRICE NINEPENCE *By Post*, 10d.

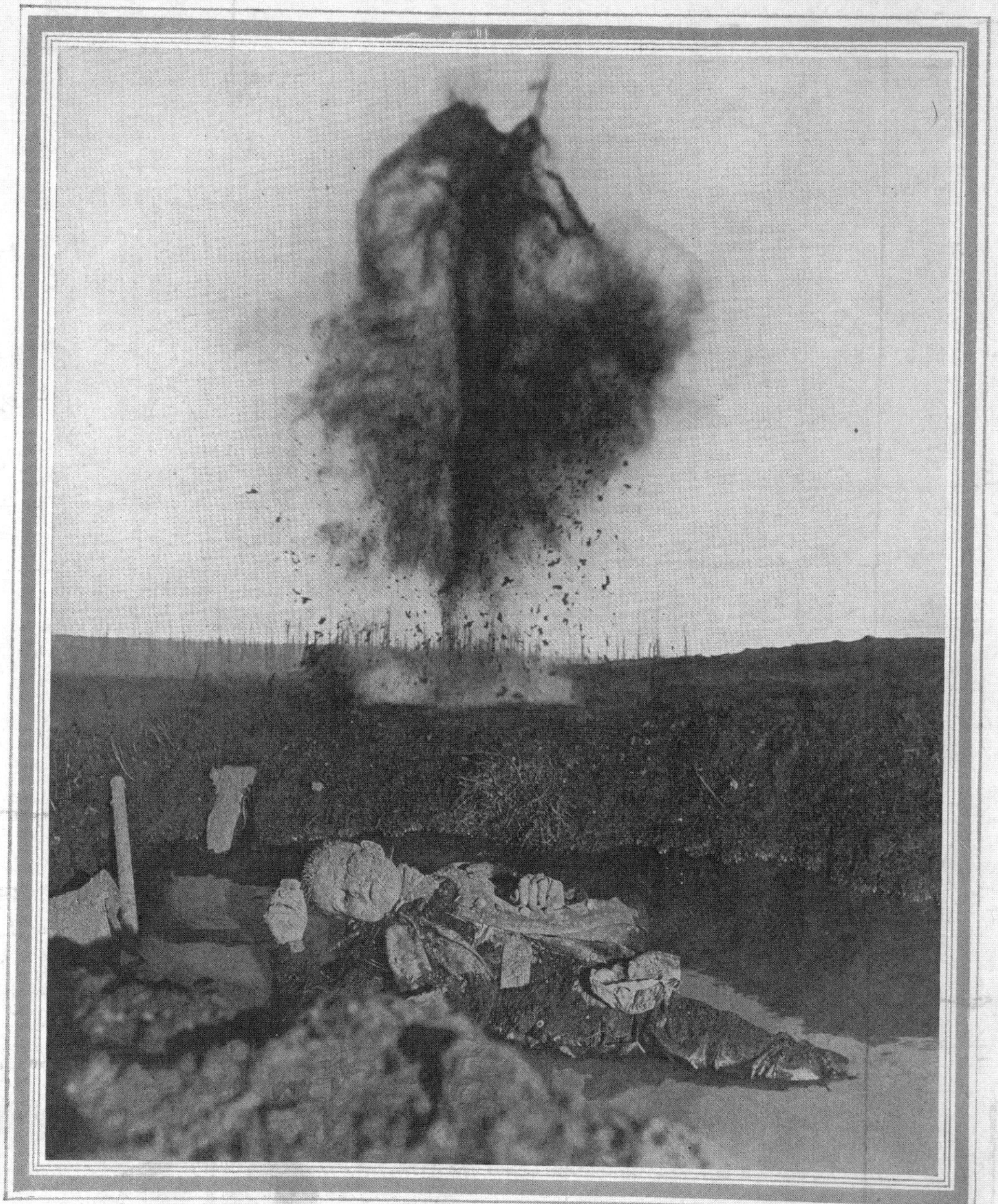

"Death the Reaper"

The Australian Battle Pictures Exhibition at the Grafton Galleries, which will be incorporated in a National Collection of War Pictures for future generations of the great Commonwealth, contains many fine sketches and photographs—none more striking than the above taken by Captain Hurley, of Mawson Expedition fame, in front of Ypres during a heavy Boche barrage.

43. *The Graphic*, front page (June 1, 1918).

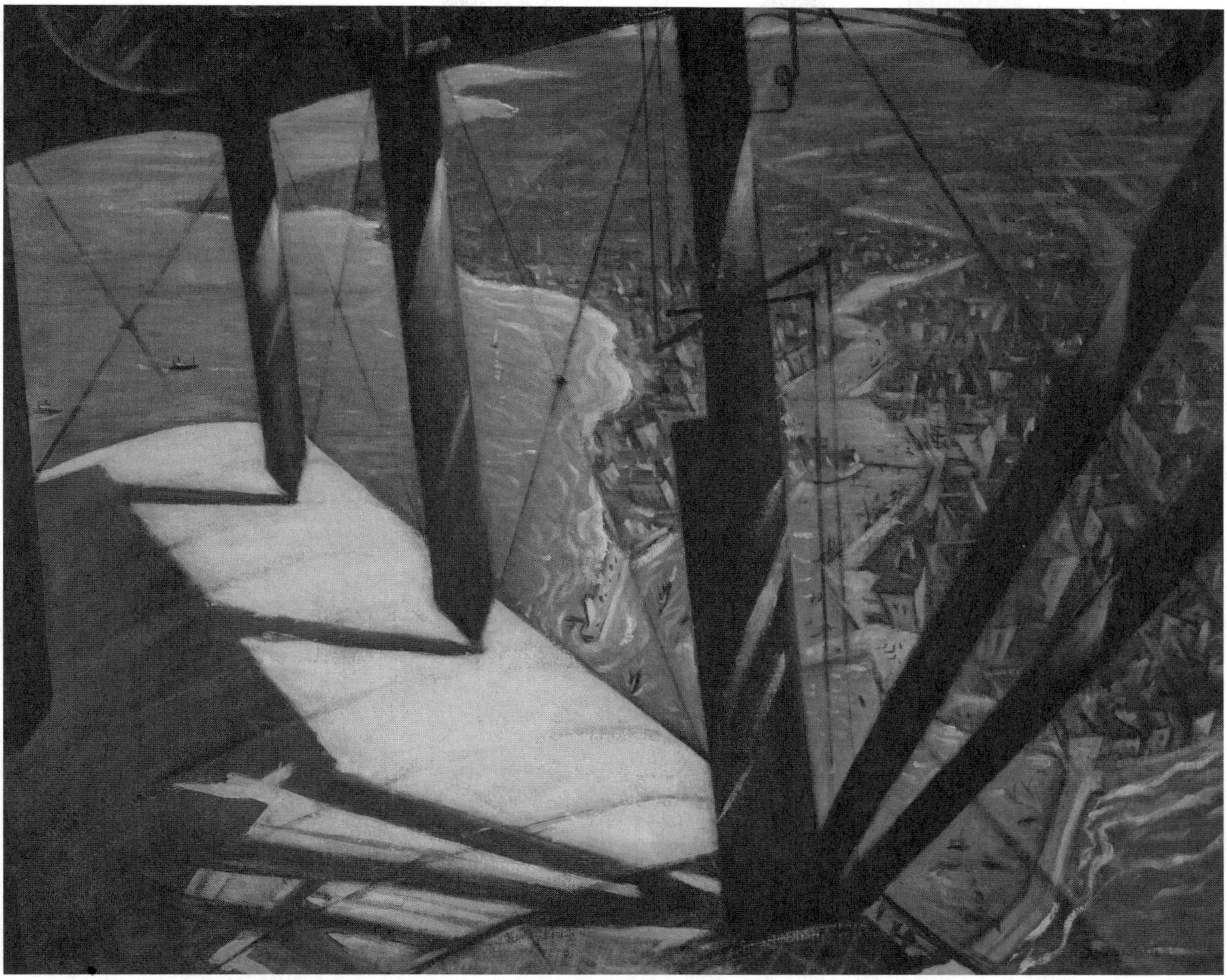

44. *Aerial View From a Paris Plane* (1919–20), oil on canvas, 60.4 × 73.7 cm. Private collection. Courtesy of Peter Nahum at the Leicester Galleries, London.

to carry an aerial image taken above terraced streets above Cricklewood, North London (fig. 46). There is a clear link between the photographic framing of the ground viewed through a strutted wing cross-supported with wire, as in the painting. The deep shadow in raking sunlight cast by the stanchions in the wing is a common facet of both images, which may have been too close a link to the painting's source, perhaps explaining Nevinson's decision not to display it in the October 1919 Exhibition of New Works which he was working toward throughout that summer. Interestingly, Nevinson chose not to exhibit the work until 1930, over ten years after it was painted.

An explanation for the specific topographical subject matter of the painting can easily be found in the fact that Richard's father Henry followed the conflict in the Dardanelles closely, reporting it for the British press and finally publishing his book *The Dardanelles Campaign* in November 1918, only months before his son's painting was begun. H. W. Nevinson explains in his book that "At the end of July [1915] about 30 planes of different types were in action, doing excellent service in observation and photography."[71] And research shows that both the *Graphic* and *War Illustrated* (fig. 47) were reporting on this particular story at the very same time. It would seem that either Richard had clipped out the article for safekeeping in 1915, or perhaps he had seen other photographs from the same reconnaissance mission in Henry's possession. If there was a series of images from this flight, it would certainly explain the slightly higher viewpoint as the photographer took his picture looking back over the tailfin as the aeroplane climbed away from the port. It is conceivable that Richard based his painting on an unpublished photograph taken a

FROM THE BIRD-MAN'S POINT OF VIEW

AEROPLANE PICTURES OF THE BATTLE LINE BY LAND AND SEA

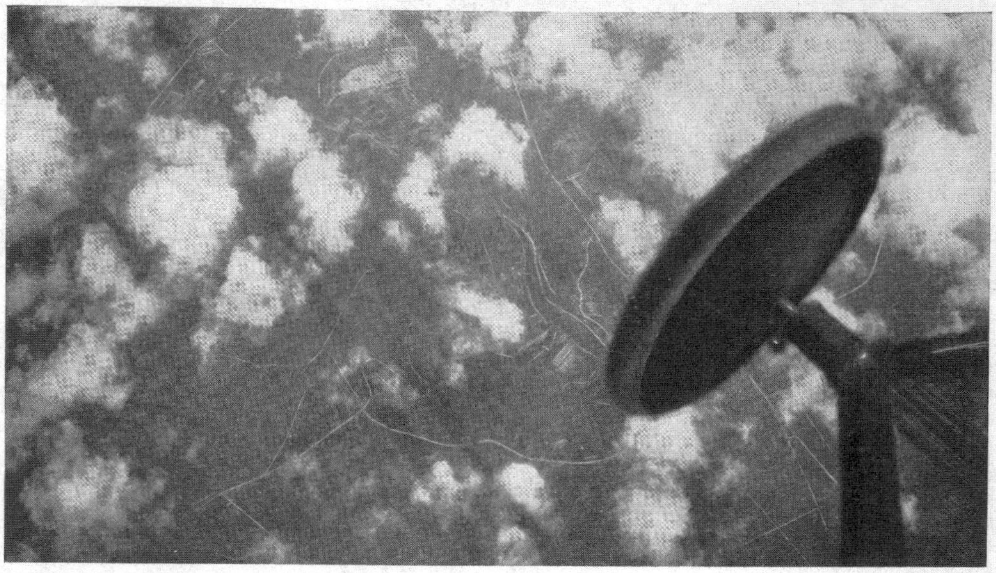

THE BATTLE LINE IN FRANCE: A PEEP THROUGH THE CLOUDS AT THE GERMAN TRENCHES IN THE CHAMPAGNE COUNTRY

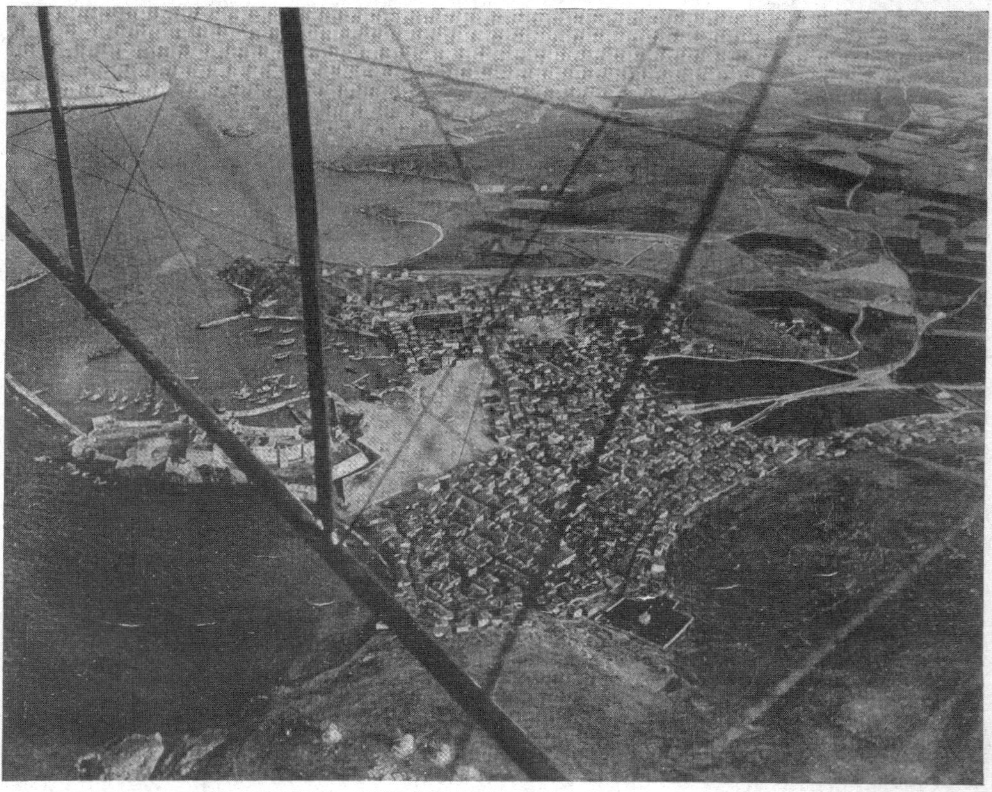

THE BATTLE LINE IN THE DARDANELLES: A VIEW FROM MID-AIR OF ONE OF THE FORTS BOMBARDED BY THE ALLIED FLEET

45. *The Graphic*, page 213 (August 14, 1915).

FLYING ABOVE LONDON : Some New Pictures.

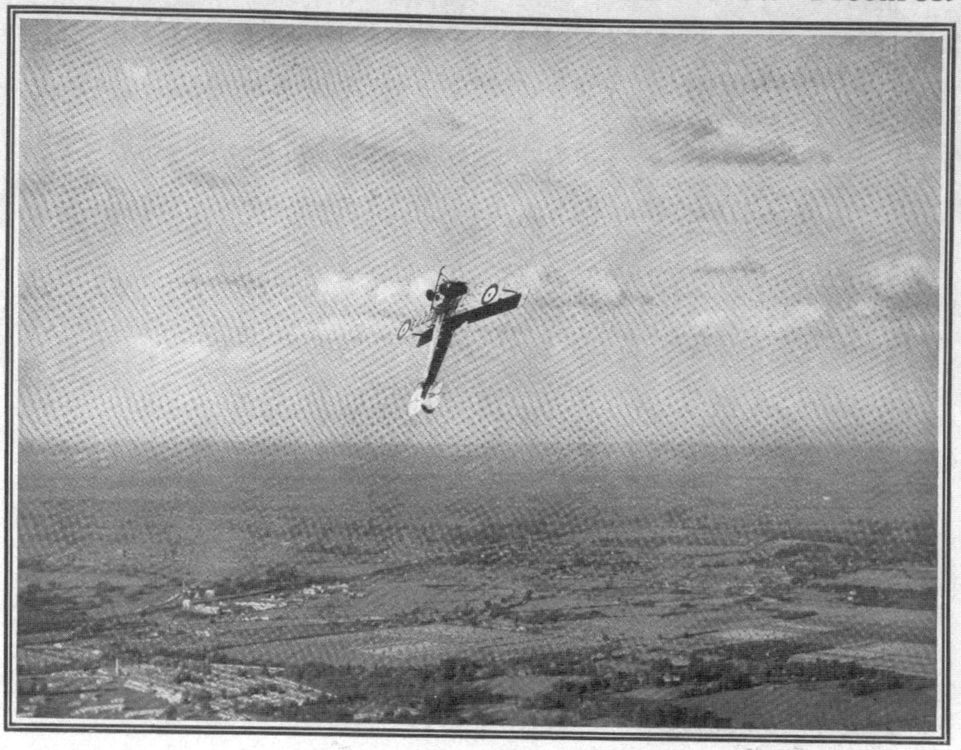

Looping the Loop over Hounslow in an Avro Machine

The machine has been photographed from another one flying at the same time, and the detail of the machine is thus shown clearly to the spectator. Below, the Middlesex meadows and market gardens stretch far into the distance

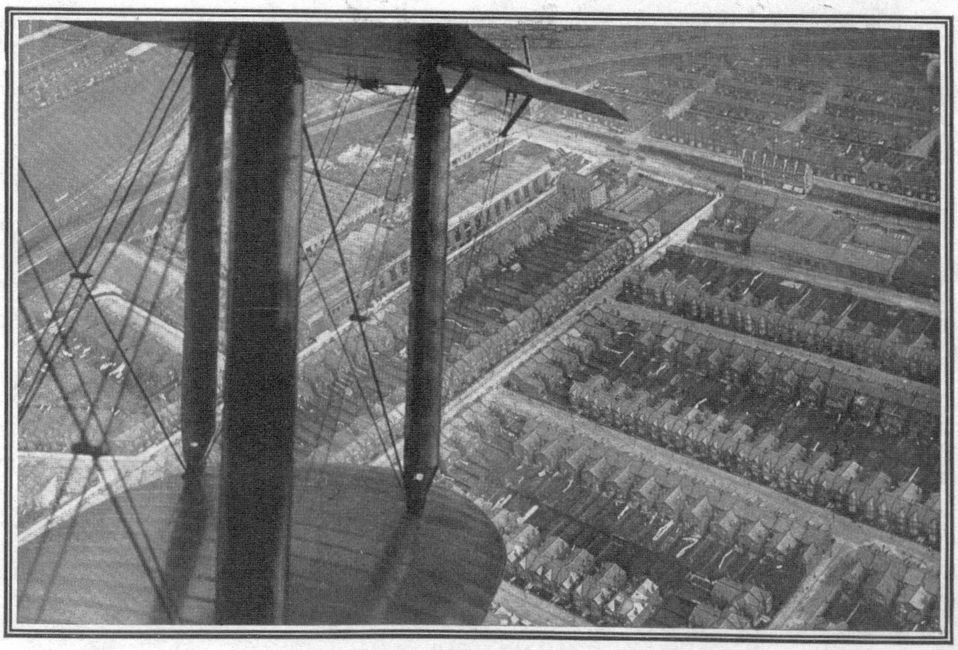

Over the Villas of Cricklewood in an Aeroplane

The spectator is looking down on rows of small houses with little gardens touching one another. Seen from above, the world looks a very neat and tidy place. It is an illusion created by distance. Many an Eastern town looks like a fairy city in the distance. So it is with these overhead views of suburbs. It is not till one is down among the 'buses and the litter that one can really gauge the nature of the place which looks so attractive from above

C

46. *The Sphere*, page 229 (June 14, 1919).

Page 599

The War Illustrated, 14th August, 1915.

The Bird-man's Peep at Turkish Strongholds

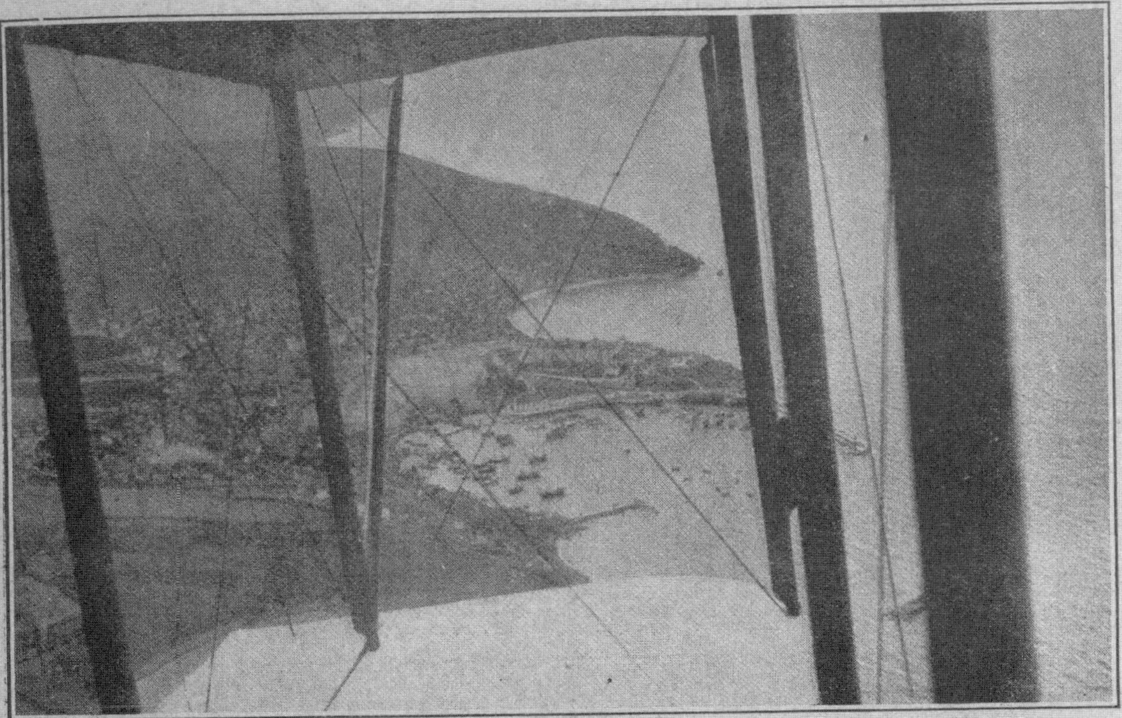

View of a Turkish town on the Gallipoli Peninsula as seen from a French aeroplane. As over Eastern and Western Europe, the Allies' aircraft services are proving invaluable in the Dardanelles operations.

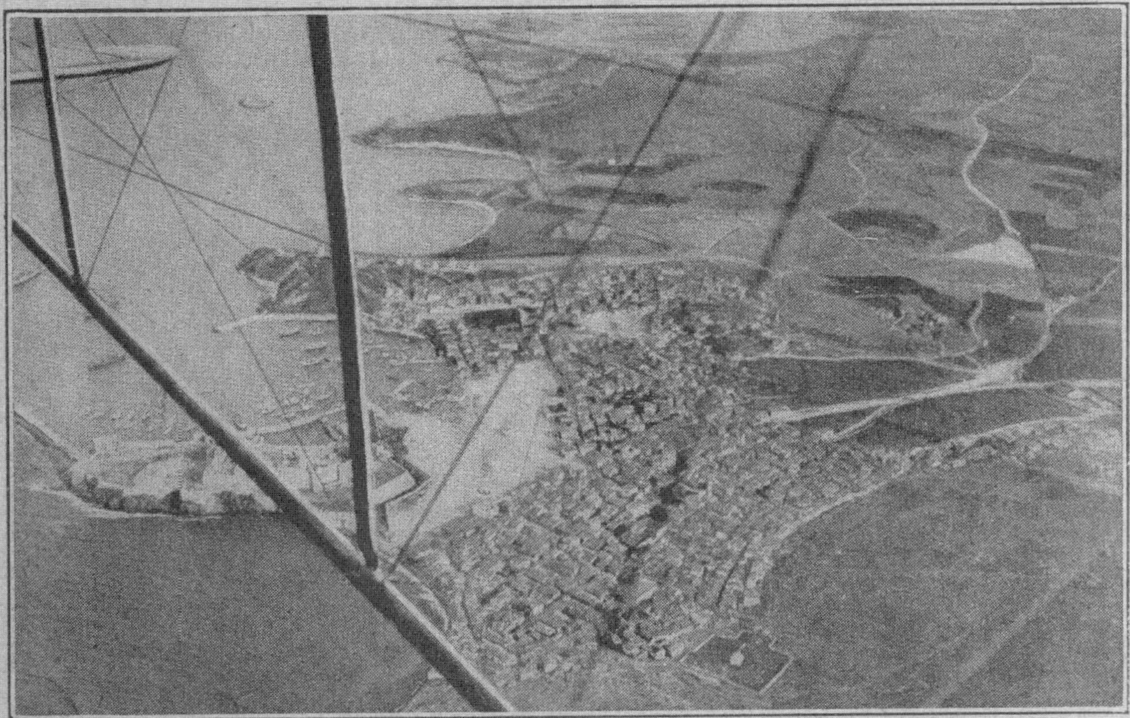

Another view of the same town from the opposite direction, showing plainly the Turkish forts guarding the mouth of the bay. These unique photographs, taken during an aerial scouting expedition, give a graphic idea of how aerial reconnaissances are carried out.

47. *War Illustrated*, page 599 (August 14, 1915).

minute or two previously, lower and closer to the harbor. In his book, Nevinson senior relates that up to eight sea planes based on *Ark Royal* could fly to a height of two thousand feet over the Dardanelles. And herein I think lies the clue to the significance of this work's title. Although the *War Illustrated* caption identifies the Allied aircraft as French, Nevinson is interested in a more subtle word association. At the time of the Dardanelles campaign, the Royal Naval Division's General Officer Commanding was Major General A. Paris, CB. Hence a pun for those in the know, to whom a "Paris" plane meant one of a select group of allied aircraft scrambled above the Gallipoli peninsula.

At his Robert Street studios the paint was still drying on *Aerial View* and *Harvest of Battle*[72] as Nevinson prepared for a journey to New York. On April 11, 1919 Nevinson attended a farewell meal held in his honor at that favorite artists' haunt the Café Royal. The dinner was presided over by Walter Sickert who with characteristic idiosyncrasy delivered an incomprehensible valediction, partly in Greek. Nevinson's first trip to the United States capital, arriving on the *Aquitania* on May 3, 1919, came about in response to an invitation from David Keppel of print publishers Frederick Keppel & Company, who successfully exhibited and sold the artist's war prints at 4 East Thirty-ninth Street. Today, the Wilshire Bank has taken over the premises, but it is still possible to see the stucco busts of those preeminent printmakers Rembrandt and Whistler set into the stone above the doorway of the building. Sales were excellent and reviews favorable; a typical article described Nevinson's style as "eminently personal, and may perhaps be defined as a compromise between Futurism and illustration."[73] Nevinson had agreed to be photographed in just such a combination of styles for *The Sketch* before he left for New York.[74] In "A Cubist Cubed for the Camera" (fig. 48) there is a playful complicity in the way Nevinson allows photographic technique to mimic and dilute the austerity of modernist painting technique. It stands as a telling marker of Nevinson's determined self-presentation at this point in his career as the acceptable face of the avant-garde and moreover his knowing exploitation of the camera for his own ends. The New York press were picking up on the theme of compromise between illustration and abstraction complemented by writers in England like Campbell Dodgson, whose *British Artists at the Front* of 1918 explained, "He has not forsworn the practice of Cubism and Futurism, but he has adapted these methods successfully to the treatment of subjects which interest the average man." Aware of the continuing commercial potential of such a stance, Keppel encouraged Nevinson to make new work in a similar vein in response to the vital island metropolis of Manhattan.

In his autobiography, Nevinson makes the unfeasible claim that his month in New York City was "probably the most extraordinary month ever lived by an artist"[75] during which incessant social invitations, combined with press interviews and speechmaking, must have made it difficult to knuckle down to image making. With typical inconsistency, though, Nevinson claims within a few pages that "the whole time I was in New York I worked hard day and night, drawing the city, which in a moment of enthusiasm I had described to a pressman as 'having been built for me.'"[76] As ever, he didn't need to devote much of his limited time to raising the hackles of the press since arrogance, and its complementary stance of wounded defensiveness, came naturally to him. Sometimes, the titles alone could cause offense, as with *The Soul of a Soulless City* (1920), a ghostly painting of New York's elevated railway, now in the Tate collection, which is visible in the lower right corner of a photograph in which Nevinson packs up works which he has painted in London following his first trip to New York (fig. 49).

Within days of arriving in New York for the second time at the end of October 1920, he was still waiting for the twenty or so paintings and etchings in the photograph to be released from customs on their way to the Bourgeois Galleries at 668 Fifth Avenue. In an impatient mood, he scratched off an irascible letter to Henry McBride, chief arts correspondent to the *New York Herald*. He bemoaned an article he had seen in the previous Sunday's edition of the newspaper, pointing out pedantically that the "Special Correspondent" credited with the piece has "plagiarised" a *Daily Mail* interview Nevinson had given on leaving England, before going on to claim as an "insult" the "one original sentence in the whole article":

> Describing me as popular as "an official war photographer." Really I think I have a right to feel sore and might I *beseech* you to contradict the foolery. I admit my work has often been photographed in fact, it has often been said of me that I am the most reproduced of any living artist but that does not make me a photographer—no more than Caruso is a Gramophonist—please, joking apart, might you come to my rescue and contradict it, surely nothing could be said of me so insulting. An artist who strives to paint what he feels rather than what he sees, "a mental impressionist" if you will.[77]

In fact, the anonymous American journalist in question had employed just such a phrase as a way of complimenting the "realistic" effect with which Nevinson

May 21, 1919 THE SKETCH. 243

A "CUBIST" CUBED—BY THE CAMERA.

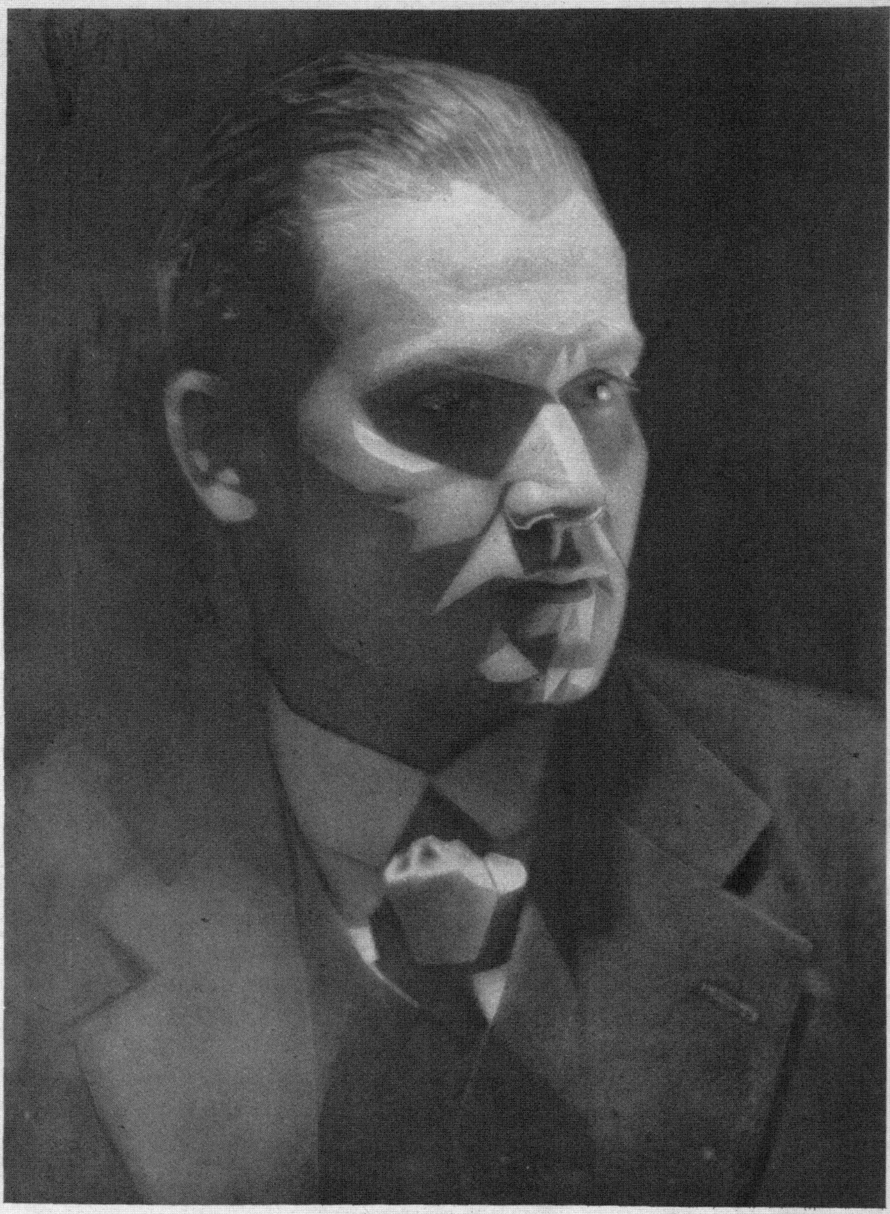

Nevinson—Reduced to His Own Artistic Formula.

Before the war, Mr. C. R. W. Nevinson was associated with the Futurist movement in art, but his peculiar style of cubism and realism combined was not developed till 1916, when he held his first War Exhibition, and was appointed an official war-artist. He has painted pictures for the Canadian War Memorials, and many of his works have been bought by Museums—at home and abroad. The above photograph of the Cubist artist as seen by a camera converted to Cubist convention was taken recently, before Mr. Nevinson sailed for America. It is, to say the least, unconventional.—[*Photograph by Bertram Park.*]

48. "A 'Cubist' cubed by the camera." Photographic portrait of Nevinson by Bertram Park, *The Sketch*, page 243 (May 21, 1919).

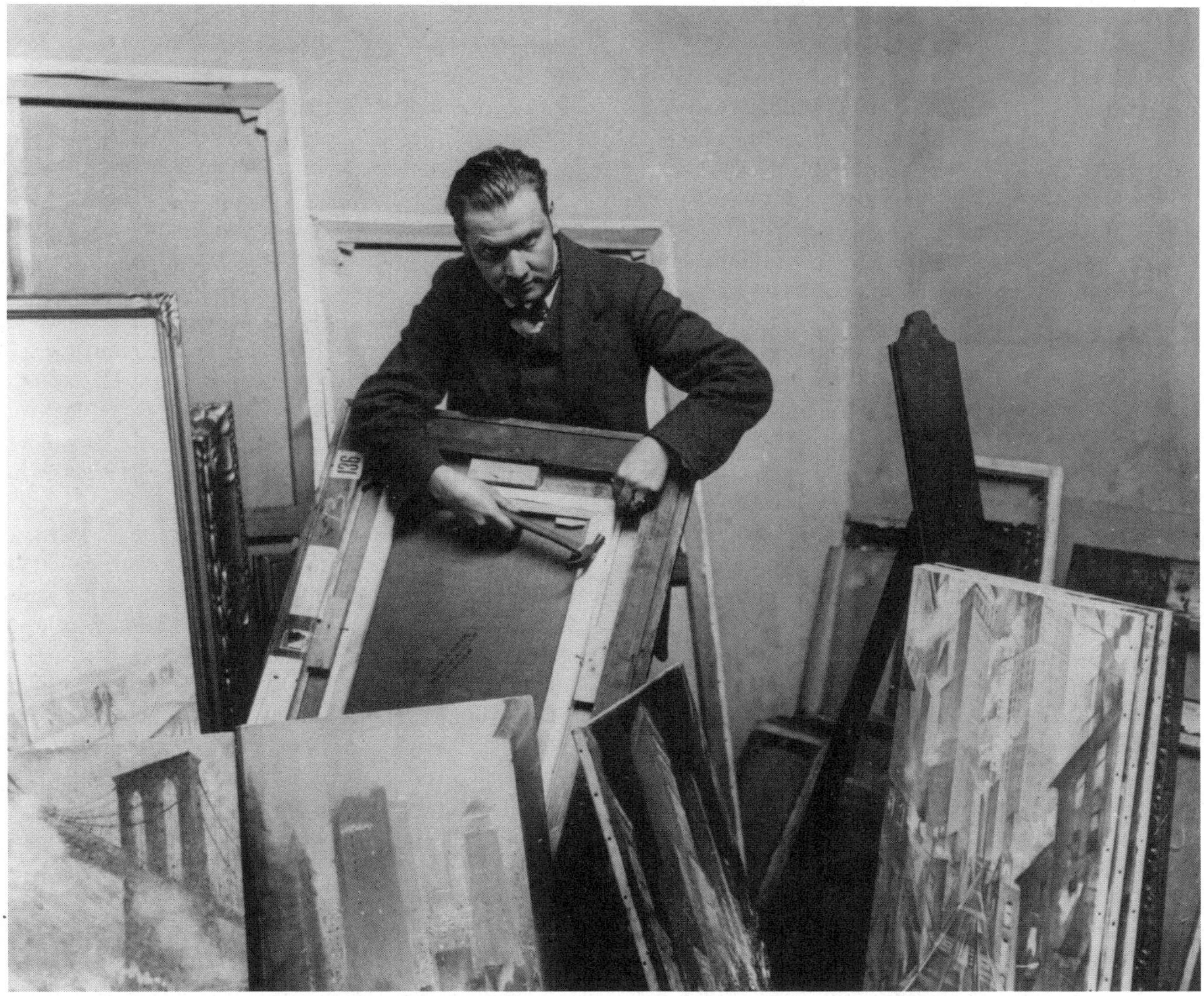

49. Nevinson arranging paintings in his studio (October 1920), photograph. Tate Gallery Archive, London.

had depicted New York's skyscrapers experienced on his first trip to the city months earlier and shortly to go on display in an exhibition entitled The Old World and the New: "He has many canvases on this subject alone, impressions left on his mind from his visit to America last year. He has reproduced the great buildings of the metropolis from all angles looking up, down, at a distance and the close-up view that so fixes the artistic eye."[78] But as we know, in no way did Nevinson want his audience to think such a photographic mode fixed *his* artistic eye; perhaps it was the use of this terminology of "angles," with its intimations of lenses and tripods, that provoked Nevinson's objections to the piece.

In Henry McBride's rejoinder of a fortnight later in his *New York Herald* column, he writes with playful hyperbole "the artist beseeches me to right this grevious wrong."[79] Hardly the retraction one feels that Nevinson sought. In delivering the gentle warning that he who "blushes often enough in the right places may become permanently noted for blushing" he alludes perceptively to the self-consciousness in Nevinson's expressions of outrage at what, in this case, was no more than a slip of the pen. He concludes: "But I was quite forgetting that Mr. Nevinson is not a photographer. Of course, Mr. Nevinson is not a photographer, though I feel quite sure that the contributor who caused Mr. Nevinson this anguish intended it as a compliment."

Naturally, McBride is not allowed the last word. It is not until Nevinson's return to London in early December 1920 that he reads McBride's review of his Bourgeois Gallery exhibition in the Sunday edition of the *Herald* dated November 21, 1920, entitled "Young

Mr. Nevinson of London Announces His 'Creed' as a Painter." McBride quotes heavily from "My Art Creed," the invective Nevinson had delivered over a year previously at the Leicester Galleries which announced the purging of "isms" from his work. Repeating the epithet "Young Mr. Nevinson" throughout, McBride witheringly criticises the artist's colour and composition as "uninspired": "He says, as though half hoping it were true, that 'There is no originality in art.' The inference here is clear—that such a stance suits an artist whose New York paintings and etchings on display at Bourgeois demonstrate a lack of originality."

Nevinson begins his letter of December 6 "Dear Old Mr. McBride," and ends the counterattack "Goodbye 'Old Man' yrs sincerely Young Nevinson," carping halfway through his diatribe that he had "unwittingly infuriated the "citizens" because I had painted the holy city & american painters [*sic*] hardly at all." His written haste here perhaps masks the sense that in his own mind he *was* the first artist to effectively paint New York City and moreover (again in his mind) that it took the artistic objectivity of the outsider to paint it with true originality. Nevinson clearly underestimated the nascency of American art and its impact on the world arena rooted in the Armory Show of 1913. Indeed, during his first visit in a speech delivered on the eve of his return to England, he made the crass judgment that America "had painters, but no artists."[80] This despite the fact that Abraham Walkowitz, Samuel Halpert, Joseph Stella, Charles Sheeler, John Marin, and Max Weber[81] had all made memorable avant-garde interpretations of the metropolis between 1909 and 1913. The point here is less the technicality of who painted the first "modern" image of this city, but more Nevinson's underlying charge that it was only his vital system of imagery, only his somehow uncategorizable radical modernist technique that had the strength to recast New York's imagery artistically.

There is enough evidence to suggest that Nevinson was far more attuned to photographs and etchings and indeed to photo-gravures of New York than he was to painted representations of the city. Or put another way, that the capacity of the photographic image to concentrate the city pictorially caught his magpie eye and offered up a scopic simulation of reality he could not resist rebranding in paint. In an unpublished paper delivered at the Yale Center for British Art,[82] Metropolitan Museum of Art curator Lisa Messinger has suggested the debt Nevinson's New York works owe to a number of American artists he came into contact with, notably etcher Joseph Pennell and photographer Alvin Langdon Coburn. Messinger begins by making a convincing stylistic and compositional link between Coburn's work of between 1905 and 1910, *Brooklyn Bridge from a Roof Top* (fig. 50), and Nevinson's *Under Brooklyn Bridge* which shows particularly strong similarities when viewed in its 1920 drypoint version (fig. 51). Coburn was well known in London where he exhibited frequently and became affiliated to the Vorticist movement, making iconic photographic portraits known as "Vortographs" of Wyndham Lewis and Ezra Pound.

From my own research, I set alongside these works Joseph Pennell's *The Bridge*, possibly as early as 1908 (fig. 52), whose tight photographic framing and sweeping arc of Brooklyn Bridge itself seem to lend heavily to Nevinson's later work. According to Nevinson, Pennell was a great friend to him, setting him up with "facilities for sketching in New York and Brooklyn,"[83] although in his widow's 1929 two-volume biography of Pennell's life and work, there is no reference to the young British ex-Futurist. Nevinson praised the generosity of Pennell in finding the time to help him: "Particularly as he himself was doing a series of etchings of New York and the Hudson from his home in Brooklyn Heights."[84] But Nevinson's memory is faulty here, perhaps deliberately. In fact, Pennell had already done two sets of etchings focusing on New York City, one a set of twelve shown as early as 1908 at the Grolier Club and the other in 1911, published as the book *The Great New York*.[85] Pennell's exhibition of war lithographs at London's Leicester Galleries which opened on February 26, 1916 (and coincidentally precedes Nevinson's debut solo exhibition in the same location precisely seven months later) coincided with Nevinson's honorable discharge, increasing the likelihood that Nevinson was already long conversant with Pennell's work by the time he arrived in New York. This is reinforced by the fact that Keppel and Company sold Pennell's etchings. Significantly, Nevinson compresses time in his memoirs to blur the boundaries surrounding the inception of New York imagery. Nevinson imposes a self-serving time frame on Pennell's work which allows that his own pictorializations of the city might be seen as somehow simultaneous with Pennell's. Records show that they were not even nearly concurrent; and this fact Nevinson carefully avoids.

Further echoes of Pennell's *Among the Sky-Scrapers in New York* (1911) are to be found in Nevinson's etchings *The Temples of New York* (1919, Victoria and Albert Museum, London) or *Looking Down on Downtown* (1921, private collection), while the tension between sinuousness and geometric austerity in Pennell's *The Elevated* (1911) clearly informs *The Soul of a Soulless City* (1920, Tate Gallery, London) later known as an etching by the less disparaging title *New York: An Abstraction* (1921, Private

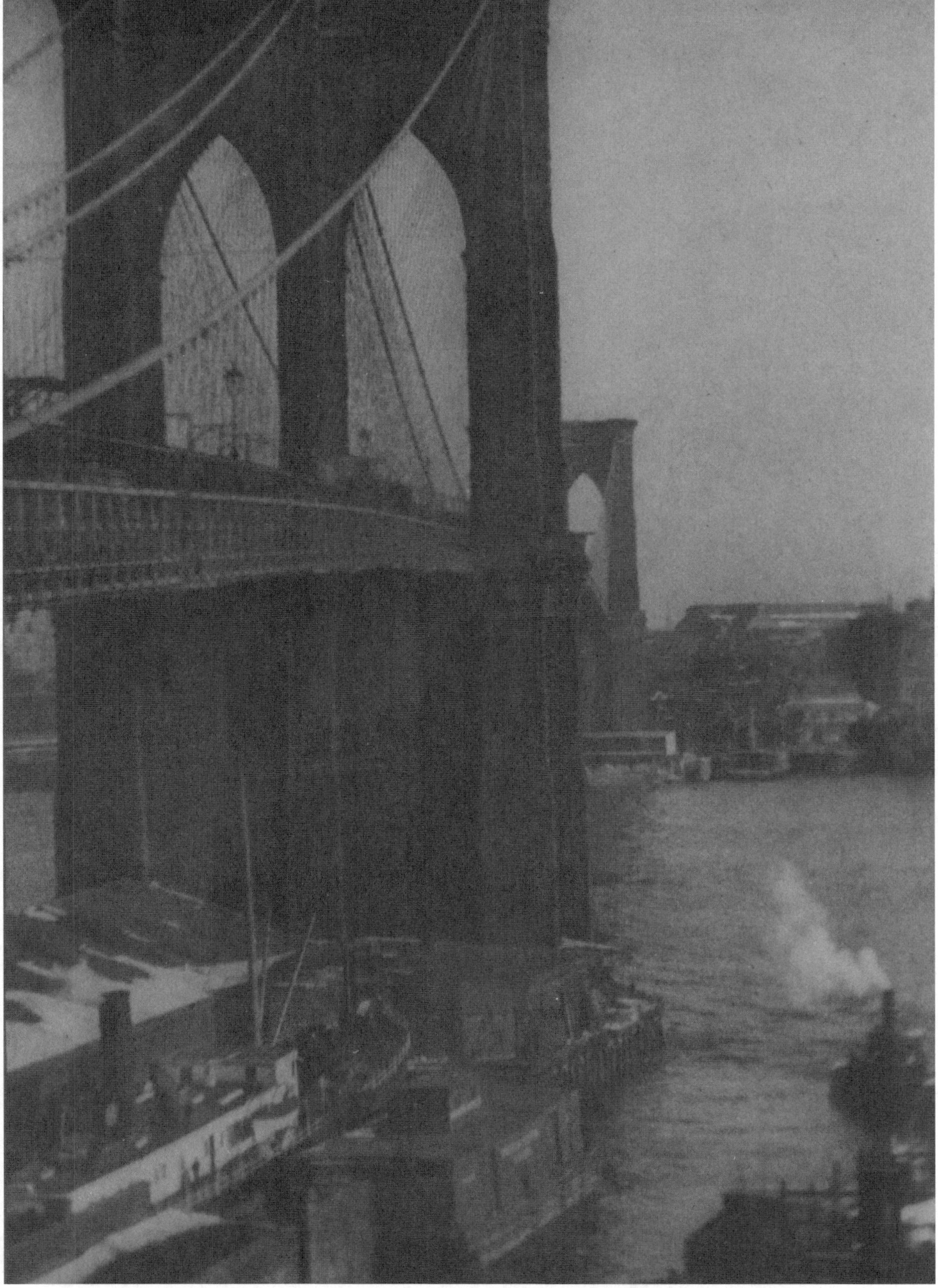

50. ***Brooklyn Bridge from a Roof Top*** **by Alvin Langdon Coburn (1905–10), photograph.**

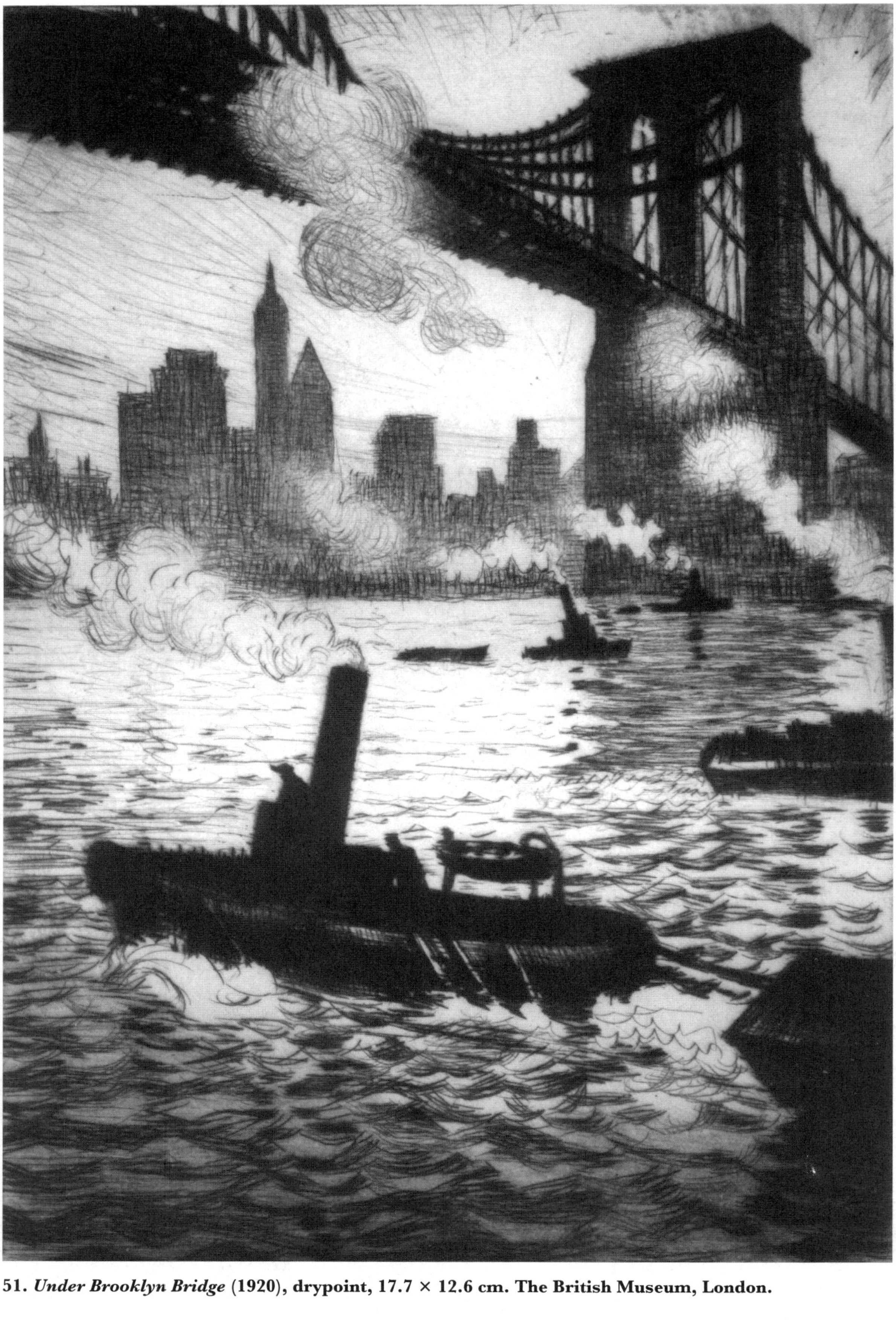

51. ***Under Brooklyn Bridge*** **(1920), drypoint, 17.7 × 12.6 cm. The British Museum, London.**

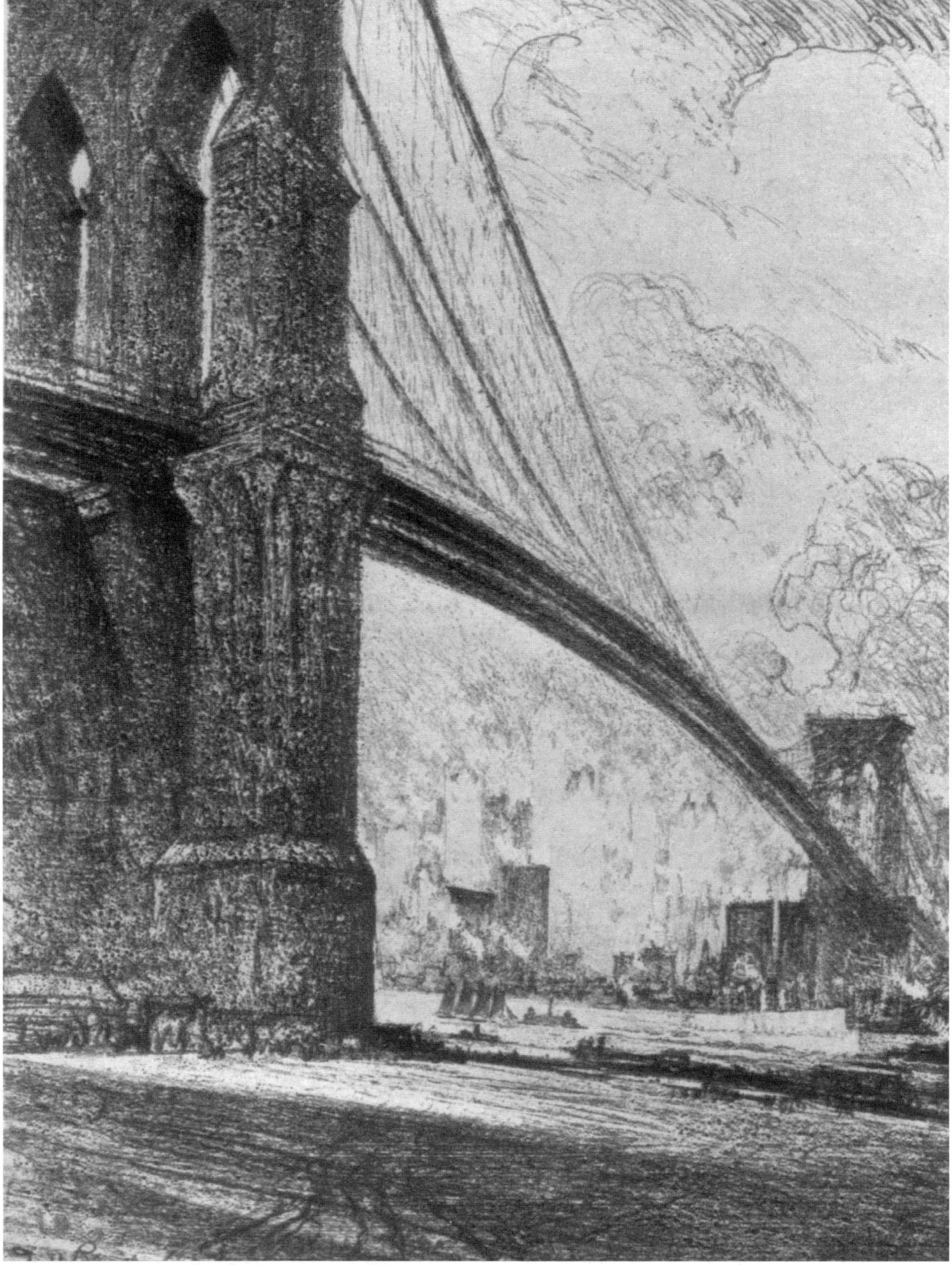

52. *The Bridge* by Joseph Pennell (ca. 1908), etching.

Collection). In Nevinson's tautly effective drypoint *Looking Through Brooklyn Bridge* (1920–22) (fig. 53), two pictures by different artists have been synthesized. Firstly, the dramatic backdrop of skyscrapers is cropped at almost precisely the same left and right edge as in Pennell's *New York from Brooklyn Bridge* (ca. 1911) (fig. 54), with the minor adjustment that the skyline has been shunted down to the center of Nevinson's picture, while the diagonally receding river lower left to upper middle right is effectively overlaid in the same formation by the bridge itself, which the Pennell chooses not to depict. The other key image is British photographer Emil Otto Hoppé's 1921 *Brooklyn Bridge* (fig. 55), one of the earliest and most iconic photographs to be created looking through the high tensile steel cables toward a Manhattan skyline cropped once again to centralize the dominating forty-seven-story Singer Building.[86] It was probably taken on Hoppé's second or third visit to New York. In his autobiography *100,000 Exposures*, he cites Pennell's lithographs as attracting him to the pictorial possibilities of a city he felt was full of "loneliness and grandeur." Nevinson would have known Hoppé as the cofounder of the London Salon of Photography and perhaps would have visited his February 1913 solo exhibition of photographs at the Goupil Gallery. "Hundreds of photographers picked up the motif," Hoppé wrote later of *Brooklyn Bridge*, "some improved on my original, some did not."[87]

Evidence from the Tate Gallery archive offers a rare insight into how Nevinson went about making etched versions of his paintings. In one example, a photograph dating back to the early 1920s of the painting *Looking Through Brooklyn Bridge*[88] bears the telltale indentations of scored pencil marks. We know that Nevinson employed the London photographic reproduction specialists Hudson and Kearns to make prints of his paintings, since he kept a personal catalog of wide-format photographs of his paintings taken two or three at a time. In one of these, Nevinson's handwriting is detectable in pencil on the photograph and identifies the painting on the left as "Sold 'The Mitrailleuse'" continuing below in a reminder to himself that this was a "present to the Tate Gallery since removed at my request now in Imperial War Museum."[89] Partly, such photographs served as a record of his output as work was sold, but they also had a more specific application to his working practice. In a letter to Alfred Yockney in the Office of Information dated December 26, 1917, Nevinson expresses his anxiousness for the return of certain paintings being photographed by Hudson and Kearns. At the same time, he asks that photographs of his paintings *The Mule Team*, *The Tank*, and *The Hindenburg Line* be sent to him urgently: "I wish to do some etchings or lithographs of these subjects."[90]

In the instance of *Looking Through Brooklyn Bridge*, Nevinson makes a photographic reduction of his painting to single six-by-four-inch format, ensuring that the photographic process reverse-prints the image. Then by using a stylus to score along key linear features of the surface of the photograph, the artist allows the image to be precisely traced to the copperplate, re-reversing it as it were to replicate in positive the architectural detail of the painting. It is a technique that Nevinson freely admits to in E. S. Lumsden's *The Art Of Etching* in 1924: "My drypoints are invariably traced onto the surface of a smoked liquid ground: cut through with a ruby point and then the ground cleaned off."[91]

But should the technique of reversal be so particular to the New York period? Drypointed versions of *Returning to the Trenches* (1914/16) or *Loading Timber at Southampton Docks* (1916/17), for example, simply reverse the original composition to its negative image. In the New York series, this decision concerning the precise transfer of image from paint to print is no doubt founded commercially in presenting the topographical detail of the city correctly to an American audience. But the decision also crucially reflects a desire in Nevinson to match technique to subject, each of which in the case of New York is inextricably linked to photography.

One could argue that the city was imagined, perpetually brought into being as Henri Bergson might have said, photographically. From our perspective nearly a century later, Nevinson's paintings can be usefully interpreted as subconscious engagements with as well as reinforcements of the photographically dominated image system that post-avant-gardism had become by the early 1920s. Nevinson's use of photography was conscious, but the admission of it repressed, the result being that the work becomes stylistically subsumed into the idea of city as self-presenting. This has a crucial bearing on the degree to which we believe Nevinson transfers the image of the city to canvas or metal plate as the direct imprint of that city on his retina, or whether he merely rehearses that immediacy by employing photography as a mnemonic substitute for scopic originality. Since Nevinson has ensured that none of the preparatory work remains from this or any other part of his career, and the only clear indication he ever gave of his working method is that he never made paintings *in situ*—confessing in Lumsden's *Art of Etching* "I never work on the spot. I can't compose out of doors"[92]—there remains a considerable area of doubt surrounding the means by which this artist was able to make full-scale paintings with such a high degree of topographical

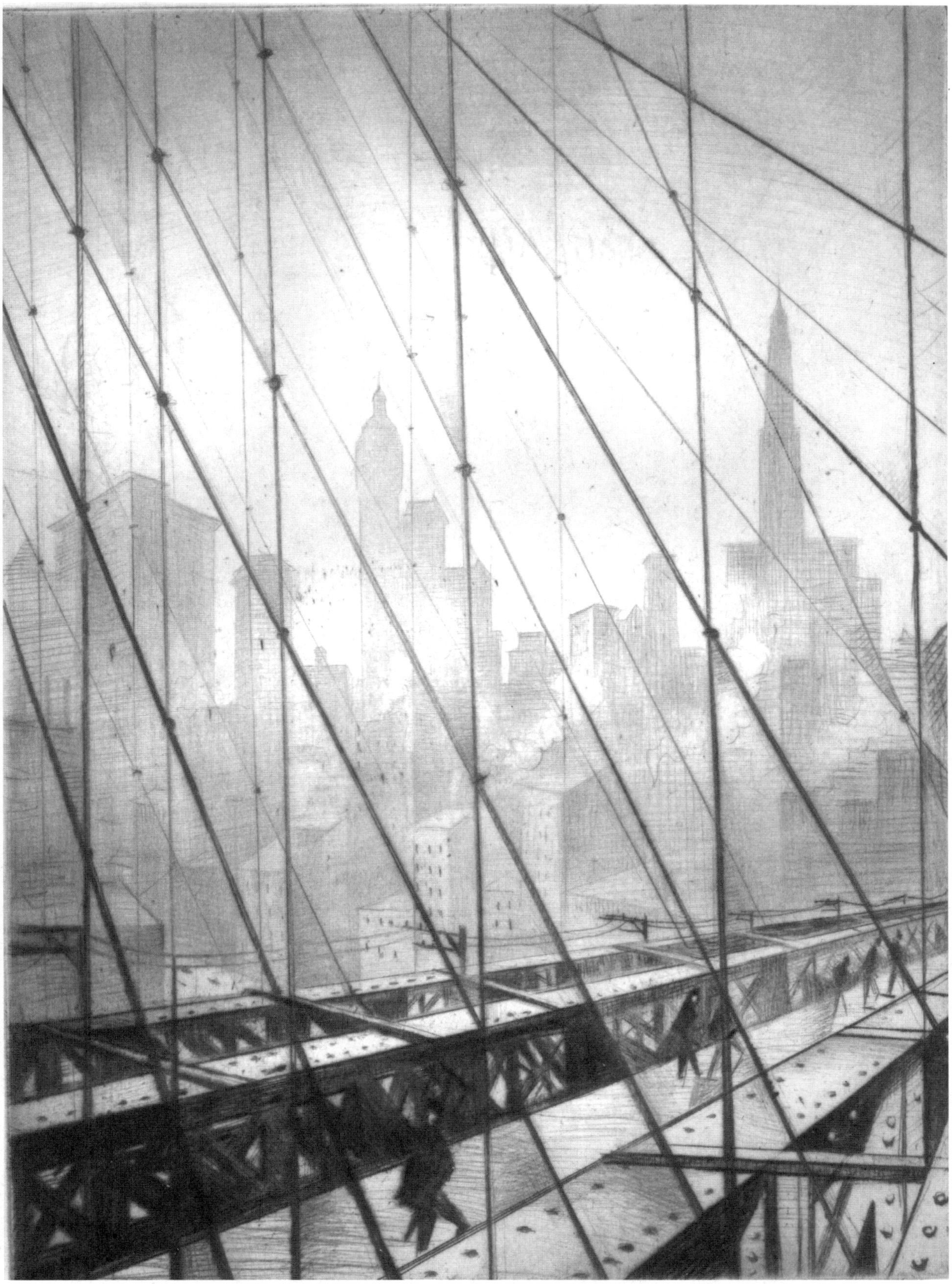

53. ***Looking Through Brooklyn Bridge*** **(1920–22), drypoint, 23.5 × 17.5 cm. The British Museum, London.**

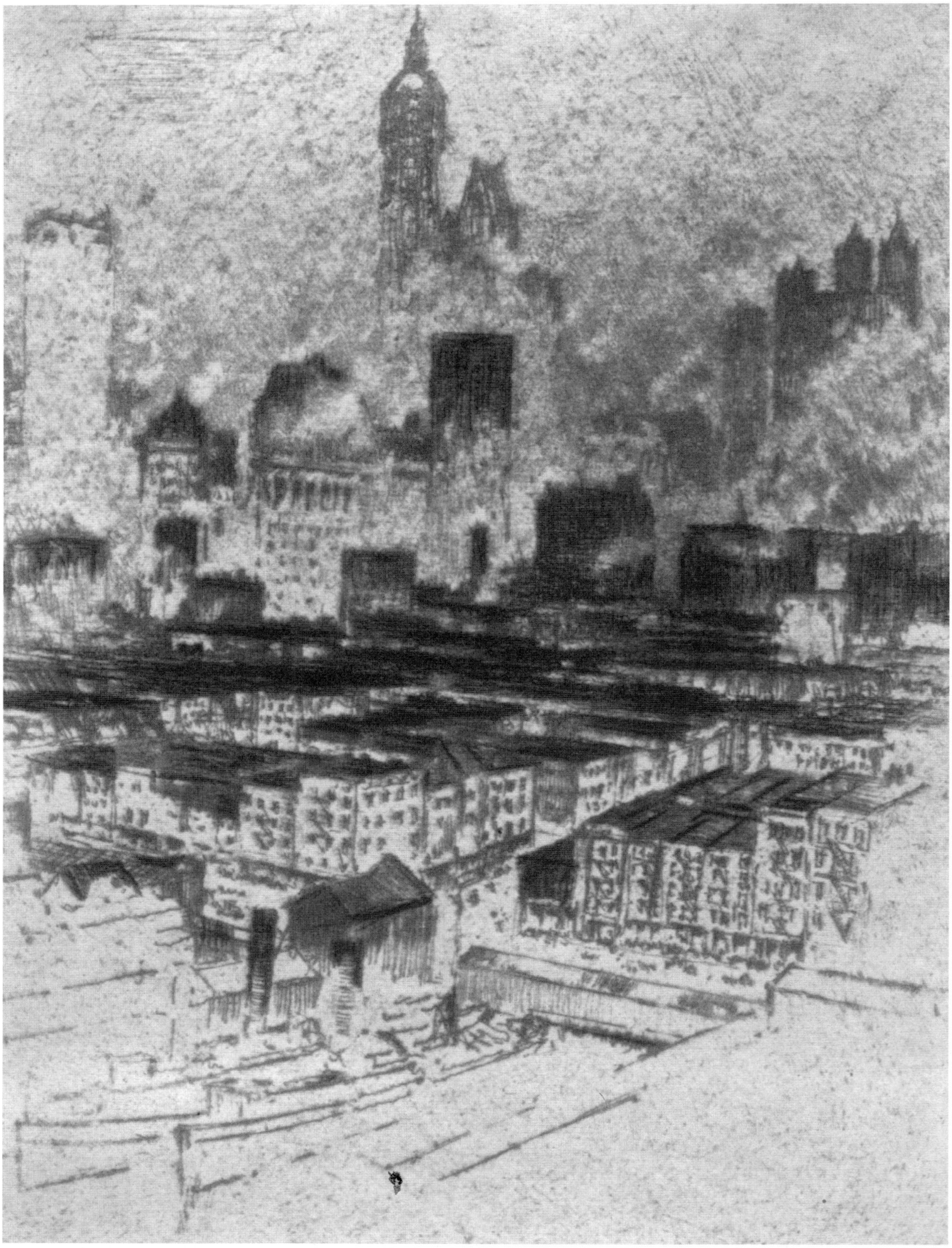

54. *New York from Brooklyn Bridge* by Joseph Pennell (ca. 1911), etching.

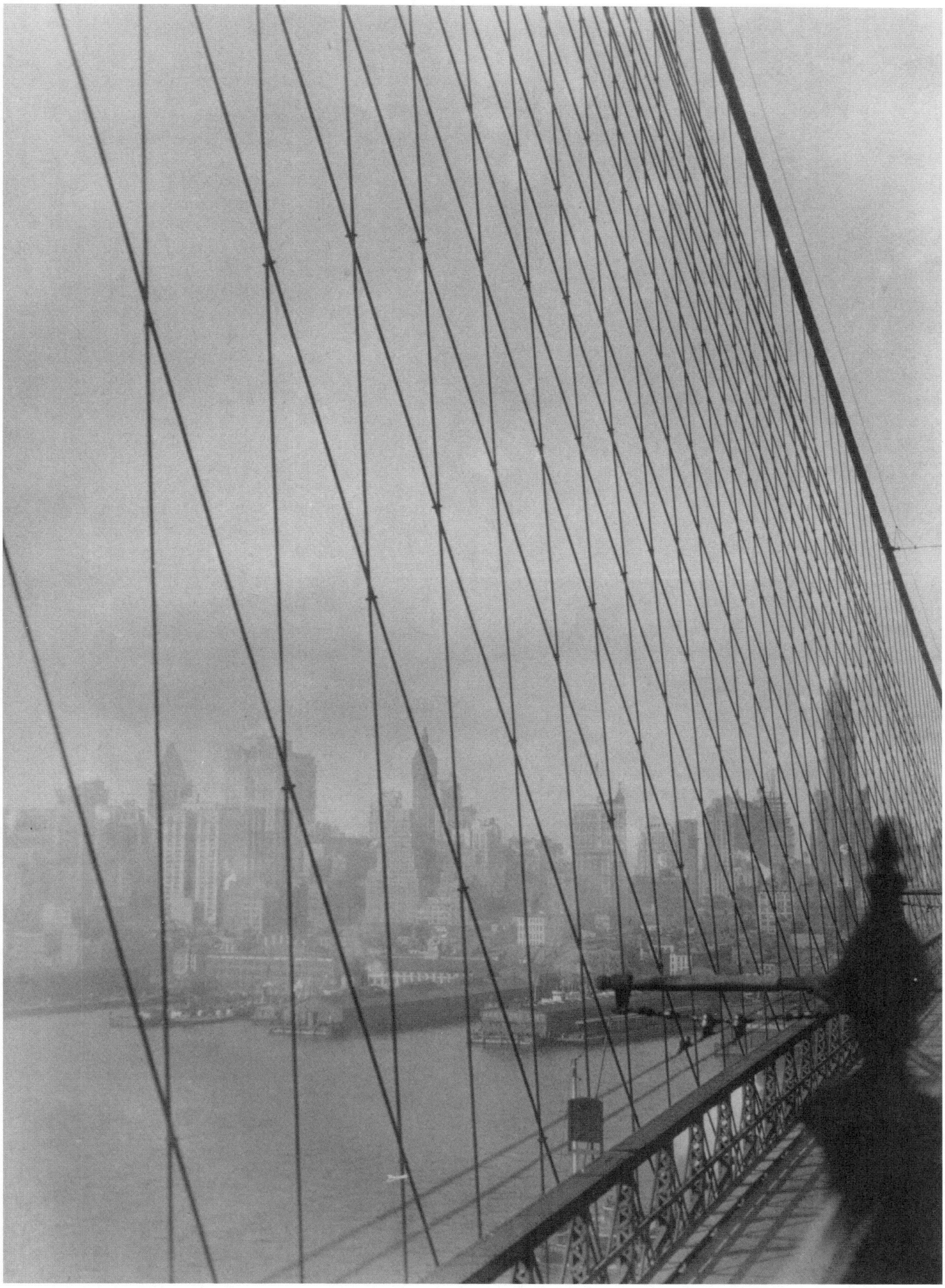

55. ***Brooklyn Bridge***, **by Emil Otto Hoppé (1921), photograph courtesy of Curatorial Assistance, Inc. and the E. O. Hoppé Trust, Los Angeles, California.**

and anecdotal detail while relying on no more than "a few pencil notes" and "a wonderful memory."[93]

During Nevinson's lifetime, the closest any critic seems to have come to addressing such an apparently paradoxical creative practice is the anonymous reviewer of a 1926 Nevinson exhibition at the Leicester Galleries:

> Mr. Nevinson is a difficult artist to "place." One has the queer feeling that his most striking qualities are somehow outside his craft. He is versatile, alert, emotional, impressionable and dramatic, but these qualities are, so to speak, illustrated by his painting rather than expressed in it. There is a missing link somewhere. It is difficult to judge, for instance, whether his unorganized handling proceeds from "damning the consequences" or from incapacity.[94]

Had the reviewer looked more closely, the "missing link" would have revealed itself to be photography.

Notes

1. Kathleen Nevinson, introduction to 1936 exhibition *Paintings of Flowers*.

2. Nevinson was the sole British signatory to Marinetti's English Futurist Manifesto, *Vital English Art*, published in the *Observer*, June 7, 1914.

3. Interview in unidentified postwar magazine, Tate Gallery Archive (hereafter: T.G.A.)—T.G.A. 7311.2A.34.

4. Introduction to Bourgeois Gallery cat., Lewis Hind, C "An Appreciation" The Old World and the New (Bourgeois Galleries 10 November–4 December, 1920) New York, November 1920.

5. Michael Walsh, *C. R. W. Nevinson: This Cult of Violence* (New Haven, CT: Yale University Press, 2002), 95–96.

6. A "tag" which Wyndham Lewis in *BLAST I*, June 1914, 143, declares is waning: "there are practically no Futurists, or at least Automobilists, left."

7. *Catalogue of an Exhibition of paintings and Drawings of War by C. R. W. Nevinson (Late Private R.A.M.C.)*, Leicester Galleries, 1916, 6.

8. C. Harrison, *English Art and Modernism 1900–1939* (Bloomington, Indiana University Press. Allen Lane, 1981), 131.

9. Letter to Masterman, July 30, 1917, T.G.A. 724.9.38.

10. Herry Bergson, *Matter and Memory*, authorized translation of *Matière et Memoire 6*, Nancy Margaret Paul and W. Scott Palmer (London: Swan Sonnenscheir, 1896), 80.

11. C. R. W. Nevinson, *Paint and Prejudice* (New York: Harcourt Brace and Company, 1938), 43.

12. Ibid., 107; Nevinson recalls the response of Harold Monro to the three paintings he submitted March 1915 London Group "What on earth are you doing journalistic clippings for?"

13. *Daily Mirror*, November 22, 1915.

14. Nevinson's own preface to his 1918 Leicester Galleries. Exhibition of Pictures of War reproduced verbatim in *Paint and Prejudice*, p. 146.

15. Nevinson, *Paint and Prejudice*, 107; note 12.

16. Ibid., 106.

17. J. Taylor, *War Photography: Realism in the British Press* (London: Routledge, 1991), 46.

18. Nevinson, *Paint and Prejudice*, 110.

19. At Neuville St. Vaast, June 5, 1915.

20. Sickert, *Burlington* (April 1916), 34.

21. Sickert, *Burlington* (January 1916), 164.

22. R. Cork, "A Bitter Truth: Avant-Garde Art and the Great War (London: Yale University Press, 1994), 74.

23. Both Sickert's and Nevinson's works clearly owe a wider debt to Goya's *The Shooting of the Third of May 1808* (1814) and might even be read as centenary reworkings of the painting. While continuing his training in Paris at Matisse's *Cercle Russe*, Nevinson described himself as "obsessed" by the recent William Rothenstein and Albert Calvert books on Goya and there is a strong sense of Nevinson emulating the audacious attitude and technique of the Spaniard. Indeed, one can imagine the description of Goya as an artist who "lived, as he worked, in a condition of unconventional, even arrogant independence" being adopted for Nevinson's as a blueprint for artistic life. See Albert F. Calvert, *The Spanish Series: Goya* (London: John Lane, 1908).

24. W. Baron, *Sickert* (London: Phaidon, 1973).

25. Nevinson's Slade colleague Stanley Spencer recalled in a letter of 1911 (T.G.A.) Tonks's admonishing words: "your drawing is too much of a photograph."

26. As demonstrated by his letter to Masterman sarcastically offering retrospective permission to the War Bond department to "crib" his poster design for the *War* exhibition of 1918.

27. T.G.A. 881.15.

28. Imperial War Museum Photographic Archive (IWMPA), Q 4437.

29. May 11, 1918, 575.

30. *Graphic*, September 15, 1917, 339. Also to be found advertised in the *Graphic* of September 1, 1917, 279.

31. Unidentified letter in the author's possession.

32. Nevinson, *Paint and Prejudice*, 143.

33. Nevinson letter to Major Lee, intercepted by Masterman, November 25, 1917 IWMA 226A-6.148.

34. Published by Wellington House in association with *Country Life* under the title *The Western Front.*

35. "Art and the Camera," *New Witness*, December 21, 1916, T.G.A. 7311.2B-400.

36. "Personality or Process: Mr. Nevinson's Pictures of Men as War Machines," *Times*, September 29, 1916.

37. *Manchester Guardian*, March 7, 1917, T.G.A. 7311.2C-450.

38. From the preface to the edition of five issues of Bone's *The Western Front* paintings, published November 1917.

39. Sue Malvern, *Art History*, no. 9 (1986), 488.

40. *Burlington* review quoted, Malvern, 497.

41. Nevinson's own introduction to his 1918 solo exhibition, Leicester Galleries. See note 14.

42. "The Bloomsburies accused me of every form of pushfulness and publicity." *Paint and Prejudice*, 114.

43. Technically the words of J. E. Crawford Flitch, *The Great War Fourth Year: Paintings by C R W Nevinson*, 1918 (London: Grant Richards, 1918).

44. Nevinson would have come across the same photo as a smaller inset in the *Graphic* of September 1, 1917, 262.

45. Letter from Nevinson to Major Lee, November 27, 1917.

46. The artist's preface to his catalog of an *Exhibition of Pictures of War*, Leicester Galleries, March 1, 1918.

47. Ultimately, the row subsided and Sir Martin Conway bought the painting for the National War Museum for £100 along with six other Nevinsons at a total of £510.

48. Preface to the catalog for Nevinson's 1918 solo exhibition, Leicester Galleries.

49. Letter to Rothenstein, October 22, 1916.

50. *Evening News*, September 27, 1916, T.G.A. 7311.2B-293.

51. Exhibited separately as *War in the Air*, January 1917, at the Grosvenor Galleries.

52. Margaret Nevinson records in her 1926 autobiography *Life's Fitful Fever*, 247, that her son "was the first artist to draw from an aeroplane over the German lines" although it was actually from an observation balloon.

53. Jamieson B. Hurry, *The Vicious Circles of Neurasthenia and their Treatment*, (London: J & A Churchill, 1915), xiii.

54. *Manchester Guardian*, June 13, 1914.

55. See IWMA 226B-6 file for correspondence which includes letters from Nevinson's father to friends in high places.

56. Masterman to Buchan, May 18, 1918.

57. Derrick to Masterman, October 16, 1917, IWMA 226A-6.192.

58. Ibid.

59. *New York Evening Post*, May 31, 1919, T.G.A. 7311.4.788.

60. Letter to Masterman, July 30, 1917, T.G.A. 724.9.38.

61. Ibid.

62. "War Neurosis and Military Training: A Report to the Medical Research Commission," *London Mental Hygiene* 2, no. 4 (1918): 513–33.

63. In terms of official army intelligence alone, between May and September 1916, 4,000 stills were distributed to newspapers. By October 1918, 23,000 negatives had reproduced themselves into 650,000 prints, John Taylor, *War Photography*, 21.

64. W. Baron *Perfect Moderns: A History of the Camden Town Group* (Aldershot, UK: Ashgate, 2000), 181.

65. Letter to Robert Ross, April 21, 1918 IWM l. 56–59.

66. "Australian First World War Photography: Frank Hurley and Charles Bean," *History of Photography* 23, no. 2 (Summer 1999).

67. Fought, April 9, 1917.

68. *Graphic*, March 9, 1918, p. 293

69. IWM l.130-1.

70. Nevinson, *Paint and Prejudice*, 143.

71. H. W. Nevinson, *The Dardarelles Campaign*, (London: Nisbet, 1918), 219.

72. *London Evening Standard*, April 9, 1919 reported that the painting was ready.

73. *New York Evening World*, May 31, 1919.

74. May 21, 1919, photographer Bertram Park.

75. *Paint and Prejudice*, 182.

76. Ibid., 179.

77. Written from the National Arts Club, Gramercy Park, October 28, 1920. (Henry McBride Papers—YCAL MSS 31, Box 9, Folder 243—Beinecke Rare Books and Manuscript Library, Yale University Library, New Haven, CT.)

78. October 24, 1920 edition, section 4, 8.

79. *Herald*, November 7, 1920.

80. Reported *Evening Standard and St. James's Gazette*, July 3, 1919.

81. Cf. Weber's *New York* (1913, Thyssen Collection) and *Grand Central Station at Rush Hour* (1915); Marin's *New York Downtown* (ca. 1914, St. Louis Art Museum); Walkowitz's *Cityscape New York Improvisation* (1909) and *Brooklyn Bridge* (ca. 1912); Stella, *Factories at Night* (n.d., Portland Art Museum); Halpert, *Brooklyn Bridge* (1913).

82. Lisa M. Messinger, "Nevinson in New York" (Lecture delivered at the Yale Center for British Art, New Haven, CT, March 1, 2000).

83. C. R. W. Nevinson, *Paint and Prejudice*, 177.

84. Ibid.

85. Text on page 6 explains that "The etchings of skyscrapers done in New York date from the Autumn of 1904."

86. Messinger has also pointed this out.

87. *Cities and Industry: Camera Pictures* by E. O. Hoppé, introduction (York, UK: Impressions Gallery of Photography, 1978).

88. See Messinger on this specific image's telltale indentations, but also a year earlier Ingleby et al. (p. 82) with the same observation made in the Tate Archive but pertaining to *Motor Ambulance Driver* (1916).

89. T.G.A. photographic ephemera.

90. IWM 226A-6 l. 131.

91. See also Denys Sutton's biography *Walter Sickert: A Biography* (London: Joseph, 1976), 293, in which he quotes Nevinson detailing the technique Sickert taught him of etching "a prepared plate on which your drawing had been photographed."

92. Published 1962, after Nevinson's death.

93. Charles Lewis Hind introduction to the Bourgeois Galleries catalog, November 1920.

94. *Times*, March 6, 1917.

C. R. W. Nevinson's "bad boy" Modernisms and Fascism in the 1930s

Sue Malvern

In 1936, the *Star* newspaper termed Nevinson "eternally the bad boy . . . among the artists."[1] The occasion was some advance publicity for the artist's memoirs, which he was writing at the rate of two thousand words a day. His book appeared the following year as *Paint and Prejudice*, the same year as Wyndham Lewis's reminiscences *Blasting and Bombardiering*. The artist explained his urgency to the *Star* as a fear that no one would be around to read it, declaring with a degree of insight "I will live to see the destruction of Europe" (he died in 1946).

Nevinson's standing among critics and the general public was based almost entirely on the reputation he established in the First World War as a war artist. He was one of the earliest artists to exhibit works in London based on firsthand experience—a brief excursion to the front as an ambulance driver. After 1917, he was an official war artist employed by the British government, initially for the propaganda organization at Wellington House and then for the British War Memorials Committee based at the Ministry of Information. His employment culminated in a major memorial canvas *The Harvest of Battle* shown at the Royal Academy in 1919–20 as part of the exhibition "The Nation's War Paintings." By the end of the war, Nevinson had published three monographs of war paintings, by P. G. Konody, by Crawford Flitch, and an official publication *British Artists at the Front*. He had held two exhibitions at the Leicester Galleries, the leading avant-garde dealers of the day, in 1916 and 1918; he had had a work, *La Mitrailleuse*, presented to the Tate by the Contemporary Art Society. Numerous works were in public collections, principally the Imperial War Museum, established in 1917, and in Canada. In the mid-30s, this work was again highly visible. In part, the renewal of interest in Nevinson's war paintings was a consequence of new publications and exhibitions. In 1931, John Rothenstein published *British Artists and the War*, consisting of a short essay that was a polemic against Roger Fry's formalist aesthetics, accompanied by extensive reproductions. Works by Nevinson such as *La Patrie* (1916), then in a private collection, and *The Road from Arras to Bapaume* (1917) in the Imperial War Museum, were reproduced in the many press notices that appeared with the book. In 1936, the Imperial War Museum, with its major collection of official art including Nevinson's, moved from the Imperial Institute in South Kensington to reopen at the former Bethlem Hospital in Southwark and its visitor numbers increased.

Coinciding with the publication of his autobiography, Nevinson also wrote a series of articles for the *Sunday Despatch* that included two about his war experiences, titled "My Crime Was This—I Painted What I Saw" (April 4, 1937) and "I Visit the Forbidden Zone" (April 11, 1937) in which he gave a straightforward account of the censorship of his *Paths of Glory* in 1918. Both articles reproduced war paintings that by 1937 were clearly intended to be read as condemnations of the war. These were the final panel of the Canadian-owned four-part *The Roads of France* with its devastated frontline landscape, *The Harvest of Battle*, and the version of this he painted in 1924, *Glittering Prizes*.

But publications and exhibitions only account for part of the reason these works seemed newly relevant to audiences in the 1930s. The tenth anniversary of the ending of the war saw a flood of war memoirs appear in print. The war poets were also republished and new films were produced such as Lewis Milestone's *All Quiet on the Western Front* (1930) based on Eric Maria Remarque's novel, published in English in 1929, and Frank Borgaze's film version of Hemingway's *A Farewell to Arms* (1932). This was also the period when Stanley Spencer completed the painted narrative of his war experiences at Burghclere, 1932. New books, poems, and films reached a new audience, specifically a generation too young to have fought in the war. But the reshaping of war memories and the reception of war imagery coincided with the stock market crash, the onset of the Great Depression, and the rise of fascism. Cultural preoccupation with the Great War was also marked by growing and widespread anxiety about the inevitability of a new European conflict that put an end to the myth that the Great War had been the "war to end all wars." Popular fascination with the look and meaning of the Great War was especially invested in the testimonies of participants. Anxieties about war were accelerated when the 1932 World Disarmament Conference collapsed with the withdrawal of Germany after Hitler came to power in 1933. Fascism was a direct threat to cultural freedom, often focused on modern art and avant-garde writers. In 1935, the year the German National Socialists first condemned modern art as degenerate, Jacob Epstein's controversial and modernist Hyde Park relief *Rima* was defaced by the Independent Fascist League. When Nevinson's epic war paintings such as *The Harvest of Battle* were reproduced in the 1930s, they stood both for telling indictments of the tragedy of a wasted generation and as ominous premonitions of a war to come.

When the *Star* called Nevinson the "bad boy" among the modernists, it summarized a career of courting controversy and press coverage, beginning with his association with the Italian futurist impresario, Marinetti in 1914 and sustained throughout the 1920s and 1930s by frequent rumpuses in the press, often carefully orchestrated by the artist himself. It was not coincidental that at the high point of controversy over Epstein's *Rima* panel for the Hudson Memorial in 1925, Nevinson demanded, rather absurdly, that the Tate should remove his *La Mitrailleuse* from public display because he was ashamed of it. The *Yorkshire Evening Post* published a cartoon of the figure of *Rima* telling off Epstein, with a caption suggesting he should do the same as Nevinson.[2]

The *Star* implied that Nevinson's "badness" was a consequence of his nonconformity, calling him "a revolutionary among artists." The question that arises is whether or not Nevinson's "rebellion" equaled a coherent intellectual position, or, put another way, just how much integrity there was in Nevinson's practice, including his politics and extending to his war paintings. It is a question that had exercised serious art critics in the second half of the Great War when Nevinson's work included a turn to realism, a kind of visual greyness, typical of *The Harvest of Battle* and *The Road from Arras to Bapaume*. His eclecticism, ranging from modernist geometries to illustrative realism, especially explicit in his "Peace Show" exhibition held at the Leicester Galleries in 1919, was excoriated by the opinion of connoisseurs and celebrated by populist, sometimes commonsensical, critics. In the 1930s, the ambivalence of Nevinson's works, posed between the specialism of modern art and vulgar illustrative narrative, continued to preoccupy critics. Anthony Blunt, writing in the *Spectator* about his show at the Leicester Galleries in 1934, called him "facile and frivolous"; the *New Statesman* put it more obliquely, describing the work as "a curious and fascinating jumble."[3] Critical appraisals of Nevinson's work have never managed to establish a critical consensus about the artist. Recently, Richard Ingelby, writing in the catalog to a major retrospective of Nevinson's work described him as "really a conservative figure," a view that is hardly compatible with the *Star*'s bad boy revolutionary.[4]

The question of the integrity of Nevinson's practice is compounded by how disparate his oeuvre is. The *Times* wrote in 1930 "In the strict sense Mr. Nevinson can hardly be said to have any artistic aims."[5] In the 1920s and 1930s, he produced paintings and prints of cityscapes, usually of London and New York, occasionally Paris, along with stylized landscapes and images of urban living, for example, *Any Wintry Afternoon in England*, a football match set in an industrialized landscape in a loosely faceted futurist style, for example. These were competent, though scarcely exceptional images. *Truth* wrote that "when . . . he is out to be a serious painter he is dull."[6] But there are other works from the period that are cursorily and flatly painted, and some where intellectual ambition seems to exceed painterly investment. This is particularly the case with a series of allegories that Nevinson began around 1930, known as his "problem pictures."[7]

"Problem pictures," popular at the Royal Academy in the late nineteenth and early twentieth century, were illustrative paintings that pictured indeterminate narratives, most often involving female figures, designed to provoke viewers into devising different solutions to the moral issues supposedly posed. A well-known example is Luke Fildes, *The Doctor*, 1891; the leading exponent was John Collier. When the Royal Academy shows opened, "problem pictures" were eagerly anticipated and often debated in letters and competitions run in newspapers. Pamela Fletcher has argued that such paintings were closely aligned with the commodification of modern life and paralleled developing forms of advertising, so that the viewer's desires stirred by the "problem picture" were akin to the desires mobilized by commodities and advertisements, making artistic meaning itself a commodity. Because, she says, the "problem picture" crossed the boundary from poetic ambiguity, proper to fine art, into populist problem solving, it was antimodern, associated with unsophisticated viewers and became a dead end in the forms of modern painting.[8]

Nevinson's first appeared at his eighth solo exhibition at the Leicester Galleries in 1930 and included *Kultur Modern*, an image of sunbathers in the Mediterranean; *Sex Appeal*, a satire on the film industry, retitled *A Comment on Vulgarity; or World Definition of Beauty and Grace* when it was shown in 1934; and a monumental self-portrait with his wife and cat, called *With*

Nothing to Lose—Not Even Chains. In 1931, he showed *Pan Triumphant*, an allegory of New York, at the National Society. Most of the paintings used fragmentation and overlapping images, as is found in prewar futurist works. Reviewers at the time said they recalled cinematic montage.[9] *With Nothing to Lose—Not Even Chains* includes glimpses of soldiers marching with bayonettes, troops embarking on a ship, a telephone, and is inscribed with texts: "Modern," "Modern," "Press," "Press," "News," "News." Flying above the artist's head is a bat.

Nevinson's "problem pictures" in 1930 were certainly intended to supply newspaper copy. Photographs of *With Nothing to Lose—Not Even Chains* were released in advance of the exhibition. Nevinson appeared dressed in a dinner jacket alongside the canvas in the *Illustrated London News* and the *Sunday Pictorial* obliged with a photograph of three viewers gazing quizzically at the painting hung in the Leicester Galleries and titled "Problem Picture in Nevinson Show."[10] In reproductions published after the show's opening, the texts, "Modern," "Press," and "News" had been painted out, presumably to make it more of a puzzle. From the press responses, comprehensively assembled in Nevinson's press cutting collection in the Tate Archive, only P. G. Konody, long a champion of the artist, supplied the requisite attempt at interpretation, but in rather acid terms: "The title can be regarded only as an attempt at mystification on the artist's part, for the meaning of the picture, if not its entangled construction, seems quite clear." The bat, he suggested ironically, "indicates the shadow thrown upon the artist's life by envious detractors and critics."[11] These "problem" paintings were recognizably modern, in a way intended to be accessible to broad audiences by being stylized in a reductive version of futurism via cubism. The reviewer of the Plymouth-based *Western Morning News and Mercury*, with self-confessed "old-fashioned ideals," provided an appropriately provincial perspective. The work, he wrote, represented "the age we live in, an age of abnormal speed, of unrest, and, to use an Americanism, that rather smarty superficiality which has invaded most of our great cities."[12]

Smarty superficiality was more of an issue with the allegories that Nevinson exhibited at his next solo exhibition at the Leicester Galleries in 1934 and which Blunt called facile and frivolous. These included *Crucify, Sacrifice: A Symbolic Picture Suggested by the Religion of Race and the Cult of Human Sacrifice*, now known as *The Unending Cult of Human Sacrifice*, and *"They All Know the Way": A Symbolic Satire on Fascists, Socialists, Capitalists, Hedonists, Ascetics, Intellectuals, and Priests*. The *Sketch* published a selection under the heading "The Modernisms of C. R, W. Nevinson." What marked this new work was a preoccupation with contemporary politics. He ended the year with the publication of a novel, *Exodus A.D. A Warning to Citizens*, that predicted gas attacks and aerial bombardment, in the same genre as H. G. Wells's *The Shape of Things to Come* (1933), the basis of Alexander Korda's epic science-fiction film *Things to Come* (1935). The jacket of Nevinson's novel was illustrated with another of his allegories *Ave Homo Sapiens*, shown at the Royal Society of Painters in 1935 and reproduced in *Studio*.[13] The last in the series was *The Twentieth Century*, shown at the Royal Institute of Oil Painters in 1935 and described as "A Cartoon for a Mural Decoration of a Public Building or Seat of Learning, suggested by the Clash between Thought, Mechanical Invention, Race Idolatry, and the Regimentation of Youth" (fig. 56). In 1943, Nevinson presented the painting to the Laing Art Gallery, Newcastle, UK.

These paintings all use a similar formula of a montage of imagery, usually incorporating marching troops and bayonets. *The Unending Cult of Human Sacrifice* includes a nun and two angels or saints, all sporting haloes, priests and a crucifix, along with an array of armies ranging from crusaders on horseback to modern howitzers and bombers. The foreground is filled with three naked dead bodies pierced with bayonets. *The Twentieth Century* has a badly drawn version of Rodin's antihero, *The Thinker*, reworked from the gas-masked colossus in *Ave Homo Sapiens*. The figure broods amid a cityscape of skyscrapers, aeroplanes, troops, and bayonets. Flags, including a Union Jack, the red flag of revolution, and a swastika, range over crowds addressed by heckling demagogues in a city of mass hysteria. Here the soldiers are evidently Great War troops emerging open-mouthed from the fog of the city, like ghosts peopling the unconscious of modernity. The image is framed with riveted steel girders, cog wheels, and a chain, making it clear that this is an image of modern war. The subtitle of *The Twentieth Century* indicates that Nevinson imagined it, perhaps ironically, as a mural for a public location or a modern version of a history painting. Admonitory and apocalyptic imagery was not absent from British art in the period. For example, Eric Kennington's woodcuts designed as endpapers for T. E. Lawrence's *The Seven Pillars of Wisdom* (1926), titled *The Eternal Itch*, also explore themes of idolatry and mass hysteria as endemic to war. Kennington also carved *The War God*, a squat and malevolent figure, which he amended in 1935 to make it resemble Mussolini and exhibited at the Artists International Association Exhibition, Artists against Fascism and War, where it was titled *Mammon*.[14]

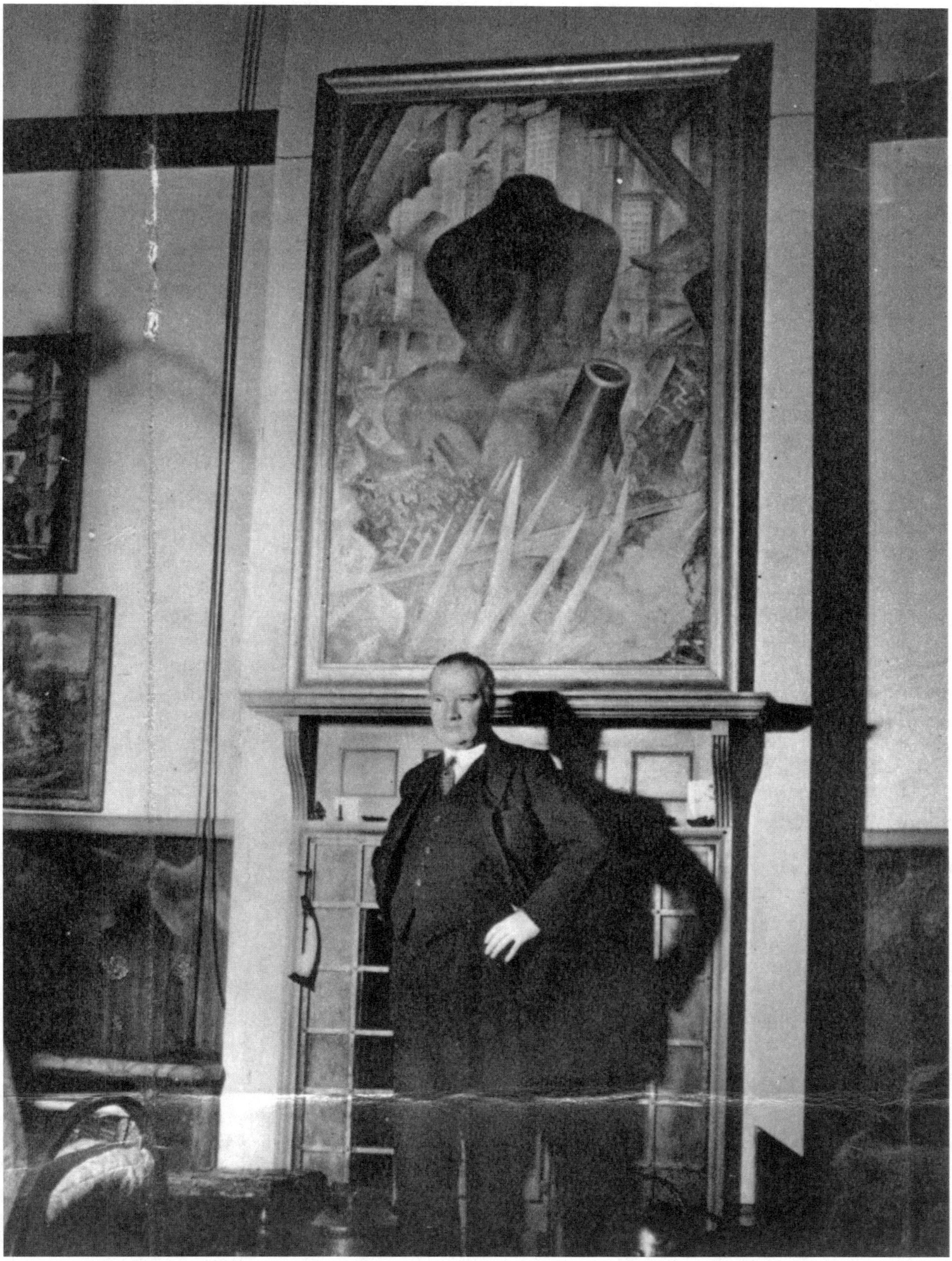

56. ***Let's Mobilise Art*****, November 1, 1939,** ***The Bystander.*** **Nevinson posing in front of** ***The Twentieth Century.***

The mid-30s was a period when artists began to organize in political forums to protest against fascism and war. In Britain, the primary organization was the Artists International Association that included artists of all persuasions from the avant-garde such as Henry Moore, Paul Nash, and Eric Gill to more established figures such as Muirhead Bone, Britain's first official war artist in 1916 and a trustee of the Imperial War Museum and the Tate. Collectivizing to represent liberty and freedom of expression gained additional impetus with the outbreak of the Spanish Civil War in 1936 and numerous artists made works of art to raise funds for the republican cause or participated in demonstrations against the government's policy of nonintervention. Nevinson, despite his standing as a war artist and the visibility of his war paintings in the 1930s, was not a participant in any of these forums.

Nevinson's absence from artists' antiwar and antifascist activism in the 1930s raises the question of the perplexity and elusiveness of his political position, in an age when it was not possible to be neutral about the pressures that faced intellectuals and artists. Among official artists of the Great War who were active in the prewar avant-garde, that is Nevinson, Wyndham Lewis, David Bomberg, and William Roberts, none was involved in organizations like the Artists International Association in the run up to the Second World War.[15] Unlike Bomberg and Roberts, however, Nevinson maintained his visibility by providing pithy copy and polemical articles for popular newspapers that extended to pronouncements on the contemporary political situation.

In the midst of economic and escalating unemployment in 1930, Nevinson called for a new national leader to address what he called the matter of national apathy in modern culture. Nevinson had a long-standing association with Futurism and Marinetti, and, in the 1920s, he had sometimes sported a black shirt, leading him to be compared to the Italian fascists.[16] In 1928 *Everybody's Weekly* claimed that Mussolini was one of his patrons.[17] His call for a great national leader could look like an endorsement of fascist politics. He concluded by demanding a British leader of "intense nationalism in reaction to the internationalism of our present day Socialists." But Nevinson's description of Mussolini was markedly satiric. He was, he said, a "rather dictatorial, theatrical braggart with few other ideals but those of Chauvinism and militarism." But despite his limitations, Mussolini had "been able to raise the vast majority of a nation into an enthusiasm which makes all the tragedy and stupidity of everyday life tolerable."[18]

Nevinson was a founder member and vice chairman of the National Society (in 1934 he chaired the organization) established in 1930 to provide an annual exhibition on behalf of artists "of every creed and outlook."[19] Its middle ground shows matched its aesthetics of consensus. Prominent members included Leon Underwood, whose circle, based in Hammersmith, extended to artists such as Henry Moore and Eileen Agar. Underwood's group published a short-lived journal, funded and edited by Agar's husband Joseph Bard, called the *Island*, with a platform of opposition to commercialism in art and the promotion of spirituality. In its fourth and last issue, Nevinson published an appraisal of modern art in England in which he denounced Marinetti as the John the Baptist of Fascism, for his deplorable chauvinism and the harmful antagonism he had provoked in the English avant-garde.[20] The same year, however, he described in an article "Italian Modern Art" for *Harper's Bazaar* "my friend" Marinetti, traced the genealogy of fascism from Futurism and discussed Boccioni, killed in the war: "the Futurist and Fascist movements owe a lot to his pugnacity and energy."[21]

It is difficult to disentangle from the evidence of Nevinson's work and writings a consistent political position. On the one hand, he published belligerent and truculent pronouncements on all aspects of contemporary culture that were often conservative and could look like endorsements of Italian Fascism. On the other hand, he was prominently associated with middle-ground art groups, even, in the case of Underwood's circle, those with a taste for romantic almost pacifist lyricism. His large scale montaged "problem pictures" are no easier to decipher. Their subject matter is melodramatic; their meanings seem superficial; their aesthetic merit is questionable.

In 1936, however, Nevinson made two contributions that align him more clearly with an antifascist position. He was a contributor to an edited collection of articles arguing against war, *The Seven Pillars of Fire*, written by a varied range of academics and intellectuals, including the architect A. E. Richardson, the feminist theologian Maude Royden, but also eccentrics such as the Marquis of Tavistock, pacifist and apologist for Hitler. Nevinson's contribution, "The Arts within this Bellicose Civilization," did not amount to a coherent intellectual argument. He stated clearly and unequivocally, however, that "Fascism has become the enemy of tolerant culture, independent intellectual thought, free speech"[22] With characteristic hyperbole, he pronounced: "I detest the tyrannies of the Soviet, American Big Business, the German Fascist, and the Italian thug."[23] He also sent *The Twentieth Century* to the 1936 exhibition De Olympiade Onder Dictatuur, held in August in Amsterdam. Abbreviated to D.O.O.D., which means "death" in Dutch, the exhibition was co-organized by De Bond van Kunstenaars ter Verdedig-ing von de Kulturele Rechter (the Association of Artists for the Defence of Cultural Rights) and the Comité de Bescherming van de Olympische Gedachte (the Committee for the Protection of the Olympic Idea) to protest against the Berlin Olympics.

Just as the Artists International Association organized Artists Against Fascism and War held in London the previous year, D.O.O.D. consisted of a section documenting the implication of Nazism for human rights, racism, children's education, the peace movement, and the status of women, and a section on the arts including literature, theater, music, and film. Works of art were separated into national sections including French artists such as Leger, Lurçat, Zadkine, and Masereel, and work from Belgium and German artists in exile. The English section was organized by the Artists International Association and included Jessica Dismorr, the émigré sculptor Laszlo Peri, Lucien Pissarro, Betty Rea, Elizabeth Watson, Cliff Rowe (all three active in the Allied Artists Association), and Carel Weight. D.O.O.D. was intended to make a case for the cultural freedoms under threat from National Socialism. The documentary material was to show the fatal destruction of culture that race theories founded in evil must lead to.[24]

Events between 1931 and 1936, including Italy's invasion of Abyssinia in 1935 and Mussolini's declaration of empire in 1936, made the issues at stake very clear. By 1935, when Nevinson first exhibited *The Twentieth Century*, the image of the dictator and the totalitarian state was fully formed. The cult of "il Duce" in Italy is usually assumed to have been inaugurated by the 1932 *Mostra dell rivoluzio fascista* in Rome where a display in twenty-three rooms set out to tell the story of the fascist revolution in Italy culminating in a *Sala de Duce*.[25] In the Soviet Union, the term *vozh'd* was first defined in dictionaries as an ideological leader, with overtones of Führer and Duce in 1935.[26] The term came to mean Nietzschean superhero, and by the mid-1930s the cult of Lenin had merged with the cult of Stalin. The visual propaganda of dictatorship, for which the myth of Mussolini provided the paradigm, made particular use of montage. Photomontages of mass rallies were often combined with enlarged images of the leader, viewed from below to emphasize his superhuman status, to which Nevinson's political allegories of 1933–35, and especially *The Twentieth Century* may be counterpoised. Where totalitarian and fascist propaganda celebrated technical proficiency and modernity through the use of photomontage or idealized superrealism, *The Twentieth Century* is painterly and confused. Where images of the fascist leader emphasized his invincibility and farsightedness, Nevinson's version of Rodin's *Thinker* is bogged down in brooding introspection.

Throughout the 1920s and 1930s, Nevinson was often paired with Jacob Epstein as artists out to "*épater le bourgeois*."[27] In the 1930s, Epstein returned to carving with a series of monumental sculptures beginning with *Genesis*, shown 1931, *Primeval Gods* (1932), *Behold the Man* (1935), *Consummatum Est* (1937), *Adam* (1939) and *Jacob and the Angel* (1942). These carvings look like a set of returns to the preoccupations of the pre-1914 work, but also like returns of the repressed. The 1930s were an era when political agendas were self-consciously pursued and taking a position on contemporary events was a necessity. It was also a period of anxieties and premonitions. In Britain these were often articulated around a fear of the return of war and apprehensions that future wars would mean aerial bombardment and invasion. It became impossible to sustain the fiction that Britain was an island fortress impregnable and invulnerable. Such anxieties were often projected into male bodies and images of masculinity. An example might be the twisted, contorted and vulnerable form of Leon Underwood's *Mindslave* (1934). There is also Eric Kennington's *War God* with its helmeted head, club, and shield, and its penetrating stare. Its priapic character with overly enlarged genitals and overdetermined markers of phallic display such as the club and serpent, suggest an excess of masculinity, a burlesque and grotesque male body. When set against the images of modern dictators, Kennington's *War God* and Epstein's gigantic almost anxious and overwrought masculine figures read as deflationary projects, emblems of masculine failure and impotence. Certainly the way Epstein's work was constantly projected into the public sphere, and often in order to be excoriated and vilified especially in the popular press, needs to be read against the new and very threatening but also preposterous images of masculinity that were increasingly projected through the bodies of fascist leaders.

In his political satires, especially *The Twentieth Century* and *Ave Homo Sapiens*, Nevinson centered his depictions on enlarged male bodies of antiheroes set in a montage of imagery including the swirling crowds of the masses. These forms were borrowed from cinema but also from the political propaganda of dictatorships, especially Mussolini and Italian Fascism. Nevinson's gigantic browbeaten and downcast male figures do not inspire confidence. Moreover, as unattractive canvases that are cursorily painted and confused, they function in a way that is similar to his war paintings from the second part of the Great War. The war work that Nevinson began to produce after 1917 has been seen as a turn away from modernism and into illustrative realism. But these are also paintings that do not offer visual pleasure to the spectator searching for an affirmation of good taste, pointing up a question about the price to be paid for good, or aesthetically satisfying, war paintings. Frank Rutter wrote about the political satires in Nevinson's 1934 exhibition that, although he granted their sincerity, "Pictorially these imaginative works may not be quite so satisfying esthetically nor so easy to understand as the artist's clean-hewn landscapes, river scenes and marines," and these works "had not yet acquired a corresponding clarity and nobility of utterance to match the seriousness of their subject matter."[28] What Rutter finds lacking in this work is expressed as failures of aesthetic satisfaction, of clarity and what he calls nobility. Nevinson's political paintings offered the spectator no visual gratification.

Throughout the 1920s and 1930s, Nevinson postured as a *bon viveur* and socialite, at the same time as he constantly complained of persecution. Nevinson's aptly titled autobiography *Paint and Prejudice* is what Ingleby terms "an unappealing mixture of self-importance and self-pity."[29] Nevinson's persona, his endless pursuit of publicity and courting of controversy, even his brief flirtation with fascism, amount to the performance of a wounded masculinity that could also be read as a parody of the paranoia and self-importance of dictators. In the end, although Nevinson's posturing and his work were ambivalent and contradictory, earning a notoriety as English modernism's "bad boy" does not add up to an image that is in any way useful for the promotion of fascism.

Notes

1. April 18, 1936.
2. October 26, 1925.
3. *Spectator*, October 19, 1934; *New Statesman*, October 20, 1934.
4. "Utterly Tired of Chaos. The Life of C. R. W. Nevinson," in *C. R. W. Nevinson, The Twentieth Century*, ed. Richard Ingleby (London: Merrell Holberton in association with the Imperial War Museum, 1999), 24.
5. October 6, 1930.
6. October 15, 1930.
7. See for example, *Daily Express*, October 3, 1930; *News Chronicle*, October 4, 1930.
8. Pamela M Fletcher, "Masculinity, Money and Modern Art: 'The Sentence of Death' by John Collier," in *English Art 1860–1914. Modern Artists and Identity*, ed. David P. Corbett and L. Perry (Manchester, UK: Manchester University Press, 2000), 84, 96–97, 99.
9. See, for example, *Manchester Guardian*, October 4, 1930.
10. *Illustrated London News*, October 4, 1930.
11. *Daily Mail*, October 6, 1930.
12. October 7, 1930.
13. August 1935, CX, 509, p. 78.
14. See the discussion in Sue Malvern, *Things to Come. Eric Kennington's "War God,"* The Henry Moore Institute, Essays on Sculpture, 33 (Leeds, UK: The Henry Moore Institute, 2001).
15. David Bomberg did visit Soviet Russia, was briefly a member of the Communist Party, and as an artist who worked extensively in Spain, a supporter of the Republican cause. Wyndham Lewis had a brief flirtation with fascism. William Roberts stayed aloof. These issues are discussed in chapter 5 of my book, *Modern Art, Britain and the Great War* (New Haven, CT: Yale University Press, 2004).
16. *World's Pictorial News*, June 9, 1923; see also *Birmingham Gazette and Express*, October 13, 1923, where it was reported that he was "leaving for Rome. His working garb already shows the traces of the Mussolini influence."
17. September 1, 1928.
18. *Daily Record and Mail*, August 26, 1930.
19. Introduction, *National Society. Painters, Sculptors, Engravers, Potters. Catalogue of the First Annual Exhibition*, Grafton Galleries, London, May 10–June 6, 1930, 5.
20. *Island*, December 1931, 114
21. March 1931.
22. Maude Royden, L. P. Jacks, A. E. Richardson, Marquis of Tavistock, Christopher Richard Wynne Nevinson, Bernard Acworth, and Bernard Denison Ross, *The Seven Pillars of Fire. A Symposium* (London: Herbert Jenkins, 1936), 186.
23. *The Seven Pillars of Fire*, 220.
24. "Het documentatie-materiaal toont aan tot welke noodlottige cultuur-vernietiging kwalijk gefundeerde rassen-theoriëen en schijn-weteschappelijke grondslagen voor een nieuwe maatschappijleer moeten leiden." Paul F. Sanders and J. J. Voskuil, "Voorwoord," *de olympiade oner dictatuur. tentoonstelling: sport, kunst, wetenschap, documenten*, Amsterdam, 1936, n.p. republished by the Amsterdam Gemeentearchief, 1996 and see Betsy Dokter and Carry van Lakerveld, eds., *Een Kunstolympiade in Amsterdam. Reconstructie van de tentoostelling D.O.O.D. 1936* (Amsterdam: Gemeentearchief, 1996).
25. Marla Stone, *The Patron State: Culture and Politics in Fascist Italy* (Princeton, NJ: Princeton University Press, 1998), 162–63.
26. See Victoria E. Bonnell, *Iconography of Power: Soviet Political Posters under Lenin and Stalin* (Berkeley and Los Angeles: University of California Press, 1997), 306.
27. See, for example, *Liverpool Courier*, February 19, 1923.
28. *Christian Science Monitor*, November 10, 1934.
29. "Utterly Tired of Chaos," 9.

Appendix

Editor's note:

The appendix is an essay written in 1925 by Sir Osbert Sitwell and represents an important re-introduction to Nevinson at a time when we tend to accept that his influence had waned. Sitwell, in a real period piece of art-historical or critical writing, previously unpublished in this form, makes no such claim; instead, he extols the merits of a great living artist, demonstrating that the transition from war to peace, from rebel to master, was now, by the first quarter of the century, complete, and part of a natural evolutionary cycle in which "art rules the artist." The essay is a personal one (though written from the standpoint of "we" and not "I") by the pen of a friend, admirer, and collector of Nevinson's work; and so it must be treated with a degree of caution. It also provides a pleasant, if sometimes meandering, commentary on the life and work of his great friend from a contemporary perspective. More importantly, it allows the reader one last chance to peruse the legend that Nevinson, with his colleagues, built up around himself during his own lifetime and which, as we have noted, fell into decline after his death. Sitwell's essay, written in 1925, goes some way toward counterbalancing this heavily weighted, though dubious and bludgeoning, argument. It also introduces many of the points raised in the earlier essays of the anthology brushing, as it does, against the subjects of his parents, his "modern" eclecticism, his abilities as a printmaker, the jealousy and violence that characterized the remainder of his career, his contempt for the Royal Academy, the values of Futurism and Cubism, his longing for a positive modernity and indeed, the realization that, in 1925, the artist was far from finished. To capture the true sentiments as expressed by Sitwell I have reproduced the entire draft of the essay, including mistakes, corrections, alterations, and later additions. In order to do this I have applied the following methods to reproduce the document as faithfully as possible. The finished piece appeared in *Contemporary British Artists: C. R. W. Nevinson* ed. Albert Rutherston (New York: Charles Scribner's Sons, 1925). This early draft is housed at the Harry Ransom Humanities Research Center, Austin, Texas and is reproduced with their permission.

A word that has been scored out, or otherwise deleted from the text, appears in square brackets [ ].

Words or expressions that have been inserted appear in round brackets ( ).

(Sic) simply denotes an acknowledged mistake in the original text.

Where one word has been scored out to make way for a different one, I have included the original in the text, then followed it with the replacement words inside { }.

* Denotes brackets in the original text.

Where a longer explanation is required I have added endnotes.

C. R. W. Nevinson

Osbert Sitwell

It is a curious phenomenon associated with the public taste that one of the most evident of Mr. Nevinson's virtues as an artist is precisely that [one] which has done the least to make him popular. The quality to which we allude is his curiosity, his love of aesthetic and technical discovery; an interest rather rare among English artists of any period. Dr. Haveloch (*sic*) Ellis, in the "Dance of Life," has suggested that art and poetry are always in the nature of exploration, and that it is not without significance the great age of poetry in England should have been coincident with the great age of (geographical) discovery. If this is true, it is, we are afraid, equally certain that the British Public prefers an explorer of the Antartic to a painter or writer. Yet those who are fond of tales of adventure should especially welcome Mr. Nevinson; for his career has ever been one of discovery. But then this painter comes of an adventurous stock, for his father is H. W. Nevinson, the famous writer and war-correspondent, whose experiences in Africa, Ireland, Russia, and even in England, are ever a delight to the reader; while his mother, whose name is as well known as her husband's and son's, has also made for herself, by her active interest {part}in politics and Poor-Law Reform, a career that has been scarcely less adventurous {interesting}.

Mr. Nevinson's existence, apart from his life as a soldier, of which we find so many records of an undeniable truth and beauty, has ever been an exciting one. A born explorer, he was the first English painter to be influenced by those waves of experiment which were passing over the Continent, (though his) alert mind, [however], prevented him from ever being caught in an artistic cul-de-sac. [and] Just as he was the first English painter to be influenced by Futurism, so, when he had absorbed the virtue that was in it, was he the first to reject it as a final doctrine; the first English artist to adopt, and absorb Cubism, so was he the first to discard that part of it which was of no value to his art. But if the latter should at any time again demand the hard schooling of Cubism, he would, whether he wished it or not, once more adopt it; for art rules the artist. Thus it is ever unsafe to prophesy about Mr. Nevinson's work, or to label him with any definite ticket. As soon as we had {have} concluded that this artist has passed into a realistic stage, he becomes abstract, or fantastic; and the only statement we can positively advance about him is that, whatever the phase through which he is passing, it is one which will be fully realised, and which will produce work of first rate interest.

Without being in absolute agreement with Mr. Walter Sichert's (*sic*) dictum that "The Public is Always Right," we must admit [it] that while it is extremely creditable to Mr. Nevinson to be an explorer, the fact that each phase through which he passes has won its own especial body of fervent admirers is equally honourable to the public. For the general public does not like change[s] in art or in much else. Anything to which through long suffering it has become accustomed—a music hall joke or even the income-tax is, in the end, perfection. And the public likes {prefers} the artist (,too,) to remain in a phase of his art to which it has become tolerant. But to be ever forced to repeat himself is to the artist death, for his art is comparable to his own body, in which every fibre, every tissue is totally destroyed and renewed by nature within the space of each successive seven years: while, if this metamopphosis {metamorphosis} is in any way impeded, the body becomes sickly and unhealthy. Only the subtle permeation, therefore (,) of personality, which remains unchanging and inimitable, through every pore of every canvas he paints should assure us that the late and early work of a painter are by the same hand. Indeed the most, and perhaps only, helpful advice that can be given to a young artist is "Never do what your friends and admirers expect of you—which will [inevitably] be the same thing, over and over again!"

To the test we have mentioned, Mr. Nevinson's work invariably responds; for however unlike one of his pictures is to another, we can never fail to recognise by whom it was painted. Each phase through which he has developed is unmistakably his own. But to the true artist, each successive aspect of his art, though to be cherished by him as a separate blossom, is in realty only valuable to him for the residue of experience with which, as itself withers away, it endows him and, beyond him, all art. Each phase, when dead, is absorbed in him, is one more sectional ring that has gone to build-up the tree-trunk; while, at the same time, his own life, when it is ended, becomes one more circle in the greater trunk of the Tree of Art. And as a result of this process, just as the human body is said to examplify in itself, during the short years between birth and maturity (,) every successive stage which the race of men has, [been] through (,) so many million years and with such difficulty (,) conquered so, through spiritual inheritance, can the young artist with ease[1] make use in his art of those discoveries which it took earlier painters a lifetime to exhaust finally. Thus, with a little preliminary trouble, the young artist may perhaps be able to produce effects which cost Raphael or (Ingres), Manet or Cézanne, a life-time to discover. And here enters in the danger of "Facility"—for since those effects will never be so much felt as by those who first explored them, it is no use for the young artist to be content (illegible) {satisfied} with them or their variations. He may only make use of them to that extent to which they enable him to wring from Art fresh and unexpected concessions. This is an inexorable law; and it is often, therefore, rather an advantage to the artist if he lacks quickness, and is slow in his reactions.

There can be no doubt, if we look for example at "le Port," the earliest work here reproduced, that Mr. Nevinson started with a natural facility and quickness of re-action, which might have constituted a danger. But since {because}he was also an artist who lived in and for his painting, it became, on the contrary, of the greatest advantage to him. For since he is never content with his achievement, and is always striving after some far, and to many indiscernible, peak, his natural talent, fully made use of, offered him a good start; and enabled him to make explorations (,) that might have taken up a life-time, within a more reasonable period.

Besides passing through such ordinary and necessary apprenticeship (sic) as the Slade School and various art schools at Paris (offered) this painter has inflicted on himself schooling after schooling. Nor has he been afraid to benefit by them (,) any more than by his natural ability: no slight triumph in days when many an artist seems bent only on disclaiming those gifts of vision and hand with which nature endowed him, and on blotting-out the craft which it took him many years to acquire. This gesture of giving up and forgetting, which is so popular in the studios of to-day, is not an act of rebellion (which in art is always to the good, and is indeed the tradition of it) as is so often supposed, but one of sheer silly abnegation, comparable to that of Essau in selling his birthright for a "mess of pottage." Incidentally the renunciation is one infinitely more perilous to the artist than he can ever have imagined, and has everywhere led to a rebellion on the part of his public. For the public now insist on taking part in every performance. This phenomenon is what Mr. Wyndham Lewis has elsewhere termed "The Revolt of the Spectator." In abandoning his art-inheritance of drawing and of surface, and of traditional technique, the naïve is in reality only opening the door to the impostor! He is giving his country over to an invasion of rebel-spectators, who believe that "they can do that sort of thing too," and who, seizing paintbrushes from their masters as the rebel slaves under Spartacus seized [their] weapons from the Romans, have proceeded to lay waste the art-galleries of Paris and London. And if the naïve thus insists in putting himself on a level with the knave, it is easy to hazard who {which} will gain most advantage from the transaction. Because it is as simple an affair for the amateur to throw away a technique he has never acquired as it is for the genuine artist to divest himself of one which has cost him twenty most tedious years to amass: and the gain of time (in which the artist was learning his craft)* and of money to the impostor is obvious.

The gradual accumulation of a technique which he can squander in his old age is to the painter as important as is the building up of an old-age pension to the working man. For alas! there must come to every artist who lives long enough a time when fire, imagination, even genius, will fail him and only the technique acquired through these will be of any avail. Then technique comes to the rescue of the ageing artist (,) making his work of as much interest by reason of its method, as it was originally by (his) intense creative ability. And when he dies, this technique is bequeathed to his spiritual heirs and successors, a rich inheritance of acquired knowledge and applied sensibility. This fact it is which makes the long discipline of a technique so necessary to the artist, and in Mr. Nevinson we find a painter who has benefited by many schoolings and has never sought to shirk the problem before him. And, since he has never sold his birthright, it is possible to find in his work traces of many earlier artists, of Cézanne, of Manet and through him of Gaza {Goya} [and] of Renoir, and through him of Watteau and a host of earlier painters, French and Italian. But this inheritance is latent, as they {it} should be, in the eye and hand of the painter, as his physical inheritance is manifest in his own form. They {it} should not be exterior to him; and in Mr. Nevinson these traces never obtrude, are never allowed to harass our vision by a self-conscious parade.

The academic painting of the mid-nineteenth century in England had so entirely lost touch with art in running after sentiment, the Pre-Raphaelite School (,) and such painters as Burne-Jones (,) had so lost themselves in the mists of antiquity and the denser fog of Ruskin's political aestheticism, that it was with a feeling of overwhelming relief that modern art-lovers turn/ed toward the works and gospel of Cézanne, or toward such naïveté as that of the (Douanier) Rousseau. Ever since the discovery of the Post-Impressionists, any other quality than theirs have {has} been at rather a discount in a painter. Intelligence, even, has come to be regarded rather as a drawback, as in the nature of a hindrance to pure painting. If this be a fault, it is one, we fear, of which it is difficult to acquit Mr. Nevinson, for behind the eye of this artist a keen and vigorous intelligence is most evidently at work: while [,] often (,) except in his purely lyrical compositions, there is to be detected a sub-flavour of satire, though never, we think, of caricature—a quality more common in modern painting. Yet as a painter born, it is neither with his head nor his hand that the {this} artist works, but with his heart—his emotions—from a natural interest in colour and love of form.

There are perhaps few artists of established reputation who are as young as Mr. Nevinson, and few indeed to whom their art has already brought such varied gifts. As a lithographer, etcher, and water-colourist he has broken new ground with an equal degree of persistence (,) and with the same success that has attended him as a painter. The unusual combination of energy and diverse talent which is his, and the constantly varying fruit of them, have made of Mr. Nevinson a public figure, winning him a continual volley of enthusiastic praise. Alas (!) [though,] since the appearance of a new star in the heavens sometimes dims, or even eclipses, the refulgence of another longer established, the arrival and constant re-arrival of Mr. Nevinson have also earned him an equivalent bombardment of abuse. It is, we believe, [supposed] commonly (held) that personal attacks on a man (,) when they are the obvious fruit of jealousy, are a subtle form of flattery, and one by which the object of all the turmoil should not allow himself to be harassed unduly. But, as a matter of fact, such onslaughts may—if the victim is sensitive (and if he is not he should not be an artist)*—by bothering him, seriously interfere with his work. This Mr. Nevinson has never allowed them to do, but has continued to follow his own pioneer-path, unperturbed and impenitent, if slightly disgusted! Sometime, however, he has allowed himself to hit-back, and because the gift of hard-hitting was also bestowed upon him (presumably by the Wicked Fairy at his Christening)* the public only remembers the very effective knock-outs (s) he has delivered {administered}, and not the endless and fidgeting attacks that occasioned them. His success, therefore, has made of kind, gentle, and rather melancholy (though witty), Mr. Nevinson an almost legendary figure of violence. For since round him the whirlwind has so often spun its boisterous course, it has endowed him in the eyes of many who have never seen him with an almost heroic quality of turbulence, - a quality which Nature never included with her other gifts to him. And many an admirer of his work (,) who has been led up trembling to meet the fiery of leonine artist of popular imagination, has come away from the encounter as much astonished as must have been Androcles at his unexpectedly genial reception from that other lion!

Although modern of the moderns in his art, it seems occasionally as if Mr. Nevinson were an anachronism. Let us turn to any of his portraits ((to our mind) the most interesting of his later phases),[2] or to his pastel "Head of a Pretty Girl." Here (,) when most young painters are resolutely flying from prettiness—so resolutely that the "ugly-ugly" threatens to become as wearisome as the "pretty-pretty," the sardine-tin as desolating as the chocolate-box—we find him alone in facing it as a problem. For prettiness is an artistic problem and one that most artists of the last fifty years in France, and twenty in England, have been content to shirk or altogether ignore. Renoir, almost alone of the masters of the last half-century, faced the question boldly; and, as we have before suggested, there is more that a little of the great Frenchman's influence to be found in Mr. Nevinson's work. Over and over again Renoir conquered prettiness, in his early period, in the "Two Waltzes (,)" or (in) the "Parapluie" of the (Lang) bequest, and even in those amazing pictures of his old age, in which the figures, incidentally, bear so much resemblance to the heroic forms in the last paintings of Titian. (Compare, for example, that Titian in the Mond bequest with a late Renoir).[3] In the footsteps of the great French master, then, Mr. Nevinson is attempting to grapple with the dangerous and most perplexing artistic problem of prettiness. His portraits are usually portraits of pretty women; seldom are his models chosen for their possession of a sepia-complexion, of an incipient strabismus, which "gives interest to the model," or of a nervous twitch the rhythm of which is difficult to prison in paint. When however he takes a type divergent from that of prettiness, or in any way unusual he is equally successful with it. His painting "Head of a Poet," is remarkable in its characterisation and force. It is not merely "imitated"—the word which Mr. {M}. Ambrose Volland {Vollard} tells us Cézanne was for ever using of those who only wished for actual reality. Yet, on the whole, Mr. Nevinson boldly chooses models that are pretty; and even ordinary. He is not like that other modern artist, whom I once heard remark to a friend, as he showed him the portrait he was doing of a lady who was {quite} unconscious of the nature of the fascination who {she} exercised over him (,) "You see my object. I want to bring out the essential coarse brutality of the face."

Yet is {if} there is about Mr. Nevinson's portraits nothing of caricature, there is undoubtedly a subtle distortion, a wringing out of hidden truth that makes the portrait more absolute in its veris-similitude (sic) than if it were merely "imitated." The painter is undaunted by the fear of prettiness, and, since fear paralyses the artist, the absence of it has given him the courage to go forward and seek a solution of the questions before him. There are still those however, who, standing in front of one of these portraits, refuse to understand them, saying finally, "Well, at any rate it isn't at all my idea of her!" The retort to such an objection is that which the late Professor Ker is said to have made to another eminent literary figure, when {whom}, following a celebrated judicial lead, we shall, for purposes of anonymity, refer to as "Mr. A." Both these two distinguished men were staying in a country-house. Before dinner they collected in a drawing-room, of which the chief ornament, placed on a central table, and unassumingly mounted in rococo (curly) [of] gilded (illegible), was a stuffed flamingo! "Mr. A." gazed at it, and then asked to what species the bird belonged. "It's a flamingo" he was informed by his host. "A flamingo," said "Mr. A." rather testily, "Well, it's not at all my idea of a flamingo," and the northern voice of Professor Ker murmured, behind him, "No (my dear) "A.," No, but it's God's idea of a flamingo!" Thus it is, too, with Mr. Nevinson's portraits.

It may well be that the very quality which enables him to tackle prettiness is the one that has also made him a master of the subtle effects of grotesque humour {horror}. And that such he is, his war-pictures have proved over and over again. Prettiness is at the same time the opposite and complementary quality of the grotesque! While the reason that "prettiness" has been brought down in the world to its present significance as a term of aesthetic abuse (,) is that it has been treated by painters, who, unable to grasp its nature, have unwittingly allowed its complement (,) the grotesque, to break through suddenly into their work, destroying its unity. This makes (evident a) lapse of logic. It is as though some artist (,) who believed in the (use of) distortion of {in} drawing, became for a moment realistic, in the drawing of an arm or a foot: or, equally, as if some very realistic draughtsman had (made) an unexpected break into [a] distortion, in the middle of an obtruse {otherwise} typical drawing. It is (,) in fact (,) like the obvious delusion which suddenly betrays the lunatic (,) [who is] perfectly sane on (e)very other point. Indeed the drawings executed by lunatics suffer from this very deficiency. We are often told (,) by certain doctors with and aversion for {from} modern art, that the paintings and drawings of lunatics are akin to it. It is possible, of course, that there are lunatics, like the late Richard Du{a}dd, who are also geniuses in their own line; but an examination of the drawings and paintings of the ordinary Asylum-hand will soon prove to anyone that the work which the average (if we may use the word in this connection)* lunatic turns out much nearer ([in quality]) to that annually displayed in great quantities on the walls of Burlington House, than to paintings displayed in more modern exhibitions. Lunatics show no grasp of the possibilities of distortion in drawing; they will not sacrifice superficial reality to composition, or diminish {simplify} in any way. Detail is everything to them: and an academy picture is their (ambition). Usually they avoid "morbid" subjects and choose some cheerful and (,) at the same time (,) sentimental one. All is going beautifully, and Burlington House is within sight almost, when, alas, some lapse of logic occurs in the work, and its prettiness becomes more gruesome than any Inquisition Scene by Gaza {Goya}. For to grasp the nature of the grotesque, it is necessary to understand prettiness, and the very genius that empowered Gaza {Goya}to paint his terrible studies of the "togged-out" old Queen, Maria-(Luisa)—to draw his awe-inspiring bull-fights and capriccios, also allowed him to revel in painting {depicting} the prettiness and fêtes champêtres and in the design of those gay and delightful Tapestries that hang in the Royal Palace at Madrid.

Now Mr. Nevinson, another master of the grotesque, never allows it to peep through into his portraits, nor by mere "imitation" does he [make them] transform them into life-less waxworks, another peril to the portraitist. In these days portrait-painting has been brought into disrepute either by cheap trickery or through a slavish attempt to copy nature. Yet it must be remembered that even such a great modern master, and revolutionary, as Cézanne thought portraiture perhaps the highest aim of art. And if the painter would consider the curious problem of the waxworks in shop-windows, he might learn something of interest (to him), for the often perfectly executed wax models of pretty ladies, so frighteningly displayed behind the glass slabs of hair-dresser or dress-maker, are worth a short examination. While these models, of life-size, are as pretty as such things can be (,) and of (an) extreme realism (,) it is these very attributes that make of them so awe-inspiring a spectacle. The absolute lack of movement and breathing, never to be found except in (the) dead or cataleptic, contrasts horribly with their extremely "life-like" rendering. To come upon them suddenly, if we were fortunate enough to be unaccustomed to them, would be to see so many coy corpses coquetting in a shop-window. This quality, indeed, imparts to them all the horror that invests the death of Bramwell Brontë, who died standing up! This it is, too, which explains why a bad painter's portrait of a pretty woman ("such an excellent likeness")* is so often akin to the works shown at Madame Tussaud's. For the realistic artistic should only aim at appearing realistic, and not {moreover} at realism itself. This [it is indeed that] Mr. Nevinson (fully) comprehends, and his portraits are even infused with vitality and life, however life-like he may make them appear to us.

Though each phase (,) through which Mr. Nevinson, in the course of his ceaseless explorations (,) has passed, is an interesting one, yet the very variety of his gifts, the very quantity of his experiments, has tended to give to his life, from the point of view of the onlooker, a false perspective. As, in one of the conventional alleys leading on to the stage of the 17th century, the multiplicity and arrangement of the statues made the vista one of unnatural length, seeming to the audience who sat in front of it to stretch to at least five times its real extent, so the many phases of Mr. Nevinson's art make his artistic career appear to cover a great many more years than it does in reality. We are apt, thus, to forget that he is still at the beginning of it. How many years it seems since his first Futurist investigations; and what an immense period must have elapsed since some of us who were then in France happened to find in some (various) old illustrated papers left about in our billets, the reproductions of work by a young painter who was the first—and to many remains the only artist able by his allied qualities of eye and mind, to translate modern warfare into terms of art and truth (veracity and art).

It must remain an odd coincidence that in times when every artist (each painter) was more free than ever before to sacrifice the last vestige of the facts before him to the composition of a broad decorative treatment or of an almost abstract pattern, an artist should have arisen, who, without sacrificing these to a false realism, was yet able to enliven them with the deadly power of truth. It is possible that one of the things which helped Mr. Nevinson to accomplish his fine and unique work of this period, was the long and severe schooling of cubism, to which, at the time amid much derision, he had submitted himself. The necessity and practice of condensation which he had learned there gave him the necessary power. In his war-pictures was to be found no empty, corpse-fed and sentimental lyricism, no primroses bloomed from his trenches. No pale pre-Raphaelite men, crowned with tin-helmets as the Greek-athletes with their straw sun-guards, were allowed to look out from them, "alone and palely loitering." Nor (,) on the other hand (,) did he reduce warfare to an abstract and rather unmeaning arrangement of planes and cones, tokens of men and guns, transmuted into one indistinguishable mass, beneath (smoke) that creaked through the air (,) as if cut out in {from} flat yellow cardboard and sent (whirling) by a hurricane. These conventions, of which the former, as being more sentimental and less original, is undoubtedly the most trying {most tedious}, were pitfalls for many artists of genuine talent. But in Mr. Nevinson's pictures we are given the whole business of modern warfare. And that/this is a rare achievement becomes very evident when we consider that (,) of all subjects, war, as it is now carried on, must be the most alien and antipathetic to the artist! For the artist lives for construction, and not destruction: while war is, and has been for the last century such a mad thing that, when captured in a drawing, as by Gaza {Goya} the spectator is at first inclined to lay the blame (up) on the artist, to conclude that the artist, instead of the thing pictured, was {is} mad!

It was not always thus. To Ucello {Uccello}, for instance, a medieval battlefield offered the most perfect of all subjects, only comparable to the *bals masqués* of the 18th Century. The war was an affair of tender sentiment and fancy-dress; the scenes of parting between the knight and his lady were emotional, but since no one was likely to be injured, they were scenes of pleasurable sentiment, given a halo of romance to those who indulged [in] them. The battlefield was fluttering with plumes, pennons and oriflamme(s), and dancing with little miniature suns (,) thrown back into the air by the cunning {curving} surfaces of cuirass, visor and gauntlet, while the constant shifting of pattern and colour added to the scene all the fascination of watching a kaleidoscope. Death was a remote, and at the same time a personal, contingency for those engaged in battle, aimed at on(c)e opponent by another with whom he could struggle. Both were equally human and honourable: and one {each} might even make his enemy laugh and talk, in the very heat of battle. In fact the mediaeval battleground appears to us as a transcendentalised prize-fight; except (that) it was (at once) less dangerous (to be the participants) and more interesting to watch {to the onlooker}.

But, with the discoveries of gunpowder, war ceased to be this chivalrous {chivalresque} affair. The attractive, swaggering side of battle, which had led men to regard it as a welcome opportunity to "show off"—to adopt for it special plumage {plumes} like the use that {those which} the male-birds of certain species develop at the season of their courting—gradually began to fade, and has by now altogether disappeared. Death became [new] even {ever} more abstract, until finally {now} it is aimed impersonally at a microscopically small unit from a vast distance. War thus became (,too,) an even {ever} more difficult subject for the painter: one, perhaps, with which no artist could be successful who lacked a subtle sense of pictorial satire. In the 300 years before the last war, the only artists whose war-scenes are interesting are Callott and Gaza, {Goya} who (invariably) underline the contrasts of war; the {its}fearful penalty and ludicrous aim {lack} of purpose: while the battle—(field) [pictures] of such good painters as Casanova (the third) MichelAngelo, (Salvator Rosa), and such bad ones as Lady Butler, lack interest, because seen through the rosy mists of optimism and false romance.

This ability to realise scenes of horror, and pin them down, is found in the work of Mr. Nevinson, as in that of Gaza {Goya}. Yet it is even more difficult now to find a satisfactory convention for war, than it was in Gaza's {Goya's} time—even if the very extent and monotony of the "Great War," made it a little more impressive.{,} [But, as regards, "picturesqueness"] the relation between the Peninsular and the Great War as wars (in this), is (about) the same as between Crippen and Landru as murderers.

This realisation of great horror, recorded with intense feeling but without sentimentality, is the quality that we find in Mr. Nevinson's war-period pictures. Let us examine "La Patrie," where each man in his torture is Everyman: for physical suffering, though not mental, makes all men alike, whether the least or the most intelligent. This we can see for ourselves (,) easily enough, in any street: for whenever we see the face of a man who has lost an arm, even before we notice his deprivation, we are reminded by his expression of some friend who has undergone the same loss. A lengthy period of identical suffering has incised the same lines on both faces (,) however unlike in their original mould: in each case the torn nerves have told the brain the same story. And how alike facially are all hunchbacks, and all dwarfs! Any hunchback we see hobbling along will [for some] resemble Richard III in the cast of his countenance (,) more than (he resembles any) normally-made men: While the Velasquez dwarfs might be the very fathers of those we see in the streets of Spanish towns to-day. Similarly the eye and cheek of those afflicted with consumption burn with the same fever: to such an extent that we often hear someone say casually about an invalid "he looks like a consumptive!"—without comprehending the full story of the agony denoted by this remark. And in this tragic summing-up of the debris of war—La Patrie—the unshaven men lying on their stretchers, suffering or dying at the hand of the same cruel and intolerable folly, reveal faces that are notched and dented into masks of pain. The rigidity of death is already asserting itself in some of the forms, their hands are already coffin-cold, though clenched in suffering. Through the open door in the background, the pyramid of a man's updrawn knees under a blanket is seen being carried in by the stretcher-bearers, one more unit of disablement or death, borne into this enormous cavern full of writhing or too-motionless bodies; When the man is (laid) down, and his countenance gradually shapes itself in the gloom, it will be visible as one more of those bleached {bearded} masks of tragedy, indistinguishable from those others that lie around it on all sides, pallidly illuminated by the grey light that creeps through the two windows.

That was one side of the war—a side which almost alone of modern artists, Mr. Nevinson had the eye, skill, and courage to depict. But in his "Column on the March" we are given an even more difficult and daring conception. Here we have all that is left of the romantic part of war, the megalomaniac quality of it, the Great War, which was fought in more places, cost more living {LIVES}, wrought more ruin, and was more expensive (,) than any other war in history. The column stretches on for ever: Here we have the endless tramping of feet, endless sky above and road beneath, endless men bent to a task without purpose, endless waste. The column stretches on forever; yet we know that one or two shells would disperse it utterly and for ever {all time}! And another column (,) that would seem the same, would step into its place. For war is the great example of equality in working, forcing all men into the same uniform, giving them the same task, (and) the same food upon which to perform them.

The treatment of this picture is most interesting, the painting of the column bold and rhythmic in the extreme. The soft thud of the men's feet as they march along the road can almost be caught by our ears, and we can almost see the shadows on the cobbles moving as they march.

Taking these two pictures as typical of Mr. Nevinson's war-pictures, we might feel that he had here given us all that we could ask of an artist still young in years. So complete was the artistic convention that he had invented for his subject, so realized was it, that to many it must have seemed as though (,) with this period of his art (,) his progress would end. But no sooner has the genuine artist conquered one form or (one) medium, that he bigns (sic) to strive after another. So it was with Mr. Nevinson. There is, for example, the "Office Window" which the artist executed in 1917, and which has always seemed to us to reveal for the first time a new quality of loveliness.

The vista through the open window is very three-divisional, and through the various shafts that are sunk like valleys {wells} between the high (brown) buildings, of which only the top windows, flat roofs, and gables are visible to us, float[s] up the unmistakable voices of London. Down there in the streets the song would be fragmentary and broken-up; but when the whole chorus rings out echoing among these roof-tops, the deep-toned and angry roaring, so vocal, so different to the strident cries of the South, or the metallic and Edisonised voices of the Transatlantic cities, can never be forgotten. But even if this leonine uproar was not here to guide us, there could be no mistaking the identity of the prospect which the window discloses. The angles and curves of pale blue smoke, those cylindrical chimneypots that turn in the wind with the sound of a ghost in chains and clanging {clanking} armour, the black shadows and grey lights, the telegraph-wires for ever intensify {intersecting} the line of vision and delicately framing-in new vistas, even the rather worn tassel of the blind, all proclaim the name of their native city.

Indeed this window is as much a window looking into the soul of the artist (,) as onto to (the) London Streets {streets}. Here we can see the power and the energy and emotion that have enabled him to accomplish so much in a few short years, and will undoubtedly empower him to do more. We wonder what he will do (?) and {And} then remember that with Mr. Nevinson it is useless to prophesy. Only, if we may for a minute wear the mantle, we should foretell, that contrary to so much expectation, the Mr. Nevinson of the grotesque and fantastic pencil is not laid to {at} rest, and that (t)his ghost will one day again cause a considerable commotion having grown stronger and more substantial from the realistic and material phases in which he has hidden himself for the last few years.

Osbert Sitwell, January, 1925.

Notes

1. In this draft "with ease" is circled, though not deleted or altered.

2. The words "to our minds" was inserted here as were the outer brackets.

3. These brackets were added later.

Selected Bibliography

Abbott, C., and Anthony Bertram, eds. *Poet and Painter: Being the Correspondence Between Gordon Bottomley and Paul Nash, 1910–1946.* London: Oxford University Press, 1955.

Aldington, R., et al. "The Futurist Manifesto." Letters to the Editor, *Observer*, June 14, 1914.

American Art News, October 29, 1921.

American Heritage Dictionary of the English Language. Fourth Edition. Boston: Houghton Mifflin, 2000.

Anderson, B. *Imagined Communities: Reflections on the Origin and Spread of Nationalism.* London and New York: Verso, 1983. Revised and reprinted 1992.

Apollonio, U., ed. *Futurist Manifestoes.* Translated by Robert Brain, R. W. Flint, J. C. Higgitt, and Caroline Tisdall. New York: Viking Press, 1973.

"Art: C. R. W. Nevinson." *Nation*, December 8, 1920.

"Artist's War Cry, An." *Observer*, April 13, 1919.

Austin, J. L. "Performative Utterances." In *The Norton Anthology of Theory and Criticism*, general editor, Vincent B. Leitch. New York: W. W. Norton, 2001, 1430–42.

Baron, W. *Perfect Moderns: A History of the Camden Town Group* Aldershot, UK: Ashgate, 2000.

———. *Sickert.* London: Phaidon, 1973.

Beechey, J. "C. R. W. Nevinson: A Controversial Modernist." *Lancet*, January 15, 2000.

Bell, Q., and Stephen Chaplin, "The Ideal Home Rumpus." *Apollo*, October 1964.

———. "Rumpus Revived." *Apollo*, January 1966.

Benjamin, W. "The Work of Art in the Age of Mechanical Reproduction," in *Illuminations*, translated by Harry Zohn, and edited by Hannah Arendt. New York: Schocken Books, 1969.

Bennett, A. *The Journals.* ed. F. Swinnerton. Harmondsworth, UK: Penguin, 1971. First published in 1885. In the United States it was called *Slum Stories of London.*

Bergson, Henry. *Matter and Memory.* Authorized translation of *Matière et memoire 6* by Nancy Margaret Paul and W. Scott Palmer. London: Swan, Sonnenschein, 1891.

Bing, S. *Artistic America, Tiffany Glass and Art Nouveau.* Paris, 1896. Reprint Cambridge, MA: MIT Press, 1970.

Birmingham Gazette and Express, October 13, 1923

Black, J. "A Curious, Cold Intensity: C. R. W. Nevinson as a War Artist, 1914–1918." In *C. R. W. Nevinson: The Twentieth Century*, edited by Richard Ingleby, et al. London: Merrell Holberton in association with the Imperial War Museum, 1999. An exhibition catalog.

———. "Neither Beasts, nor Gods, But Men': Constructions of Masculinity and the Image of the British Soldier (or "Tommy") in the First World War Art of: C. R. W. Nevinson (1889–1946); Eric H. Kennington (1888–1960) and Charles Sargeant Jagger (1885–1934)." PhD diss., University College, London, 2003.

Black, J., Michael J. K. Walsh, Chris Adams, and Jon Wood. *Blasting the Future! Vorticism in Britain 1910–1920.* London: Philip Wilson, 2004.

Blind Man: Independent's Number, April 10, 1917.

Bonnell, V. E. *Iconography of Power: Soviet Political Posters under Lenin and Stalin.* Berkeley and Los Angeles: University of California Press, 1997.

Brex, T. "Old Masters and Modern Humbug." *Daily Mail*, June 30, 1914.

Brookfarmer, C. "Futile-ism. Or, All Cackle and No Osses." *New Age* 15, no. 7 (June 18, 1914).

Bullen, J. B. ed. *Post-Impressionists in England.* London: Routledge, 1988.

Burlington Magazine, April 1987.

"Buzzers, Whistlers, Gurglers and Roarers. Terrifying instruments with which Luigi Russolo's Futurist band will accompany Signor Marinetti's forthcoming lecture on noise music at the Coliseum" (photograph). *Daily Express*, London, June 11, 1914.

"C. R. W. Nevinson." *Antiques and The Arts Weekly*, February 11, 2000.

"C. R. W. Nevinson: Practical Modernist." *Christian Science Monitor* (n.d.).

"C. R. W. Nevinson's New York Show." *Tribune*, November 14, 1920.

Cannan, G. *Mendel: A Story of Youth.* London: T. Fisher Unwin, 1916.

Carey, F., Anthony Griffiths, and Stephen Coppel. *Avant-Garde British Printmaking: 1914–1960.* London: British Museum, 1990.

Carrieri, R. *Futurism.* Trans. Leslie van Rensselaer White. Milan: Edizioni del Milione, 1963.

Carrington, N. *Carrington: Paintings, Drawings and Decorations.* London: Thames & Hudson, 1980.

Carrington, N., ed. *Mark Gertler: Selected Letters.* London: Rupert Hart-Davis, 1965.

Causey, A. "Wyndham Lewis and History Painting in the later 1930s." In *Wyndham Lewis and the Art of War*, edited by David Peters Corbett. Cambridge: Cambridge University Press, 1998.

Cavalcade, May 31, 1947.

Christian Science Monitor, June 9, 1919.

Christian Science Monitor, June 16, 1920.

Christian Science Monitor, November 10, 1934.

Christie, A. *Murder is Easy.* London: Collins, 1939.

Clough, R. T. *Futurism: The Story of a Modern Art Movement. A New Appraisal.* Philosophical Library, 1961. Reprint New York: Greenwood Press, 1969.

Coady, R. "The Ineps." *Soil*, July 1917.

Coady, R. to Jean Crotti, published in *Soil*, December 1916.

Corbett, D. P. " 'Grief with a Yard-Wide Grin': War and Wyndham Lewis's Tyros." In *Wyndham Lewis and the Art of Modern War*, ed. David Peters Corbett. Cambridge: Cambridge University Press, 1998.

———. *The Modernity of English Art, 1914–30.* Manchester, UK: Manchester University Press, 1997.

Cork, R. *A Bitter Truth: Avant-Garde Art and the Great War.* London: Yale University Press, 1994.

———. *David Bomberg.* London: Tate Gallery, 1988.

Corn, W. *The Great American Thing*. Berkeley and Los Angeles: University of California Press, 1999.

Crawford Flitch, J. E. *The Great War: Fourth Year, by C. R. W. Nevinson*. London: Grant Richards, 1918.

D'Acierno, P. "The Manifesto as Text," in *Comparative Literary History as Discourse. In Honor of Anna Balakian* ed. Mario J. Valdes, Daniel Javitch and A. Owen Aldridge. (Bern: Peter Lang, 1992).

Daily Express, February 25, 1915.

Daily Express, May 21, 1919.

Daily Express, March 1, 1930.

Daily Express, October 3, 1930.

Daily Herald, September 28, 1920.

Daily Mail, October 6, 1930.

Daily Mail, October 8, 1946, and *Scotsman*, October 8, 1946.

Daily News and Leader, September 28, 1920.

Daily Record and Mail, August 26, 1930.

Daily Sketch, February 16, 1927.

Daily Telegraph, November 24, 1933.

Dangerfield, G. *Strange Death of Liberal England*. London: University of Ottawa Press, 1935).

De Villers, J-P. *Le Premier manifeste du futurisme. Édition critique avec, en facsimilé, le manuscript original de F. T. Marinetti*. Ottawa: Éditions de l'Université d'Ottawa, 1986.

Denvir, B. *The Café Royalists: An Exhibition of Café Royal Artists*. London: Eyre & Spottiswoode, 1956.

Doherty, C. "Nash, Nevinson and Roberts at War: A Catalogue Raisonne of first World War Paintings, Drawings and Prints by Paul Nash, C. R. W. Nevinson and William Roberts." PhD diss., University of Madison, Wisconsin, 1989.

Dokter, B., and Carry van Lakerveld, eds. *Een Kunstolympiade in Amsterdam. Reconstructie van de tentoostelling D.O.O.D. 1936*. Amsterdam: Gemeentearchief, 1996.

Eagle, May 25, 1919.

Edwards, P. "Wyndham Lewis and the *Rappel à l'ordre*: Classicism and Significant Form, 1919–21." In *The Geographies of Englishness: Landscape and the National Past 1880–1940*, edited by David Peters Corbett, Ysanne Holt, and Fiona Russell. New Haven, CT: Yale University Press, 2002.

———. "Wyndham Lewis at the Second Post-Impressionist Exhibition: Reproductions of Three Lost Works." *Wyndham Lewis Annual* 9–10 (2002–3).

———. *Wyndham Lewis: Painter and Writer*. New Haven, CT: Yale University Press, 2000.

Eliot, T. S. *The Waste Land*. New York: Boni & Liveright, 1922.

Eliot, V., ed. *The Waste Land: A Facsimile and Trancript of the Original Drafts including the Annotations of Ezra Pound*. London: Faber, 1971.

Evening News, August 29, 1922.

Evening Post, May 31, 1919.

Evening Standard, October 7, 1946.

Ferrall, C. " 'Melodramas of Modernity': The Interaction of Vorticism and Futurism before the Great War." *University of Toronto Quarterly* 63, no. 2 (Winter 1993/94).

Fewster, K. ed. *Gallipoli Correspondent. The Front-line Diary of C. E. W. Bean*. Sydney: Unwin Hyman, 1983.

Firbank, R. *The Flower Beneath the Foot*. London: Grant Richards, 1923.

———. *The Flower Beneath the Foot*. New York: Brentano's, 1924.

———. *Prancing Nigger*. New York: Brentano's, 1924.

———. *Sorrow in Sunlight*. London: Brentano's, 1924.

Fletcher, P. "Masculinity, Money and Modern Art: 'The Sentence of Death' by John Collier." In *English Art 1860–1914. Modern Artists and Identity*. Edited by David Peters Corbett and L. Perry. Manchester, UK: Manchester University Press, 2000.

Flint, R. W. ed. *Marinetti: Selected Writings* Translated by R. W. Flint and Arthur A. Coppotelli. New York: Farrar, Straus & Giroux, 1972.

Fulleylove, J. RI, and H. W. Nevinson. *Pictures of Classic Greek Landscape and Architecture*. London: Dent, 1897.

"Futurists and the Past." *Times*, Thursday, June 11, 1914.

"Futurist Squabbles. English Artists' Counterblast to Signor Marinetti." *Daily Express*, London, June 11, 1914.

Gallatin, A. E. Introduction to *Etchings and Lithographs by C. R. W. Nevinson*. New Galleries, November 10–December 4, 1920. An exhibition catalog.

Gallatin, E. Papers. C. R. W. Nevinson to Albert Eugene Gallatin. Reels 507, 508, & 1293. New York Historical Society, Manuscript Division. Copies at the Archives of American Art, Smithsonian Institution, Washington, D.C. (Smithsonian-Gallatin).

Gibbs, P. *The Street of Adventure*. London: Heinemann, 1909.

Gilbert, W. S., and A. S. Sullivan. *Patience*. In *The Complete Plays of Gilbert and Sullivan*. Illustrated by W. S. Gilbert. New York: Garden City Publishing Co., 1941. Reprint New York: W. W. Norton, 1976.

Gilder, R. W. *The Poems of Richard Watson Gilder*. Boston, 1908.

Giles, S., ed. *Theorizing Modernism. Essays in Critical Theory*. London: Routledge, 1993.

Glasgow Evening Times, September 28, 1920.

Glew, A. *Stanley Spencer: Letters and Writings*. London: Tate Publishing, 2001.

Graphic, series no 2: of "Wild Parties in Three Countries: America," May 17, 1930.

Greenwood, J., and Richard Cork. *The Graphic Work of Edward Wadsworth*. London: Wood Lea Press, 2002.

Gresty, H. *C. R. W. Nevinson: Retrospective Exhibition of Paintings, Drawings and Prints*. Cambridge, UK: Kettle's Yard Gallery, 1988. An exhibition catalog.

Guichard, K. M. *British Etchers: 1850–1940*. London, UK: Robin Garton, 1977.

Hall, M. "Modernism, Militarism and Masculinity: British Modern Art Discourses and Official War Art During the First World War." PhD diss., State University of New York at Binghampton, 1994.

Halliday, N. V. "The Identity of Wyndham Lewis's Painting at Group X." Burlington Magazine 1009 (April 1987): 245–47.

Hamilton, J. *Wood Engraving in Britain 1890–1990*. London: Barrie & Jenkins, 1994.

"Hansoms, Pictures, Books, Plays." *Bristol Times & Mirror*, April 16, 1919.

Harris, W. "H. W. Nevinson, Margaret Wynne Nevinson, Evelyn Sharp: Little-Known Writers and Crusaders." *English Literature in Transition* 45, no. 3 (2002).

Harrison, C. *English Art and Modernism 1900–1939*. Bloomington: Indiana University Press and London: Allen Lane 1981.

Haskell, B. *The American Century*. New York: W. W. Norton, 1999.

Hewitt, A. *Fascist Modernism. Aesthetics, Politics, and the Avant-Garde*. Stanford, CA: Stanford University Press, 1993.

Higginbottom, W. H. *The Frightfulness of Modern Art*. London: Cecil Palmer, 1928.

Holman-Hunt, D. *Latin Among Lions: Alvaro Guevara*. London: Michael Joseph, 1974.

Huddleston, S. *Back to Montparnasse*. London: Harrap, 1931.

———. *Mr Paname: A Paris Fantasia*. New York: Doran, 1927.

Hulten, P., ed. *Futurism and Futurisms*. Venice: Palazzo Grassi / New York: Abbeville Press, 1986.

Hynes, S. *A War Imagined—The First World War and English Culture*. London: The Bodley Head, 1990.

Illustrated London News, October 4, 1930.

Isaak, J. A. *The Ruin of Representation in Modernist Art and Texts*. Ann Arbor, Michigan: UMI Research Press, 1982.

Island, December 1931.

Jeffrey, I. "C. R. W. Nevinson: Artist Celebrity." In *C. R. W. Nevinson, 1889–1946: Retrospective Exhibition of Paintings, Drawings and Prints*. Cambridge, UK: Kettle's Yard Gallery, [1988]. An exhibition catalog.

John, A. V. "Imag(in)ing H. W. Nevinson: War Correspondent, Literary Journalist and Rebel." In *Representing Victorian Lives*. Edited by M. Hewitt, 146–51. Leeds: Leeds Centre Working Papers in Victorian Studies, 1999.

———. "Margaret Wynne Nevinson: Gender and National Identity in the Early Twentieth Century." In *From Medieval to Modern Wales: Historical Essays in Honour of Kenneth O. Morgan and Ralph A. Griffiths*, edited by G. H. Jenkins and R. R. Davies. Cardiff: University of Wales Press, 2004.

Jones, M. W. *Fragments of Life: Tales and Sketches*. London: Allen & Unwin, 1922.

Juvenal. *IVNII IVVENALIS SATVRAE*. Latin text based on Bucheler, 1893, at The Latin Library Web Page, http://www.thelatinlibrary.com/juvenal.html. Accessed 02/16/05.

King, J. *Interior Landscapes: A Life of Paul Nash*. London: George Weidenfeld & Nicolson, 1987.

Kirby, M. *Futurist Performance* With manifestos and playscripts translated from the Italian by Victoria Nes Kirby. New York: Dutton, 1971.

Konody, P. G. *Modern War: Paintings by C. R. W. Nevinson*. London: Grant Richards, 1917.

Krauss, R. "The Originality of the Avant-Garde." In *The Originality of the Avant-Garde and Other Modernist Myths*. Cambridge, MA: MIT Press, 1985.

Kuspit, D. *The Cult of the Avant-Garde Artist*. Cambridge: Cambridge University Press, 1993.

Lawton, A., ed. *Russian Futurism through Its Manifestoes, 1912–1928*. Translated by Anna Lawton and Herbet Eagle. Ithaca, NY: Cornell University Press, 1988.

Lewis, P. W., ed. *Blast: Review of the Great English Vortex*, nos. 1–2 (1914–1915). London: John Lane, The Bodley Head / New York: John Lane Company, 1914, 1915. Reprinted by Millwood, NY: Kraus Reprint Co., 1974.

Lewis, S. *Martin Arrowsmith*. London: Cape, 1925. Published in the United States of America as *Arrowsmith*. New York: Harcourt Brace, 1925.

Lewis, W. *Blasting and Bombardiering*. London: Eyre & Spottiswoode, 1937.

———. Letter to Charles Handley-Read, September 2, 1949. In *The Letters of Wyndham Lewis*, edited by W. K. Rose, 504–5. London: Methuen, 1963.

———. "Marinetti Man of the Week." *New Weekly*, May 14, 1914.

———. "A Review of Contemporary Art." (1915). In *Wyndham Lewis on Art*, edited by C. J. Fox and Walter Michel, 68. London: Thames and Hudson, 1969.

Lewis Hind, C. "An Appreciation." *The Old World and the New*. Bourgeois Galleries, November 10–December 4, 1920. An exhibition catalog.

Lista, G., ed. *Futurisme. Manifestes—Proclamations—Documents*. Lausanne: L'Age d'Homme, 1973.

Listener, August 8, 1940.

Liverpool Courier, February 19, 1923.

Lowry, H. B. In the *Evening Post*, May 24, 1919.

Lumsden, E. *The Art of Etching*. London: Seeley, Service, 1925.

Lyon, J. "Militant Discourse, Strange Bedfellows: Suffragettes and Vorticists before the War." *Differences: A Journal of Feminist Cultural Studies* 4, no. 2 (1992).

MacDougall, S. *Mark Gertler*. London: John Murray, 2002.

Malvern, S. "Art, Patronage and Propaganda: British Modern Art Discourses and Official War Art During the First World War ." PhD diss., Reading University, UK, 1981.

———. *Modern Art, Britain and the Great War*. New Haven, CT: Yale University Press, 2004.

———. *Things to Come. Eric Kennington's "War God."* The Henry Moore Institute. Essays on Sculpture, 33. Leeds, UK: The Henry Moore Institute, 2001.

Manchester Guardian, June 27, 1930.

Manchester Guardian, October 4, 1930.

Mann, P. *The Theory-Death of the Avant-Garde*. Bloomington: Indiana University Press, 1991.

Mannin, E. *Confessions and Impressions*. London: Jarrolds, 1930.

———. *Sounding Brass*. London: Jarrolds, 1926.

Marinetti, F. T., and C. R. W. Nevinson. "Contre l'art anglais, Manifeste futuriste lu à la Doré Galerie (Exposition des peintres futuristes Boccioni, Carrà, Russolo, Balla, Severini, Soffici) et à l'Université de Cambridge.—Juin 1914" (pamphlet). London, June 11, 1914. Yale University Library, Beinecke Collection (Marinetti +M317 79).

———. "Futurism and English Art" (newspaper publication). *Observer*, London, June 7, 1914.

———. "Futurism and English Art" (digital image). "Marinetti Libroni," in *Digital Images Online*, Yale University Library, Beinecke Collection. Master CD Number: 0259-3231-0455; Carousel 8, Slots 20 and 69).

———. "Manifesto Futurista." *Lacerba*, 15 Luglio II, no. 14; 2–10; 210–11.

———. "Vital English Art." *Lacerba*, 15 Luglio II, no. 14; 2–10; 209–10.

———. "Vital English Art: Futurist Manifesto" pamphlet. Yale University Library, Beinecke Collection (Marinetti +M317 78).

———. "Vital English Art: A Futurist Manifesto." *Observer*, June 7, 1914.

Marriott, C. "Stunting in Art." *Outlook*, November 8, 1919.

Martin, M. W. *Futurist Art and Theory 1909–1915*. New York: Hacker Art Books, 1978.

Marx, K. *Towards a Critique of Hegel's Philosophy of Right: An Introduction*. Cited in: Chloe Johnson, "CRW Nevinson: The Soul of a Soulless City," *British Art in Focus*, 4. London: Tate Publishing, 2001.

McNally, O. "Images from the Front Lines." *Hartford Courant*, February 24, 2000.

Meyers, J. in *The Enemy: A Biography of Wyndham Lewis*. London: Routledge, 1980.

Moore, G. *Conversations in Ebury Street*. London: William Heinemann, 1924.

Morris, L., ed. *Henry Tonks and the "Art of Pure Drawing."* Norwich, UK: Norwich School of Art Gallery, 1985.

"Mr. Nevinson, British Artist, Thinks New York is Too Modest." *Herald*, May 18, 1919.

Murray, A. H. H., accompanied by H. W. Nevinson and M. Carmichael. *Sketches On The Old Road Through France to Florence*. London: John Murray; New York: Dutton, 1904.

Murray, G. Papers, MSS 15, fol. 87. Nevinson to Murray, January 18, 1909. Bodleian Library.

Nash, P. *Outline: An Autobiography and Other Writings*, with a preface by Herbert Read. London: Faber and Faber, 1949.

Nation, January 4, 1913.

"Nevinson—a Painter who is Developing." *American Art News*, November 20, 1920.

"Nevinson Dinner, A." *Daily Mirror*, March 15, 1919.

"Nevinson for New York," *Daily Express*, September 16, 1920.

"The Nevinson Palace of Varieties." *Westminster Gazette*, November 4, 1919.

Nevinson Papers, John Lea Nevinson Diaries, 111, September 15, 1924. British Library.

"Nevinson Talks on Art." *New York Times*, May 30, 1919.

"Nevinson with a Horsewhip." *Daily Express*, September 9, 1921.

Nevinson, C. R. W. "The Arts Within this Bellicose Civilization," *The Seven Pillars of Fire: A Symposium by Dr Maude Royden, Dr L. P. Jacks, Prof. A. E. Richardson, the Marquis of Tavistock, C. R. W. Nevinson, Capt. Bernard Acworth, and Sir E. Denison Ross*. London: Barrie Jenkins, 1936.

———. "The Futurist Manifesto." Letters to the Editor, *Observer*, June 21, 1914.

———. "My Art Creed," *The Old World and the New* (Bourgeois Galleries, November 10–December 4, 1920).

———. *Paint and Prejudice*. London: Methuen, 1937; and New York: Harcourt, Brace, 1938.

———. "Vital English Art. Lecture at the Doré Galleries." *New Age* 15, no. 7, 154–62 (June 18, 1914).

Nevinson, C. R. W. to Carrington, January 14, 1913. Harry Ransom Humanities Research Center, Austin, Texas.

Nevinson, H. W. *Changes and Chances*. London: Nisbet, 1923.

———. Journals, June 19–28, 1921, Henry Woodd Nevinson Papers, MS.Eng.e.621/4, Bodleian Library, Oxford University.

———. *Last Changes, Last Chances*. London: Nisbet, 1928.

———. "Marinetti: Futurist." Reprinted from *Atlantic Monthly*, November 1914. In *Visions and Memories*, collected by Evelyn Sharp; introduction by Gilbert Murray. 1944. Reprint London: Oxford University Press, 1946, repr. 1946.

———. *The Natives of England*. New York: Alfred A. Knopf, 1930.

———. Papers, Diaries, MSS Eng. Misc. e615/1, October 8, 1908. Bodleian Library, Oxford University.

———. *The Plea of Pan*. London: John Murray, 1901.

———. *Rough Islanders*. London: Routledge, 1930.

Nevinson, H. W. to Murray January 18, 1909, Gilbert Murray Papers, MSS 15, fol. 87. Bodleian Library, Oxford University.

Nevinson, Mrs. H. W. "Juvenal on Latter-Day Problems: an Unscholarly Gossip." *Fortnightly Review* 87 (1907).

Nevinson, M. W. *Fragments of Life*. London, 1922.

———. *Life's Fitful Fever*. London: Black, 1926.

Nevinson, M. to Edith How Martyn, February 11, 1915. The Women's Library, London.

Nevinson, W. to John Lea, April 10, 1900. British Library MSS RP2679 (ii),

News Chronicle, October 4, 1930.

News Chronicle, October 8, 1946, and *Liverpool Daily*, October 8, 1946.

"The New Slave-Trade of Portuguese Africa." *Harper's Monthly Magazine* 111, no. 663 (1905).

New Statesman, October 20, 1934.

New Statesman, December 11, 1937.

New York City Herald, May 25, 1919.

New York Times Magazine, May 25, 1919.

"Notes From New York." *Evening Standard and St. James Gazette*, July 3, 1919.

"Painter of Modern Life, A." *Observer*, November (n.d.), 1919.

Parsons, I., ed. *The Collected Works of Isaac Rosenberg: Poetry, Prose, Letters, Paintings and Drawings*. London: Chatto & Windus, 1979.

Perloff, M. *The Futurist Moment. Avant-Garde, Avant Guerre, and the Language of Rupture*. Chicago: University of Chicago Press, 1986.

Petrie, Sir C. *The Edwardians*. London: W. W. Norton, 1965.

Pirandello, L. *The One-act Plays of Luigi Pirandello*. New York: Dutton, 1928.

Pittsburgh Gazette, June 23, 1919.

Poggioli, R. *The Theory of the Avant-Garde*. Translated by Gerald Fitzgerald. Cambridge, MA: Harvard University Press, 1968.

Pound, E. "Affirmations VI." *New Age* 16, no. 15 (1915): 393–416.

———. *New York Times*, August 9, 1914.

———. "Small Magazines." In *Ezra Pound. The Image and the Real*. Edited by H. N. Schneidau. Baton Rouge: Louisiana State University Press, 1969.

Quinn, J. to Wyndham Lewis, dated June 16, 1919. Letter Box 21. New York Public Library.

Rainey, L. "The Creation of the Avant-Garde: F. T. Marinetti and Ezra Pound," *Modernism/Modernity* 1, no. 3 (1994).

"Rebels in Art. Exhibition of the London Salon," *Times*, June 16, 1914.

Robins, E. Papers, Nevinson to Robins, June 4, 1932, Series 2B, Box 6, folder 136. Fales Library, Elmer Holmes Bobst Library, New York University.

Ross, M. *Robert Ross: Friend of Friends*. London: Cape, 1952.

Rothenstein, J. *Modern English Painters, Volume 2: Lewis to Moore.* London: Eyre & Spottiswoode, 1957.

Rothenstein, W. *Men and Memories: Recollections of William Rothenstein, 1900–1922.* London: Faber & Faber, 1932.

Russell, T. J. "The Big Show: C. R. W. Nevinson." *Times*, October 30, 1999.

Rutter, F. *Art in my Time.* London: Rich & Cowan, 1933.

———. *Some Contemporary Artists.* London: Leonard Parsons, 1922.

Salaman, M. C. *Modern Masters of Etching: C. R. W. Nevinson.* London: Studio Publications, 1932.

———. *Modern Woodcuts and Lithographs.* London: A. & C. Black.

"Sane Modernism." *Tribune* (New York City), November 14, 1920.

Schorer, M. *Sinclair Lewis: An American Life.* London: Heinemann, 1961.

Schwabe, R. "Reminiscences of Fellow Students." *Burlington Magazine* 82, 1943.

Scotsman, November 15, 1934.

Sewell, B. "Pictures that pack a punch." *Evening Standard*, November 19, 1999.

Sharp, E. Nevinson Papers, Diary 1, d668, September 21, 1942. Bodleian Library, Oxford University.

Sinclair, M. *Tree of Heaven.* London: Classic Books, 2000.

Sitwell, O. *C. R. W. Nevinson.* London: Ernest Benn, 1925.

———. *Memorial Exhibition of Pictures by C. R. W. Nevinson.* London: Leicester Galleries, 1947.

"Some Famous Figures in the Foreign News," *Union*, Springfield, MA, October 31, 1920.

Somigli, L. "Towards a Theory of the Avant-Garde Manifesto." PhD diss., State University of New York at Stony Brook, 1996; DAI, 57, no. 11A, (1996): 4726.

Southam, B. C. *A Student's Guide to the Selected Poems of T. S. Eliot.* London: Faber, 1974.

Spalding, F. *Roger Fry: Art and Life.* London: Granada Publishing, 1980.

Spectator, October 19, 1934.

Spencer, G. *Memoirs of a Painter.* London: Chatto & Windus, 1974.

Stanstell, C. *American Moderns: Bohemian New York and the Creation of a New Century.* New York: Metropolitan Books, 2000.

Stella, J. "The Brooklyn Bridge," *Transitions.* Published privately, 1929.

Stone, M. *The Patron State: Culture and Politics in Fascist Italy.* Princeton, NJ: Princeton University Press, 1998.

Sun, May 18, 1919.

Sutton, D., ed. *Letters of Roger Fry.* London: Chatto & Windus, 1972.

Taylor, J. *War Photography: Realism in the British Press.* London: Routledge, 1991.

Times, July 15, 1930.

T. K. L. "Pastiche. Wake up, England!" *New Age* 15, no. 8, Thursday, June 25, 1914.

Thorn, A. F. "Speeditis: Addressed to Certain Modern Maniacs." *New Age* 15, no. 17 (August 27, 1914).

Tisdall, C., and Angelo Bozzolla. *Futurism.* New York: Oxford University Press, 1978.

Titterton, W. R. *A Candle To The Stars.* London: Grayson & Grayson, 1932.

Tonks, H. "Notes from 'Wander Years.'" *Artwork* 5, no. 20 (1929).

Tosh, J. *A Man's Place. Masculinity and the Middle-Class Home in Victorian England.* New Haven, CT: Yale University Press, 1999.

Touchstone. "A Futurist's Holiday" (poem). *Daily Mail*, June 17, 1914.

Trotter, D. *Paranoid Modernism: Literary Experiment, Psychosis, and the Professionalization of English Society.* Oxford: Oxford University Press, 2001.

Troubetzkoy, Princess P. *Gallow's Seed.* London: Grayson & Grayson, 1934.

Troubetzkoy, Princess P., and C. R. W. Nevinson. *Exodus A.D.: A Warning to Civilians.* London: Hutchinson, n.d [1934].

"Vorticist Art." *Times*, June 13, 1914.

Vote, December 31, 1910.

Wadsworth, B. *Edward Wadsworth: A Painter's Life.* Salisbury, UK: Michael Russell, 1989.

Walsh, M. J. K. "C. R. W. Nevinson at the Slade." *Apollo*, October 2001.

———. "C.R.W. Nevinson: The Modern Artist of Modern War." *Apollo*, July 2004.

———. "'The Eminent English Futurist': C. R. W. Nevinson and English Futurism in Peace and War." In *Blasting the Future: Vorticism in Britain 1910–1920*, edited by Jonathan Black et al., 19–26 London: Philip Wilson Publishers, 2004.

———. *C. R. W. Nevinson: This Cult of Violence.* New Haven, CT: Yale University Press, 2002.

———. "This Tumult in the Clouds." *British Art Journal*, Summer 2004.

———. "Vital English Art: Futurism and the Vortex of London 1910–14." *Apollo*, February 2005.

Wees, W. *Vorticism and the English Avant-Garde.* Toronto: University of Toronto Press, 1972.

Wells, H. G. *The Shape of Things to Come: The Ultimate Revolution.* London: Hutchinson, 1933.

———. *War and the Future: Italy, France and Britain at War.* London: Cassell, 1917.

———. *The War of the Worlds.* London: Heinemann, 1951; originally published: 1898.

Westminster Gazette, October 1916.

White, J. J. *Literary Futurism: Aspects of the First Avant Garde.* Oxford: Clarendon Press, 1990.

Williamson, A. *Henry Williamson: Tarka and the Last Romantic.* Stroud, UK: Sutton, 1995.

Williamson, H. *The Gold Falcon, or The Haggard of Love.* London: Faber, 1933.

———. *The Linhay on the Downs and Other Adventures in the Old and the New World.* London: Faber, 1934.

———. *The Phoenix Generation.* London: Macdonald, 1965.

———. *The Power of the Dead.* London: Macdonald, 1963.

———. *A Test to Destruction.* London: Macdonald, 1960.

———. *The Wet Flanders Plain.* London: Faber, 1929.

Woodeson, J. *Mark Gertler: Biography of a Painter, 1891–1939.* London: Sidgwick & Jackson, 1973.

Woolf, V. *Mr. Bennett and Mr. Brown*, in H. Read. *Contemporary British Art*. Harmondsworth, UK: Penguin Books, 1951, 20. Woolf wrote "On, or around December 1910, human character changed."

World's Pictorial News, June 9, 1923.

Yeats, W. B. "The Second Coming." In *The Norton Anthology of English Literature*. Seventh edition. Volume 2. New York: W. W. Norton, 2000.

Yockney, A. to C. F. G. Masterman. December 4, 1917, 226-A6-129, Imperial War Museum Archive, London.

Contributors

Jonathan Black is the author of *The Sculpture of Eric Kennington* (2002), *Form, Feeling and Calculation: The Paintings and Drawings of Edward Wadsworth: 1907–1949* (2006), and curator of *Blasting the Future: Vorticism in Britain 1910–1920* (Estorick Collection, London and the Whitworth Gallery, Manchester, UK). He is currently AHRB Research Fellow in History of Art at Dorich House Museum, Kingston University, London. Dr. Black's essay on the sculptor Dora Gordine (1898–1991) appeared in the Ben Uri Gallery Exhibition Catalogue *Embracing the Exotic: Jacob Epstein and Dora Gordine* in 2006.

Paul Edwards is Professor of English and History of Art at Bath Spa University. He is the author of *Wyndham Lewis: Painter and Writer* (2000), and editor of *Blast: Vorticism 1914–1918* (2000).

David Boyd Haycock is Wellcome Research Fellow at the London School of Economics. He is the author of *Paul Nash* (2002) and *William Stukeley* (2002), and is a regular arts reviewer for the *Times Literary Supplement.* His latest book, *A Crisis of Brilliance: Five Young British Artists, 1908–1919,* has just been completed.

Angela V. John was, until recently, Professor of History at the University of Greenwich, London. Here she co-organized, with Michael Walsh, the 2002 conference "C. R. W. Nevinson: Life, Art and Legacy." She now has an Honorary Professorship at the University of Wales, Aberystwyth, and is the author of *War, Journalism and the Shaping of the 20th Century. The Life and Times of Henry W. Nevinson* (2006).

Ben Jones is a freelance art historian and educator running programs in Modern and Contemporary Art Studies at London institutions including Christie's Education and the Tate Gallery. He also lectures widely to student and adult groups across the United Kingdom.

Sue Malvern is a Senior Lecturer in History of Art and Head of the Department of History of Art at the University of Reading. She is the author of *Modern Art, Britain and the Great War* (2004).

Christopher Martin is a librarian at the University of Portsmouth. His book of poetry, entitled *Chicken Factory,* was published by Peter Way in 1972, and more recently he has contributed to the anthology *My Rebellious and Imperfect Eye: Observing Geoffrey Grigson* (2002). He has been preparing the complete *catalogue raisonné* of Nevinson's work for over a decade, a project which is nearing completion.

Anber Onar is a practicing artist and Senior Lecturer in the Department of Archaeology and Art History at Eastern Mediterranean University, where she teaches courses in the visual arts with a special focus on interpretation and analysis in the areas of modernism and postmodernism.

Johann Pillai is an Associate Professor of Comparative Literature and Dean of the Faculty of Arts and Sciences, Eastern Mediterranean University. His research is focused on the aesthetics of Dada and Surrealism, relations between literature and the visual arts, and critical theory. He is currently completing a book on the German Romantic philosophy of irony, and a series of articles on visual and sound poetry.

Sir Osbert Sitwell was a critic of contemporary art, music and literature. Some of his works included: *Triple Fugue* (1924); *Before the Bombardment* (1926); *Collected Poems and Satires* (1931); *Selected Poems* (1943); *Four Songs of the Italian Earth* (1948); *Collected Stories* (1953); *The Four Continents* (1954), and *Tales My Father Taught Me* (1962). He died in 1969.

Michael Walsh is the author of *C. R. W. Nevinson: This Cult of Violence* (2002) and numerous articles on the pre-war avant-garde in London. He is currently Associate Professor of Art History at Eastern Mediterranean University, North Cyprus and Visiting Research Collaborator at the Department of Art and Archaeology, Princeton University. His biographical study, *Hanging a Rebel: The Life and Work of C. R. W. Nevinson,* is due for publication in 2007.

Index

Page numbers in *italics* refer to illustrations.